CENSUS

OF MODERN GREEK LITERATURE

NOT ADDED BY
UNIVERSITY OF MICHIGAN

The Modern Greek Studies Association, a nonprofit organization established in 1968, is devoted to the study of the language, history, literature, and institutions of modern Greece. It sponsors symposia, seminars, and publications and serves as a center of information on programs and scholarly activities in the field.

MODERN GREEK STUDIES ASSOCIATION SERIES

1. *Modern Greek Writers*. Edmund Keeley and Peter Bien, editors. Princeton, N.J.: Princeton University Press, 1972.

2. *Hellenism and the First Greek War of Liberation, 1821-1830: Continuity and Change*. P.N. Diamandouros, J. Anton, J. Petropulos, and P. Topping, editors. Thessaloniki: Institute for Balkan Studies, 1976.

3. The "Past" in Medieval and Modern Greek Culture. Speros Vryonis, Jr., editor. Malibu, Calif.: Undena Publications, 1978.

4. *Greece in the 1940s: A Nation in Crisis*. John O. Iatrides, editor. Hanover, N.H.: University Press of New England, 1981.

5. *Greece in the 1940s: A Bibliographic Companion*. John O. Iatrides, editor. Hanover, N.H.: University Press of New England, 1981.

6. *New Trends in Modern Greek Historiography*. A. Lily Macrakis and P. Nikiforos Diamandouros, editors. Occasional Papers of the MGSA, 1. Hanover, N.H.: MGSA, 1982.

7. *CENSUS of Modern Greek Literature: Check-list of English-Language Sources Useful in the Study of Modern Greek Literature*. Dia M.L. Philippides. Occasional Papers of the MGSA, 2. New Haven, Conn.: MGSA, 1990.

CENSUS

OF MODERN GREEK LITERATURE

Check-list of ENglish-Language Sources
Useful in the Study
of Modern Greek Literature
(1824 - 1987)

Dia M. L. Philippides

MODERN GREEK STUDIES ASSOCIATION

OCCASIONAL PAPERS, 2

NEW HAVEN

© 1990 by Dia M. L. Philippides. All rights reserved
Published 1990
Printed in the United States of America

On the front cover, drawing of the façade of the Gennadius Library
of the American School of Classical Studies at Athens,
by Charles Dennis.
Used by permission of the American School of Classical Studies.

          Library of Congress Cataloging-in-Publication Data

Philippides, Dia Mary L.
  Census of modern Greek literature : check-list of English-language sources useful in the study of modern Greek literature (1824-1987) / Dia M.L. Philippides.
    p.   cm. -- (Occasional papers / Modern Greek Studies Association ; 2)
   Includes bibliographical references and index.
   ISBN 0-912105-01-1 (paper : text) : $15.00
   1. Greek literature, Modern--19th century--History and criticism--Bibliography. 2. Greek literature, Modern--20th century--History and criticism--Bibliography. 3. Greek literature, Modern--19th century--Translations into English--Bibliography. 4. English literature--19th century--Translations from Greek, Modern--Bibliography. 5. Greek literature, Modern--20th century--Translations into English--Bibliography. 6. English literature--20th century--Translations from Greek, Modern--Bibliography. I. Title. II. Series: Occasional papers (Modern Greek Studies Association) ; 2.
Z2294.C8P46 1990
[PA5210]
016.889'09--dc20   90-6441
                                                                   CIP

To George and Lena Savidis

CONTENTS

Introduction	ix
Abbreviations Used for Journals	xx
List of Journals Cited	xxi

1. BIBLIOGRAPHICAL SOURCES
    i. Bibliographies Wholly Concerned with Modern Greek — 1
    ii. General Bibliographies with Sections on Modern Greek Literature — 3
    iii. Library Catalogues and Surveys of Collections — 4

2. JOURNALS
    i. Indexed — 5
    ii. Not Indexed — 7

3. SPECIAL ISSUES OF JOURNALS — 9

4. ANTHOLOGIES
    i. Prose *and* Poetry — 17
    ii. Prose — 19
    iii. Poetry — 20
    iv. Regional — 30
        a. *Cyprus* — 30
        b. *Epirus* — 32
        c. *Thessaloniki* — 32
        d. *Other* — 32

5. COLLECTED ESSAYS
    i. Works by Individual Authors — 35
    ii. Collective Works — 36

6. LITERARY HISTORY
    i. General — 39
        a. *Entirely Concerned with Modern Greek Literature* — 39
        b. *Partially Concerned with Modern Greek Literature* — 40
    ii. Pre-1800 — 41
        a. *Literature Before the Fall of Constantinople (Eleventh to Fifteenth Centuries* — 41
        b. *After the Fall of Constantinople (Fifteenth to Seventeenth Centuries)* — 47
        c. *The Great Age of Cretan Literature (ca. 1570-1669)* — 48
        d. *The Eighteenth Century: Modern Greek Enlightenment* — 50
        e. *The Folk Song* — 53
    iii. The Nineteenth and Twentieth Centuries — 57

7. AUTHORS — 71

Index — 229

INTRODUCTION

1. Aims and scope of the check-list

The check-list began in the form of a prototype presented at the Conference on the Teaching of Modern Greek Literature in American Universities (at Princeton University in April 1984) with the idea of providing a means by which speakers of English could approach Modern Greek literature through translations and works of criticism.[1] The response then and since has been so encouraging that the original list, initially intended for use in a survey course, has now been expanded. It is not aimed at the specialist but at a wider variety of readers: university students, instructors, librarians considering acquisitions—indeed anyone interested in the literature of Modern Greece. Some of the material (translations of Modern Greek literature and critical essays in English about the literature) had been listed elsewhere, but nowhere was there available a comprehensive catalogue both of English versions of the literature itself in book form and of the contents (itemized) of anthologies, journals, and collections of essays. As the text has been set up on the computer, the addition of new material or the correction of errors should be relatively easy in the case of any future edition.

By calling this compilation a 'check-list' rather than a 'bibliography', I believe that I am remaining truer to its nature and scope. It has become more than evident to me over the last six years of checking and rechecking that the compilation of an authentic bibliography is no easy task, but one requiring a professional bibliographer or a team of trained co-workers with access to the larger libraries both of the U.S. and Europe. I have done the best I could with the means available and am now presenting this book in the hope of stirring up greater interest in Modern Greek literature and of encouraging people to send us any possible additional sources of information.

"Census", the first word in the main title, *Census of Modern Greek Literature,* as well as forming an acronym for the subtitle (see letters given in outline form on title page), is related to the word's original meanings as cited in the *Oxford Latin Dictionary,*[2] 'the registration and classification of property', or more generally, 'property, substance and wealth'. The check-list is intended to record and classify the works of Modern Greek literature available in English in the hope of producing a fuller realization of our present wealth of material. Its classification could also point to possibilities of further translation or critical writing in areas so far unexplored.

---

[1] See *Bulletin of the Modern Greek Studies Association* XVI, No. 2 (Fall 1984), pp. 31-32.
[2] *Oxford Latin Dictionary.* P.G.W. Glare, ed. Oxford: Clarendon Press, 1982.

Most of the entries in this list refer to C.P. Cavafy, Odysseus Elytis, Nikos Kazantzakis, Yannis Ritsos, and George Seferis. Some important Greek authors seem not to have been translated into English at all; others have received minimal attention. Poetry has been more translated than prose, modern drama particularly neglected. The critical studies about the literature seem far fewer than the translations. I hope that English-speaking translators of, and commentators on, Modern Greek literature will be encouraged by this check-list to fill some of the outstanding gaps.[3]

In a remarkable article written on the occasion of George Katsimbalis' bibliography of Palamas[4] Ioannis Sykoutris states that the bibliographer should provide a clear report of the sources he has examined, attempt to be as accurate as possible, and aim at making his bibliography easy to use. He concludes with a 'more general recommendation to all prospective bibliographers': "One should not keep one's material long shut up in a drawer from fear of missing something that one could have added...For the advantage of scholarship it is necessary that bibliographies be published as soon as possible...The publication itself constitutes an invitation for the collaboration of others who, without negative critical disposition and with complete gratitude to the compiler of the aid, may complement or correct the work".[5] We trust that the present check-list will be received with his type of understanding.

2. Content and format of the check-list

The check-list is divided into the following chapters: (1) bibliographical sources useful in locating Modern Greek literary works and studies; (2) journals frequently containing Modern Greek literary subjects; (3) special issues of other journals dedicated for a single time to Modern Greek literature; (4) anthologies; (5) books of collected essays; (6) literary history (including general works on literature but also most of the literary material prior to the nineteenth century); and (7) authors, arranged in alphabetical order. In each chapter it is recommended to the reader that he read the initial brief introduction.

This list relies heavily on the specialized bibliographies of Evro Layton and Peter Mackridge published in Μαντατοφόρος 20 (Nov. 1982); Richard and Mary Jo Clogg's general bibliography entitled *Greece* (1980); the bibliography on Modern Greek Culture compiled by C.Th. Dimaras, C. Koumarianou, and L. Droulia (4th ed., 1974); and the Modern Greek section of the international bibliography published annually by the Modern Language Association of America (for Modern Greek literature, 1968-). The English

---

[3] See Dia Philippides, "Computers in Literary and Bibliographic Research" (in Greek), forthcoming in the Proceedings of the First International Conference on Greek Bibliography, held in Athens in October 1989.
[4] Γ. Κατσίμπαλη, Παλαμική Βιβλιογραφία 1926-1931. 'Αθήνα: Τυπ. 'Εστία, 1932. 62 p.
[5] 'Ιωάννου Συκουτρή, "Ἡ βιβλιογραφία τῆς Νεοελληνικῆς Λογοτεχνίας ἐξ αἰτίας ἑνός βιβλίου". In his Μελέται καί Ἄρθρα. 'Αθῆναι: 'Εκδόσεις τοῦ Αἰγαίου, 1956, pp. 319-328, esp. pp. 320ff. and 328.

entries in the recent bibliography of translations of Modern Greek literature compiled by E.-L. Stavropoulou for the Ἑλληνικό Λογοτεχνικό καί Ἱστορικό Ἀρχεῖο (1986) have been incorporated as completely as possible. Additionally, all available issues of the journals with regular entries in English on Modern Greek literature have been indexed[6] (from their first issue up through 1987—list given below under "Journals"), as well as material from unpublished bibliographies, from syllabuses intended for courses, or from comments provided by colleagues.

The literature included in the check-list ranges from approximately the eleventh century (*Digenis Akritas*) to the present day. This accords in scope and outline with that of the *History of Modern Greek Literature* by Linos Politis.[7] Literary subjects and authors prior to 1800 are listed in the chapter on literary history. All publications in the check-list appeared between 1824 and the end of 1987. The latter date was a conscious choice—it was necessary to choose a firm and manageable stopping point; the former resulted from the availability of material. I regret not having been able to include later publications.

The present check-list differs from other bibliographies in that it is not critical or annotated, but instead includes all the appropriate material that the compiler was able to find. It makes specific reference to articles and shorter literary pieces usually hidden within larger collective works such as anthologies, by listing the contents of anthologies, books of collected essays, and special issues of journals, and then by repeating the individual items in the appropriate places of the chapters on literary history and authors (Chapters 6 and 7). Only a few comments have been added as possibly useful (for instance, in the description of works of literary history).

It was recommended that the first, original, publication of individual items, such as a poem in translation, be omitted if it were possible to show that these items had been included in later collections. However, all the separate entries discovered have been kept in the check-list in the hope that the information regarding the first publication will be of interest to some readers. Subsequent books of collected works are not always clear in this respect. From reading translations or the comments of scholars one learns that translations (or essays) quite often have been revised in later editions. Thus it can be of particular interest to follow the separate versions.

For the purpose of cross-reference each entry in the check-list has been given an individual number in boldface, consisting of an initial Arabic numeral (the chapter) separated by a period from a second number (its individual accession number within the chapter). The running heads on the even pages indicate the section of the chapter with which the page begins. Cross-references are denoted by placing entry numbers within curly brackets.

---

[6] All documents within the scope of this bibliography have been included, with the exception of book reviews.

[7] Linos Politis, *A History of Modern Greek Literature*. [Robert Liddell, tr.] Oxford: The Clarendon Press, 1973. Reprinted with corrections, 1975 {Entry 6.5}.

The main alphabet followed in the sorting is the English one. The rare Greek names or titles have been interpolated according to their transcription under the scheme generally followed (see "Transcription" below).

The governing principle in the arrangement of the entries is the name of the author or the editor (or the title, when necessary). The variety of the material in the chapters, the frequent lack of a definite original date of publication in the case of books, the fact that often only later editions could be seen and described, all are factors that have led to avoidance of a chronological arrangement. The check-list is not intended as a research tool. As already stated, it is primarily meant to be useful to students and instructors of Modern Greek literature, and its present arrangement has been considered more likely to serve this purpose.

An asterisk placed at the beginning of an entry or at the start of a reference indicates that it has not been possible to inspect that item personally: the information is that available from bibliographical sources. Square brackets have been used not only to indicate information supplied independently of the title page of a bibliographical source, but also in order to distinguish categories, such as the titles or translators of shorter works listed as part of the contents of larger ones.

Bibliographical Sources (Chapter 1)

The chapter on bibliographical sources is divided into three sections: (I) Modern Greek bibliographies; (II) General bibliographies with sections on Modern Greek literature; (III) Library catalogues and surveys of collections. Each section is arranged alphabetically by editor or compiler. More specific bibliographies referring to individual authors are placed in the chapter on authors (Chapter 7).

Journals (Chapter 2)

This chapter includes journals regularly containing articles in English on Modern Greek literary subjects. The journals are arranged alphabetically by title. Not all the journals in this chapter have been completely indexed. This fact is indicated by the division of the chapter into two parts. Besides the journals *Byzantine and Modern Greek Studies, The Charioteer, Epsilon, Folia Neohellenica, Το Γιοφύρι, Greek Letters, Journal of the Hellenic Diaspora, Journal of Modern Greek Studies, Journal of Modern Hellenism, Μαντατοφόρος, Modern Greek Studies Yearbook, Neo-Hellenika,* and *Scandinavian Studies in Modern Greek*, the periodical *Classical and Modern Literature* has been scanned for relevant entries. The journals have been indexed from their first issue until the last one of the end of 1987 (the entries give precise indications of the numbers and dates of the issues in square brackets).[8]

---

[8] Two further lists related to journals appear at the end of this introduction: a list of abbreviations for the titles of journals most commonly met in the bibliography (p. xx) and a general list of all the journals encountered in the compilation (including subtitles and place of publication, to facilitate clarity in the case of possible ambiguity [pp. xxi-xxviii]).

Special Issues of Journals (Chapter 3)

This chapter contains issues of journals dedicated for a single time to Modern Greek literature. Special issues of journals dedicated to a specific author are listed under that author's name in the chapter on authors (Chapter 7).

The special issues are arranged alphabetically by title, with the contents described in full in each case.

Anthologies (Chapter 4)

The anthologies are divided into four sections: (I) Prose *and* poetry; (II) Prose; (III) Poetry; (IV) Regional. The fourth section is further sub-divided: a. Cyprus; b. Epirus; c. Thessaloniki; d. Other.

Within each section the anthologies are listed alphabetically by the name of their compiler. A list is provided for the authors (and in certain cases, the works) contained in each anthology.

Collected Essays (Chapter 5)

This chapter is divided into two sections: (I) Works by individual authors; (II) Collective works. Within each section the books are listed alphabetically by their authors or editors. The complete contents are given for each book.

Chapters 3, 4, and 5

In the description of the contents of special issues, anthologies, and collections of essays, the following have been consistently given: the names of the Greek authors whose works appear in translation (in the actual forms in which the names appear); the authors and titles of critical essays. The titles of works translated, the translators and the page numbers have generally been given whenever available through inspection of the volume or through information provided elsewhere, except in cases where the number of separate works was prohibitive (this is especially true for special issues and anthologies containing poems).

Items described in the contents of special issues, anthologies, and collections of essays (i.e., translations where the titles of works and page numbers have been given, or individual essays) are repeated in the appropriate places in the chapters on literary history and authors (Chapters 6 and 7).

Literary History (Chapter 6)

The chapter on literary history is divided into three major parts: (I) General works; (II) Pre-1800; (III) The nineteenth and twentieth centuries. It incorporates general histories of literature, most of the literary material preceding the nineteenth century, and specific critical essays which do not refer to a single author. Within each part the ordering is alphabetical by author.

Part I is further sub-divided into: (a) Works entirely concerned with Modern Greek literature, (b) Works partially concerned with Modern Greek literature.

Part II is sub-divided into five divisions in accordance with the partitions in Linos Politis' *History of Modern Greek Literature*: (a) Literature prior to 1453; (b) Literature from the fifteenth to the seventeenth century; (c) The great age of Cretan literature (1570-1669);

(d) The eighteenth century (the Enlightenment); (e) The folk song. The five divisions all distinguish texts from studies. The category of 'folk song' includes certain items of folk narrative and culture, especially when they had been cited in the bibliography of the Modern Language Association.[9]

Authors (Chapter 7)

The authors (of the nineteenth and twentieth centuries) are listed alphabetically by their last names. In the entries (especially in the description of contents) the names have been given in the actual forms in which they appear in the sources. In the headings, however, the spelling has been generally standardized to follow that of Linos Politis' *History of Modern Greek Literature*. A guide to the transcription used here is given below; however, exceptions are made when the name is already well-known in a different form, viz. Demetrios Capetanakis, C.P. Cavafy (not Kavafis), John Chioles, Kay Cicellis, Andonis Decavalles, N.C. Germanacos, Stratis Haviaras, Vasso Kalamaras, George Thaniel, usually as the author has lived extensively outside Greece.

Under each author's name are four categories:
    a. translations in the form of books;
    b. translations of shorter works appearing within other works;
    c. book-length studies on the author himself;
    d. shorter studies on the author in larger works.

In other words, the first two categories refer to works by the author[10] and the second two to studies about him and his works. Within each of the four categories the entries are arranged first, alphabetically by author and secondly, by title. In the alphabetical arrangement the word "from", when it comes at the beginning of a title to indicate the source of an excerpt, is ignored. This chiefly occurs in category (b).

In describing shorter selections from the works of authors, especially entries entitled "5 poems" or the like, I have tried to list also the titles of the poems, when the selection included fewer than three. Occasionally I was able to go beyond that number, but to do so for all selections would have extended the work past practical bounds. I have done my best within the time available and should welcome supplements and emendations.

Special issues of journals devoted to a single author are listed with their full contents, at the end of category (c). Abstracts for dissertations are listed under (d), whereas the few dissertations which are cited as a whole are found under (c).

The chapter on authors does not include all the Greek authors mentioned in the checklist. As stated, authors prior to the nineteenth century are incorporated in Part II of the chapter on literary history. Chapter 7 incorporates all subsequent authors translations of whose works have appeared in the form of books or about whom a book (or books) has been written in English. It also, however, includes authors of whom the translation of a single poem has been printed in a journal or book not described in Chapters 3-6. No 'value' judgement whatever is implied in the inclusion or omission of an author in Chapter

---

[9] The annual section on Modern Greek literature includes entries under the heading "Folklore".
[10] Especially for authors such as those named above, categories (a) and (b) may occasionally include works written directly in English.

7. The other authors appearing only in special issues, anthologies, books of collected essays, or literary history, can be located with the help of the index.

Some overlap and repetition of items occurs among the chapters on special issues, anthologies, collected essays, literary history, and authors. In later chapters the repeated items are cited with a reference to the earlier occurrence(s) of the entry. The repetition is intended to make it easier for readers to locate material which might interest them. It also means, however, that readers hoping to compile statistics on the basis of the total count of entries found in a chapter or listed in the index under the name of an author, translator, or editor risk producing inaccurate results if they do not check their counts with the contents of the book in general.

Index

The index at the back of the book includes in a single alphabet: (1) all the Greek authors, both those with individual entries in the chapter on authors (Chapter 7) (page numbers in bold type) and those appearing in special issues, anthologies, books of collected essays or under the category of literary history (page numbers in regular type); (2) all translators, authors, and editors responsible for translations, essays, introductions, or comments in the chapters on special issues, anthologies, collected essays, literary history, or the chapter on authors (page numbers given in italics); (3) the titles of anonymous works, e.g., *Digenis Akritas* and *The Sacrifice of Abraham*; (4) Καραγκιόζης and the category 'folk song'.

As in the chapter on authors, the spelling of the Greek authors' names in English has been reduced to a unified scheme. (This has been done so that readers should not have to look repeatedly in different places for the works of a single author.) However, the actual alternative spellings encountered in the sources have been preserved in the index, where they are given with a cross-reference to the standardized spelling. Users of the card catalogue in libraries should be aware of all these variant spellings.

Transcription

As is evident from the many forms in which the names of Greek authors appear in English, there is no standard system of transcription.[11] Yet it would be cumbersome for the user of the check-list to have to search for each author, in either the chapter on authors or the index, under different forms of his or her name. Thus a unified system, such as that used by Linos Politis in his *History of Modern Greek Literature*,[12] has been followed. Greek letters (and combinations) lacking a unique equivalent in the Latin alphabet have been transcribed as follows:

---

[11] In the compilation of both the chapter on authors and the index, difficulties were caused by the lack of a standard transliteration of the Greek authors' names into English. The formation of such a standard would be a tool of great use, and it is hoped that librarians, bibliographers, and philologists will soon reach a joint conclusion.

[12] *op.cit.* (cf. note 7). See especially his "Note on Transcription" immediately following his table of contents. Linos Politis' system of transcription has been adopted, though not without a few reservations as to its consistency, e.g. ντ might perhaps better have been transcribed as 'nd' in place of 'nt'.

β:	v
γ:	g
δ:	d
η:	i
θ:	th
κ:	k (not c)
υ:	y
φ:	f (not ph)
χ:	ch (not h or kh)

Diphthongs ει and οι: i   αι: ai   ου: ou

Double consonants μπ: mb (b in word-initial position);

νт: nt (d in word initial position);

γγ, γκ: ng (g in word-initial position).

The last names of women authors have been given in the genitive case (without -ς).

The names of editors, translators, and authors of critical studies have not been transcribed under the scheme used for the Greek authors: instead, their names have been unified under their fullest and most frequent form.

The computer

As originally mentioned, the check-list has been compiled on the computer and thus should be easier to correct and supplement for a subsequent version. (The fact of compiling the present version of the check-list on the computer did not necessarily save time.) Although it might have been preferable to enter the material into a data-base program, initial investigations into such programs as were commercially available did not produce an obvious candidate. The use of multiple alphabets (with different "sorting" orders and different initial words to be ignored), the variety of the types of material that appeared successively (books, articles, short poems, anthologies and special issues with varied contents, etc.), as well as the many sections in which they were to be arranged made it seem preferable to choose a word-processing program. The check-list has been developed on a Macintosh Plus computer in Microsoft Word 4.0. The Greek font is Smyrna, developed by the Boston College Font Project (Prof. M.J. Connolly, director).[13]

3. Caveat lector

No attempt has been made to provide a complete history of the translation of Modern Greek literature into English or a history of scholarship in English on Modern Greek literature. Others may indeed use the check-list as a springboard for such studies, always with the warning that nineteenth and early twentieth-century translations have been sketchily recorded (and with a further warning as to the mechanical nature of the index: see below). Nor has the check-list indexed very specialized Greek bibliographies on particular

---

[13] A Greek laser font, Samos, is forthcoming.

authors—although I had access to them—all of which, besides Greek references, cite foreign-language publications.[14]

This book, then, is intended as a guide to the literature itself: to present, to the speaker of English, references to the works of Greek authors translated into English and to the critical essays written in English on Modern Greek literature within the dates stated. Originally it was organized to be self-contained and, where necessary, to guide its reader by the use of subject headings and cross-references. Only at a later stage was an index added. The book does not intend to constitute a prosopography of all those who have occupied themselves with publishing English translations, or (in English) essays, anthologies, etc. on Modern Greek literature. The information on this topic available in this book comes as an extra benefit, with an apology to all the translators and others whose names may have been omitted through pressure of time. Perhaps a compiler of a future edition or another bibliographic source will concentrate on this subject, one of interest to historians of the reception and spread of Modern Greek literature in the English-speaking world. (Someone might also investigate a matter on which I had little information: the frequency and volume of publication of works contained in this list [the frequency may be somewhat gleaned from the successive publishers and dates of publication cited, but information as to the number of books published each time would require special research].)

The index has been mechanically prepared in accordance with the specifications of the program Microsoft Word 4.0. From its mechanical nature it incorporates occasional repetitions of names which increase the count of entries for an editor, translator, or author of an essay, when, for instance, an item is listed in more than one place (although double-indexing of repeated items has been kept to a minimum). Furthermore, a person listed with a page number in the index may actually appear on that page more than once. These facts are mentioned as a caveat to readers who might wish to use the simple counts of page numbers listed in the index as indicative of volume of production. They should inspect the book itself before coming to conclusions. The index is intended as a guide and aid to locating the material in the book, not in evaluating it quantitatively.

A different approach to the bibliography of Modern Greek literature is promised by the forthcoming bibliography currently under preparation by the Modern Greek Studies Association. It presents a chapter on each of the major fields of Modern Greek Studies which has been prepared by a specialist in that field. The entries are annotated and the bibliography aims at being authoritative: containing the major sources, mostly books but

---

[14] Such are the works: Δημήτρης Δασκαλόπουλος, Ἐργογραφία Σεφέρη (1931-1979): Βιβλιογραφική Δοκιμή (Ἀθήνα: Ἑλληνικό Λογοτεχνικό καί Ἱστορικό Ἀρχεῖο, 1979), Diana Haas-Μιχάλης Πιερής, Βιβλιογραφικός Ὁδηγός στά 154 Ποιήματα τοῦ Καβάφη (Ἀθήνα: Ἑρμῆς, 1985), and Mario Vitti, Ὀδυσσέας Ἐλύτης: Βιβλιογραφία 1935-1975 (Συνεργασία Ἀγγελικῆς Γαβαθᾶ. Ἀθήνα: Ἴκαρος, 1977), and the forthcoming bibliography of C.P. Cavafy, now in its final stages of preparation by Dimitris Daskalopoulos.

also articles, published in any language, though mainly in English, chiefly since 1945. The chapter on Modern Greek literature contains 400 entries and has been compiled by Roderick Beaton (who has generously allowed me to preview his work). Readers interested in being informed of recent periodical literature should be helped by current surveys published in the periodical Μαντατοφόρος which include material in English.[15] The compilers have indexed approximately 80 periodicals.

4. Acknowledgments

Much of the original impetus for this enterprise was provided by George Savidis, former incumbent of the George Seferis Chair of Modern Greek Studies at Harvard University from 1977 to 1984. He also provided a substantial part of the material which formed the original basis for this collection and offered valuable comments throughout the compilation. To him I am especially grateful.

Paula Touliopoulos, a graduate of Harvard University and advanced student of Modern Greek, began the project as its co-author, but was forced to withdraw at the end of 1986 because of the pressure of her studies at medical school. Her contributions to the contents and form of this work are inestimable.

This work would have not been possible without the help of many people to whom I should also like to express my gratitude. Colleagues, students, and friends at several universities and locations have been most generous with the material they have sent and with other assistance: Charles Ahern, Joseph Appleyard, S.J., John Atteberry, Kallifroni Avramidou, Alan Boegehold, Jacques Bouchard, Catherine Bouffides, Robert Bridges, Richard Burgi, Eugene Bushala, Katharine Butterworth, Yorghos Chouliaras, Elizabeth Constantinides, William Coulson, Loring Danforth, Effie Flessas, Dorothy Gregory, Diana Haas, Emily Hanawalt, Stratis Haviaras, David Holton, Lawrence Jones, Irene Kacandes, Maria Kakavas, Helen Kalogerakis, Isadora Kamarinea-Rosenthal, Mary Keeley, Helen Kyrkos, Fotios Litsas, Thanasis Maskaleris, Evangelia Mastichiadou, Martin McKinsey, Gareth Morgan, Rebecca Mosher, Kostas Myrsiades, Rick Newton, David W. Packard, Sophie Papageorgiou, Leandros Papathanasiou, John and Mary Zelia Philippides, Costas Proussis, Lillian Reisman, Martha Richardson, Alkesti Souloyianni, Erasmia Stavropoulou, Theofanis Stavrou, Christus Synadinos, Ruth Temple, George Thaniel, Maria Touliopoulos, Nassos Vayenas, Vasilis Vitsaxis, Mary Philippides Vlantikas, Louise Zarmati, Deborah Zimic. The following institutions have contributed their help: American School of Classical Studies in Athens, Boston College, Byzantijns-Nieuwgrieks Seminarium of the University of Amsterdam, Ελληνικό Λογοτεχνικό και Ιστορικό Αρχείο, Fulbright Program of the United States Educational Foundation in

---

[15] Wim Bakker-Δημήτρης Δασκαλόπουλος, "Μελέτες σε περιοδικά για τη νεοελληνική λογοτεχνία. Βιβλιογραφική καταγραφή". Μαντατοφόρος 27 (Ιούν. 1988), pp. 7-46 (covers 1 Jan. 1986 - 1 Apr. 1987); 29 (Ιούν. 1989), pp. 101-121 (covers 1 Apr. 1987 - 31 Dec. 1987); and (forthcoming) 31 (Ιούν. 1990) (covers 1988).

Greece, Gennadius Library, Charles and Mary Maliotis Charitable Foundation, Modern Greek Studies Association (through its Executive Committee), Tiffany Printing Company in Cheshire, Conn., Widener Library of Harvard University.

I am particularly indebted to Wim Bakker for unstintingly contributing his editorial expertise and his newly-acquired computer skills towards giving the material its proper shape. To Roderick Beaton for sending two unpublished bibliographies of his own and offering suggestions based on my manuscript. To Peter Bien for sending an unpublished bibliography, for reviewing the introduction and the section on Kazantzakis, and for standing as constant mentor over the check-list. To M.J. Connolly for authoritative guidance in formatting the typescript on the computer and designing the cover. To John Iatrides for inspired patience and ingenuity in leading the typescript through all the complex steps of in-house publication. To Edmund Keeley for responding to many requests for edification. To Lena Savidis for providing expert finishing touches to the cover and the overall format of the book.

One of the greatest pleasures resulting from the preparation of the check-list has been the chance of being enlightened by experienced bibliographers. Dimitris Daskalopoulos has repeatedly granted free access to his invaluable library and archive of references, his first-hand knowledge of Modern Greek literature, and his unique proficiency in bibliographic compilation. Other bibliographers have also impressed me with their generosity: Kyriakos Delopoulos, Loukia Droulia, and Manos Haritatos offered information and access to material; Evro Layton and John Zenelis gave very helpful comments based on the manuscript at various stages. My work has been considerably enhanced by their advice.

As I have come to appreciate increasingly throughout the compilation of this check-list, bibliographic compilation, especially in the area of Modern Greek literature, is not a task to be undertaken lightly by the uninitiated (see p. ix). It takes endless patience and many resources (time and travel). Missing data (e.g., the name of the publisher, the date of publication or the number of the issue) in references or in the publications themselves cause hours of extra worry. Inadequate tables of content or discrepancies in the description of items from more than one source lead to confusion and delays. Erroneous information wastes even more time in the attempt to verify it. The trouble in ascertaining an author's year of birth (or death) has been considerable. I should like to close with a plea to authors, publishers, and scholars that they assist their readers by providing correctly the basic facts. Perhaps a second, revised and enlarged, edition of the present check-list will be able to rely on more plentiful and accurate information.

Cambridge and Chestnut Hill, Mass. -   Dia M.L. Philippides
Athens and Aegina -
London and Cambridge -
Amsterdam
1984-1990

ABBREVIATIONS USED FOR JOURNALS

BMGS	*Byzantine and Modern Greek Studies*
CML	*Classical and Modern Literature*
JHD	*Journal of the Hellenic Diaspora*
JMGS	*Journal of Modern Greek Studies*
JMH	*Journal of Modern Hellenism*
JML	*Journal of Modern Literature*
MGSY	*Modern Greek Studies Yearbook*
SSMG	*Scandinavian Studies in Modern Greek*
TLS	*[London] Times Literary Supplement*
WLT	*World Literature Today*

Byzantine and Modern Greek Studies (Oxford)
Byzantinische Zeitschrift (München: C.H. Beck)
Byzantinoslavica: International Journal of Byzantine Studies / Revue Internationale des Études Byzantines (Prague)
Byzantion: Revue Internationale des Études Byzantines (Brussels)
Canadian Review of Comparative Literature / Revue Canadienne de Littérature Comparée (University of Toronto Press for the Canadian Comparative Literature Association)
Canto: Review of the Arts (Andover, Mass.)
Cave: An International Review of Arts and Ideas (Hamilton, New Zealand: Outriggers Publishers)
Central Park: A Journal of Arts and Social Theory (New York)
Chapman (Perthshire, Scotland)
The Charioteer: A Quarterly Review of Modern Greek Culture (New York: Pella Publishing Company)
Chelsea (New York)
Chicago Review (Chicago: University of Chicago)
The Christian Science Monitor (Boston, Mass.)
Christianity & Literature (Grand Rapids, Mich.: Conference on Christianity & Literature)
Christopher Street (New York)
Classical and Modern Literature: A Quarterly (Terre Haute, Ind.)
Classical Journal (Gainesville, Fla.: Classical Association of the Middle West and South)
The Classical Outlook (New York: American Classical League)
The Coffeehouse / Τό καφενεῖο: Contemporary Greek Arts and Letters (San Francisco). Continued by *Aegean Review*
College Literature (West Chester, Pa.: West Chester State College)
The Colorado Quarterly (Boulder: The University of Colorado)
Columbia: A Magazine of Poetry & Prose (New York: School of the Arts, Columbia University)
Comparative Drama (Kalamazoo, Mich.)
Comparative Literature (Eugene, Oreg.: University of Oregon)
Comparative Literature Studies (Urbana: University of Illinois Press)
Conspectus of History (Muncie, Ind.: Ball State University)
Contemporary Literature in Translation (Vancouver, British Columbia)
The Contemporary Review (Edinburgh and Dublin)
Cornhill Magazine (London)
Crete
The Critical Survey (Hull, England)
Crosscurrents (Westlake Village, Calif.)
Daily Telegraph (London)
Dance Perspectives (Brooklyn, N.Y.)
Denver Quarterly (The University of Denver)
Descant (Toronto)
Deus Loci: The Lawrence Durrell Newsletter (Kelowa, British Columbia)
Dissertation Abstracts International (Ann Arbor, Mich.)
Δωδώνη: Ἐπιστημονική Ἐπετηρίς τῆς Φιλοσοφικῆς Σχολῆς τοῦ Πανεπιστημίου Ἰωαννίνων
The Drama Review (New York University School of the Arts)
Dumbarton Oaks Papers (Washington, D.C.)
Durak: An International Magazine of Poetry (Eerin, N.Y.)
The Dutton Review (New York: Dutton)
East European Quarterly (Boulder: University of Colorado)
The Eastern and Western Review (London)

JOURNALS CITED

This list contains all the journals cited in this bibliography. For each journal its (original) place of publication and/or publishing agent are given, when known. Subtitles have been provided as found, but they may vary throughout the life of the journal.

Greek titles have been interpolated according to their standardized transcription (see introduction).

Accent: A Quarterly of New Literature (University of Illinois, Urbana)
Aegean Review (New York). Continues *The Coffeehouse*
Agenda (London)
The Amaranth: Bulletin of the Modern Greek Studies Program, University of Toronto
American Imago: A Psychoanalytic Journal for the Arts and Sciences (Detroit, Mich.: Wayne State University Press)
American Journal of Philology (Baltimore, Md.: Johns Hopkins University Press)
The American Poetry Review (Philadelphia, Pa.: World Poetry Inc.)
The American Scholar: A Quarterly for the Independent Thinker (Washington, D.C.)
Ἀγγλο-ελληνική Ἐπιθεώρηση / *Anglo-Greek Review* (Athens)
Antaeus: A Literary Magazine (Tangier)
The Antioch Review (Yellow Springs, Ohio)
Antipodes (Melbourne, Australia)
Ararat (New York)
Arion's Dolphin: A Quarterly of Poetry (Cambridge, Mass.)
Arizona Quarterly (Tucson: The University of Arizona)
Athenaeum (London)
Athene: The American Magazine of Hellenic Thought (Chicago)
The Athenian: Greece's English Language Monthly (Athens)
The Atlantic Monthly (Boston, Mass.)
[Monthly Illustrated] *Atlantis* / Μηνιαία Εἰκονογραφημένη Ἀτλαντίς (New York)
Balkan Studies: Biannual Publication of the Institute for Balkan Studies (Thessaloniki)
Ball State University Forum (Muncie, Ind.)
Baltic Avenue Poetry Journal
The Beloit Poetry Journal (Beloit, Wis.)
The Bentham Newsletter
Books Abroad: An International Literary Quarterly (Norman, Okla.). Continued by *World Literature Today*
Book Week (New York: World Journal Tribune, Inc.)
Books at Iowa (Iowa City: University of Iowa)
Boston Globe (Boston, Mass.: Globe Newspaper Co.)
Boston Latin School Register (Boston, Mass.)
Boston Review (Cambridge, Mass.: Boston Critic, Inc.)
Boston University Journal (Boston, Mass.)
Boundary 2: A Journal of Postmodern Literature and Culture (Binghamton, N.Y.)
Brown Classical Journal (Providence, R.I.: Brown University)
Bulletin of Bibliography (Boston, Mass.: The Boston Book Company)

Educational Theatre Journal (Washington, D.C.)
Eleutheria: A Journal of Opinion Devoted to Discussion of the Realities of Greek Politics, Arts and Letters (Waltham, Mass.)
Ἑλληνικά: Φιλολογικόν, Ἱστορικόν καί Λαογραφικόν Περιοδικόν Σύγγραμμα (Thessaloniki)
Ἑλληνισμός Ἀμερικῆς (New York)
Encounter (London)
English Review of Salem State College (Salem, Mass.)
Envoy
Ἐπετηρίς τοῦ Κέντρου Ἐπιστημονικῶν Ἐρευνῶν Κύπρου
Ἐπιστημονική Ἐπετηρίς τῆς Φιλοσοφικῆς Σχολῆς τοῦ Πανεπιστημίου Ἀθηνῶν
Ἐπιθεώρηση Κοινωνικῶν Ἐρευνῶν / *The Greek Review of Social Research* (Athens)
Epoch (Ithaca, N.Y.: Cornell University)
Epsilon: Modern Greek and Balkan Studies (Copenhagen: University of Copenhagen, Department of Modern Greek and Balkan Studies). Continues *Scandinavian Studies in Modern Greek*
Ὁ Ἐρανιστής (Athens)
Ἡ Ἑσπερία (London)
Essays in Criticism: A Quarterly Journal of Literary Criticism (Oxford)
Études Helléniques / Hellenic Studies (Montréal, Québec)
Evergreen Review (New York)
The Falcon (Mansfield, Pa.)
Feats and Seasons
Field: Contemporary Poetry and Poetics (Oberlin, Ohio: Oberlin College)
Filologia Moderna (Madrid)
Folia Neohellenica: Zeitschrift für Neogräzistik (Amsterdam: A.M. Hakkert)
Folklore (London: The Folklore Society)
Footprint Magazine (Somerville, N.J.)
Forum for Modern Language Studies (St. Andrews, Scotland)
Fulbright Review (Athens)
The Georgia Review (Athens, Ga.: University of Georgia)
Τὸ Γιοφύρι: Περιοδικό νεοελληνικῶν σπουδῶν / *The Yofiri: Periodical of Modern Greek Studies* (Sydney, Australia: University of Sydney)
Graham House Review (Englewood, N.J.: Graham House Press)
Grand Street (New York: Grand Street Public.)
Greece
Greek Heritage: The American Quarterly of Greek Culture (Chicago: Athenian Corp.)
Greek Letters: A Modern Greek Literature Annual (Athens)
The Greek Orthodox Theological Review (Brookline, Mass.: Holy Cross School of Theology, Hellenic College)
The Greek Report (London)
The Greek Review of Social Research, see Ἐπιθεώρηση Κοινωνικῶν Ἐρευνῶν
Greek, Roman, and Byzantine Studies (Cambridge, Mass.)
Greek World (New York)
Grove: Contemporary Poetry and Translation (Claremont, Calif.: Pitzer College)
Harvard Library Bulletin (Cambridge, Mass.: Harvard University Library)
Harvard Slavic Studies (Cambridge, Mass.)
Harvard Studies in Classical Philology (Cambridge, Mass.)
Helios: Journal of the Classical Association of the Southwest (Lubbock, Tex.)
The Hellenic Herald (London)

The Hellenic Journal (San Francisco)
Hesperia: Journal of the American School of Classical Studies at Athens (Cambridge, Mass.)
Hispania: A Journal Devoted to the Interests of the Teaching of Spanish and Portuguese (Appleton, Wis.)
Horizon: A Review of Literature and Art (London)
The Hudson Review (New York: Hudson Review, Inc.)
Humanitas: Journal of the Institute of Man (Pittsburgh, Pa.: Duquesne University)
Imprint
Indiana Social Studies Quarterly (Muncie, Ind.: Ball State University)
The International Fiction Review (Fredericton, New Brunswick, Canada)
The International Journal of Psycho-Analysis and Bulletin of the International Psycho-Analytical Association (London: The Institute of Psycho-Analysis)
International Poetry Review (Greensboro, N.C.)
The International Portland Review (Portland, Oreg.)
Interpretations: Studies in Language and Literature (Memphis State University, Dept. of English)
The Iowa Review: A Literary Quarterly (Iowa City: University of Iowa)
Iron (North Shields, Tyneside, England)
Ironwood (Tucson, Ariz.: Ironwood Press)
Jahrbuch der Österreichischen Byzantinistik (Wien: Verlag der Österreichischen Akademie der Wissenschaften)
Journal of American Folklore (Boston and New York: Published for the American Folklore Society by Houghton, Mifflin, and Co.)
Journal of English
Journal of Hellenic Studies (London)
Journal of Modern Greek Studies (Baltimore, Md.: The Johns Hopkins University Press)
Journal of Modern Hellenism (Brookline, Mass.: Hellenic College Press)
The Journal of Modern History (Chicago: University of Chicago Press)
Journal of Modern Literature (Philadelphia: Temple University)
Journal of Popular Culture (Bowling Green, Ohio: Bowling Green State University)
Journal of the Hellenic American Society (Indianapolis, Ind.). Continued by *Journal of the Hellenic Diaspora*
Journal of the Hellenic Diaspora (Indianapolis, Ind.: Hellenic American Society)
Kayak (Santa Cruz, Calif.)
The Kenyon Review (Gambier, Ohio: Kenyon College)
Κρίκος / The Link (London)
Κρητικά Χρονικά: Τετραμηνιαία ἐπιστημονικὴ ἔκδοσις (Ἡράκλειον Κρήτης)
Κρητολογία: Περιοδικὴ ἐπιστημονικὴ ἔκδοσις (Ἡράκλειον Κρήτης)
Κυπριακαὶ Σπουδαί: Δελτίον τῆς Ἑταιρείας Κυπριακῶν Σπουδῶν (Λευκωσία Κύπρου)
Labrys (Hayes, Middlesex, England)
Λαογραφία: Δελτίον τῆς Ἑλληνικῆς Λαογραφικῆς Ἑταιρείας (Athens)
Life and Letters and the London Mercury: An International Monthly of Living Literature (London)
Linguistics: An International Review (The Hague)
Link: A Review of Medieval and Modern Greek (Oxford)
The Listener (London)
The Literary Gazette and Journal of the Belles Lettres

The Literary Review (Edinburgh: Sunlight Press). Herein: *The Literary Review* (Edinburgh)
The Literary Review: An International Journal of Contemporary Writing (Madison, N.J.: Fairleigh Dickinson Univ.)
Literature and Psychology (Teaneck, N.J.)
Literature in North Queensland
London Magazine (London)
[London] Times Literary Supplement
The Los Angeles Times (Los Angeles)
Madrona (Seattle, Wash.: Gemini Press)
Makedonski Folklor / Le Folklore Macédonien (Skopje)
The Malahat Review: An International Quarterly of Life and Letters (Victoria, B.C.: University of Victoria)
Manna: A Review of Contemporary Poetry (Toronto)
Μαντατοφόρος: Δελτίο Νεοελληνικῶν Σπουδῶν (Birmingham, England)
Margin: At the Edge of Literature & Ideas (Dunning, Scotland)
The Massachusetts Review: A Quarterly of Literature, the Arts and Public Affairs (Amherst: Massachusetts Review, Inc.)
Meanjin (Parkville, Victoria, Australia: University of Melbourne)
Mediterranean Review (Oakdale, N.Y.)
Mews (Cambridge, England: Cambridge University English Society)
The Miami Herald (Miami, Fla.: Herald Print and Pub. Co.)
Michigan Academician: Papers of the Michigan Academy of Science, Arts, and Letters (Ann Arbor, Mich.)
Micromegas (Amherst, Mass.)
Milkweed Chronicle (Edina, Minn.)
The Missouri Review (Columbia: Dept. of English of the University of Missouri, Columbia)
Modern Greek Studies Association Bulletin (Princeton, N.J.)
Modern Greek Studies Yearbook (Minneapolis, Minn.: University of Minnesota)
The Modern Language Review (Belfast: Modern Humanities Research Association)
Modern Poetry in Translation (London)
Modern Writing
Mosaic: A Journal for the Comparative Study of Literature (Winnipeg, Manitoba: University of Manitoba Press)
Mundus Artium: A Journal of International Literature and the Arts (Athens, Ohio)
The Nassau Literary Review (Princeton, N.J.)
The Nation
Neohelicon: Acta Comparationis Litterarum Universarum (Budapest: Akademiai Kiado)
Neo-Hellenika: Annual Publication of the Center for Neo-Hellenic Studies (Austin, Tex.)
Neophilologus: Modern Language Quarterly (Groningen)
New Directions in Prose and Poetry (New York)
New England Review and Bread Loaf Quarterly (Hanover, N.H.: Kenyon Hill Pub.)
New Jersey Folklore: A Statewide Journal (New Brunswick, N.J.: Douglass College, American Studies Dept.)
New Letters: A Magazine of Fine Writing (Kansas City: University of Missouri). A continuation of *The University Review*
The New Orleans Review (New Orleans, La.: Loyola University)
The New Republic (New York: The Republic Pub. Co.)
The New World
New World Writing (Philadelphia & New York: J.B. Lippincott Co.)
New Writing and Daylight (London: John Lehmann). Superseded by *Orpheus*

The New York Review of Books (New York)
The New York Times (New York)
The New York Times Book Review (New York)
The New Yorker (New York: New Yorker Magazine, Inc.)
Newsweek (Los Angeles, Calif.: Newsweek, Inc.)
Nine: A Magazine of Literature and the Arts (London)
The Nineteenth Century: A Monthly Review (London)
The Noiseless Spider (New Haven, Conn.)
Northwest Review (Eugene, Oreg.)
Notes on Contemporary Literature (Carrollton, Ga.)
Ohio Journal (Columbus, Ohio: Ohio State University, Dept. of English)
Omphalos: A Mediterranean Review (Athens)
The Ontario Review (Windsor, Ont.)
Oral Tradition (Columbus, Ohio: Slavica Publishers)
Orpheus: A Symposium of the Arts (London: John Lehmann)
Oxford Slavonic Papers (Oxford: The Clarendon Press)
Pacific Quarterly Moana (Hamilton, New Zealand: Outrigger Publishers)
The Pacific Review
Paintbrush: A Journal of Poetry, Translations, and Letters (Laramie, Wyo.: Ishtar Publications)
Ὁ Παλίμψηστος / The Palimpsest (Montreal)
Panjandrum (San Francisco: Panjandrum Press)
Papers on Language and Literature: Journal of the Midwest MLA for Scholars and Critics of Language and Literature (Edwardsville: Southern Illinois University)
The Paris Review (Flushing, N.Y.)
Parnassus: Poetry in Review (New York: S. Lewis)
Partisan Review (New York: Partisan Review, Inc.)
The Patristic and Byzantine Review (Kingston, N.Y.: American Institute for Patristic and Byzantine Studies)
PEN American Center Newsletter (New York: American Center of PEN International)
The Penguin New Writing (Harmondsworth, Middlesex, England)
Pequod: A Journal of Contemporary Literature and Literary Criticism (Forest Knolls, Calif.)
Perfect Bound (Cambridge, England)
Perspective: A Quarterly of Literature and the Arts (Louisville, Ky.)
Philological Quarterly (Iowa City, Iowa: Univ. of Iowa)
Philosophy and Literature (Dearnborn, Mich.: University of Michigan-Dearborn)
Phylon: The Atlanta University Review of Race and Culture (Atlanta, Ga.)
Πλάτων: Δελτίον τῆς Ἑταιρείας Ἑλλήνων Φιλολόγων (Athens)
Ploughshares: A Quarterly of the Arts (Cambridge, Mass.)
Πνευματική Κύπρος (Λευκωσία Κύπρου)
Poet Lore (Philadelphia, Pa.)
Poetics Today: International Journal for Theory and Analysis of Literature and Communication (Tel Aviv: Porter Institute for Poetics and Semiotics)
Poetry (Chicago: Modern Poetry Association)
Poetry (Madras, India). Herein *Poetry* (Madras)
Poetry Pilot (New York: Academy of American Poets)
Poetry Review (London: The Poetry Society)
Poetry Society of America Bulletin (New York)
Poetry Wales (Swansea: C. Davies)
Prairie Schooner (Lincoln, Nebr.: University of Nebraska Press)
Princeton Alumni Weekly (Princeton, N.J.: Princeton University)

Prism International: A Magazine of Contemporary Writing (Vancouver: University of British Columbia)
Proceedings of the Cambridge Philological Society (London: Trübner)
Proceedings (of the) Pacific Northwest Council on Foreign Languages
Πρωϊνή (New York: Petellides Pub.)
Prose (New York)
Quadrant (Sydney, Australia: Quadrant Magazine Co., Ltd.)
Quarterly Review of Literature (Chapel Hill, N.C.)
Raccoon (Memphis, Tenn.)
Rackham Literary Studies (Ann Arbor, Mich.)
Raritan: A Quarterly Review (New Brunswick, N.J.: Rutgers University)
Regionalism and the Female Imagination (Univ. Park, Pa.: Pennsylvania State University, Dept. of English)
The Review
Review of National Literatures (New York: St. John's University Press)
St. Andrews Review: A Twice-yearly Magazine of the Arts and Humanities (Laurinburg, N.C.: St. Andrews Presbyterian College)
Saturday Review of Literature (New York)
Scandinavian Studies in Modern Greek / Νεοελληνικά Μελετήματα (Copenhagen: University of Copenhagen, Dept. of Modern Greek). Continued by *Epsilon*
Scripsi (Parkville, Victoria, Australia: Scripsi Society)
Seneca Review (Geneva, N.Y.)
Sequoia (Stanford, Calif.: Associated Students of Stanford University)
Shakespeare Translation (Tokyo: Yushodo Shoten)
The Shaw Review (University Park, Pa.: The Shaw Society of America and the Pennsylvania State University Press)
Shenandoah: The Washington and Lee University Review (Lexington, Va.)
Skylark: A Quarterly of Contemporary Indian Literature (India)
The Slavonic and East European Review (London: University of London)
Small Moon (Somerville, Mass.)
Soundings (Santa Barbara, Calif.: University of California Library)
The South Atlantic Quarterly (Durham, N.C.: Duke University Press)
Southern Humanities Review (Auburn, Alabama: Auburn University)
Southern Review (Baton Rouge: Louisiana State University)
Southwest Review (Dallas, Tex.: Southern Methodist University Press)
Speculum: A Journal of Medieval Studies (Cambridge, Mass.: Medieval Academy of America)
Spirit: A Magazine of Poetry (South Orange, N.J.: Seton Hall University)
Στασῖνος: Δελτίον τοῦ Συνδέσμου Ἑλλήνων Φιλολόγων Κύπρου "Στασῖνος" (Λευκωσία Κύπρου)
Steinbeck Quarterly (Muncie, Ind.: Steinbeck Society)
Studies in Browning and His Circle: A Journal of Criticism, History, and Bibliography (Waco, Tex.: Baylor University)
Studies in Medieval Culture (Kalamazoo, Mich.: Western Michigan University)
Sumac (Fremont, Mich.)
Svenska Forskningsinstitutet i Istanbul, Meddelanden (Stockholm: Institutet)
Σύγχρονα Θέματα: Τριμηνιαία ἔκδοση ἐπιστημονικοῦ προβληματισμοῦ καί παιδείας (Athens)
Temenos: A Review Devoted to the Arts of the Imagination (Dulverton, England: Watkins; West Stockbridge, Mass.: Lindisfarne Press)
Texas Quarterly (Austin: University of Texas)

Theatre Research: The Journal of the International Federation for Theatre Research (Roma). Continued by *Theatre Research International*
Theatre Research International (London: Oxford University Press)
Theatre Survey: The American Journal of Theatre History (Pittsburgh, Pa.: American Society for Theatre Research)
Thespis: Bulletin of the Greek Center of the I.T.I. (Athens)
Third Rail (Los Angeles, Calif.: Third Rail)
Θησαυρίσματα (Venice, Italy: Ἑλληνικόν Ἰνστιτοῦτον Βενετίας)
Thought (Bronx, N.Y.: Fordham University Press)
Transactions of the Philological Society (London)
The Transatlantic Review (London and New York)
Translation: The Journal of Literary Translation (New York: Columbia University)
Translation Review (Richardson, Tex.: The University of Texas at Dallas)
University: A Princeton Magazine (Princeton, N.J.)
University of Birmingham Historical Journal (Birmingham, England)
University Publishing (Berkeley, Calif.: University of California Press)
Verse (Oxford)
The Virginia Quarterly Review: A National Journal of Literature & Discussion (Charlotteville, Va.: University of Virginia)
Wake: The Creative Magazine (New York)
The Western Humanities Review (Salt Lake City: University of Utah)
The Western Review: A Literary Quarterly (Iowa City: State University of Iowa)
Willow Springs Magazine (Cheney, Wash.: Literary Guild on the Campus at Eastern Washington University)
Women's Studies: An Interdisciplinary Journal (National Women's Studies Association; New York: Gordon and Breach Science Publishers)
World Literature Today: A Literary Quarterly of the University of Oklahoma (Norman, Okla.: University of Oklahoma Press). Continues *Books Abroad*
The Yale Review (New Haven, Conn.: Yale University)
Yearbook of Comparative and General Literature (Bloomington, Ind.: Indiana University)
The Yofiri, see [Το] Γιοφύρι
Zenos (Nottingham, England)

1. BIBLIOGRAPHICAL SOURCES

This chapter is divided into three sections:
    I. Bibliographies Wholly Concerned with Modern Greek;
    II. General Bibliographies with Sections on Modern Greek Literature;
    III. Library Catalogues and Surveys of Collections.

In each section the works are arranged alphabetically by the last names of their editors. More specific bibliographies referring to individual (Greek) authors are placed in Chapter 7.

I. Bibliographies Wholly Concerned with Modern Greek

1.1 Bislani-Dalipi, Bessie, ed. *Τά Νεοελληνικά Γράμματα στή Δύση / La Littérature Néohéllenique en Occident / Modern Greek Literature in the West / (1941-1980): Κατάλογος Βιβλίων / Catalogues de Livres / Catalogue of Books.* Ἑλληνική Δημοκρατία, Ὑπουργεῖο Ἐξωτερικῶν, Διεύθυνση Μορφωτικῶν Ὑποθέσεων. République Hellénique, Ministère des Affaires Étrangères, Direction des Affaires Culturelles. Hellenic Republic, Ministry for Foreign Affairs, Direction of Cultural Affairs. Initiative of Dimitrios Voudouris, Deputy Foreign Minister. Athens: "Manoutios" Printing House, 1981. 95 p.

    A catalogue of books in English, French, German, Italian, Spanish, Portuguese, Swedish, Norwegian, Danish, Finnish, and Dutch, arranged alphabetically by authors (pp. 13-86), followed by a list of anthologies, arranged chronologically (pp. 87-93). Not on the market.

1.2 Clark, Richard C. "Modern Greek Literature: Bibliographical Spectrum and Review Article". *Review of National Literatures* 5, No. 2 (Fall 1974), pp. 137-159.

1.3 Clogg, Mary Jo and Richard Clogg, comps. *Greece.* World Bibliographical Series, Vol. 17. Oxford and Santa Barbara: Clio Press, 1980. 225 p.

    Arranged in sections by subjects such as geography, history, language, politics, the arts, and bibliography. The section on literature, pp. 153-165, contains 69 entries, arranged alphabetically by author and including brief comments.

1.4 Dimaras, C.Th., C. Koumarianou, and L. Droulia. *Modern Greek Culture: A Selected Bibliography* (in English, French, German, Italian). Fourth revised edition. Offered on the occasion of the Third International Congress of South Eastern European Studies. Athens, 1974. 119 p.

    Entries on literature are mostly found under the sections entitled: History of Literature (pp. 42-45); Texts (pp. 50-59); Greek Authors (pp. 60-91).

1.5 Feeney, William R. and Martha J. Feeney. "A Bibliography of Doctoral Dissertations in the Non-Science Fields of Modern Greek Studies Accepted by the

Universities of Athens and Thessaloniki". *Modern Greek Studies Association Bulletin* 6, No. 1 (June 1974), pp. 3-8.
    The authors' names and the field of the dissertation are given in English, but the titles are given in Greek.

1.6 Giannaris, George, comp. "A Bibliography of Doctoral and Masters Dissertations on Greece". *Modern Greek Studies Association Bulletin* 5, No. 1 (June 1973), pp. 3-12.
    Lists separately doctoral dissertations and masters theses arranged alphabetically by name of author. Subject matter starts after A.D. 800. Supplementary list published in *Modern Greek Studies Association Bulletin* 7, No. 1 (June 1975), pp. 5-6.

1.7 Karathanassis, A.A., C. Dimadis, and E.-L. Stavropoulou. "Modern Greek Literature: A Bibliography 1981-1982". *Greek Letters* 1 (1982), pp. 341-412.
    Subdivided into: I. Poetry; II. Prose; III. Theatre; IV. Studies-Essays; V. Book reviews; VI. Interviews. The authors' names are given in English; the titles of their works have also been translated into English. Most of the publications listed, however, are in Greek.

1.8 Layton, Evro. "'Επισκόπηση μεταφράσεων καί μεταφραστῶν: Ἡνωμένες Πολιτεῖες (καί Καναδᾶς) 1945-1981" (Survey of Translations and Translators: United States and Canada 1945-1981). *Μαντατοφόρος* 20 (Nov. 1982), pp. 30-48.
    Fundamental publication for translations of Modern Greek literature into English. Includes books arranged under the headings: anthologies; [authors in alphabetical order]; studies/essays; journals; forthcoming publications; and a section on English translations from Greece, Cyprus and elsewhere.

1.9 Layton, Evro, comp. "Selective List of Books on Modern Greece Published in English 1968-1971". *Modern Greek Studies Association Bulletin* 3, No. 2 (Dec. 1971), pp. 6-8.

1.10 Mackridge, Peter. "'Επισκόπηση μεταφράσεων καί μεταφραστῶν: Μεγάλη Βρεταννία καί 'Ιρλανδία 1945-1981" (Survey of Translations and Translators: Great Britain and Ireland 1945-1981). *Μαντατοφόρος* 20 (Nov. 1982), pp. 49-61.
    Complements entry 1.8.

1.11 Σταυροπούλου, 'Ερασμία-Λουΐζα. *Βιβλιογραφία Μεταφράσεων Νεοελληνικῆς Λογοτεχνίας* (Bibliography of the Translations of Modern Greek Literature). 'Αθήνα: 'Εταιρεία 'Ελληνικοῦ Λογοτεχνικοῦ καί 'Ιστορικοῦ 'Αρχείου, 1986. 318 p.
    Lists the translations of works (books) by Modern Greek authors into more than 30 languages. Comprises 1895 titles. The main section (pp. 21-233) is arranged alphabetically by author. Anthologies follow (pp. 235-264). The book concludes with a supplement (pp. 265-275) and three indexes (of authors, of translators, and by language).

1.12 Swanson, Donald C. *Modern Greek Studies in the West: A Critical Bibliography of Studies on Modern Greek Linguistics, Philology and Folklore, in Languages other than Greek.* New York: New York Public Library, 1960. 93 p.
    Contains two major sections: Books and Monographs; Periodical Articles. The literary entries are restricted mainly to early Modern Greek literature or to popular folk literature.

1.13 Will, Frederic. "Translations into English of Modern Greek Poetry". *Yearbook of Comparative and General Literature* 5 (1956), pp. 17-20.

II. General Bibliographies with Sections on Modern Greek Literature

1.14 *The American Bibliography of Slavic and East European Studies*. Prepared at the Library of Congress for The American Association for the Advancement of Slavic Studies. Stanford, Calif., 1956-[1987].
   Annual. The most recent volume available refers to 1987 (Barbara L. Dash, comp. and ed.). The bibliography contains sections on [Modern] Greek under the heading of "Literature" irregularly until 1967, regularly thereafter.

1.15 Horecky, Paul L., ed. *Southeastern Europe: A Guide to Basic Publications*. Chicago: University of Chicago Press, 1969.
   Part Four refers to Greece; entries on literature are given on pp. 298-303.

1.16 Koundouros, Roussos. *On Greece and Cyprus: Theses Index in Britain (1949-1974)*. London: Greek Press and Information Office, 1977.
   By the same author: *On Greece: Theses Index in Britain (1874-1950)*. London: Greek Press and Information Office, 1980. 16 p. The two collections are joined as "Ἑλληνικές Διατριβές σέ Ἀγγλικά Πανεπιστήμια", in *Σύγχρονα Θέματα* 9 (Oct. 1980), pp. 47-66. Arranged in two sections: A. 1874-1950; B. 1950-1975. An index of theses on Greek subjects, starting with antiquity. Theses are arranged chronologically and listed by author, title and university.

1.17 *MLA International Bibliography of Books and Articles on the Modern Languages and Literatures*. New York: The Modern Language Association of America, 1968-[1987].
   Annual. The separate section on Modern Greek literature began in 1968 and is based on contributions by noted bibliographers and scholars of Modern Greek, including Evro Layton, Costas Proussis, and Mario Vitti. A bibliography of each year's publications on Modern Greek literature in all languages, especially full in its early years. Currently (starting with the volume for 1984) Modern Greek literature is listed under "Balkan Literature".
   Prior to 1969 the bibliography was published as part of *PMLA (Publications of the Modern Language Association)*.

1.18 Parks, George B. and Ruth Z. Temple, eds. *The Literatures of the World in English Translation: A Bibliography*. Volume I: *The Greek and Latin Literatures*. New York: Frederick Ungar Publishing Co., 1968.
   Aims at listing the English translations of all Greek and Latin works published up to 1965. Section entitled "Modern Greek Literature from A.D. 1453" (pp. 183-200) compiled from contributions by Procope S. Costas and William V. Pappas.

1.19 Reinhold, Meyer and Emily Albu Hanawalt. "Bibliography of the Classical Tradition". *CML* 5, No. 3 (Spring 1985) ["for 1980-1982"]; 6, No. 3 (Spring 1986) ["for 1983"]; 7, No. 3 (Spring 1987) ["for 1984"].
   In each case the bibliography occupies the entire issue; it contains some references to Modern Greek literature.

III. Library Catalogues and Surveys of Collections

1.20 *Catalog of the Modern Greek Collection at the University of Cincinnati.* 5 vols. Boston, Mass.: G.K. Hall, 1978.
　　The ca. 69,000 catalogue cards of the collection are reproduced by offset, with 21 cards per page.

1.21 *Catalogue of the Gennadius Library.* American School of Classical Studies at Athens. 7 vols. Boston, Mass.: G.K. Hall, 1968. Supplements I (1973) and II (1981).
　　Catalogue cards reproduced 21 to a page. The collection is specialized: it originally incorporated early editions of classical, patristic and Byzantine authors; has been supplemented by later Greek material to double its initial size.

1.22 Clogg, Richard. "Early Modern Greek Printed Books in the Library of the British School at Athens". Ὁ Ἐρανιστής 5, No. 27-28 (June-Aug. 1967), pp. 98-104.

1.23 Horecky, Paul L., chief editor, and David H. Kraus, associate editor. *East Central and South East Europe: A Handbook of Library and Archival Resources in North America.* Santa Barbara, Calif.; Oxford, England: Clio Press, 1976. 467 p.
　　Descriptions of the Modern Greek collections of the Universities of California (Berkeley and Los Angeles), Chicago, Cincinnati, Harvard (including Dumbarton Oaks), Toronto, Yale, the Library of Congress, and the New York Public Library.

1.24 *Jackson, Robert F. "Sixteenth-Century Greek Editions at Iowa". *Books at Iowa* 12 (1970), pp. 3-12.

1.25 Layton, Evro. "The Modern Greek Collection in the Harvard College Library". *Harvard Library Bulletin* 19, No. 3 (July 1971), pp. 221-243.
　　Article full of references, especially to early publications.

1.26 Perry, George E. "The Modern Greek Collection in the Library of Congress: A Survey". *The Greek Review of Social Research* 15-16 (Jan.-June 1973), pp. 14-25.

1.27 Topping, Peter. "Modern Greek Studies and Materials in the United States". *Byzantion* 15 (1940-1941), pp. 414-442.

1.28 Walton, Francis R. "Gennadeion Gleanings". Ὁ Ἐρανιστής 4, No. 24 (Dec. 1966), pp. 215-221.
　　Rare items relevant to Neohellenic studies in the Gennadius Library.

2. JOURNALS

This chapter is divided into two sections:
  I. Journals indexed;
  II. Journals not indexed.

The journals listed below regularly contain Modern Greek literary items in English. The contents of the journals in the first section have been fully indexed, from their first issue until the last one published before the end of 1987 (enclosed in square brackets). In order to help readers who might be interested in ordering back issues of journals, an attempt has been made to list for each journal its most recent place of publication.

I. Indexed

2.1 *Aegean Review.* New York: Wire Press. Premier issue (Fall/Winter 1986) - [No. 3 (Fall/Winter 1987)]. Semi-annual.

2.2 *The Amaranth: Bulletin of the Modern Greek Studies Program, University of Toronto.* G. Thaniel, ed. No. 1 (1981) - [No. 10 (1987)].
   This publication is not for sale.

2.3 Ἀγγλο-ελληνική Ἐπιθεώρηση / *Anglo-Greek Review.* Athens. Vol. 1 published by the Anglo-Greek Information Service. Vols. 2-7 published by the British Council. Vol. 1, No. 1 (March 1945) - [Vol. 7, No. 8 (Spring 1955)]. Monthly to quarterly.
   Bilingual only through Vol. 1, No. 3 (May 1945). Subsequently in Greek. Only the bilingual numbers have been indexed. Has ceased publication.

2.4 *Byzantine and Modern Greek Studies.* Currently published by the Centre for Byzantine Studies and Modern Greek, The University of Birmingham, England. Vol. 1 (1975) - [Vol. 11 (1987)]. Annual.

2.5 *The Charioteer: An Annual Review of Modern Greek Culture.* Currently published by Pella Publishing Company, New York. Vol. 1, No. 1 (Summer 1960) - [Nos. 29/30 (1987-88)]. Quarterly to annual.

2.6 *Classical and Modern Literature.* Terre Haute, Indiana. Vol. 1, No. 1 (Fall 1980) - [Vol. 8, No. 1 (Fall 1987)]. Quarterly.
   This journal devotes less of its contents to Modern Greek literature than most of the others in this section.

2.7 *The Coffeehouse / Τό καφενεῖο: Contemporary Greek Arts and Letters*. San Francisco, California. No. 1 (Fall 1975) - No. 11/12 (1982). Semi-annual.
Ceased publication in 1982. The same editor (Dino Siotis) now produces the *Aegean Review* (see above).

2.8 *Epsilon: Modern Greek and Balkan Studies*. University of Copenhagen, Department of Modern Greek and Balkan Studies. No. 1 (1987) - . Annual.
Continues *Scandinavian Studies in Modern Greek* (see below).

2.9 *Études Helléniques / Hellenic Studies*. Montréal, Québec. Vol. 1, No. 1 (Spring 1983) - [Vol. 2, No. 2 (Autumn 1984)]. Semi-annual.

2.10 *Folia Neohellenica: Zeitschrift für Neogräzistik*. Neugriechische und byzantinische Philologie / Ruhr-Universität Bochum. Amsterdam: A.M. Hakkert. Vol. 1 (1975) - [Vol. 7 (1985-1986)].

2.11 *Το Γιοφύρι / To Yofiri: Περιοδικό Νεοελληνικῶν Σπουδῶν / Periodical of Modern Greek Studies*. University of Sydney, Australia. No. 1 (Feb. 1978) - [No. 9 (Aug. 1980)]. Semi-annual.
Has recently resumed publication.

2.12 *Greek Letters: A Modern Greek Literature Annual*. Athens. Currently published by The Hellenic Society of Translators of Literature. Vol. 1 (1982) - [Vol. 4 (1986-1989)].

2.13 *Journal of Modern Greek Studies*. Baltimore, Maryland: The Johns Hopkins University Press. Sponsored by the Modern Greek Studies Association. Vol. 1, No. 1 (May 1983) - [Vol. 5, No. 2 (October 1987)]. Semi-annual.

2.14 *Journal of Modern Hellenism*. Brookline, Massachusetts: Hellenic College Press. No. 1 (April 1984) - [No. 4 (Autumn 1987)]. Annual.

2.15 *Journal of the Hellenic Diaspora*. Currently published by Pella Publishing Company, New York. Vol. 1, No. 1 (1974) - [Vol. 14, Nos. 3 & 4 (Fall-Winter 1987)]. Quarterly.

2.16 *Μαντατοφόρος / Mantatoforos: Δελτίο Νεοελληνικῶν Σπουδῶν*. Currently edited by the Byzantijns-Nieuwgrieks Seminarium, University of Amsterdam, and published by the Ἑταιρεία Ἑλληνικοῦ Λογοτεχνικοῦ καί Ἱστορικοῦ Ἀρχείου, Athens. No. 1 (Nov. 1972) - [Nos. 25-26 (Nov. 1987)]. Semi-annual.

2.17 *Modern Greek Studies Yearbook*. Minneapolis, Minnesota: University of Minnesota. Vol. 1 (1985) - [Vol. 3 (1987)]. Annual.

2.18 *Neo-Hellenika: Annual Publication of the Center for Neo-Hellenic Studies*. Austin, Texas. Vols. 1-4: 1970-1981.
Ceased publication in 1981.

2.19 *Omphalos: A Mediterranean Review.* Published by John G. Zervos. Athens. Vol. 1, No. 1 (March 1972) - [Vol. 1, No. 3 (Winter 1973)].
   Has ceased publication.

2.20 *Scandinavian Studies in Modern Greek:* Νεοελληνικά Μελετήματα. Published jointly by the Departments of Modern Greek, Universities of Copenhagen and Gothenburg. No. 1 (1977) - [No. 7/8 (1984)]. Annual.
   Ceased publication in 1984. Currently continued by *Epsilon* (see above).

II. Not indexed

2.21 Ἀντίποδες / *Antipodes*. Published by the Greek-Australian Cultural League of Melbourne. Currently edited by Pavlos Andronikos, Dept. of Classical Studies, Monash University, Clayton, Victoria 3168, Australia.
   The journal began publication in the mid 1970s.

2.22 *Athene: The American Magazine of Hellenic Thought.* Chicago. Vol. 1, No. 1 (Nov. 1940) - [Vol. 28 (Spring/Summer 1967)]. Quarterly, 1944- .
   Has ceased publication.

2.23 *Balkan Studies.* Thessaloniki: Institute of Balkan Studies, Society for Macedonian Studies. Vol. 1 (1960) - . Semi-annual.

3. SPECIAL ISSUES OF JOURNALS

This chapter contains issues of journals not included in Chapter 2 which are, however, devoted to a Modern Greek literary topic. Special issues dedicated to a specific author are listed under the author's name in Chapter 7.

The spellings of the names of the Greek authors are taken directly from the publications.

3.1 *Agenda*, Vol. 7, No. 1 (Winter 1969). *Greek Poetry Special Issue*. Peter Levi, S.J., ed. 95 p.

Translation and discussion of Greek literature, both ancient and modern. Includes: Vitzentzos Kornaros, "from *The Erotokritos*" [Iain Watson, tr.] (pp. 30-31); "Four Folksongs" [Hilary Pym, tr.] (pp. 32-34); "Folksong" [Peter Levi, tr.] (p. 34); George Seferis, *Three Private Poems* [Peter Thompson, tr.] (pp. 35-49); George Seferis, "Conversation with Fabrice" (pp. 50-57); Nikos Gatsos, "Song of the Old Days" [Peter Levi, tr.] (pp. 58-59); Odysseus Elytis, "*Axion Esti*, Part III: The Gloria" [Edmund Keeley and George Savidis, trs.] (pp. 60-68); Odysseus Elytis, "Six and a Single Remorse for the Sky" [Stuart Montgomery, tr.] (pp. 69-77); Captain Antoniou, "The Bad Businessmen" [Peter Levi, tr.] (p. 78); Nanos Valaoritis, "World War" [Nikos Stangos, tr.] (p. 79); Markos Meskos, "Two Poems" ["Mute Poem"; "Love"] [John A. Goumas, tr.] (p. 80); Nikos Stangos, "That Man" (p. 81); N.H. Ghika, "Scholia on the Translation into Modern Greek of Edward Lear's Poem *The Courtship of the Yonghy-Bonghy-Bò*. London, July, 1968" (pp. 83-86); Robin Fletcher, "The Literary-Historical Background of Modern Greek Literature" (pp. 87-95).

Address: Editor, Agenda, 5 Cranbourne Court, Albert Bridge Road, London, S.W. 11 4PE, United Kingdom. Out of print in 1984.

3.2 *Arion's Dolphin: A Quarterly of Poetry*, Vol. 1, Nos. 4-5 (Summer-Autumn 1972). *35 Post-War Greek Poets*. Stratis Haviaras, ed. and intro. 125 p.

Includes poems (pp. 13-60 and 71-124) by: Franghiski Abatzopoulou, Ares Alexandrou, Manolis Anagnostakis, Nikos Alexis Aslanoglou, V.N. Bonos, Dinos Christianopoulos, Dimitris Christodoulou, Andonis Decavalles, Dimitris Doukaris, Th.D. Frangopoulos, George Gavalas, Stratis Haviaras, George Kaftantzis, Ektor Kaknavatos, Socrates Kapsaskis, Nikos Karachalios, N.D. Karouzos, Michael Katsaros, Loukas Kousoulas, Rovyros Manthoulis, Matthaios Moundes, Dimitris Papaditsas, Titos Patrikios, Miltos Sachtouris, Teos Salapassidis, Takis Sinopoulos, Yannis Thallas, George Thaniel, Panos K. Thassitis, Loukas Theodorakopoulos, Eleni Vakalo, Nanos Valaoritis, Nikos Vranas, Leonidas Zenakos, Nikos Zoumboulakis, and a portfolio of photographs by Constantine Manos (pp. 61-70).

Translators include: Athan Anagnostopoulos, James Damaskos, Andonis Decavalles, Stavros Deligiorgis, George Economou, John Fludas, Stratis Haviaras, Sarah Kafatou, Thanasis Maskaleris, Paul Merchant, T.K. Scuris, Stuart Silverman, George Thaniel, Nanos Valaoritis, Ruth Whitman.

Address: Arion's Dolphin, P.O. Box 313, Cambridge, Mass. 02138.

3.3 *The Atlantic Monthly*, Vol. 195, No. 6 (June 1955), pp. 97-168. *Perspective of Greece: An Atlantic Supplement*. Kimon Friar and Ronald Freelander, eds. Also published as a separatum. 74 p.

Contains: Lincoln MacVeagh, "Introduction" (p. 100); George Theotokas, "The Modern Greeks" [Conn Hadjilia, tr.] (pp. 101-105); Takis Papatzonis, "Before the First Coming" [Kimon Friar, tr.] (p. 105); Andreas Karandonis, "In the Greek Islands" [Robert Liddell, tr.] (pp. 106-109); Nikos Kazantzakis, "The Return of Odysseus" [Kimon Friar, tr.] (pp. 110-112); Stephen G. Xydis, "Where Greece Stands Today" (pp. 113-116); Elias Venezis, "The Sea Gulls" [Robert Liddell and Constantine Trypanis, trs.] (pp. 117-119); C.P. Rodocanachi, "Eternal Athens" (pp. 120-125); Demetrios Capetanakis, "The Isles of Greece" (p. 125); Constantine Kavafis, "Expecting the Barbarians" [Marguerite Yourcenar and W.H. Auden, trs.] (p.

126); Manolis Hadjidakis, "Some Aspects of Modern Greek Art" [John Leatham, tr.] (pp. 127-138); Cosmas Politis, "The Funeral Games" [Robert Liddell and Andreas Cambas, trs.] (pp. 139-141); Odysseus Elytis, "I Know the Night No Longer" [Kimon Friar, tr.] (p. 141); C.Th. Dimaras, "Literary Renaissance" [H.L.R. and Epy Edwards, trs.] (pp. 142-146); Constantine Tsatsos, "The Language Problem" [Conn Hadjilia, tr.] (p. 143); Andreas Embirikos, "Daybreak" [Kimon Friar, tr.] (p. 146); Henry Miller, "Coming into Poros Harbor" (pp. 147-148); Nikos Engonopoulos, "Poetry 1948" [Kimon Friar, tr.] (p. 148); Kay Cicellis, "Orpheus in Hades" (pp. 149-152); Kostis Palamas, "Two Octaves" [Kimon Friar, tr.] (p. 152); George Mylonas, "Archaeology in Greece" (pp. 153-157); George Seferis, "Three Poems" ["The King of Asine"; "The Smile of the Statues"; "Calligraphy"] [Kimon Friar, Lawrence Durrell, Bernard Spencer, Nanos Valaoritis, trs.] (pp. 158-159); Stratis Myrivilis, "To the Country of Statues" [Robert Liddell, tr.] (pp. 160-164); Angelos Sikelianos, "Unrecorded" [Kimon Friar, tr.] (p. 165).

Address: The Atlantic Monthly, 8 Arlington St., Boston, Mass. 02116. Out of print in 1984.

3.4 *Books Abroad,* Vol. 49, No. 4 (Autumn 1975). *Analogies of Light: The Greek Poet Odysseus Elytis.*
See Chapter 7 (O. Elytis).

3.5 *Boundary 2: A Journal of Postmodern Literature and Culture,* Vol. 1, No. 2 (Winter 1973). A Special Issue on Contemporary Greek Writing. N.C. Germanacos (Greek ed.) and William V. Spanos, eds. In memoriam George Seferis 1900-1971. Pages 255-539.

Includes: William V. Spanos and Robert Kroetsch, "Greek Writing and the Boundary: A Foreword" (pp. 261-263); George Seferis, "Across Gorse..." [Walter Kaiser, tr.] (pp. 264-265); N.C. Germanacos, "An Interview with Three Greek Prose Writers (May 1972): Stratis Tsirkas, Thanassis Valtinos, George Ioannou" (pp. 266-313); Stratis Tsirkas, "The Fight with the Moray-Eel" [Kevin Andrews, tr.] (pp. 315-320); Thanassis Valtinos, "The Descent of the Nine" [N.C. Germanacos, tr.] (pp. 321-347); George Ioannou, "The Dogs of Seikh-Sou" [Calliope Doxiadis, tr.] (pp. 349-355); C.P. Cavafy, "Five Poems" [Edmund Keeley and Philip Sherrard, trs.] (pp. 369-378); Yannis Ritsos, "Poems from *Corridors and Stairs"* [N.C. Germanacos, tr.] (p. 379-399); Odysseus Elytis, "Poems" [Kimon Friar, tr.] (pp. 401-418); Manolis Anaghnostakis, "Poems" [Kimon Friar, tr.] (pp. 419-432); Nikos Karouzos, "Poems" [Philip Ramp and Katerina Angelaki-Rooke, trs.] (pp. 433-440); George Themelis, "De Rerum Natura" [Kimon Friar, tr.] (pp. 441-453); Theodore Antoniou, "Searching for the Theme of an Article about Contemporary Theater Music" (pp. 454-468); "Moirologia for Jani Christou" [Th. Maskaleris, tr.] (p. 469); Nikos Kasdaglis, "Blessed are the Merciful..." [N.C. Germanacos, tr.] (pp. 470-505); "Three Young Poets: Jenny Mastoraki, Haris Megalinos and Lefteris Poulios" [N.C. Germanacos, William V. Spanos, Philip Ramp, Katerina Angelaki-Rooke, trs.] (pp. 507-518); Kostas Taktsis, "Small Change" [N.C. Germanacos, tr.] (pp. 519-523); Peter Bien, "Arrogance and Intoxication: A Review of *Eighteen Texts"* (pp. 524-536).

Address: Boundary 2, SUNY-Binghamton, Binghamton, N.Y. 13901. Out of print in 1984.

3.6 *Chicago Review,* Vol. 21, No. 2 (Aug. 1969). 114 p.

Contains: Minas Savvas, "Eight Parasyntheta after Cavafy" (pp. 5-13); "Eighteen Post-War Greek Poets: Takis Sinopoulos, Minas Dhimakis, George Yeralis, Takis Varvitsiotis, Miltos Sahtouris, Ares Dhikteos, Andonis Decavalles, George Kotsiras, Nanos Valaoritis, Klitos Kirou, Eleni Vakalo, D.M. Papadhitsas, Manolis Anaghnostakis, Nikos Karouzos, Nikos Phocas, Mando Aravandinou, Dinos Christianopoulos, Lydia Stephanou" [Kimon Friar, tr.] (pp. 14-82); Thomas Doulis, "Loula Anagnostaki and the New Theatre of Greece" (pp. 83-87); Loula Anagnostaki, *"The Town:* A Play in One Act" [Aliki Halls, tr.] (pp. 88-105); Konstantinos Lardas, "Nine Poems from the Folksongs of Modern Greece" (pp. 106-108); Dan Georgakas, "Two Greek Commentaries" (pp. 109-114) [the latter refer respectively to the translations of Vassilis Vassilikos, *Z* and Miltos Sahtouris, *With Face to the Wall*].

Address: Chicago Review, University of Chicago, Chicago, Ill. 60637.

3.7 *Contemporary Literature in Translation* 27 (Summer 1977). Andreas Schroeder, ed.; Yannis Goumas, guest ed. and intro. 31 p.

Contains works of: Elias Papadimitrakopoulos, Yannis Efstathiadis, Andreas Embiricos, Nikos Engonopoulos, Marios Pontikas, Yannis Kondos, Nassos Vayenas, Sakis Papadimitriou, Kostas Ritsonis, Tassos Roussos, Maria Laina. Translations by: Yannis Goumas, John Stathatos, and Gillian Tweed.

Address: The Editor, Contemporary Literature in Translation, P.O. Box 3127, Mission, B.C., Canada V2V4J3.

3.8 *Descant XVIII,* Vol. 8, No. 2 (1977). *Contemporary Greek Literature.* Karen Mulhallen, ed. Donna McDonald, contributing editor for this issue. 101 p.

Translations of 24 poets and prose writers. Introduction by Kay Cicellis (pp. 8-10). Poetry includes works by: Nasos Vayenas, Eleni Vakalo, Nikos Phocas, George Hronas, Nana Isaia, Lefteris Poulios, Vasilis Steryadis, D.M. Papadhitsas, Nikos Dokas, Miltos Sahtouris, Yannis Kondos, Takis Sinopoulos, Manolis Anagnostakis, Mihalis Katsaros, Mando Aravantinou, Katerina Anghelaki Rooke, Yannis Ritsos (pp. 11-59). Translators of poetry include: Kimon Friar, John Stathatos, Peter Thompson, Philip Ramp, Gwendolyn MacEwan, Nikos Tsingos. Prose includes: Nasos Vayenas, "Foreword to the Second Edition of 'Vertigo'" [Kay Cicellis, tr.] (pp. 60-63); Kay Cicellis, "Cephalonia the First" (pp. 64-68); Alexander Kotzias, "from *Brave Telemachus*" [John Stathatos, tr.] (pp. 69-72); Stratis Tsirkas, "from *The Lost Spring*" [Kay Cicellis, tr.] (pp. 73-80); George Cheimonas, "from *The Wedding*" [Kay Cicellis, tr.] (pp. 81-84); Costas Tachtsis, "A Visit" [Philip Ramp, tr.] (pp. 85-88); Dimitris Hadzis, "From Fifty-fifty to Love" [Edward Fenton, tr.] (pp. 89-97).

Address: Descant, Department of English, Texas Christian University Station, Fort Worth, Texas 76129, or Descant, Oxus Press, 16 Haslemere Road, London, N. 8, United Kingdom.

3.09 *The Falcon,* Vol. 9, No. 16 (Spring 1978). The Poetry of Yannis Ritsos.
See Chapter 7 (G. Ritsos).

3.10 *Grand Street,* Vol. 2, No. 3 (Spring 1983). Issue dedicated to C.P. Cavafy.
See Chapter 7 (C.P. Cavafy).

3.11 *Greek Heritage: The American Quarterly of Greek Culture,* Vol. 1, No. 2 (Spring 1964). Homage to George Seferis.
See Chapter 7 (G. Seferis).

3.12 **Grove: Contemporary Poetry and Translation,* Vol. 5 (Winter 1979). Kostas Myrsiades, guest ed.

Introduction: "Contemporary Greek Poetry of the Sixties and Seventies" (pp. 1-2). Translations of 28 poets by various translators. Includes poems by: Yannis Kondos, Lefteris Poulios, George Thaniel, Katerina Angelaki-Rooke, Dino Siotis, Nana Isaiah, Tasos Denegris, Dhimitris Potamitis, Jenny Mastorakis, Pavlina Pamboudhi, Kostas Kindhinis, and others.

Address: Grove, Pitzer College, Claremont, Calif. 91711.

3.13 *Journal of Modern Literature,* Vol. 2, No. 2 (Second issue 1971-1972). Nikos Kazantzakis Special Number.
See Chapter 7 (N. Kazantzakis).

3.14 *Labrys* 8 (Apr. 1983). Issue dedicated to George Seferis.
See Chapter 7 (G. Seferis).

3.15 *The Literary Review,* Vol. 16, No. 3 (Spring 1973). *Greece.* Marios Byron Raizis, guest ed. Pages 251-392.

Includes: Andonis Decavalles, "Cycles" [Kimon Friar, tr.] (p. 252); an essay by M. Byron Raizis, "The Literary Renaissance in Post-War Greece" (pp. 253-267); Nikos Pentzikis, "from 'The Dead and the Resurrection'" [Stavros Deligiorgis, tr.] (pp. 268-272); Nikephoros Vrettakos, "Fever" [M. Byron Raizis, tr.] (p. 273); Triandafillos Pittas, "The Monsters are Coming" [Theodora Vasils, tr.] (pp. 274-289); Nikos Karouzos, "Terrifying Joy" [Kimon Friar, tr.] (p. 289); Nikos Phocas, "The Three Knocks" [Kimon Friar, tr.] (pp. 290-292); Takis Varvitsiotis, "Two Poems" ["Dreams are Hung by a Thread"; "October Blood"] [Kimon Friar, tr.] (pp. 293-294); George Seferis, "Two Poems" ["On Stage"; "from 'Summer Solstice'"] [M. Byron Raizis, tr.] (pp. 295-302); George Ioannou, "The Bed" [M. Byron Raizis, tr.] (pp. 303-308);

Eleni Vakalo, "The Mythology of Taste" [Kimon Friar, tr.] (p. 308); Ph.D. Drakodaides, "Christ, or The Condemnation" [Andreas K. Poulakidas, tr.] (pp. 309-317); Yannis Papadhopoulos, "Two Poems" ["Mosaic Stones"; "Athens, Spring A.D. 1966"] [Kimon Friar, tr.] (pp. 318-320); Ph.D. Drakodaides, "Pylades" [M. Byron Raizis, tr.] (p. 321); Ares Dhikteos, "The Dead Youth" [Kimon Friar, tr.] (pp. 322-324); Antonis Samarakis, "50 Kilos of Mothballs" [Catherine Raizis, tr.] (pp. 325-337); Takis Sinopoulos, "Two Poems" ["Elpenor"; "Song of Songs"] [Kimon Friar, tr.] (pp. 338-341); Vassilis Vassilikos, "The Departure" [M. Byron Raizis, tr.] (pp. 342-349); Nanos Valaoritis, "The Gods" [Kimon Friar, tr.] (pp. 350-351); Nikos Kazantzakis, "from *Odysseus*, A Drama" [M. Byron Raizis, tr.] (p. 352); Yannis Ritsos, "Two Poems" ["If I Had the Water of Immortality"; "My Sweet One, You Did Not Vanish"] [Thanasis Maskaleris, tr.] (p. 353); Odysseus Elytis, "Two Poems" ["Ode VII"; "Ode X"] [Nanos Valaoritis, tr.] (pp. 354-356); Menis Koumandareas, "The Burnt Ones" [Stavros Deligiorgis, tr.] (pp. 357-386); Dinos Christianopoulos, "Ithaca" [Kimon Friar, tr.] (p. 387); Zoë Karelli, "Poet" [Kimon Friar, tr.] (pp. 388-389).

Out of print. May be obtained in reprint form from Kraus Reprints Co., Route 100, Millwood, N.Y. 10546.

3.16 *The Literary Review*, Vol. 18, No. 4 (Summer 1975). *Kazantzakis*.
See Chapter 7 (N. Kazantzakis).

3.17 *The Literary Review*, Vol. 19, No. 2 (Winter 1976). *Kazantzakis*.
See Chapter 7 (N. Kazantzakis).

3.18 *Manna: A Review of Contemporary Poetry* 5 (1974). Special: *The Poets of Greece*. Lorne Shirinian, ed.; George Thaniel, special co-editor. 63 p.

Contains: an introduction (pp. 1-5) by George Thaniel; poems (pp. 6-34 and 38-61) by: Alexander Baras, Nikos Engonopoulos, Melissanthi, Eleni Vakalo, Nikos Spanias, Andonis Decavalles, Dhimitris Dhoukaris, Nikos Karouzos, Nadhina Dhimitriou, Loukas Theodorakopoulos, Tassos Korfis, Kostas Kovanis, Nana Issaia, Prodhromos Markoghlou, Stratis Haviaras, Anestis Evanghellou, George Thaniel, Phaedra Zabatha-Paghoulatou, Katerina Anghelaki-Rooke, Zephi Dharaki, Philippos Dracontaidis, Andhreas Anghelakis, Yannis Kontos, Dino Siotis, Nasos Vayenas, Stephanos Bekatoros, Yorghos Chronas, Yorghos Markopoulos; an interview with Nikos Engonopoulos (pp. 34-38).

Various translators, including Kimon Friar, Stratis Haviaras, George Thaniel, Athan Anagnostopoulos, Daniel Sahas, Fotoula Pantazis, Thanassis Photiou, Lorne Shirinian, Nana Issaia, Heather Ellen Cole, George Economou, George Kirikopoulos, Jim Pantazis, Philip Ramp, Marios Byron Raizis, Paul Vlachogiannis, Dino Siotis, Nini Papatheodorou.

Address: Manna Publishing, 21 Don Valley Dr., Toronto, Ontario, Canada M4K 2J1.

3.19 *Micromegas* 5, No. 1 (1971). *Greek issue*. Frederic Will, ed.; Stavros Deligiorgis, guest ed. 43 p.

Includes: Vasilis Vasilikos, [5 Poems]; Nanos Valaoritis, [3 Poems]; Stratis Haviaras, [4 Poems]; Andonis Decavalles, [3 Poems]; Iannis Goudelis, [3 Poems]; George Themelis, "Naked Window"; Panos Thasites, "Home on Earth"; Thanasis Papadopoulos, [4 Poems]; Traditional, Anonymous "From the Deme"; Frangiske Abatzopoulou, [3 Poems]; Dimitris Christodoulou, "Kastalia".

Stavros Deligiorgis, Nanos Valaoritis, Thanasis Maskaleris, George Economou, M. Byron Raizis, trs.
Address: The Editor, 84 High Point Drive, Amherst, Mass.

3.20 *Modern Poetry in Translation*, No. 4 (1968). *Greece*. Paul Merchant, tr. [42 unnumbered pages.]

Poems by: George Seferis, Andreas Embiricos, Yannis Ritsos, Odysseus Elytis, Takis Sinopoulos, and Eleni Vakalo.

Address: Modern Poetry in Translation, 46a Woodside Park Road, London N12 8RP, United Kingdom.

3.21 *Modern Poetry in Translation*, No. 34 (Summer 1978). *Greek*. Pages 3-22.

Includes: Katerina Anghelaki Rooke, "A Note on Greek Poetry in the 1970's" (pp. 3-4); poems by: George Themelis, Zoi Karelli, Rita Boumi-Papa, Melissanthi, Eleni Vakalo, Nikos Karouzos, Lena Pappa, Kiki Dimoula, Nana Isaia, Katerina Anghelaki Rooke, Lefteris Poulios, Tzeni Mastoraki, and Nasos

Vayenas (pp. 5-22). Various translators, including Stephen Kerce, Maria Kotzamanidou, Michael Heldman, Philip Ramp, Katerina Anghelaki Rooke, Nana Isaia, Richard Burns.
Address: Modern Poetry in Translation (as above).

3.22 *Pacific Quarterly Moana,* Vol. 5, No. 3 (July 1980). *Greek & Turkish Poets of Today.* An International Review of Arts and Ideas. A Special Issue of Pacific Quarterly Moana. Yannis Goumas and Talât Sait Halman, eds.

Greek poets include: Mihalis Ganas, Aryiris Hionis, Yannis Ifantis, Yorghos Karavassilis, Yannis Kondos, Maria Laïna, Nikos Lazaris, Christoforos Liontakis, Yorghos Markopoulos, Kostas Mavroudis, Kostas G. Papageorgiou, Yannis Varveris, Alexandros Issaris. All translations (pp. 273-324) by Yannis Goumas.
Address: Outrigger Publishers Limited, P.O. Box 13-049, Hamilton, New Zealand.

3.23 *'Ο Παλίμψηστος / The Palimpsest* 2 (1967). Nicholas Kachtitsis, ed.
Includes: D. Fotiadis, G. Seferis, N.-G. Pentzikis, T. Sinopoulos, E.C. Gonatas, J.C. Stathatos, N. Spanias, P. Trogadis.

3.24 *Perspective of Greece: An* Atlantic *Supplement* (June 1955). See *The Atlantic Monthly* above.

3.25 *Ploughshares,* Vol. 11, No. 4 [June 1986]. *International Writing Issue.* Stratis Haviaras, ed. Pages 11-37.

Greek contents include: Stratis Haviaras, "Advertisement (Or, Sr. Calvino's Shaving Brush)" (pp. 11-14); Alan Dugan, "Mock Translation from the Greek" (p. 15); Odysseus Elytis, "Three Poems" [Martin McKinsey, tr.] (pp. 16-19); C.P. Cavafy, "Notes on Poetics and Ethics" [Martin McKinsey, tr.] (pp. 20-26); Yannis Ritsos, "Eight Paper Poems" [Edmund Keeley, tr.] (pp. 27-30); George Seferis, "Two Prose Excerpts" (from *A Poet's Journal: Days of 1925-31* and from *Six Nights on the Acropolis*) [Athan Anagnostopoulos, tr.] (pp. 31-37).
Address: Ploughshares, Box 529, Cambridge, Mass. 02139-0529.

3.26 *Poetry* (Chicago), Vol. 78, No. 3 (June 1951). *New Greek Poets: An Anthology and Commentary.* Kimon Friar, ed. and tr. Pages 145-183.

Includes: Kimon Friar, "Contemporary Greek Poetry" (pp. 145-151) and "A Note on the Prosody" (pp. 152-153). "Greek Poems of the 20th Century" (pp. 154-183) includes poems by: Anghelos Sikelianos, George Seferis, Nikos Kazantzakis, Takis Papatzonis, Andreas Emberikos, Demetrios Antoniou, Nikiforos Vrettakos, Alexander Matsas, Nikos Engonopoulos, Odysseus Elytis, Nikos Gatsos, Miltos Sahtouris, Adonis Decavallas, Nanos Valaoritis.
Address: Poetry Magazine, 601 S. Morgan St., P.O. Box 4348, Chicago, Ill. 60680. Out of print in 1984.

3.27 *Poetry* (Chicago), Vol. 105, No. 1 (Oct. 1964). *Greek Number.* Edmund Keeley, Philip Sherrard, George Savidis et al., trs. 74 p.

Includes: Odysseus Elytis, "from *Axion Esti:* The Genesis" [Edmund Keeley and George Savidis, trs.] (pp. 1-15); Edmund Keeley, "'The Genesis': A Commentary" (pp. 16-20); Odysseus Elytis, "from *Axion Esti:* This Then is I" and "from *Six and One Regrets for the Sky:* The Sleep of the Brave" [Ruth Whitman, tr.] (pp. 21-23); Nikos Gatsos, "Amorgos" [Edmund Keeley, tr.] (pp. 24-32); Edmund Keeley, "*Amorgos:* A Commentary" (pp. 33-35); Takis Sinopoulos, "Magda", "Sophia and the Rest", "Sight and Vision", "Ioanna's Invitation", "One of Constantine's Nights", "The Beheading" [Edmund Keeley and George Savidis, trs.] (pp. 36-42); George Savidis, "A Note on Takis Sinopoulos" (p. 43); George Seferis, "Santorini", "Salamis in Cyprus", "Three Mules" [Edmund Keeley and Philip Sherrard, trs.] (pp. 44-49) and "Letter to a Foreign Friend" [Nanos Valaoritis, tr.; appended by Edmund Keeley] (pp. 50-59); Vassilis Vassilikos, "Letter from Athens" [re. poetry] [Kriton Hourmousiades, tr.] (pp. 60-64); Andonis Decavalles, "A Poet's Novel" [re. *The Plant, The Well, The Angel: A Trilogy* by Vassilis Vassilikos. Edmund and Mary Keeley, trs.] (pp. 65-67).
Address: Poetry Magazine (as above).

3.28 *Poetry* (Chicago), Vol. 139, No. 2 (Nov. 1981). "Thirteen Post-War Greek Poets: Translations and an Essay" (pp. 76-107).

Includes poems by: Takis Varvitsiotis, Aris Dhikteos, Andonis Decavalles, Eleni Vakalo, Athos Dhimoulas, P.D. Papadhitsas (sic), Aristotle Nikolaidis, Aris Alexandhrou, T.D. Frangopoulos, Tasos Livadhitis, Dhimitris Dhoukaris, Nikos Karouzos, and Yannis Papadhopoulos [Kimon Friar, tr.] (pp. 76-98); Kimon Friar, "Comment: Post-War Greek Poets" (pp. 99-107).

Address: Poetry Magazine (as above).

3.29 **Poetry* (Madras), Vol. 9, No. 2 (1968). *Modern Poetry of Greece*. Agnes Sotiracopoulou, tr.

Contains: Hugh McKinley, "Introduction" (pp. 1-2); Melissanthi, "Lyric Confession" (p. 2); Nikiforos Vrettakos, "Muster" (p. 3); Agnes Sotiracopoulou, "Critical Hour" (pp. 3-4); Giorgis Saradis, "Prologue" (pp. 4-5); Nikos Pappas, "Pyros King of Epiros" (p. 5); Zoe Karelli, "As Beautiful Naked Women" (pp. 5-6); Yannis Hondroyannis, "Moment" (p. 6); Tassos Livaditis, "From Day to Day" (pp. 6-7); Aris Dicteos, "The Story of Paradise" (pp. 7-9); Basil Liaskas, "The Murderer's Face" (p. 9); Nikos Pappas, "Splendid Treasury", "I Cry", "88 Charilaou Trikoupi Street" (pp. 10-11); Agnes Sotiracopoulou, "Ionia" (p. 11); Rita Boumi-Pappa, "If You Knew how Sorrowful I Came" (pp. 11-12); Tilla Bali, "Anatomy of Memory" (pp. 12-13); Yannis Negrepontis, "Preveza—The Poet's City" (p. 13); Gregory Nazianzinos, "Not to be Frugal" (p. 14); Agnes Sotiracopoulou, "I Count the Nights" (p. 14); Yannis Negrepontis, "The Irreconcilables" (p. 15); Tilla Bali, "The Sepulchral Urn of Larnakos" (p. 15), "Midnight" (p. 16); Minas Dimakis, "There are Roads ..." (p. 16); Yannis Ritsos, "The Hill" (pp. 16-17); Yannis Goudelis, "Borinage" (pp. 17-18); Nikos Gatsos, "In the Courtyard of the Afflicted" (p. 18); Sophia Mavroidi-Papadaki, "Flower of Ashes" (pp. 18-19); Andreas Karandonis, "Description", "Little Lights in the Night" (pp. 19-20).

3.30 *Review of National Literatures*, Vol. 5, No. 2 (Fall 1974). *Greece: The Modern Voice*. Anne Paolucci, ed.; Peter A. Mackridge, special ed. 159 p.

Includes a collection of essays: Katerina Anghelaki-Rooke, "The Greek Poetic Landscape: Recent Trends in Greek Poetry" (pp. 13-26); Mario Vitti, "Rural Greekness in Greek Prose Fiction" (pp. 27-40); Christopher Robinson, "Greece in the Poetry of Costis Palamas" (pp. 41-65); Edmund Keeley, "Cavafy's Hellenism" (pp. 66-89); Philip Sherrard, "Anghelos Sikelianos and His Vision of Greece" (pp. 90-112); Peter Bien, "The Mellowed Nationalism of Kazantzakis' *Zorba the Greek*" (pp. 113-136); Richard C. Clark, "Modern Greek Literature: Bibliographical Spectrum and Review Article" (pp. 137-159).

Address: CNL, P.O. Box 81, Whitestone, N.Y. 11357.

3.31 *Shenandoah: The Washington and Lee University Review*, Vol. 26, No. 3 (Spring 1975). James Boatwright, ed. 171 p.

This issue is described as a 'response' to Greece and contains: Kenneth O. Hanson, "Two Poems" (pp. 3-9); W.S. Merwin, "Aspects of a Mountain" [Mt. Athos] (pp. 10-89); Edmund Keeley, "Cavafy's Sensual City" (pp. 90-121); Robin Magowan, "Panegyri" (pp. 122-145); Richard Howard, "On Michael Lekakis" [sculptor] (pp. 146-155); James Boatwright, "Are You Tourists?" [a journal/review dated June 5-Aug. 16, 1974; esp. re. Stratis Tsirkas and Kay Cicellis] (pp. 156-171).

Address: Shenandoah, Washington and Lee University, Box 722, Lexington, Virginia 24450.

3.32 *Shenandoah: The Washington and Lee University Review*, Vol. 27, No. 1 (Fall 1975). James Boatwright, ed. 144 p.

The second of two special issues dealing with Greece. Selections and translations mostly by N.C. Germanacos. Contains: Marios Hakkas, "The Bidet" [Kay Cicellis, tr.] (pp. 3-5); Margarita Karapanou, "from *Kassandra and the Wolf*" [N.C. Germanacos, tr.] (pp. 6-19); Thanassis Valtinos, "August '48" [N.C. Germanacos, tr.] (pp. 20-25); Kay Cicellis, "Proportions" (pp. 26-34); Andreas Lendakis, "In the Noonday Heat" [Kevin Andrews, tr.] (pp. 35-43); Vassili Vasilikos, "The Three T's" [James Merrill, tr.] (pp. 44-48); Yannis Ritsos, "A Portfolio", including: "from *The Wall in the Mirror*" [N.C. Germanacos, tr.] (pp. 51-52), "from *The Paper Poems*" [N.C. Germanacos, tr.] (pp. 53-55), "Stones, Bones, Roots" [Kay Cicellis, tr.] (pp. 56-67), and "Philoctetes" (The Ultimate Mask) [Peter Bien, tr.] (pp. 68-87); Kostas Taktsis, "The

First Image" [N.C. Germanacos, tr.] (pp. 89-94); Zissimos Lorenzatos, "Freedom and Language" [Edmund and Mary Keeley, trs.] (pp. 95-98); Stratis Tsirkas, "from *The Journal of the Trilogy*" [Kay Cicellis, tr.] (pp. 99-103); Giorgos Ioannou, "'Voungari'" [Roderick Beaton, tr.] (pp. 104-117); Dimitris Hatzis, "Outworn Symbols" [Roderick Beaton, tr.] (pp. 118-124); Nikos Kasdaglis, "The Sponge-Diver" [Roderick Beaton, tr.] (pp. 125-142).

Address: Shenandoah (as above).

3.33 *Skylark* (India), No. 25 (1970). *Special Greek Poetry Number*. Baldev Mirza, ed. 48 p.

Contains poems of: A. Argyriou, G. Seferis, K. Ouranis, K. Karyotakis, Melissanthi, Y. Ritsos, T. Livaditis, A. Dikteos, V. Vitsaxis, Kr. Athanasoulis, N. Pappas, K. Kokorovits, A. Sotiracopoulou-Skina, N. Isaia, K. Angelaki Rooke, Victoria Roda, Y. Negrepontis, Georgia Moraki, George Savidis, Timos Pontis, Lucretia Dounavi.

Translators include Agnes Sotiracopoulou-Skina, Victor Hill, V. Vitsaxis, Byron Raizis, Hugh McKinley, Kimon Friar, Philip Ramp, Manolis Keramianakis.

Address: Skylark, Kothi Zamirabad, Raghubirpuri, Aligarh, India.

3.34 *Translation: The Journal of Literary Translation,* Vol. 14 (Spring 1985). *Greek Issue*. John Chioles and Edmund Keeley, guest eds.

Greek Feature Section (pp. 1-166) includes: Yannis Ritsos, "Seven Poems" [Edmund Keeley, tr.] (pp. 3-9); Odysseus Elytis, "Odyssey" [John Chioles and Edmund Keeley, trs.] (pp. 10-14); Ersi Sotiropoulou, "Interview" [Kay Cicellis, tr.] (pp. 15-22); Jenny Mastoraki, "Four Poems" [John Stathatos, tr.] (pp. 23-27); Zirana Zatelli, "Birds" [Kay Cicellis, tr.] (pp. 28-37); S.S. Harkianakis, "Six Poems" [Peter Bien, tr.] (pp. 38-42); Yannis Kondos, "Three Poems" [James Stone, tr.] and "Two Poems" [Edmund Keeley, tr.] (pp. 43-46); Dimitri Nollas, "Tender Skin" [Mary Keeley, tr.] (pp. 47-50); Manolis Anagnostakis, "Four Poems" [James Stone, tr.] (pp. 51-53); Kay Cicellis, "Puppet Show" [Kay Cicellis, tr.] (pp. 54-62); Miltos Sahtouris, "Four Poems" [John Stathatos, tr.] (pp. 63-65); Katerina Anghelaki-Rooke, "Four Poems" [Gail Holst Warhaft, tr.] (pp. 66-70); Mihalis Katsaros, "Three Poems" [John Stathatos, tr.] (pp. 71-72); Mihalis Ghanas, "Four Poems" [John Stathatos, tr.] (pp. 73-75); Costas Taktsis, "On Being a Student" [John Chioles, tr.] (pp. 76-85); "Twelve Poems by Younger Greek Poets" (Nasos Vayenas, Lefteris Poulios, Yiorgos Chouliaras, Dino Siotis, Yannis Varveris, Dimitris Kalokyris, Giorgos Chronas, Giorgos Veis, Costas Gouliamos) [John Chioles, tr.] (pp. 86-97); Nikos Karouzos, "Lindos" [Maria Kotzamanidou and N.C. Germanacos, trs.] (pp. 98-102); Anastassis Vistonitis, "Egnatia 1958" [John Chioles, tr.] (pp. 103-105); Vassilis Vassilikos, "I / He" [John Chioles, tr.] (pp. 106-109); Dimitris Kehaidis, *The Wedding Band* (A One-Act Play) [John Chioles, tr.] (pp. 110-166).

Address: The Translation Center, 307A Mathematics Building, Columbia University, New York, N.Y. 10027.

3.35 *Zenos,* No. 2 (1982). *Poetry, British & International. Includes 4 Greek Poets.*

Greek Feature section (pp. 29-44) includes poems of 'the generation of the seventies': Katerina Anghelaki-Rooke, Kostas Mavroudis, Yorghos Chronas, Nana Issaia, Natassa Hadjidaki, Dinos Siotis, Nassos Vayenas Yannis Kontos, Pavlina Pamboudi. Various translators, including Timothy Gallagher, Yannis Goumas, Dinos Siotis, Robert Rowe, Nana Issaia, Thanasis Maskaleris, John Stathatos, Kostas Myrsiades, Kimon Friar.

Address: Zenos Publications, 61B Ilkeston Rd., Nottingham NG7 3GR, United Kingdom.

4. ANTHOLOGIES

This chapter is separated into several sections:
 I. Prose *and* Poetry;
 II. Prose;
 III. Poetry;
 IV. Regional: a. Cyprus; b. Epirus; c. Thessaloniki; d. Other.

The category 'prose' includes both fiction and drama. All anthologies within each section are arranged by the names of their editors. At the end of Sections II, III, and IVa are found subsections listing anthologies contained within journals; they are arranged chronologically under the headings of the journals.

The spellings of the names of the Greek authors are taken directly from the publications.

I. Prose *and* Poetry

4.1 Barnstone, Willis, ed. *Eighteen Texts: Writings by Contemporary Greek Authors*. Cedric Whitman, foreword; Stratis Haviaras, intro. Cambridge, Mass.: Harvard University Press, 1972. 187 p.

Includes: George Seferis, "The Cats of Saint Nicholas" [Edmund Keeley, tr.] (pp. 1-3); Kay Cicellis, "Brief Dialogue" [Kay Cicellis, tr.] (pp. 5-9); Takis Koufopoulos, "The Actor" [Rodis Roufos, tr.] (pp. 11-17); Spiros Plaskovitis, "The Radar" [N.C. Germanakos, tr.] (pp. 19-36); Alexandros Kotzias, "Going Home" [Sarah Kafatou, tr.] (pp. 37-51); Takis Sinopoulos, "Nights" (from the poem "Chronicle") [Willis Barnstone, tr.] (pp. 53-62); Nora Anagnostakis, "A Testimony" [Kay Cicellis, tr.] (pp. 63-67); Rodis Roufos, "The Candidate" [Rodis Roufos and Sarah Kafatou, trs.] (pp. 69-81); George Himonas, "Dr. Ineotis" [Willis Barnstone, tr.] (pp. 83-87); T.D. Frangopoulos, "El Procurador" [Rodis Roufos, tr.] (pp. 89-96); Stratis Tsirkas, "Weather-Change" [Kevin Andrews, tr.] (pp. 97-102); Manolis Anagnostakis, "The Target" [Edmund and Mary Keeley, trs.] (pp. 103-116); D.N. Maronitis, "Arrogance and Intoxication: The Poet and History in Cavafy" [A.A. Fatouros, tr.] (pp. 117-134); Nikos Kasdaglis, "Athos" [N.C. Germanakos, tr.] (pp. 135-151); Thanasis Valtinos, "The Plaster Cast" [Theodora Vasils, tr.] (pp. 153-159); Menis Koumandareas, "Holy Sunday on the Rock" [Stavros Deligiorgis, tr.] (pp. 161-166); Lina Kasdaglis, "Traffic Lights" [Edmund and Mary Keeley, trs.] (pp. 167-168); Alexandros Arghyriou, "The Style of a Language and the Language of a Style" [Kevin Andrews, tr.] (pp. 169-182).

4.2 Fourtouni, Eleni, sel., tr., and intro. *Greek Women in Resistance. Journals—Oral Histories*. [New Haven, Conn.]: Thelphini Press, 1986. 215 p. Chicago, Ill.: Lake View Press, distributors.

Part II, "The Journals", includes: Victoria Theodorou, "Prologue" (pp. 95-96); from *Picnic* [a poem] (p. 97); Evanghelia Fotaki, "White Terror" (pp. 98-104); Victoria Theodorou, "The Trikeri Journal" (pp. 105-143); Aphrodite Mavroede-Pandeleskou, "The Makronisos Journal" (pp. 144-183); Rena Hatzidaki, "Marina" from *The State of Siege* [a poem] (p. 184); Victoria Theodorou, "Back to Trikeri" (pp. 185-187); from *Picnic* [a poem] (p. 189).

4.3 Gianos, Mary P., ed. and tr. *Introduction to Modern Greek Literature: An Anthology of Fiction, Drama, and Poetry.* Kimon Friar, tr. of poetry. New York: Twayne Publishers, Inc., 1969. 548 p.

Aims at a chronological presentation of Greek writers born between 1850 and 1914. I. 'Fiction' includes works of: Panayiotis Kanellopoulos, I.M. Panayotopoulos, Emmanuel Roidis, Alexandros Papadiamantis, Konstantinos Theotokis, Andreas Karkavitsas, Konstantinos Hadzopoulos, Stratis Myrivilis, Elias Venezis, Kosmas Politis, Petros Haris, Takis Doxas, Yiannis Manglis, Markos Lazaridis, Demetrios Yiakos. II. 'Drama': Gregorios Xenopoulos, George Theotokas, Pandelis Prevelakis, Loukis Akritas. III. 'Poetry': Constantine Cavafis, Angelos Sikelianos, Nikos Kazantzakis, Kostas Ouranis, Takis Papatzonis, Kostas Kariotakis, George Seferis, George Themelis, Zoë Karelli, Andreas Embiricos, George Thomas Vafopoulos, Alexander Baras, George Sarandaris, Melissanthi, Yannis Ritsos, Nikos Engonopoulos, Alexander Matsas, Odysseus Elytis, Nikiphoros Vrettakos, Nikos Gatsos, Takis Varvitsiotis.

4.4 *Harlow, Michael, ed. *Events, Greece 1967-1974.* Athens: Anglo-Hellenic, n.d. 88 p.

Includes: P. Korovesis, Y. Ritsos, M. Karapanou, J. Mastoraki, K. Cicellis, S. Yemenaki, M. Anaghnostopoulos, G.C. Savvides, Y. Goumas.

4.5 Pappageotes, George C., Philip D. Emmanuel, and Artemis P. Emmanuel, eds. and trs. *Modern Greek Literary Gems / Ἐκλεκτές Σελίδες.* New York: R.D. Cortina Company, 1962. 64 p. Bilingual edition.

Contains "The Bridge of Arta", and selections from the works of: Regas Pheraios, Andreas Kalvos, Dionysios Solomos, Alexandros Rangavis, Aristotelis Valaoritis, Kostas Krystallis, Lorentzos Mavilis, Alexandros Papadiamantis, John Psycharis, John Vlachoyannis, Kostis Palamas, George Drosinis, Aristomenis Provelengios, Gregorios Xenopoulos, C.P. Cavafy, Angelos Sikelianos, George Seferis, Spyros Melas, Stratis Myrivilis, Nikos Kazantzakis, Pantelis Prevelakis.

4.6 Sherrard, Philip, ed. *The Pursuit of Greece. An Anthology.* Dimitri, photographs. Athens: Denise Harvey & Company, 1987. 291 p. First published: London: John Murray, 1964. 291 p.

The texts include a number of short excerpts translated from the works of Modern Greek authors.

4.7 Stoneman, Richard, ed. *The Literary Companion to Travel to Greece.* Harmondsworth, Middlesex, England: Penguin Books, 1984. 321 p.

Includes several translations from Modern Greek literature.

4.8 Stuart-Glennie, J.S., ed. *Greek Folk Poesy: Annotated Translations, from the Whole Cycle of Romaic Folk-Verse and Folk-Prose.* Lucy M.J. Garnett, tr. Edited with essays on The Science of Folklore, Greek Folkspeech, and The Survival of Paganism by J.S. Stuart-Glennie. 2 vols. *Vol. I: Folk-Verse.* Guildford: Printed for the Authors by Billing and Sons, 1896. 477 p. *Vol. II: Folk-Prose.* Guildford: Printed for the Authors by Billing and Sons, 1896. 541 p.

4.9 Vlachos, Helen, comp. and ed. *Free Greek Voices. A Political Anthology.* London: Doric Publications Ltd., 1971. 162 p.

Includes statements (in prose or poetry) by: Helen Kazantzaki, Menelaos Loundemis, Yannis Ritsos, Rodis Roufos, George Seferis, Vassilis Vassilikos, Nikiforos Vrettakos.

II. Prose

4.10 Dawkins, R.M., sel. and tr. *Modern Greek Folktales*. Oxford: The Clarendon Press, 1953. 491 p.
   84 stories.

4.11 Dawkins, R.M., ed. and tr. *More Greek Folktales*. Oxford: The Clarendon Press, 1955. 178 p. Also *Westport, Conn., 1974.
   26 stories.

4.12 Delopoulos, Kyr., ed. *Modern Greek Short Stories*. Vol. 1. Theodore Sampson, tr.; [translation revised by Dorothy Trollope]. Athens: Kathimerini Publications, 1980. 333 p.
   Stories, given in chronological order, according to the year of birth of their writers. Includes: Iakovos Polylas, "The Error" (pp. 11-28); Demetrios Vikelas, "The Rabid Boy" (pp. 29-41); Emmanuel Roidis, "The Story of a Dog" (pp. 43-54); George Vizyinos, "My Mother's Sin" (pp. 55-83); Argyris Eftaliotis, "Angelica" (pp. 85-97); Alexandros Moraitidis, "The Saint of the Seas" (pp. 99-114); Alexandros Papadiamandis, "Love in the Snow" (pp. 115-122); Yannis Psycharis, "The Earrings" (pp. 123-134); Costis Palamas, "Death of a Young Man" (pp. 135-169); Ioannis Kondylakis, "The Funeral Oration" (pp. 171-181); Andreas Karkavitsas, "The Black Coral" (pp. 183-195); Pavlos Nirvanas, "Behold the Bridegroom Cometh..." (pp. 197-210); Antonis Travlantonis, "The Complaint" (pp. 211-224); Gregorios Xenopoulos, "Warblings" (pp. 225-235); Michael Mitsakis, "The Kiss" (pp. 237-241); Constantinos Hadjopoulos, "The Sister" (pp. 243-249); Yannis Vlachoyannis, "The Miserly Old Woman's Chest" (pp. 251-260); Demosthenes Voutyras, "Pararlama" (pp. 261-266); Constantinos Theotokis, "Face Down!" (pp. 267-271); Zacharias Papantoniou, "The Good Wife of Malis" (pp. 273-280); Costas Paroritis, "The Ferry-Barge" (pp. 281-291); Galatea Kazantzaki, "The Shopping Window" (pp. 293-306); Nikos Kazantzakis, "Father Yanaros" [from his novel *The Fratricides*] (pp. 307-333).
   This volume out of print in 1986.

4.13 Delopoulos, Kyr., ed. *Modern Greek Short Stories*. Vol. 2. Theodore Sampson, sel. and tr.; [translation revised by Dorothy Trollope]. Athens: Kathimerini Publications, 1981. 349 p.
   Includes: Spyros Melas, "The Ship of Redemption" (pp. 9-24); Dionysios Cokkinos, "The Brave Hand" (pp. 25-34); Kosmas Politis, "Julia" (pp. 35-64); Stratis Myrivilis, "The Step-Daughter" (pp. 65-83); G. Athanas, "The Return" (pp. 85-104); Elli Alexiou, "The Fountain of Brahim-Baba" (pp. 105-115); Fotis Condoglou, "Stringaros" (pp. 117-126); Alcis Yannopoulos, "The Buddha's Tooth" (pp. 127-135); Yannis Scarimbas, "Jack's Master" (pp. 137-155); Tatiana Stavrou, "The Pink Dress" (pp. 157-173); Thrasos Kastanakis, "A Common Story" (pp. 175-191); I.M. Panayotopoulos, "The Englishwoman on the Pier" (pp. 193-204); Costis Bastias, "Kavo-Malias. A Sea Story" (pp. 205-221); Petros Haris, "Lights in the Sea" (pp. 223-232); Lilika Nakou, "The Companions" (pp. 233-244); Elias Venezis, "The Seagulls" (pp. 245-256); Th. Petsalis-Diomidis, "Contrasts" (pp. 257-276); George Theotokas, "Simone" (pp. 277-286); Angelos Terzakis, "Calm" (pp. 287-295); M. Karagatsis, "The Man who Loved Cats" (pp. 297-322); Pandelis Prevelakis, "The Smile of Maya" [from his novel *The Bread of Angels*] (pp. 323-337); Menelaos Loundemis, "One Cold Night..." (pp. 339-349).

4.14 *Haviland Virginia, tr. *Favorite Fairy Tales Told in Greece*. Nonny Hogrogian, illustr. Boston: Little, Brown, 1970.

4.15 Megas, Georgios A., ed. *Folktales of Greece*. Helen Colaclides, tr.; Richard M. Dorson, foreword. Chicago and London: The University of Chicago Press, 1970. 287 p.

4.16 Vaka, Demetra and Aristides Phoutrides, trs. *Modern Greek Stories*. Demetra Vaka, foreword. New York: Duffield and Company, 1920. 270 p. Also *New York: AMS Press, 1971. 270 p. Reprint of 1920 edition.

Includes: A. Karkavitsas, "Sea" (pp. 21-53); George T. Bizyenos, "The Sin of My Mother" (pp. 55-89); George Drosines, "The God-Father" (pp. 91-101); Gregorios Xenopoulos, "Mangalos" (pp. 103-129); Iakovos Polylas, "Forgiveness" (pp. 131-154); Argyres Eftaliotes, "Angelica" (pp. 155-170); Kostes Palamas, "A Man's Death" (pp. 171-218); Thrasyvoulos Kastanakis, "The Frightened Soul" (pp. 219-233); A. Papadiamanty, "She that was Homesick" (pp. 235-270).

ANTHOLOGIES OF PROSE CONTAINED WITHIN JOURNALS

The Charioteer

4.17 "The Short Story in Greece: Six Pioneers". *The Charioteer* 4 (1962), pp. 82-145.

Contains: Dimitrios Vikelas, "Why I Remained a Lawyer" [Alice-Mary Maffry, tr.] (pp. 82-93); Yannis Psyharis, "The Earrings" [Alice-Mary Maffry, tr.] (pp. 93-100); Alexandros Papadiamandis, "The Yearly Victim" [JoAnne Cacoullos, tr.] (pp. 100-107); Alexandros Moraïtidis, "The Upside-Down Man" [Merella Psarakis Assmus, tr.] (pp. 108-117); Ioannis Kondylakis, "The Funeral Oration" [Alice-Mary Maffry, tr.] (pp. 117-123); Andreas Karkavitsas, "The Sea" [Christina Pappas and staff, trs.] (pp. 123-137); Andreas Karkavitsas, "The Yousouri" [Fotine Nicholas, tr.] (pp. 138-145).

4.18 "An Anthology of Modern Greek One-Act Plays". *The Charioteer* 26 (1984). Special Issue. George Valamvanos, guest ed. George Valamvanos and Kenneth MacKinnon, trs.

Includes: Iakovos Kambanellis, *He and his Pants* (pp. 9-15); Iakovos Kambanellis, *The Woman and the Wrong Man* (pp. 17-35); Loula Anagnostakis, "The City: A Trilogy of One-Act Plays" [*The Overnight Visitor, The City, The Parade*] (pp. 37-88); Dimitris Kehaides, *Backgammon* (pp. 89-121); George Maniotis, *The Match* (pp. 123-148); George Maniotis, "Three Dramatic Monologues" [*The Little Wooden Man, The Electric Lamp, The Snow*] (pp. 149-154).

New Jersey Folklore

4.19 "Greek Folk Tales". Peri Hionis, coll. *New Jersey Folklore* 1, No. 2 (1977), pp. 8-11.

"Three Gold Pieces"; "The Twelve Months"; "The Lion and the Mouse".

III. Poetry

4.20 Abbott, G.F. *Songs of Modern Greece*. With introductions, translations, and notes. Cambridge, [England]: The University Press, 1900. 307 p. Bilingual texts. Also *Abbott, George F. *Songs of Modern Greece*. Maza Dazla, intro., tr., and notes. Athens: Σκέψη, 1974. 244 p.

4.21 *Alevizos, Susan and Ted Alevizos, eds. and trs. *Folk Songs of Greece*. New York: Oak Publications, 1968. 96 p.

4.22 Barnstone, Aliki and Willis Barnstone, eds. *A Book of Women Poets from Antiquity to Now*. New York: Schocken Books, 1980. 612 p.

Modern Greek Section (pp. 48-56) includes: Moirologia (Traditional Funeral Songs), and works of: Eleni Vakalo, Lydia Stephanou, Lina Kasdaglis, Nana Issaia, Eva Mylonas, Jenny Mastoraki.

4.23 *Barnstone, Willis et al., eds. *Modern European Poetry: French, German, Greek, Italian, Russian, Spanish*. New York; Toronto; London: Bantam Books Inc., 1966. 605 p.

"Greek Poetry" [Kimon Friar, ed. and tr.] (pp. 187-268): Introduction, and poems of: Angelos Sikelianos, Nikos Kazantzakis, George Seferis, George Themelis, Demetrius Antoniou, Yannis Ritsos, Alexander Matsas, Nikos Engonopoulos, Odysseus Elytis, Nikos Gatsos, Miltos Sahtouris, Eleni Vakalo, Nanos Valaoritis, Nikos Karouzos, Dinos Christianopoulos.

4.24 Butterworth, Katharine and Sara Schneider, eds. *Rebetika: Songs from the Old Greek Underworld*. Athens: Komboloi, 1975. 168 p.

Contains preface by the editors (pp. 9-10); Elias Petropoulos, "Rebetika" (pp. 1-15); Markos Dragoumis, "The Music of the Rebetes" (pp. 16-25); Ted Petrides, "The Dances of the Rebetes" (pp. 27-33); Sakis Papadimitriou, "Rebetika and Blues" (pp. 34-37); "Collection of Song Lyrics" from the anthology of Elias Petropoulos (bilingual version) [Katharine Butterworth and Sara Schneider, trs.] (pp. 39-147); Markos Dragoumis, "Musical Examples" (pp. 149-157); "Glossary of Transliterated Words" (pp. 161-163).

4.25 *Creekmore, Hubert, ed. and intro. *A Little Treasury of World Poetry: Translations from the Great Poets of Other Languages, 2600 B.C. to 1950 A.D.* New York: Charles Scribner's Sons, 1952. 904 p.

Modern Greek Section [Kimon Friar, tr.] (pp. 256-261) contains works of: C.P. Cavafis, Anghelos Sikelianos, George Seferis, Odysseus Elytis, Nikos Engonopoulos.

4.26 Dalven, Rae, tr. and ed. *Modern Greek Poetry*. Second edition, revised and enlarged. New York: Russell & Russell, 1971. 375 p. *1st edition: New York: Gaer, 1949.

The second edition includes: Rae Dalven, "The Growth of Modern Greek Poetry" (essay) (pp. 23-40) and "The Folk Song: Source of Modern Greek Poetry" (essay) (pp. 41-56); Vincenzo Kornaros, "Erotokritos" (excerpt); works of Modern Greek poetry by the following authors: Rhigas Pheraios, Yiannis Vilaras, Andreas Calvos, Dionysios Solomos, Julius Typaldos, Aristotelis Valaoritis, Gerasimos Markoras, Georgios Vizinos, Alexandros Pallis, Kostes Palamas, Georgios Drossinis, Lorenzo Mavilis, C.P. Cavafy, Kostas Krystallis, Kostes Hatzopoulos, Miltiades Malakassis, Yiannis Griparis, Petros Vlastos, Lambros Porphyras, Zacharias Papandoniou, Apostolos Melachrinos, Nicholas Karvounis, Sotiris Skipis, Myrtiotissa, Angelos Sikelianos, Kostas Varnalis, Markos Avgeris, Nikos Kazantzakis, Galatea Kazantzakis, Kostas Ouranis, Kostas Kariotakis, Georgios Seferis, Tefcros Anthias, Joseph Eliyia, Kassaris Emmanuel, Michalis Stasinopoulos, Sophia Mavroidi Papadaky, Nicholas Pappas, Rita Boumy Pappas, Yiannis Sphakianakis, Yiannis Ritsos, Nicephorus Vrettakos, Odysseus Elytis, Georgios Themelis, Andreas Embirikos, Zoe Karelli, I.M. Panayiotopoulos, Georgios Thomas Vafopoulos, Georgios Sarandaris, Nikos Engonopoulos, Melissanthi, Nikos Gatsos, Takis Varvitsiotis, Minas Dimakis, Crito Athanasoulis, Georgios Geralis, Ares Diktaios, Georgios Kotsiras, Kostas Kovanis.

4.27 Edmonds, E.M., tr. *Greek Lays, Idylls, Legends, &c.: A Selection from Recent and Contemporary Poets*. With introduction and notes. Revised and enlarged edition: London: Trübner & Co., Ludgate Hill, 1886. 288 p. *1st edition: London: Trübner & Co., Ludgate Hill, 1885. 264 p.

In the revised and enlarged edition, 'recent' poets include: Athanasius Chrystopoulos, Dionysius Solomos, George Zalakostas (sic), Alexander Soutsos, John Karasutsas, Elias Tantalidês, Aristotle Valaôritês, Julius Typaldos. 'Contemporary' poets include: Alexander Rhangabes, Demetrius Bikelas, Angelus Vlachos, Spyridon Lambros, Achilles Paraschos, Kostes Palamas, George Viziênós, Aristomenês Provilegios, George Drosinês, Stamatos Valvês. A poem by Theodore Orphanidês is also included.

4.28 Fotheringham, David Ross. *War Songs of the Greeks and Other Poems*. With a preface by G.W.E. Russell. Cambridge, [England]: Deighton Bell & Co.; London: George Bell & Sons, 1907. 88 p.

The 'Hellenic' contents include: "Ballads of Modern Greece—War Songs" (pp. 15-39); "Hellenic Poems" (pp. 40-50); "Leaves from the Roll of Honour" [prose] (pp. 51-59).

4.29 Fourtouni, Eleni, tr. *Contemporary Greek Women Poets*. New Haven, Conn.: Thelphini Press, 1978. 74 p.

Includes works by: Victoria Theodorou, Rita Boumi-Pappas, Melpo Axiote, Lili Bita, Katerina Anghelaki-Rooke, Kiki Dimoula, Jenny Mastoraki, Eleni Fourtouni.

4.30 Fourtouni, Eleni, tr. *4 Greek Women: Love Poems*. [New Haven, Conn.]: Thelphini Press, 1982. 79 p.

Poems by Victoria Theodorou, Angeliki Pavlopoulou, Katerina Anghelaki-Rooke, Eleni Fourtouni.

4.31 Friar, Kimon, tr. *Contemporary Greek Poetry*. With introduction, biographies, and notes. Athens: The Greek Ministry of Culture, 1985. 486 p.

Contains works by: Minas Dhimakis, Takis Varvitsiotis, Kritos Athanasoulis (sic), Takis Sinopoulos, Sarandos Pavleas, Yorgos Yeralis, Nikos Karidhis, Ares Dhikteos, Miltos Sahtouris, Andonis Decavalles, Hector Kaknavatos, Yoryis Kotsiras, Nanos Valaoritis, Klitos Kirou, Heleni Vakalo, Athos Dhimoulas, Tasos Livadhitis, P.D. Papadhitsas (sic), Ares Alexandrou, Aristotle Nikolaidis, T.D. Frangopoulos, George Pavlopoulos, Mihalis Katsaros, Yannis Dhallas, Manolis Anagnostakis, Dhimitris Dhoukaris, Stavros Vavouris, Nikos Spanias, Panos Thasitis, Mando Aravandinou, Kostas Steryopoulos, Nikos Karouzos, Nikos Phocas, Lydia Stephanou, Yannis Papadhopoulos, Titos Patrikios, Maria Servaki, Dinos Christianopoulos, Kiki Dhimoula, Nikos-Alexis Aslanoglou, Byron Leondaris, Nana Isaïa, Markos Meskos, Tasos Denegris, Prodhromos X. Markoglou, Anestis Evangelou, George Thaniel, Eva Mylona, Katerina Angelaki-Rooke, Zephy Dharaki, Kyriakos Haralambhidhis, Yannis Kondos, Christos Valavanidhis, Alexis Traïanos, Lefteris Poulios, Dinos Siotis, Nasos Vayenas, Dhimitris Potamitis, Natasa Hadjidhaki, Nikos Lazaris, Yannis Patilis, Vasilis Steryadhis, Pavlina Pampoudhi, Yorgos Hronas, Jenny Mastoraki, Yannis Ifandis, Andonis Fostieris.

Not available on the market.

4.32 Friar, Kimon, ed., tr., and epilogue. *The Greeks: A Celebration of the Greek People through Poetry and Photographs*. John Veltri, photography; Lawrence Durrell, preface; Odysseus Elytis, commentary. Garden City, N.Y.: Doubleday & Company, Inc., 1984. 144 p.

Contains poetry of: George Seféris, Yánnis Rítsos, George Thémelis, Odysseus Elytis, Alexander Mátsas, Níkos Kazantzákis, Eléni Vakaló, D.P. Papadhítsas, George Sarandáris, G.T. Vafópoulos.

4.33 Friar, Kimon, tr. *Modern Greek Poetry: From Cavafis to Elytis*. With introduction, an essay on translation, and notes. New York: Simon and Schuster, 1973. 780 p.

Introduction (pp. 1-130) includes: The Historical Background; Language and Literature; The Schools; Forerunners and Traditionalists; Traditions and Transitions; The Turning Point and the Surrealists; The Social Poets; Religious and Existentialist Modes; A Few Observations. Poetry translations (pp. 131-645) include works of: Constantine Cavafis, Nikos Kazantzakis, Kostas Varnalis, Angelos Sikelianos, Kostas Ouranis, Takis Papatsonis, Kostas Kariotakis, George Seferis, George Themelis, Zoe Karelli, Andreas Embiricos, I.M. Panayotopoulos, G.T. Vafopoulos, Nikos Pappas, Rita Boumi-Pappas, D.I. Antoniou, Alexander Baras, George Sarandaris, Nicolas Calas, Nikos Ghavriil Pendzikis, Pandelis Prevelakis, Yannis Ritsos, Nikos Kavadhias, Andreas Karandonis, Melissanthi, Alexander Matsas, Nikos Engonopoulos, Odysseus Elytis, Nikos Gatsos, Nikiphoros Vrettakos. Concludes with a section containing essays on translation (pp. 647-678); biographies, bibliographies, notes (pp. 679-759); and a select general bibliography (pp. 761-769).

4.34 Friar, Kimon, tr. *Modern Greek Poetry*. Including: George Seferis, Nobel Prize 1963; Odysseus Elytis, Nobel Prize 1976. With introduction, commentaries, and notes. Athens: Efstathiadis Group, 1982. 326 p.
   Contains: an introduction (pp. 13-31) and works of: Constantine Cavafis, Nikos Kazantzakis, Kostas Varnalis, Angelos Sikelianos, Kostas Ouranis, Takis Papatsonis, Kostas Kariotakis, George Seferis, George Themelis, Zoë Karelli, Andreas Embiricos, I.M. Panayotopoulos, G.T. Vafopoulos, Nikos Pappas, Rita Boumi-Pappa, D.I. Antoniou, Alexander Baras, George Sarandaris, Nicolas Calas, Nikos Gavriil Pendzikis, Pandelis Prevelakis, Yannis Ritsos, Nikos Kavadhias, George Stoyannidhis, Andreas Karandonis, Melissanthi, Alexander Matsas, Nikos Engonopoulos, Zisis Economou, Odysseus Elytis, Nikos Gatsos, Nikiphoros Vrettakos. Concludes with biographies, bibliographies, commentary and notes (pp. 279-319).
   Is a condensed version of the preceding entry.

4.35 Frye, Ellen. *The Marble Threshing Floor: A Collection of Greek Folksongs*. Publications of the American Folklore Society. Memoir Series, Vol. 57. Published for the American Folklore Society. Austin and London: The University of Texas Press, 1973. 327 p.

4.36 *Gaist, Jack, tr. *Poems from the Modern Greek*. Nicosia, Cyprus: Pnevmatiki Kypros, 1976. 42 p.
   Includes poems by J. Tsatsos, G. Vafopoulos, T. Papatsonis, C. Karyotakis, K. Chrysanthis, G. Athanas, A. Karantonis, C. Montis, C. Ouranis, C. Steryiopoulos, C. Varnalis, T. Agras, I. Gryparis, A. Sikelianos.

4.37 *Georgakas, Dan, ed. *Z: An Anthology of Revolutionary Poetry*. New York: Smyrna Press, 1968.
   Contains Greek and American Poetry.

4.38 Goumas, John A., tr. *Nine Greek Poets*. Athens: Athens Publishing Center, 1968. 123 p.
   Poems by: Alexandros Baras, Dimitris Christodoulou, Akos Daskalopoulos, George Sarantaris, Andreas Embiricos, Nikos Engonopoulos, Anestis Evangelou, Markos Meskos, Tassos Roussos.

4.39 *Halpern, Daniel, ed. *The Antaeus Anthology*. Toronto; New York: Bantam Books, 1986.
   Includes: C.P. Cavafy, "Myris", "Their Beginning", "In the Evening", "In the Tavernas", "On Board Ship", "Dareios"; Yannis Ritsos, "Disfigurement", "Penelope's Despair", "Philomela", "Marpessa's Choice", "Our Land"; George Seferis, "Summer Solstice" [Edmund Keeley, sometimes in collaboration with Philip Sherrard, trs.].

4.40 Joss, Paul Maria Leopold. Παραδείγματα 'Ρωμαϊκῆς Ποιητικῆς. *Specimens of Romaic Lyric Poetry*. With a translation into English to which is prefixed a concise treatise on music. London: Printed for Richard Glynn, 1826. 144 p. Bilingual edition.
   Amatory Songs, Brigand Songs (one by Spiridion Trikupi of Missolonghi, "Deemos, A Brigand Tale" [pp. 37-57]), and Patriotic Songs.

4.41 Junkins, Donald, ed. *The Contemporary World Poets*. New York: Harcourt Brace Jovanovich, Inc., 1976. 415 p.

"Greece" (pp. 115-132) includes works of: Odysseus Elytis [Edmund Keeley, George Savidis, Paul Merchant, and Stuart Montgomery, trs.] (pp. 115-121); Yannis Ritsos [Nikos Stangos and Paul Merchant, trs.] (pp. 121-125); and George Seferis [Rex Warner, Walter Kaiser, and John Chioles, trs.] (pp. 126-132).

4.42 Keeley, Edmund and Philip Sherrard, eds. and trs. *The Dark Crystal. An Anthology of Modern Greek Poetry by Cavafy, Sikelianos, Seferis, Elytis, Gatsos.* Athens: Denise Harvey & Company, 1981. 202 p.

Contents identical to those of their *Voices of Modern Greece* {4.45}.

4.43 Keeley, Edmund and Philip Sherrard, trs. and eds. *Four Greek Poets: C.P. Cavafy, George Seferis, Odysseus Elytis, Nikos Gatsos.* Penguin Modern European Poets, D91. Harmondsworth, Middlesex, England: Penguin Books Ltd., 1966. 110 p. Reprinted, 1970.

Much overlap with their *Six Poets of Modern Greece* {4.44}.

4.44 Keeley, Edmund and Philip Sherrard, eds., trs. and intro. *Six Poets of Modern Greece.* Unesco Collection of Contemporary Works. European Series. London: Thames and Hudson, 1960 [1969]. 192 p. Also New York: Alfred A. Knopf, 1961 and 1970. 183 p.

Includes poems of: C.P. Cavafy, Anghelos Sikelianos, George Seferis, D.I. Antoniou, Odysseus Elytis, Nikos Gatsos.

Out of print. Cf. *Four Greek Poets* {4.43} and *Voices of Greece* {4.45}.

4.45 Keeley, Edmund and Philip Sherrard, trs. and eds. *Voices of Modern Greece: Selected Poems by C.P. Cavafy, Angelos Sikelianos, George Seferis, Odysseus Elytis, Nikos Gatsos.* Princeton, N.J.: Princeton University Press, 1981. 202 p.

Contains poems of: Constantine P. Cavafy (pp. 3-51); Angelos Sikelianos (pp. 55-83); George Seferis (pp. 87-130); Odysseus Elytis (pp. 133-169); Nikos Gatsos (pp. 173-186). "The anthology ... is composed of those translations that seem ... to come over most successfully into English and at the same time to be representative of the best in the poetry of the original poets". Revised versions of translations of Cavafy, Seferis, Sikelianos, and Elytis.

Also published as *The Dark Crystal* {4.42}.

4.46 Kontos, N. and P. Gravalos [photographs]. *Optikon: A New Photographic View of Greece.* Marios Ploritis, prologue; Kimon Friar, tr. Athens: Chryssos Typos, 1981. 303 p.

Many photographs of Greece interspersed with excerpts from Modern Greek poets, selected by Marios Ploritis.

4.47 *Lee, David, Elmer E. Moore, Jr. and Oliver Niles, eds. *Compass II.* Glenview, Ill.: Scott, Foresman, 1971.

Contains works of: D. Antoniou, G. Seferis, N. Vrettakos [Kimon Friar, Edmund Keeley, Philip Sherrard, Thomas Doulis, trs.].

4.48 Maskaleris, Thanasis. *Poems & Translations.* San Francisco: Kayak, 1969. 83 p.

Includes original poems of Thanasis Maskaleris (in English) and translations of selections from: C.P. Cavafy, Nanos Valaoritis, Takis Sinopoulos, Yannis Ritsos, Nikephoros Vrettakos, Nikos Kavvadias, Nikos Engonopoulos, Orpheus Xenophobos, Andreas Embirikos, and George Seferis.

4.49 McPherson, Florence, tr. *Poetry of Modern Greece: Specimens and Extracts.* London: Macmillan and Co., 1884. 183 p.
   Part I (pp. 1-55): Popular Ballads; Part II (pp. 57-183): Translations from the Works of Lettered Poets of the Present Century (Dionysios Solomos, Angelica Palli, Constantine Kokkinakes, Andrew Kalvos, Alexander and Panagiotes Soutsos, Alexander Rhizos Rhangabes, George Zalakostas (sic), Aristotle Valaorites, Theodore Aphentoules, Achilles Paraschos, George Drosines).

4.50 Mitsakis, K. *Modern Greek Music and Poetry. An Anthology.* Mikis Theodorakis, pref. Athens: Editions "Grigoris", 1979. 533 p. Bilingual edition.
   Includes works of: George Chortatsis, Vitsentzos Kornaros, Andreas Kalvos, Dionysios Solomos, George Vizyinos, Argyris Eftaliotis, Vassilis Michaelidis, Kostis Palamas, C.P. Cavafy, Dimitris Lipertis, Kostas Chatzopoulos, Zacharias Papantoniou, Nikos Kazantzakis, Angelos Sikelianos, Kostas Varnalis, Napoleon Lapathiotis, Kostas Karyotakis, Yannis Skarimbas, George Seferis, George Themelis, Pantelis Prevelakis, Yannis Ritsos, Nikos Engonopoulos, Nikos Kavadias, Odysseus Elytis, Nikiphoros Vrettakos, Menelaos Loundemis, Minas Dimakis, Manolis Anagnostakis.
   Translators include F.H. Marshall, M.B. Raizis, K. Trypanis, E. Keeley, Ph. Sherrard, J. Mavrogordato, K. Friar, J. Gaist, R. Dalven, A. Mims, G. Savidis.

4.51 *New World Writing. Second Mentor Selection.* New York: The New American Library, Nov. 1952.
   "Four Contemporary Greek Poets" [Kimon Friar, tr.] (pp. 102-108). Includes works of: Nikos Kazantzakis, Odysseus Elytis, Takis Papatzonis, George Seferis.

4.52 Ragovin, F. *Greek Love Songs.* Collected and Translated into English Verse. With Prologue and Notes. Athens: "Cnossos" Editions, 1974. 103 p.

4.53 Raizis, M. Byron. *Greek Poetry Translations: Views—Texts—Reviews.* Athens: Efstathiadis Group, 1981. 248 p.
   Includes: an introduction by Raizis on literary translation (pp. 12-29), an anthology of Greek poetry (pp. 35-171), and several critical reviews of books of Greek poetry in translation (pp. 173-240). The anthology is divided into: 'Traditional Poetry' (pp. 35-141), with works by Dionysios Solomos, John Polemis, George Drosinis, John Gryparis, Kostas Karyotakis, Michael D. Stasinopoulos, Nikos Kazantzakis, Andreas Embiricos, Nikos Engonopoulos, Markos Avyeris, Nikephoros Vrettakos, Ares Diktaios, Zoë Karelli, George Kotsiras, Dimitris Doukaris, Triandafillos Pittas, Kostes Kokorovits, Koula Yiokarini, Philip Drakodaides, Takis Antoniou, George Themelis, Takis Varvitsiotis, Nikos Alexis Aslanoglou, George X. Stoyannides, Dinos Christianopoulos, Panos Thasites, Anestis Evangelou; 'Cypriot Poems' (pp. 144-155), with works of Kypros Chrysanthis, Manos Kralis, Petros Sophas, Yannis K. Papadopoulos, Nadina Dimitriou. The final section contains works of George Seferis (pp. 157-171).

4.54 Richmond, John and Bryan McCarthy, trs. *The Singing Cells: Modern Greek Poems.* Paolo Vivante, pref. Montreal: Ingluvin Publications, 1970. 52 p.
   Includes: Nikos Engonopoulos, George Seferis, Angelos Sikelianos, Yiannis Ritsos, Tassos Spiropoulos, Pantelis Trogadis, Rita Boumi-Papa, Costas Kariotakis, Leon Koukoulas, Menelaos Loundemis, Tassos Livaditis, Nanos Valaoritis, Eleni Paidoussi, Tassos Denegris, Nikiforos Vretakos.

4.55 *A Sheaf of Greek Folk Songs, Gleaned by an Old Philhellene.* With an introductory note by Countess Evelyn Martinengo Cesaresco. Oxford: Basil Blackwell, 1922. 78 p.

4.56 Sheridan, Charles Brinsley, tr. *The Songs of Greece, from the Romaic Text*, edited by M.C. Fauriel, with additions, translated into English verse. London: printed for Longman, Hurst, Rees, Orme, Brown, and Green, 1825. 313 p.

Part the First: Historical (pp. 5-123): Class I: Songs of the Klephtai; Class II: Miscellaneous Historical Ballads. Part the Second: Ideal (pp. 125-247): Class I: Romantic Ballads; Class II: Domestic Songs, Holiday Carols, Nuptial Songs; Class III: Distichs Current on the Coast and Islands. Part the Third: Recent Odes of Greek Literati: "Dithyrambics to Liberty" (158 stanzas) [by Mr. Salomos] (pp. 249-288); "The Triumph of Greece" [by M. Rizo Neroulos] (pp. 289-305); "Epitaph on the Ever to Be Remember'd Marco Botzaris, Who Heroically Fell for Liberty at the Battle of Laspi" [by M. Gregorios Paleologos] (as stated in Preface) (pp. 306-310); "The Song of Freedom" (pp. 311-313).

4.57 Siotis, Dino, ed. *Ten Women Poets of Greece*. Katerina Anghelaki-Rooke, intro. San Francisco: Wire Press, 1982. Is *The Coffeehouse* 11-12 (1982). 96 p.

Includes: Katerina Anghelaki-Rooke, "Introduction" (pp. 7-16); works of: Demetra Christodoulou, Veroniki Dalakoura, Katerina Gogou, Natassa Hatzidaki, Andriana Ierodiaconou, Maria Laina, Jenny Mastoraki, Pavlina Pampoudi, Ersi Sotiropoulou, Ioanna Zervou (pp. 17-94).

Translators: John Chioles, Stavros Deligiorgis, Kimon Friar, Yannis Goumas, Jack Hirschman, Maria Layoun, Thanasis Maskaleris, Dino Siotis, Nikos Spanias.

4.58 Siotis, Dinos & John Chioles, eds. *Twenty Contemporary Greek Poets*. Nanos Valaoritis, intro. San Francisco: Wire Press, 1979. Is *The Coffeehouse* 7-8 (1979). 130 p.

Includes poems of: Katerina Anghelaki-Rooke, Stefanos Becatoros, Yorghos Chronas, Veroniki Dalakoura, Antonis Fostieris, Natassa Hadjidaki, Yannis Kakoulidis, Yannis Kontos, Maria Laina, Jenny Mastoraki, Pavlina Pampoudi, Yannis Patilis, Lefteris Poulios, Dinos Siotis, John Stathatos, Vassilis Steriadis, George Thaniel, Christos Valavanidis, Nassos Vayenas, Yannis Yfantis, and illustrations.

4.59 Spanias, Nikos, tr. and ed. *Resistance, Exile and Love: An Anthology of Post-War Greek Poetry*. New York: Pella Publishing Company, 1977. 170 p.

Includes: Manolis Anagnostakis, Takis Antoniou, Theodosis Athas, Yannis Dallas, Iason Depountis, Dimitris Doukaris, Thanasis Fotiadis, Stelios Geranis, Michalis Katsaros, Spyros Kokkinis, Klitos Kyrou, Tasos Livaditis, Yorgis Manousakis, Dimitris Papaditsas, Nikos Spanias, Panos Thasitis, Eleni Vakalo, Takis Varvitsiotis.

4.60 Stathatos, John, ed. and tr. *Six Modern Greek Poets*. London: Oasis Books, 1975. 90 p.

Includes poems by: George Seferis, Takis Sinopoulos, Miltos Sahtouris, Yannis Ritsos, Aris Alexandrou, Eleni Vakalo.

4.61 Steiner, George, ed. *The Penguin Book of Modern Verse Translation*. Baltimore, Md.; Harmondsworth, Middlesex, England: Penguin Books, 1966. 332 p.

The section on Modern Greek poetry contains (pp. 307-313): Anghelos Sikelianos, "The First Rain"; Odysseus Elytis, "The Mad Pomegranate Tree" and "The Body of Summer"; Nikos Gatsos, "They Say the Mountains Tremble" and "In the Griever's Courtyard" [Edmund Keeley and Philip Sherrard, trs.].

4.62 Stephanides, Theodore Ph. and George C. Katsimbalis, eds. and trs. *Modern Greek Poems*. London: printed by Hazell, Watson & Viney, Ltd., 1926. 76 p. "To Kostes Palamas, greatest poet of Modern Greece".

Includes works by: George Argyropoulos, George Athanas, Homer Bekes, Emilia Dafni, George Delis, George Drosinis, Arghyris Eftaliotis, John Gryparis, Kostas Hadjopoulos, Constantine Karyotakis, Constantine Kavafis, Kostas Krystallis, Athanasios Kyriazis, Miltiades Malakasis, Gerasimos Markoras, Lorenzos Mavilis, Andrew Michalopoulos, Myrtiotissa (Mrs. Drakopoulos), Paul Nirvanas, Kostas Ouranis, Kostes Palamas, Alexander Pallis, Zacharias Papantoniou, Nicholas Petimezas, John Polemis, Lambros Porphyras, Louis Scarpas, Stelios Seferiades, Theodore Stephanides, Panos Tangopoulos, Kostas Varnalis, Peter Vlastos, John Cl. Zervos.

4.63 Stuart Glennie, John S., ed. *Greek Folk-Songs from the Turkish Provinces of Greece*, ἡ Δούλη Ἑλλάς: *Albania, Thessaly (not yet wholly free), and Macedonia*. Literal and metrical translations by Lucy M.J. Garnett. Classified, revised, and edited with an historical introduction on the survival of paganism by the editor. London: Elliot Stock, 1885. 260 p. Second edition, revised and enlarged: John Stuart Stuart Glennie, ed. *Greek Folk-Songs from the Ottoman Provinces of Northern Hellas*. Literal and metrical trs. by Lucy M.J. Garnett. Classified, revised and edited with essays on the Survival of Paganism, and the Science of Folk-lore. London: Ward and Downey, 1888. 290 p.

4.64 Trypanis, Constantine A., intro., ed., tr. *The Penguin Book of Greek Verse*. Harmondsworth, Middlesex, England: Penguin Books Ltd., 1971. 630 p. Bilingual edition.

Includes plain prose translations of poetry from ancient Greece, the Hellenistic world, late antiquity, the Byzantine Empire (including selections from Theodore Prodromos, *Callimachus and Chrysorrhoe, The Epic of Digenis Akritas, Lybistros and Rhodamne, The Achilleïs*), Greece under Frankish and Turkish rule (including anonymous folk-songs, selections from Vizentzos Cornaros, George Chortatzis, Rhigas Pherrhaios); Modern Greek selections (pp. 499-618) are taken from the works of: Dionysios Solomos, Andreas Kalvos, Alexander Soutsos, George Zalokostas, Alexander Rizos Rangavis, Julius Typaldos, John Karasoutsas, Gerasimos Markoras, Achilles Paraschos, Demetrios Paparrhegopoulos, G. Vizyenos, Aristotle Valaoritis, George Drosinis, Kostis Palamas, John Polemis, K. Krystallis, Lorentzos Mavilis, Lambros Porphyras, Constantine Hatzopoulos, Paul Nirvanas, Miltiades Malakasis, John Gryparis, Constantine Karyotakis, Maria Polydoure, Myrtiotissa, Emily S. Daphne, C. Kavafis, Angelos Sikelianos, George Seferis, Odysseus Elytis.

ANTHOLOGIES OF POETRY CONTAINED WITHIN JOURNALS

The Amaranth

4.65 "The Garden" [an anthology of (mostly young) poets based in Greece, Cyprus and North-America]. G. Thaniel, tr. *The Amaranth* 3 (1982), pp. 19-31.

Includes works of: Mihalis Ganas, Manolis Xenakis, Niki Marangou, Andreas Anghelakis, Savas Savopoulos, Frossoula Kolossiatou, Thomas Gorpas, Nassos Vayenas, Savas Patsalidis, Dionysis Karatzas, Vanghellis Kassos, Andreas Fouskarinis, Fontas Bratsos, Christos Ziatas, Mary Kassos, Labis Mavrides, Ilias Simopoulos, Christos Laskaris.

4.66 "The Garden". Various translators. *The Amaranth* 4 (1982), pp. 3-14.

Includes poems of: Yorghos Stoyannidhis, Eleni Pappa, Dhimitris Dhoukaris, Maria Laghoureli, Maria Kentrou-Agathopoulou, Kostas Gharbis, Spiros (Spiros Zafiris), Nikos Engonopoulos, Stefanos Bekatoros, Yannis Patilis, Ilias Tsehos, Dinos Siotis, Nikos Spanias.

4.67 "The Garden: Poetry in Translation". E. Phinney, G. Thaniel et al., trs. *The Amaranth* 5 (1983), pp. 5-22.

Includes works of: Elias Kefalas, G. Thaniel, Vasilis Karavitis, Christos Laskaris, Nasos Vayenas, Nikos Karakostas, Zephi Dharaki, Yannis Kontos, Aryiris Hionis, Yoryis Pavlopoulos, Stylianos Harkianakis, Takis Varvitsiotis, Andhreas Anghelakis, Tolis Nikiforou, Antonis Fostieris.

4.68 "The Garden: Poetry in Translation". Edward Phinney, G. Thaniel and Dino Siotis, trs. *The Amaranth* 6 (1983), pp. 11-22.

Includes works of: Dhimitris Dhaskalopoulos, Manolis Pratsikas, Nikos Ghrighoriadhis, Lambis Mavrides, Rois Papangelou, Tasos Korfis, Veroniki Dhalakoura.

4.69 "The Garden: Poems in Translation". Various translators. *The Amaranth* 7 (1984), pp. 5-29.

Includes works of: Nikos Karouzos, Dinos Christianopoulos, Thanasis Papathanasopoulos, Leonidhas Bombas, Dhimitris Sourvinos, Sotiris Trivizas, Orestis Alexakis, Ilias Tsehos, Dhimitris Konidharis, Maria Lagourelli, Nikos Engonopoulos, Nikos Kavadhias.

4.70 "The Garden: Poems in Translation". Edward S. Phinney, G. Thaniel and Donald Hall, trs. *The Amaranth* 8 (1984), pp. 29-43.

Includes works of: Mattheos Moundes, Popi Sotiriou, Dhionisis Karatzas, Antonis Fostieris, Thanasis Niarchos, Kostas Papayeoryiou, Nasos Vayenas.

4.71 "Poems in Translation (from Greek to English)". Various translators. *The Amaranth* 9 (1985), pp. 16, 20-32.

Includes works of: Nikos Karouzos, Maria Lazou, Christos Roumeliotakis, Ector Kaknavatos, Kostas Ghouliamos, Dhimitris Papakonstantinou, Stylianos Harkianakis, E.C. Gonatas.

4.72 "Greek Poems in English Translation". Various translators. *The Amaranth* 10 (1987), pp. 33-55.

Includes works of: Ioanna Tsatsos, Rena Kasdhaghli, Tasos Ghalatis, Dinos Siotis, E.C. Gonatas, Peggy Korovesi-Porfiri, Nasos Vayenas, Anna Katevaini, Amalia Tsaknia.

The Beloit Poetry Journal

4.73 "Four Greek Poets". Edmund Keeley, tr. *The Beloit Poetry Journal* 7, No. 3 (Spring 1957), pp. 11-17.

George Seferis, "From *Mythical Story*, Nos. 9, 12, 22" (pp. 11-13); Odysseus Elytis, "Drinking the Sun of Corinth", "The Mad Pomegranate Tree" (pp. 13-15); Nikos Gatsos, "In the Griever's Courtyard" (p. 16); I.D. Antoniou (sic), "Obstacle to What" (p. 17).

Boundary 2

4.74 "Three Young Poets: Jenny Mastoraki, Haris Megalinos and Lefteris Poulios". N.C. Germanacos and others, trs. *Boundary 2*, Vol. 1, No. 2 (Winter 1973), pp. 507-518 {3.5}.

The Charioteer

4.75 "Poems by the Post-War Poets". Kimon Friar, tr. *The Charioteer* 15 (1974), pp. 28-101.

The issue includes: Andonis Decavalles, "Kimon Friar as Translator" (pp. 9-14); Andonis Decavalles, "Poets of Two Decades" (pp. 15-27); poems (pp. 28-101) of: Maro Aravandinou (sic), Kriton Athanasoulis, Andonis Decavalles, Ares Dhikteos, Minas Dhimakis, Nikos Karidhis, Nikos Karouzos, George Kotsiras, Dimitris Papadhitsas, Yannis Papadhopoulos, Nikos Phocas, Miltos Sahtouris, Takis Sinopoulos, Lydia Stephanou, Kostas Steryopoulos, Eleni Vakalo, Nanos Valaoritis, George Yeralis.

4.76 "The New Poets". Kimon Friar, tr. *The Charioteer* 20 (1978), pp. 42-115.

The issue includes: Andonis Decavalles, "Modernity: The Third Stage, the New Poets" (pp. 11-41); poems (pp. 42-115) by: Dhimitris Kakavelakis, Kiki Dhimoula, Nana Isaïa, Tasos Denegris, Markos Meskos, Prodhromos Markoglou, Anestis Evangelou, Eva Mylona, George Thaniel, Katerina Angelaki-Rooke, Zephy Dharaki, Yannis Kondos, Mihalis Meïmaris, Lefteris Poulios, Dinos Siotis, Dhimitris Potamitis, Nasos Vayenas, Maria Laïna, Yannis Patilis, Vasilis Steryadhis, Christos Valavanidhis, Pavlina Pamboudhi, Jenny Mastoraki, George Hronas.

Chicago Review

4.77 "Eighteen Post-War Greek Poets". Kimon Friar, tr. *Chicago Review* 21, No. 2 (Aug. 1969), pp. 14-82 {3.6}.

Contains works of: Takis Sinopoulos, Minas Dhimakis, George Yeralis, Takis Varvitsiotis, Miltos Sahtouris, Ares Dhikteos, Andonis Decavalles, George Kotsiras, Nanos Valaoritis, Klitos Kirou, Eleni Vakalo, D.M. Papadhitsas (sic), Manolis Anaghnostakis, Nikos Karouzos, Nikos Phocas, Mando Aravandinou, Dinos Christianopoulos, Lydia Stephanou.

The Colorado Quarterly

4.78 "Three Greek Poets". Edmund Keeley, tr. *The Colorado Quarterly* 8, No. 4 (Spring 1960), pp. 318-323.

Includes: George Seferis "The Last Stop" (pp. 318-320); Nikos Gatsos, "Death and the Knight (1513)" (pp. 321-322); D.I. Antoniou, "Tonight You Remembered" (pp. 322-323).

The International Portland Review

4.79 "Greece: [An Anthology of Poems]". *The International Portland Review* (1980), pp. 152-166.

Contains poems of Yannis Ritsos, Nana Isaia, Dinos Siotis, Nicos Phocas, Katerina Angelaki-Rooke, Nasos Vayenas. Bilingual. All translations by Kimon Friar except for the poem by Dinos Siotis, translated by the author himself.

The London Magazine

4.80 "Eleven Poems from Greece". *The London Magazine,* N.S. Vol. 5, No. 7 (Oct. 1965), pp. 3-8.

Includes translations of poems by Odysseus Elytis, Tasos Denegris, Takis Sinopoulos, Nanos Valaoritis, Nikos Phocas, Andreas Embirikos, Dimitris Doukaris, Miltos Saktouris. Translated by Philip Sherrard, N. Stangos, Kay Cicellis, C. Tacktsis.

Madrona

4.81 "Eleven Modern Greek Poems". Kimon Friar, tr. *Madrona* 2, No. 6 (1973), pp. 22-33.

Poems of Nikos Karidhis, Takis Varvitsiotis, Panos Thasitis, George Ioannou, G.X. Stoyiannidhis, Eleni Vakalo, Sarandos Pavleas, Nanos Valaoritis, Dim. Papadhitsas.

Mundus Artium

4.82 "Three Contemporary Greek Poets" *Mundus Artium* 4, No. 1 (Winter 1970), pp. 6-13.

Includes: Yannis Ritsos, [5 poems] [Kimon Friar, tr.] (pp. 6-7) and [6 poems] [John Constantine Stathatos, tr.] (pp. 8-9); Takis Sinopoulos, "Waiting Room" [Kimon Friar, tr.] (pp. 10-11); and Odysseus Elytis, "Sleep of the Valiant" and "Seven Days for Eternity" [Kimon Friar, tr.] (pp. 12-13).

Poetry Pilot

4.83 *"Five Contemporary Greek Poets". Edmund Keeley, tr. *Poetry Pilot* (Oct. 1982), pp. 1, 3, 4, 5, 7-9.

Poetry Wales

4.84 "Modern Greek Poetry". *Poetry Wales* 11, No. 3 (Winter 1976), pp. 21-31.

Includes: Nanos Valaoritis, Yannis Ritsos, Takis Sinopoulos, Miltos Sahtouris, Yannis Kondos, Nasos Vayenas and Ares Dhikteos. Kimon Friar, tr. into English and J. Gwyn Griffiths into Welsh.

Translation

4.85 "Twelve Poems by Younger Greek Poets". John Chioles, tr. *Translation* 14 (Spring 1985), pp. 86-97 {3.34}.

Nasos Vayenas, Lefteris Poulios, Yiorgos Chouliaras, Dino Siotis, Yannis Varveris, Dimitris Kalokyris, Giorgos Chronas, Giorgos Veis, Costas Gouliamos.

Wake

4.86 "Greece". *Wake* 12 (1953). *Contemporary Foreign Number*, pp. 52-76.

Includes: Kimon Friar, "The Greek Tradition" (pp. 52-57); Nikos Kazantzakis, [Selections from] "The Odyssey" [Kimon Friar, prose tr.] (pp. 58-65); and poems of George Seferis, Takis Papatzonis, and Odysseus Elytis [Kimon Friar, tr.] (pp. 66-76).

IV. Regional

a. Cyprus

4.87 Casdaglis, Emmanuel C., ed. *Cyprus '74: Aphrodite's Other Face*. Athens: National Bank of Greece, 1976. 219 p.

The section entitled "Cyprus in Modern Greek Literature" (pp. 113-162) includes: Pandelis Prevelakis, "Crete and Cyprus" [Kevin Andrews, tr.] (pp. 115-117); Odysseus Elytis, "Axion Esti" (Part 2: The Passion, VII) [Edmund Keeley and George Savvides, trs.] (p. 118); Constantine N. Rados, "Down to Cyprus, to Famagusta" [Amy Mims, tr.] (pp. 119-142); George Seferis, "Three Poems for Cyprus" ("Enkomi", "Memory I", "Salamis in Cyprus") [Kimon Friar, tr.] (pp. 143-147); Nikos Kazantzakis, "The Angels of Cyprus" [Amy Mims, tr.] (pp. 148-150); Thanasis Petsalis-Diomedes, "Exaltation of the Sweet Land of Cyprus" (Chronicle of the 12th century) [Amy Mims, tr.] (pp. 151-160); Yannis Ritsos, "Hymn and Lament for Cyprus" [Amy Mims, tr.] (pp. 161-162).

4.88 Decavalles, Andonis, Bebe Spanos, Katherine Hortis and Costas Proussis, eds. *The Voice of Cyprus: An Anthology of Cypriot Literature*. New York: October House Inc., 1965. 192 p. First appeared in *The Charioteer* 7-8 (1965). See "Cyprus: Its Poetry, Prose and Art from Ancient Times to the Present" {4.95}.

Includes: Costas Proussis, "The Literature and Art of Cyprus: An Introductory Note"; An Anthology of Cypriot Verse (with [Three Cypriot Medieval Lyrics] and poems of: Vassilis Michaelides, Demetrios Lipertis, Nikos Nikolaides, Glafkos Alithersis, Pavlos Liasides, Tefcros Anthias, Pavlos Krinaios, Nikos Kranidiotis, Kostas Montis, Manos Kralis, Nikos Vrahimis, Kypros Chrysanthis, Yiannis K. Papadopoulos, Petros Sophas). Prose by: Nikos Nikolaides, Melis Nikolaides, Maria Roussia, Loukis Akritas, Nikos Kranidiotis, Tassos Psaropoulos, Christakis Georghiou, Hebe Meleagrou, Spyros Papageorghiou, Panos Ioannides, Theo Stavrou.

4.89 *Kouyialis, Theoklis, ed. *Contemporary Cypriot Poetry: An Anthology*. John Vickers and Amy Mims, trs. Nicosia: Cyprus PEN Publications, 1981. 101 p.

4.90 Kouyialis, Theoklis. *27 Centuries of Cypriot Poetry. An Anthology*. John Vickers and others, trs. Nicosia: Cyprus PEN Publications, 1983. 94 p.

4.91 Montis, Costas and Andreas Christophides, eds. *Anthology of Cypriot Poetry*. Amy Mims, tr. Nicosia, Cyprus: Proodos Ltd., 1974. 247 p.

Includes ancient, religious, medieval, and folk poetry; modern poetry, with works of: Glafkos Alithersis, Andreas Andreou, Tefkros Anthias, Kyriakos Charalambides, Andreas Christophides, Kypros Chrysanthis, Stephanos Constantinides, Yiorghos Constantis, Theoklis Couyialis, Demetres Demetriades, Nadina Demetriou, Pythagoras Droussiotis, Achilleas Emilios, Rea Erel-Koumidou, Antonakis Evyeniou,

Yiorghos Fanos, Loros Fantazis, Nasos Flogas, Christodoulos Galatopoulos, Pitsa Galazi, Andreas Gavris, Tassos Georghiou, Costas Graikos, Kypros Hadjigeorghiou, Savvas Halloumas, Demetres Hamboulides, Antonis Heliakis, Yiorghos Himarrides, Mimis Iacovides, Andreas Iacovou, Antonis Indianos, Antis Ioannides, Kleitos Ioannides, Panos Ioannides, Roula Ioannidou, Niki Katsaouni, Rina Katselli, Dina Katsouri-Payiasi, Vera Korphioti-Panayiotidou, Koula Kotsapa, Manos Kralis, Nikos Kranidiotis, Pavlos Krinaios-Michaelides, Eleni Kyrri-Leontiadou, Costas Kyrris, Sophocles Lazarou, Yiannis Lefkis, Pavlos Leontiou, Evrydike Liatsou, Anthos Lykavyis, Xanthos Lyssiotis, Michalis Maratheftis, Yeorghios Markides, Pavlos Meranos, Costas Michaelides, Pantelis Mihanikos, Ninos Mikellides, Yorghos Moleskis, Costas Montis, Marios Montis, Elli Paionidou, Evyenia Palaiologou-Petronda, Myrianthi Panayiotou, Christodoulos Papachrysostomou, Yiannis K. Papadopoulos, Spyros Papageorghiou, Michalis Passiardis, Andreas Pastellas, Hector Patriotis, Maria Pattihi, Leonidas Pavlides, Louis Perentos, Antis Pernaris, Niki Philippou-Ladaki, Takis Phylaktou, Theodosis Pierides, Antonis Pillas, Kyriakos Plissis, Demetres Potamitis, Maria Pylioti-Constantinou, Achilleas Pyliotis, Anthos Rhodinis, Zenon Rossides, Avyi Sakalli, Costas Sokratous, Petros Sophas, Sophronis Sophroniou, Phoebos Stavrides, Chrystalleni Stavrou, Tassos Stephanides, Theodoros Stylianou, Avra Theophanous, Ianthi Theocharidou, Elena Toumazi, Eirini Tsoulli-Panayi, Pavlos Valdasserides, Costas Vassiliou, Ayis Voreadis, Nicos Vrahimis, Xenia Yerolemidou, Lefteris Yiannidis, Evyenios Zenon, Victor Zenon, Stephanos Zymboulakis; and Modern Poetry in Cypriot Dialect: Pavlos Liassides, Demetres Lipertis, Costas Markides, Vassilis Michaelides.

4.92 [Proussis, Costas M., ed. and intro.]. *Poems of Cyprus: A Selection from the Work of Vassilis Michaelides and Dimitris Lipertis*. Costas M. Proussis, Athan Anagnostopoulos, Kinereth Gensler, and Ruth Whitman, trs. Republic of Cyprus: The Council of Europe, 1970. 120 p.
The poems were selected by the Ministry of Education of the Republic of Cyprus through a special committee. Costas M. Proussis supervised the whole edition.

4.93 *Spanos, Nicos S. *Cypriot Prose-Writers from Antiquity to 1950*. With introduction and notes. David Bailey et al., trs. Nicosia: Cyprus PEN Publications, 1983. 126 p.

4.94 *Spanos, Nicos S. *22 Contemporary Cypriot Prose-Writers*. With introduction and biographical notes. David Bailey et al., trs. Nicosia: Cyprus PEN Publications, 1981. 111 p.

ANTHOLOGIES OF CYPRIOT LITERATURE CONTAINED WITHIN JOURNALS

The Charioteer
4.95 "Cyprus: Its Poetry, Prose, and Art from Ancient Times to the Present". *The Charioteer* 7 and 8 (1965). A Double Issue. Various translators. Cf. *The Voice of Cyprus* {4.88}.
Includes: Costas Proussis, "The Literature and Art of Cyprus: An Introductory Note" (pp. 9-14); "An Anthology of Cypriot Verse" (pp. 15-39): Stasinos, from *Cypria*; three Cypriot Medieval Lyrics; poems by Vassilis Michaelides, Demetrios Lipertis, Nikos Nikolaides, Glafkos Alithersis, Pavlos Liasides, Tefcros Anthias, Pavlos Krinaios, Nikos Kranidiotes, Kostas Montis, Manos Kralis, Nikos Vrahimis, Kypros Chrysanthis, Yannis K. Papadopoulos, Petros Sophas; prose works (pp. 40-190) by: Nikos Nikolaides, Melis Nikolaides, Maria Roussia, Loukis Akritas, Nikos Kranidiotis, Tassos Psaropoulos, Christakis Georghiou, Hebe Meleagrou, Spyros Papageorghiou, Panos Ioannides; and Theo Stavrou, "Letter from Cyprus".

Κυπριακαί Σπουδαί
4.96 Ioannides, C.D. "A Short Collection of Cyprus Folksongs". *Κυπριακαί Σπουδαί* 32 (1968), pp. 265-300.

Πνευματική Κύπρος
4.97 Thompson, Peter, tr. "Seven Poems from Cyprus". Appended to No. 100-101 (Jan. 1969) of *Πνευματική Κύπρος* with separate pagination. 15 p. Bilingual. *Also as a separatum.
Poems of: Andreas Christophides, Kypros Chrysanthis, Costas Montis, Takis G. Phylactou.

b. Epirus

4.98 Holton, D. and Panos Karageorgos, sel. and trs. *Voices from Jannina: Contemporary Greek Literature.* Thessaloniki: printed at "Hellenism", 1972. 149 p.
Contains works of: Arsenis Gerontikos, Demostenes Kokkinos, Spyros Kyriazopoulos, Lambros Malamas, Vasilis Margaris, Ioannis Nikolaidis, Kostas N. Nikolaidis, Takis Siomopoulos, Kimon Tzalias, Pavlos Vrellis.

4.99 Photos, Basil J., coll. *Epirus and Epirotic Muse.* Poems. Chicago Essays on World History and Politics, 5. Chicago: Argonaut Inc., 1963. 16 p.
Folksongs, and works of: Aristotelis Valaorites, Costas Crystallis, Sotiris Skipis.

c. Thessaloniki

4.100 Friar, Kimon, ed. and tr. "Thirteen Poets of Salonika". *The Charioteer* 10 (1968), pp. 19-65.
The issue includes: George Odysseus, "An Introduction to the Salonika Poets" (pp. 10-18); poems (pp. 19-65) of: George Themelis, Zoë Karelli, George T. Vafopoulos, Nikos Gabriel Pentzikis, G.X. Stoyiannidhis, Takis Varvitsiotis, Sarandos Pavleas, Klitos Kirou, Panos Thasitis, Manolis Anagnostakis, George Ioannou, Dinos Christianopoulos, Nikos-Alexis Aslanoglou.

d. Other

4.101 Argenti, Philip P. and H.J. Rose, eds. *The Folk-Lore of Chios.* 2 vols. [Cambridge, England]: Cambridge University Press, 1949. 1199 p. (continuous pagination). Partly bilingual.
Includes folk tales, drolls, folk songs, proverbs, riddles, etc.

4.102 Chianis, Sotirios (Sam). *Folksongs of Mantineia, Greece.* Folklore Studies, 15. Berkeley and Los Angeles: University of California Press, 1965. 171 p.

4.103 Dawkins, R.M., ed. and tr. *Forty-five Stories from the Dodekanese.* Edited and translated from the mss. of Jacob Zarraftis. Cambridge, [England]: University Press, 1950. 560 p. Bilingual.

4.104 Kanarakis, George. *Greek Voices in Australia. A Tradition of Prose, Poetry and Drama.* Sydney, Australia: Australian National University Press, 1987. 510 p. + index.
    Includes works of over 80 Greek authors in Australia. Most of the translations are by Philip Grundy.

4.105 Karageorgos, Panos, coll. and tr. *Love Folksongs of Rhodes.* 1973. 15 p.

4.106 Ragovin, F. *Cretan Mantinades: Song Poems.* Athens: "Cnossos" Editions, 1974. 71 p.

5. COLLECTED ESSAYS

This chapter, containing only books of *collected* essays, is divided into two sections:
   I. Works by Individual Authors;
   II. Collective Works.
Essays may also be found in Chapters 3, 6, and 7 and as introductions to anthologies (Chapter 4).

I. Works by Individual Authors

5.1   Bien, Peter. *Three Generations of Greek Writers. Introductions to Cavafy, Kazantzakis, Ritsos.* Athens: Efstathiadis Group, 1983. 125 p.
   Contains: 1. "Cavafy" (pp. 9-54); 2. "Kazantzakis" (pp. 55-94); 3. "Ritsos" (pp. 95-125). The three essays have been reprinted from separate publications {7.139, 7.622, 7.1114}.

5.2   Keeley, Edmund. *Modern Greek Poetry: Voice and Myth.* Princeton, N.J.: Princeton University Press, 1983. 232 p.
   Contains: "Voice, Perspective, and Context in Cavafy" (pp. 3-30); "Sikelianos: The Sublime Voice" (pp. 31-42); "Sikelianos and Greek Mythology" (pp. 43-52); "Seferis's Elpenor: A Man of No Fortune" (pp. 53-67); "Seferis and the 'Mythical Method'" (pp. 68-94); "Seferis's 'Political' Voice" (pp. 95-118); "The Voices of Elytis's *The Axion Esti*" (pp. 119-129); "Elytis and the Greek Tradition" (pp. 130-148); "Ritsos: Voice and Vision in the Shorter Poems" (pp. 149-179); "Postscript: A Conversation with Seferis" (pp. 180-217).
   A bibliographical note (pp. 219-220) clarifies the first serial publication of the essays included in this volume.

5.3   Lorenzatos, Zissimos. *The Lost Center and Other Essays in Greek Poetry.* Kay Cicellis, tr. Princeton Essays in Literature. Princeton, N.J.: Princeton University Press, 1980. 200 p. Also Guildford, Surrey: Princeton University Press, 1980.
   Contains: "Solomos" (pp. 3-69); "A Definition of Style by Solomos" (pp. 70-84); "The Lost Center" [esp. re. George Seferis] (pp. 85-146); "Solomos' *Dialogos* and Dante" (pp. 147-180); "'Ultima Verba': Solomos" (pp. 181-194).

5.4   Pallis, A.A. *Greek Miscellany: A Collection of Essays on Mediaeval and Modern Greece.* Athens, 1964. 187 p.
   Essays on Modern Greek literary subjects include: "The Chronicle of the Morea—The Age of Chivalry in Greece" (pp. 30-45); "The Chronicle of Leontios Machairas—Cyprus under the Rule of the Lusignans" (pp. 46-64); "Memoirs of the Greek War of Independence—and After" (pp. 143-163); "The Ballad-Poetry of Modern Greece" (pp. 164-187).

5.5   Seferis, George. *On the Greek Style: Selected Essays in Poetry and Hellenism.*
   See Authors Section (G. Seferis).

5.6 Sherrard, Philip. *The Marble Threshing Floor: Studies in Modern Greek Poetry.* Freeport, N.Y.: Books for Libraries Press, 1956. Reprinted 1970. 258 p. Also London: Vallentine, Mitchell & Co., 1956; Athens: Denise Harvey & Company, 1982.

Essays entitled: I. "Dionysios Solomos" (pp. 1-37); II. "Costis Palamas" (pp. 39-81); III. "Constantine Cavafis" (pp. 83-123); IV. "Anghelos Sikelianos" (pp. 125-183); V. "George Seferis" (pp. 185-231); VI. "The Poetry and the Myth" (pp. 233-255) [the last essay concerns the shared characteristics of the poetry of Solomos, Palamas, Sikelianos, Seferis].

5.7 Sherrard, Philip. *The Wound of Greece: Studies in Neo-Hellenism.* London: Rex Collings Ltd. with Athens: Anglo-Hellenic, 1978. 128 p. Also New York: St. Martin's Press, 1979; Athens: Denise Harvey & Company, 1982.

Contains: 1. "Introduction: Who are the Greeks?" (pp. 1-16); 2. "Andreas Kalvos and the Eighteenth-Century Ethos" (pp. 17-50); 3. "General Makriyannis: The Portrait of a Greek" (pp. 51-71); 4. "Anghelos Sikelianos and his Vision of Greece" (pp. 72-93); 5. "George Seferis 1900-1971: The Man and his Poetry" (pp. 94-117); 6. "Epilogue: The Figure of Aretousa (from the seventeenth-century Cretan Epic *Erotokritos*") (pp. 118-124).

II. Collective Works

5.8 Alexiou, Margaret and Vassilis Lambropoulos, eds. *The Text and its Margins: Post-Structuralist Approaches to Twentieth-Century Greek Literature.* New York: Pella Publishing Company, Inc., 1985. 288 p.

Contains: Vassilis Lambropoulos, "Towards a Genealogy of Modern Greek Literature" (pp. 15-36); Gregory Jusdanis, "C.P. Cavafy and the Politics of Poetry" (pp. 37-57); Dimitris Dimiroulis, "The 'Humble Art' and the Exquisite Rhetoric: Tropes in the Manner of George Seferis" (pp. 59-84); Pavlos Andronikos, "The Narrator of Stratis Myrivilis' *Vasilis Arvanitis:* An Exploration into Emotional Response to the Reading of Fiction" (pp. 85-122); Maria Kakavoulia, "Telling, Speaking, Naming in Melpo Axioti's *Would You Like to Dance, Maria?*" (pp. 123-156); Margaret Alexiou, "C.P. Cavafy's 'Dangerous' Drugs: Poetry, Eros and the Dissemination of Images" (pp. 157-196); Michael Herzfeld, "Interpretation from Within: Metatext for a Cretan Quarrel" (pp. 197-218); Charles Stewart, "Nymphomania: Sexuality, Insanity and Problems in Folklore Analysis" (pp. 219-252); Dimitris Tsiovas, "The Organic Discourse of Nationistic Demoticism: A Tropological Approach" (pp. 253-277).

5.9 Keeley, Edmund and Peter Bien, eds. *Modern Greek Writers: Solomos, Calvos, Matesis, Palamas, Cavafy, Kazantzakis, Seferis, Elytis.* Princeton, N.J.: Princeton University Press, 1972. 261 p.

The literary renaissance of modern Greece is the subject of essays by ten critics and scholars on the theme "Modern Greek Literature and its European Background". Contains: Peter Bien, "Introduction" (pp. 3-22); 1. Zissimos Lorenzatos, "Solomos' *Dialogos:* A Survey" (pp. 23-65); 2. Bertrand Bouvier, "Calvos in Geneva" (pp. 67-91); 3. Angelos Terzakis, "Matesis' *Vassilikos:* The First Drama of Ideas" (pp. 93-107); 4. Thanasis Maskaleris, "Palamas and World Literature" (pp. 109-122); 5. Edmund Keeley, "The 'New' Poems of Cavafy" (pp. 123-143); 6. Peter Bien, "The Demoticism of Kazantzakis" (pp. 145-169); 7. Peter Levi, S.J., "Seferis' Tone of Voice" (pp. 171-189); 8. Stavros Deligiorgis, "Elytis' Brecht and Hadzidakis' Pirandello" (pp. 191-215); 9. Mario Vitti, "Family and Alienation in Contemporary Greek Fiction" (pp. 217-233); 10. C.Th. Dimaras, "Survivances du romantisme dans la culture néo-hellénique" (pp. 235-248).

5.10 Litsas, Fotios K., ed. Ἑλληνικά Γράμματα / *(Essays in) Tribute to Hellenic Letters.* Modern Greek Studies Series. Chicago, Ill.: University of Illinois at Chicago, 1985. 304 p.

The English-language contents on Modern Greek literary subjects include: Part I, 'Hellenic Letters throughout the Centuries': Constantine Santas, "The Growth of Modern Greek Letters in the Nineteenth

Century" (pp. 46-55); Karolos Mitsakis, "Hellenic Letters in the Twentieth Century" (pp. 56-70); Part II, 'Hellenic Letters Outside of Greece': George Kanarakis, "Hellenic Letters and the Literature of the Greek Diaspora Since the Mid-Nineteenth Century" (pp. 84-109); Part III, 'The Impact of Hellenic Letters': Rev. Theodore N. Thalassinos, "Hellenic Letters and Christianity: Hellenization and Dehellenization of the Christian Gospel" (pp. 123-131); Constantine A. Trypanis, "Romanos the Melodist and Hellenic Letters" (pp. 132-143); Diane Touliatos-Banker, "The Impact of Hellenic Letters to Western Music" (pp. 149-151); Andrew J. Sopko, "Hellenic Letters and the Slavic World" (pp. 152-156); Alexander MacGregor, "The Rediscovery of Greek Letters during the Italian Renaissance (1300-1500)" (pp. 157-164); Peter Bien, "Hellenic Letters and the Language Question in Greece" (pp. 174-178); Aristotle Michopoulos, "Hellenic Letters and the Greek Language: A Burden and Resource" (pp. 179-187); Part IV, 'Hellenic Letters in the United States': Charles C. Moskos, "Hellenic Letters and Their Impact on Greek-American Studies" (pp. 195-199); Alexander Karanikas, "Greek-American Prose Writers" (pp. 200-205); Andrew T. Kopan, "Hellenic Letters in the New World: The Greek Pioneer Intellectual in Chicago" (pp. 206-213); Aris Angelopoulos, "The Greek-American Press of Chicago and Hellenic Letters" (pp. 233-235); Marianthe Karanikas, "The Descendants of Demokritos: Greek-American Scientists" (pp. 236-238); George Christakes, "Hellenic Letters and American Historiography: Historians and Greek Immigration to the United States. Recent Bibliography on Greek-American Studies Since 1968" (pp. 239-249); Part V, 'A Prosopography of Neo-Hellenic Letters': Fotios K. Litsas, "Who's Who in Neo-Hellenic Letters: A Prosopography" (pp. 253-285).

5.11 Macrakis, A. Lily and P. Nikiforos Diamandouros, eds. *New Trends in Modern Greek Historiography*. William McGrew, intro. Occasional Papers, 1. [Thessaloniki]: The Modern Greek Studies Association in cooperation with Anatolia College, 1982. 209 p.

Includes: Maria-Alke Kyriakidou-Nestoros, "Oral History and Folklore" (pp. 1-5); Paschalis M. Kitromilides, "Historiographical Interpretations of Modern Greek Reality: An Exploratory Essay" (pp. 7-11); Costas Hatzidimitriou, "From Paparrigopoulos to Vacalopoulos: Modern Greek Historiography on the Ottoman Period" (pp. 13-23); John C. Alexander, "The Klephts of the Morea: An Historiographic Essay" (pp. 31-37).

5.12 *The Mind and Art of C.P. Cavafy: Essays on his Life and Work*.
See Authors Section (C.P. Cavafy).

5.13 Vryonis, Speros, Jr., ed. *The "Past" in Medieval and Modern Greek Culture*. Byzantina kai Metabyzantina, 1. Malibu, [Calif.]: Undena Publications, 1978. 256 p. and plates.

Part II, 'The Problem of the Historical Past', contains: Dennis Skiotis, "The Nature of the Modern Greek Nation: The Romaic Strand" (pp. 155-162); John A. Petropoulos, "The Modern Greek State and the Greek Past" (pp. 163-176); Thomas Doulis, "The Asia Minor Disaster in Greek Fiction" (pp. 177-192); Evangelos Petrounias, "The Modern Greek Language and Diglossia" (pp. 193-220); Margaret Alexiou, "Modern Greek Folklore and its Relation to the Past: The Evolution of Charos in Greek Tradition" (pp. 221-236); Speros Vryonis, Jr., "Recent Scholarship on Continuity and Discontinuity of Culture: Classical Greeks, Byzantines, Modern Greeks" (pp. 237-256).

A publication of the Modern Greek Studies Association. Out of print in 1986.

6. LITERARY HISTORY

This chapter contains three major sections:
  I. General works on the history of Modern Greek literature;
  II. Material concerning the period pre-1800;
  III. Material concerning the 19th and 20th centuries.

Section I is divided into two subsections: A. [Works] entirely concerned with Modern Greek literature; B. [Works] partially concerned with Modern Greek literature.

Section II is divided into five subsections, according to the chronological divisions given in the *History of Modern Greek Literature* by Linos Politis: A. Literature before the Fall of Constantinople (eleventh to fifteenth centuries); B. [Literature] after the Fall of Constantinople (fifteenth to seventeenth centuries); C. The Great Age of Cretan literature (ca. 1570-1669); D. The Eighteenth Century: Modern Greek Enlightenment; E. The Folk Song. Each of the five subsections contains texts and studies on its period. The texts of the fifth subsection, "The Folk Song", may overlap somewhat with the anthologies in Chapter 4. Thus readers should consult both this subsection and Chapter 4, or be guided by the entry "folk song" in the index.

In all sections and subsections the works are arranged alphabetically by the name of the author (for studies), or the editor or translator; encyclopedias are listed by title. The (Greek) authors (or titles, in the case of anonymous works) in Section II may be located with the help of the index.

I. General

A. ENTIRELY CONCERNED WITH MODERN GREEK LITERATURE

6.1 Bacopoulou-Halls, Aliki. *Modern Greek Theater: Roots and Blossoms*. Athens: Diogenis, 1982. 165 p.

6.2 Dimaras, C.Th. *A History of Modern Greek Literature*. Mary P. Gianos, tr. Albany, N.Y.: State University of New York Press, 1972. 539 p. Also *London: University of London Press, 1974.

Arranged chronologically in nine parts, starting with Part One, 'The Roots—Modern Greek Literature before the Turkish Domination' and concluding with Part Nine, 'Under the Heavy Shadow of Palamas—Later Years'. The twenty-nine chapters included in the nine parts are followed by a "Supplement" (writers who appeared around 1930 but not after 1940) and a "Selected Bibliography" (pp. 503-510).

This book, along with that of Linos Politis cited below, currently constitute the two major sources for the history of Modern Greek literature. In the case of the present book, however, readers with a knowledge of Greek are encouraged to consult the original, in its current 8th edition.

6.3 Negris, Alexander. *An Outline of the Literary History of Modern Greece*. Edinburgh: Thomas Clark, 1835. 30 p. First edition: *Boston, 1829.

6.4 Pappageotes, George C. *The Story of Modern Greek Literature. From the 10th Century to the Present*. Rae Dalven, pref. New York: Athens Printing, 1972. 263 p.

6.5 Politis, Linos. *A History of Modern Greek Literature*. [Robert Liddell, tr.]. Oxford: The Clarendon Press, 1973. *Reprinted with corrections, 1975. 338 p.
Contains an introduction (pp. 1-20) and two major parts: Part One, 'From the Beginning to the Eighteenth Century' (pp. 21-97); Part Two, 'The Nineteenth and Twentieth Centuries' (pp. 99-268). Part One, containing five chapters, starts with "Literature before the Fall of Constantinople (Eleventh to Fifteenth Centuries)". Part Two, containing eleven chapters, concludes with "The Generation of 1930. Poetry" and "The Generation of 1930. Prose". Parts One and Two are followed by: "Excursus. Post-war Poetry and Prose" (pp. 269-273); "Appendix. Text of Poems Quoted" (pp. 274-282); "Chronological Tables" (pp. 283-298); "Selected Bibliography" (pp. 299-320).

6.6 *Spanias, Nikos. *The Language and Literature of the Greeks*. New York, 1965. 15 p.

6.7 Tofallis, Kypros. *Landmarks in Modern Greek Literature*. Second edition. London: The Greek Institute, 1970. 32 p. First edition, *Modern Greek Literature,* published by the author in 1969. 24 p.
Primarily designed for 'A' Level students. The second edition contains: "A Short History of Modern Greek Literature", and sections on *Abraham's Thysia,* Dionysios Solomos, "Poiemata"; A. Karkavitsas, *O Zetianos;* John Psychares, *To Taxidhi Mou;* Elias Venezis, *Aeoliki Ge.*

6.8 Trypanis, C.A., ed. *Medieval and Modern Greek Poetry. An Anthology*. Oxford: The Clarendon Press, 1951. 285 p.
Only the introduction (pp. ix-lxiii) is in English: A. The Byzantine Empire (A.D. 330-1453); B. Greece under Frankish and Turkish Domination (A.D. 1204; 1453-1821); C. Modern Greece (A.D. 1821-1949); D. Conclusion.

6.9 Vassardaki, Lucille, [tr.]. *The Modern Greek Theatre: A Concise History*. [Tr. from the Greek of John Sideris]. Athens: Difros, 1957. 67 p.
Additionally includes a two-part introduction: Emil Hourmouzios, "The Ancient Drama in Our Time" (pp. i-xiii); Linos Politis, "The Theatre in Crete during the Time of the Renaissance" (pp. xiv-xxii).

B. PARTIALLY CONCERNED WITH MODERN GREEK LITERATURE

6.10 Campbell, John and Philip Sherrard. *Modern Greece*. New York and Washington: Frederick A. Praeger Publishers, 1968. 426 p. Also *London: Ernest Benn Limited, 1968.
Contains Chapter 7: "Modern Greek Literature" (pp. 214-244).

6.11 *Columbia Dictionary of Modern European Literature*. Jean-Albert Bédé and William B. Edgerton, general eds.; Peter Bien, editor of Greek section. 2nd edition, fully revised and enlarged. New York: Columbia University Press, 1980. 895 p.
Contains summary article on Modern Greek literature by Christos Alexiou (pp. 327-330); also separate entries on a number of authors, including: C. Cavafy, O. Elytis, K. Kariotakis, N. Kazantzakis, S. Myrivilis, K. Palamas, Y. Ritsos, G. Seferis, A. Sikelianos, K. Varnalis.

6.12 *Encyclopedia International*. New York: Grolier, 1963-64.
Includes entries by Edmund Keeley on: Modern Greek literature, Konstantinos Kavafis, Nikos Kazantzakis, Kostis Palamas, George Seferis, Dionysios Solomos.

6.20 Bakker, W.F. and A.F. van Gemert. "The Ρίμα Παρηγορητική of Marinos Phalieros. A critical edition with introduction, notes and index verborum". *Studia Byzantina et Neohellenica Neerlandica* (W.F. Bakker, A.F. van Gemert, W.J. Aerts, eds. Leiden: E.J. Brill, 1972), pp. 74-195.

6.21 Holton, David, ed. Διήγησις τοῦ Ἀλεξάνδρου. *The Tale of Alexander: The Rhymed Version*. Critical edition, with an introduction and commentary. Βυζαντινή καί Νεοελληνική Βιβλιοθήκη, 1. Thessaloniki, 1974. 296 p.

6.22 Hull, Denison B. *Digenis Akritas: The Two-Blood Border Lord*. The Grottaferrata version. Translated with an introduction and notes. Athens, Ohio: Ohio University Press, 1972. 148 p.

6.23 Lurier, H[arold] E., tr. *Crusaders as Conquerors: The Chronicle of Morea*. Translated from the Greek, with notes, and introduction. New York and London: Columbia University Press, 1964. 346 p.

6.24 Mavrogordato, John, ed. *Digenes Akrites*. With an introduction, translation and commentary. Oxford: The Clarendon Press, 1956. 273 p. Bilingual text

6.25 Nørgaard, Lars and Ole L. Smith, eds. *A Byzantine Iliad: The Text of* Par. Suppl. Gr. 926. With critical apparatus, introduction and indexes. Opuscula Graecolatina, No. 5. Copenhagen: Museum Tusculanum, 1975. 75 p.

6.26 Schmitt, John, ed. *The Chronicle of Morea / Τό Χρονικόν τοῦ Μορέως*. A history in political verse, relating the establishment of feudalism in Greece by the Franks in the thirteenth century. Edited in two parallel texts from the mss. of Copenhagen and Paris, with introduction, critical notes, and indices. London: Methuen & Co., 1904. 640 p. Reprinted: Groningen: Verlag Bouma's Boekhuis, 1967.

6.27 Wagner, Wilhelm, ed. *Medieval Greek Texts: being a collection of the earliest compositions in vulgar Greek, prior to the year 1500*. Reprint: Amsterdam: Verlag B.R. Grüner, 1970. Is an unchanged reprint of the edition: *London, 1870. 190 p.

Studies

6.28 Aerts, W.J., Jos. M.M. Hermans, and Elizabeth Visser. *Alexander the Great in the Middle Ages: Ten Studies on the Last Days of Alexander in Literary and Historical Writing*. Symposium: Interfacultaire Werkgroep Mediaevistiek. Groningen, 12-15 October 1977. Medievalia Groningana, 1. Nijmegen: Alfa Nijmegen, 1978. 352 p.

6.29 Alexiou, Margaret. "The Poverty of Écriture and the Craft of Writing: Towards a Reappraisal of the Prodromic Poems". *BMGS* 10 (1986), pp. 1-40.

6.30 Alexiou, Margaret and David Holton. "The Origins and Development of 'Politikos Stichos': A Select Critical Bibliography". Μαντατοφόρος 9 (Nov. 1976), pp. 22-34.

6.13 *Encyclopedia of World Literature in the 20th Century.* Based on the first edition edited by Wolfgang Bernard Fleischmann. Leonard S. Klein, general editor. 4 vols. Revised edition. New York: Frederick Ungar Publishing Co., 1982.

Entries on Greek and Cypriot Literature and on several authors. The entry on "Greek Literature" (Vol. 2, pp. 279-284) is written by John E. Rexine.

6.14 Pilling, John. *A Reader's Guide to Fifty Modern European Poets.* London: Heinemann; Totowa, N.J.: Barnes & Noble Books, 1982. 479 p. *Also *An Introduction to Fifty Modern European Poets.* Pan Literature Guides. London and Sydney: Pan Books, 1982. 479 p.

Includes entries on: Constantine Cavafy, George Seferis, Yannis Ritsos.

6.15 *Princeton Encyclopedia of Poetry and Poetics.* Alex Preminger, ed.; Frank J. Warnke and O.B. Hardison Jr., assoc. eds. Enlarged edition. Princeton, N.J.: Princeton University Press, 1974. 992 p.

Contains entry "Greek Poetry: Modern" (pp. 330-332).

6.16 Thorlby, Anthony K., ed. *The Penguin Companion to Literature: Europe.* Revised edition. London: Allen Lane, The Penguin Press, 1971. 908 p.

Includes entries on: Digenis Akrites Basileios, the Prodromic Poems, Maksim the Greek, G. Hortatzis, the *Erotokritos*, A. Korais, A. Kalvos, D. Solomos, A. Valaoritis, E. Roidis, A. Papadiamantis, Y. Psycharis, K. Palamas, C.P. Cavafy, A. Sikelianos, N. Kazantzakis, S. Myrivilis, T. Papatsonis, G. Seferis, A. Embirikos, I. Venezis, G. Theotokas, P. Prevelakis, Y. Ritsos, D. Capetanakis, O. Elytis, N. Valaoritis, et al.

6.17 Toynbee, Arnold. *The Greeks and their Heritages.* Oxford; New York; Toronto; Melbourne: Oxford University Press, 1981. 334 p.

The reactions of Greeks to their heritages at different stages of Greek history. The last stage refers to the Modern Greeks, who "have not yet overcome their awe of their 'classical' predecessors". Modern Greek literature is mentioned especially at pp. 247-248, 251-267, 269 as part of the discussion of 'The Language Question'.

6.18 Trypanis, C.A. *Greek Poetry: From Homer to Seferis.* London & Boston: Faber and Faber, 1981. 896 p. Also *Chicago: University of Chicago Press, 1981.

Modern Greek poetry is discussed in: Part Three, "The Byzantine World", Section II (843-1204): "Poetry Composed in the Vernacular" (pp. 490-505); Section III (1204-1453): "Poetry in the Vernacular" (pp. 522-526); Part Four, "The Greeks under the Franks and the Turks" (pp. 531-602); Part Five, "Modern Greece (1829-1940)" (pp. 605-700); Bibliography (pp. 787-885).

II. Pre-1800

A. LITERATURE BEFORE THE FALL OF CONSTANTINOPLE (ELEVENTH TO FIFTEENTH CENTURIES)

Texts

6.19 Bakker, W.F. and A.F. van Gemert. *The Λόγοι Διδακτικοί of Marinos Phalieros.* A critical edition with introduction, notes and index verborum. Leiden: E.J. Brill, 1976. 140 p.

6.31 Bakker, Wim. "The Transition of Unrhymed to Rhymed: The Case of the Βελισαριάδα". In *Neograeca Medii Aevi: Text und Ausgabe; Akten zum Symposion Köln 1986* (Hans Eideneier, ed. Köln: Romiosini, 1987), pp. 25-50.

6.32 Beaton, Roderick. "Byzantine Historiography and Modern Greek Oral Poetry: The Case of Rapsomatis". *BMGS* 10 (1986), pp. 41-50.

6.33 Beaton, Roderick. "*Digenes Akrites* and Modern Greek Folk Song: A Reassessment". *Byzantion* 51, No. 1 (1981), pp. 22-43.

6.34 Beaton, Roderick. "Modern ΠΟΙΗΤΑΡΗΔΕΣ and Medieval Poetry in Vernacular Greek". In Πρακτικά Β΄ Διεθνοῦς Κυπριολογικοῦ Συνεδρίου, Τόμος Γ΄ (Λευκωσία, 1987), pp. 485-494.

6.35 Beaton, Roderick. "The Rhetoric of Poverty: The Lives and Opinions of Theodore Prodromos". *BMGS* 11 (1987), pp. 1-28.

6.36 Beaton, Roderick. "Was *Digenes Akrites* an Oral Poem?". *BMGS* 7 (1981), pp. 7-27.

6.37 Bury, J.B. *Romances of Chivalry on Greek Soil, being the Romanes Lecture for 1911*. Oxford: The Clarendon Press, 1911. 24 p.

6.38 Dyck, Andrew R. "On *Digenis Akritas*, Grottaferrata Version Book 5". *Greek, Roman, and Byzantine Studies* 24, No. 2 (Summer 1983), pp. 185-192.

6.39 Entwistle, William J. "Bride-Snatching and the 'Deeds of Digenis'". *Oxford Slavonic Papers* 4 (1953), pp. 1-16.

6.40 Fletcher, Robin. "The Epic of Digenis Akritas and the Akritic Songs: A Short Guide to Bibliography". Μαντατοφόρος 11 (Dec. 1977), pp. 8-12.

6.41 Galatariotou, Catia. "Structural Oppositions in the Grottaferrata *Digenes Akrites*". *BMGS* 11 (1987), pp. 29-68.

6.42 Gavrilovic, Zaga. "The Cosmic Symbolism of the Cross and the Emperor in Ptochoprodromos, Poem IV". *BMGS* 10 (1986), pp. 195-202.

6.43 Gemert, A.F. van. "The Cretan Poet Marinos Falieros". Θησαυρίσματα 14 (1977), pp. 7-70.

6.44 Gemert, Arnold F. van. "The New Manuscript of the History of Belisarius". *Folia Neohellenica* 1 (1975), pp. 45-72.

6.45 Graham, Hugh F. "Digenis Akritas and the *Devgenievo Dejanie*: A Reappraisal". *Studies in Medieval Culture* 4, No. 3 (1974), pp. 483-495.

6.46 Graham, Hugh F. "The Tale of Devgenij". *Byzantinoslavica* 29 (1968), pp. 51-91.

6.47 Grégoire, H. "Notes on the Byzantine Epic. The Greek Folk-Songs and their Importance for the Classification of the Russian Version and of the Greek Manuscripts". *Byzantion* 15 (1941), pp. 92-103.
   Re. Digenes Akrites.

6.48 Gunderson, Lloyd L. "Early Elements in the Alexander Romance". In Ἀρχαία Μακεδονία / *Ancient Macedonia: Papers Read at the First International Symposium held in Thessaloniki, 26-29 August 1968* (Basil Laourdas and Ch. Makaronas, eds. Thessaloniki, Institute for Balkan Studies, 1970), pp. 353-375.

6.49 Huxley, George. "Antecedents and Context of *Digenes Akrites*". *Greek, Roman, and Byzantine Studies* 15, No. 3 (Autumn 1974), pp. 317-338.

6.50 Jeffreys, Elizabeth M. "The Judgement of Paris in Later Byzantine Literature". *Byzantion* 48, No. 1 (1978), pp. 112-131. Reprinted in {6.55}.

6.51 Jeffreys, Elizabeth. "The Later Greek Verse Romances: A Survey". In *Byzantine Papers: Proceedings of the First Australian Byzantine Studies Conference, Canberra, 17-19 May 1978* (Elizabeth and Michael Jeffreys and Ann Moffatt, eds. With a preface by Ihor Sevcenko. Byzantina Australiensia, No. 1. Canberra: Humanities Research Centre, Australian National University, 1981), pp. 116-127.

6.52 Jeffreys, E. "The Manuscripts and Sources of the War of Troy". In *Actes du XIVe Congrès International des Études Byzantines, Bucarest, 6-12 septembre 1971. Rapports*, Vol. 3 (M. Berza and E. Stanescu, eds. Bucuresti: Editura Academiei Republicii Socialiste Romania, 1974-76), pp. 91-93.

6.53 Jeffreys, Elizabeth M. "The Popular Byzantine Verse Romances of Chivalry: Work since 1971". Μαντατοφόρος 14 (Nov. 1979), pp. 20-34.

6.54 Jeffreys, Elizabeth and Michael. "The Oral Background of Byzantine Popular Poetry". *Oral Tradition* 1, No. 3 (Oct. 1986), pp. 504-547.

6.55 Jeffreys, E.M. and M.J. *Popular Literature in Late Byzantium*. London: Variorum Reprints, 1983. 342 p.
   Contains reprints of a number of their articles: I. "*Imberios and Margarona:* The Manuscripts, Sources and Edition of a Byzantine Verse Romance"; II. "Formulas in the *Chronicle of the Morea*"; III. "The Traditional Style of Early Demotic Greek Verse"; IV. "The Nature and Origins of the Political Verse"; V. "*Digenes Akritas* Manuscript Z"; VI. "The Astrological Prologue of *Digenis Akritas*"; VII. "Digenis Akritas and Commagene"; VIII. "The Judgement of Paris in Later Byzantine Literature"; IX. "Constantine Hermoniakos and Byzantine Education" (Δωδώνη 4 [1975], pp. 81-109); X. "The Comnenian Background to the *romans d' antiquité*" (*Byzantion* 50 [1980], pp. 455-486). The pagination follows that of the original publications.

6.56 Jeffreys, E.M. and M.J. Jeffreys. "The Style of Byzantine Popular Poetry: Recent Work". In *Okeanos: Essays Presented to Ihor Sevcenko on his Sixtieth Birthday by his*

Colleagues and Students (Cyril Mango and Omeljan Pritsak, eds. with the assistance of Uliana M. Pasicznyk. Harvard Ukrainian Studies, 7. Cambridge, Mass.: Ukrainian Research Institute, Harvard University, 1983), pp. 309-343.

6.57 Jeffreys, E.M. and M.J. "The Traditional Style of Early Demotic Greek Verse". *BMGS* 5 (1979), pp. 115-139. Reprinted in {6.55}.

6.58 Jeffreys, Michael. "The Astrological Prologue of 'Digenis Akritas'". *Byzantion* 46, No. 2 (1976), pp. 375-397. Reprinted in {6.55}.

6.59 Jeffreys, Michael. "Byzantine Metrics: Non Literary Strata". *Jahrbuch der Österreichischen Byzantinistik* 31, No. 1 (1981), pp. 313-334.
    The history of political verse in Byzantium.

6.60 Jeffreys, M.J. "The Chronicle of the Morea: Priority of the Greek Version". *Byzantinische Zeitschrift* 68, No. 2 (Oct. 1975), pp. 304-350.

6.61 Jeffreys, Michael J. "Digenis Akritas and Commagene". *Svenska Forskningsinstitutet i Istanbul, Meddelanden* 3 (1978), pp. 5-28. Reprinted in {6.55}.

6.62 Jeffreys, Michael. "*Digenes Akritas* Manuscript Z". Δωδώνη 4 (1975), pp. 161-201. Reprinted in {6.55}.

6.63 Jeffreys, Michael J. "Formulas in the Chronicle of the Morea". *Dumbarton Oaks Papers* 27 (1973), pp. 163-195. Reprinted in {6.55}.

6.64 Jeffreys, Michael J. "The Literary Emergence of Vernacular Greek". *Mosaic* 8, No. 4 (Summer 1975), pp. 171-193.

6.65 Jeffreys, Michael J. "The Nature and Origins of the Political Verse". *Dumbarton Oaks Papers* 28 (1974), pp. 141-195. Reprinted in {6.55}.

6.66 Jeffreys, Michael and Elizabeth. "Imberios and Margarona: The Manuscripts, Sources and Edition of a Byzantine Verse Romance". *Byzantion* 41 (1971), pp. 122-160. Reprinted in {6.55}.

6.67 Kahane, Henry and Renée. "Akritas and Arcita: A Byzantine Source of Boccaccio's *Teseida*". *Speculum* 20, No. 4 (Oct. 1945), pp. 415-425.

6.68 *Kahane, H. and R. "The Hidden Narcissus in the Byzantine Romance of Belthandros and Chrysantza". *Jahrbuch der Österreichischen Byzantinistik* 33 (1983), pp. 199-219.

6.69 *Kastner, George Ronald. "Language and Romance: Plato, *Kallimachos and Chrysorrhoe* and *Konrad's Saga*". *Dissertation Abstracts International* 39 (1979), p. 7333A.

6.70 *Kastner, G. "Narrative Unity in the Digenes Akrites". In *Second Annual Byzantine Studies Conference, University of Wisconsin: Abstracts* (J.W. Barker, ed. Madison, Wisconsin, 1976), pp. 35-36.

6.71 Littlewood, A.R. "Romantic Paradises: The Rôle of the Garden in the Byzantine Romance". *BMGS* 5 (1979), pp. 95-114.

6.72 Lord, Albert B. "Notes on *Digenis Akritas* and Serbocroatian Epic". *Harvard Slavic Studies* 2 (1954), pp. 375-383.

6.73 Lord, Albert B. "Parallel Culture Traits in Ancient and Modern Greece". *BMGS* 3 (1977), pp. 71-80.

6.74 Lord, Albert B. *The Singer of Tales*. New York: Atheneum, 1973. 308 p. Original publication: *Harvard Studies in Comparative Literature, 24. Cambridge, Mass.: Harvard University Press, 1960.
    See pp. 89, 91, 127, 202-203, 206-218.

6.75 MacAlister, Suzanne. "Digenis Akritas: The First Scene with the Apelatai". *Byzantion* 54 (1984), pp. 551-574.

6.76 Marshall, Frederick Henry. "The Greek Theseid". *Byzantinische Zeitschrift* 30 (1930), pp. 131-142.

6.77 Mitsakis, K. "The Tradition of the Alexander Romance. In Ἀρχαία Μακεδονία / *Ancient Macedonia: Papers Read at the First International Symposium held in Thessaloniki, 26-29 August 1968* (Basil Laourdas and Ch. Makaronas, eds. Thessaloniki, Institute for Balkan Studies, 1970), pp. 376-386.

6.78 Notopoulos, James A. "Originality in Homeric and Akritan Formulae". Λαογραφία 18 (1959), pp. 423-431.

6.79 Pallis, A.A. "The Chronicle of the Morea—The Age of Chivalry in Greece". In his *Greek Miscellany: A Collection of Essays on Mediaeval and Modern Greece* (Athens, 1964), pp. 30-45 {5.4}.

6.80 Pickford, T.E. "*Apollonius of Tyre* as Greek Myth and Christian Mystery". *Neophilologus* 59, No. 4 (Oct. 1975), pp. 599-609.

6.81 Sevcenko, Ihor. "Three Byzantine Literatures: A Layman's Guide". *JMH* 2 (1985), pp. 1-20.

6.82 Smith, Ole L. "Versions and Manuscripts of the *Achilleid*". In *Neograeca Medii Aevi: Text und Ausgabe; Akten zum Symposion Köln 1986* (Hans Eideneier, ed. Köln: Romiosini, 1987), pp. 315-324.

6.83 Trypanis, C.A. "Byzantine Oral Poetry". *Byzantinische Zeitschrift* 56 (1963), pp. 1-3.

6.84 Winnifrith, Tom. "Homer in Byzantine Dress". In *Aspects of the Epic* (Tom Winnifrith, Penelope Murray, and K.W. Gransden, eds. New York: St. Martin's, 1983 and London: Macmillan, 1983), pp. 80-91.

B. AFTER THE FALL OF CONSTANTINOPLE (FIFTEENTH TO SEVENTEENTH CENTURIES)

Texts
6.85 Dawkins, R.M., tr. *The Chronicle of George Boustronios 1456-1489*. Translated with introduction by the late R.M. Dawkins. Melbourne: University of Melbourne Cyprus Expedition, 1964. 84 p.

6.86 Dawkins, R.M., ed. and tr. *Leontios Makhairas. Recital Concerning the Sweet Land of Cyprus Entitled 'Chronicle'*. 2 vols. Oxford: The Clarendon Press, 1932. Vol. I: 685 p.; Vol. II: 333 p. Reprinted: Famagusta, Cyprus: Les Éditions L'Oiseau.

6.87 Marshall, F.H., ed. *Old Testament Legends from a Greek Poem on Genesis and Exodus by George Chumnos*. Ed. with introduction, metrical translation, notes and glossary from a manuscript in the British Museum. Cambridge, [England]: The University Press, 1925. 116 p.

Studies
6.88 *Dawkins, R.M. *The Nature of the Cypriot Chronicle of Leontios Makhairas*. Oxford, 1945. 32 p.

6.89 Dawkins, R.M. "The Vocabulary of the Mediaeval Cypriot Chronicle of Leontios Makhairas". *Transactions of the Philological Society* (1925-1930), pp. 300-330.

6.90 Frazee, Charles. "Leon Allatios, a Greek Scholar of the Seventeenth Century". *MGSY* 1 (1985), pp. 63-78.

6.91 Geanakoplos, Deno John. *Greek Scholars in Venice: Studies in the Dissemination of Greek Learning from Byzantium to Western Europe*. Cambridge, Mass.: Harvard University Press, 1962. 348 p.

6.92 Hadjiantoniou, George A. *A Protestant Patriarch: The Life of Cyril Lucaris (1572-1638), Patriarch of Constantinople*. Richmond, Va.: John Knox Press, 1961. 160 p. Also *London, 1961.

6.93 Hionides, Harry T. *Paisius Ligarides*. Twayne's World Authors Series, 240. New York: Twayne Publishers, 1972. 169 p.

6.94 Holton, David. "A Set of Sixteenth Century Woodcuts in Greek Popular Texts". Ἑλληνικά 25 (1972), pp. 371-376.

6.95 Kotzamanidou, Maria. "The Greek Monk Arsenios and His Humanistic Activities in Seventeenth-Century Russia". *MGSY* 2 (1986), pp. 73-88.

6.96 Layton, Evro. "The First Printed Greek Book". *JHD* 5, No. 4 (Winter 1979), pp. 63-79.

6.97 Layton, Evro. "Notes on Some Printers and Publishers of 16th Century Modern Greek Books in Venice". Θησαυρίσματα 18 (1981), pp. 119-144.

6.98 Olmsted, Hugh M. "A Learned Greek Monk in Muscovite Exile: Maksim Grek and the Old Testament Prophets". *MGSY* 3 (1987), pp. 1-74.

6.99 Pallis, A.A. "The Chronicle of Leontios Machairas—Cyprus under the Rule of the Lusignans". In his *Greek Miscellany: A Collection of Essays on Mediaeval and Modern Greece* (Athens, 1964), pp. 46-64 {5.4}.

C. THE GREAT AGE OF CRETAN LITERATURE (CA. 1570-1669)

Texts

6.100 Gargilis, Stephen. *The Path of the Great*. An Adaptation of the Epic Poem Erotokritos, Written in Cretan Dialect in about the 16th Century by Vitzentzos Kornaros. Boston, [Mass.]: Athena Publishers, 1945. 480 p.
   A version in prose.

6.101 Marshall, F.H., tr. *Three Cretan Plays: The Sacrifice of Abraham, Erophile, and Gyparis (also the Cretan Pastoral Poem* The Fair Shepherdess*)*. John Mavrogordato, intro. London: Oxford University Press, H. Milford, 1929. 338 p.

6.102 Mavrogordato, John, tr. *Vincenzo Cornaros. The Erotokritos*. Stephen Gaselee, intro. Oxford: Oxford University Press, 1929. 61 p.
   An extended summary in prose.

6.103 Stephanides, Theodore Ph., tr. *Vitzentzos Kornaros. Erotocritos*. Athens: Papazissis Publishers, 1984. Also London: Merlin Press, 1985. 345 p.
   A full translation in verse.

Studies

6.104 Bakker, W.F. *The Sacrifice of Abraham: The Cretan Biblical Drama* Ἡ Θυσία τοῦ Ἀβραάμ *and Western European and Greek Tradition*. Birmingham, England: University of Birmingham Centre for Byzantine Studies, 1978. 124 p.

6.105 Bakker, W.F. "Is *The Sacrifice of Abraham* a Drama?". Κρητικά Χρονικά 21 (1969), pp. 515-518.

6.106 Bakker, W.F. "Some Remarks on Megas' Commentary on *The Sacrifice of Abraham*". Κρητικά Χρονικά 21 (1969), pp. 130-133.

6.107 Bakker, W.F. "Structural Differences between Grotto's *Lo Isach* and *The Sacrifice of Abraham*". *Folia Neohellenica* 1 (1975), pp. 1-26.

6.108 Bancroft-Marcus, Rosemary E. "The editing of *Panoria* and the Prologue of Apollo". Κρητολογία 10-11 (1980), pp. 135-163.

6.109 Bancroft-Marcus, Rosemary E. "Georgios Chortatsis and His Works: A Critical Review". Μαντατοφόρος 16 (July 1980), pp. 13-46.

6.110 Bancroft-Marcus, Rosemary. "The Language of Chortatsis: Phonetic Consistency". In *Neograeca Medii Aevi: Text und Ausgabe; Akten zum Symposion Köln 1986* (Hans Eideneier, ed. Köln: Romiosini, 1987), pp. 53-72.

6.111 Bancroft-Marcus, Rosemary E. "Literary Cryptograms and the Cretan Academies". *BMGS* 8 (1982/83), pp. 47-76.

6.112 Bancroft-Marcus, Rosemary E. "Women in the Cretan Renaissance (1570-1669)". *JMGS* 1, No. 1 (May 1983), pp. 19-38.

6.113 Hadas, Rachel. "A Reading of *The Sacrifice of Abraham*". *BMGS* 6 (1980), pp. 43-59.

6.114 Holton, David. "Exile as Theme and Motif in the *Erotokritos*". *Antipodes* 21 (July 1987), pp. 37-43.

6.115 Jenkins, R.J.H. "Some Notes on Foscolo's *Fortunatus*". *The Link,* No. 1 (June 1938), pp. 29-36.

6.116 Krikos-Davis, Katerina. "Moira at Birth in Greek Tradition". *Folia Neohellenica* 4 (1982), pp. 106-134.

6.117 Lowe, C.G. "The *Rhodolinos* of Johannes Andreas Troilos". In Εἰς μνήμην Σπυρίδωνος Λάμπρου (Athens: Ἐπιτροπή Ἐκδόσεως τῶν Καταλοίπων Σπυρίδωνος Λάμπρου, 1935), pp. 190-198.

6.118 Mavrogordato, John. "The Greek Drama in Crete in the Seventeenth Century". *Journal of Hellenic Studies* 48 (1928), pp. 75-96, and "A Postscript", pp. 243-246.

6.119 Morgan, Gareth. "Cretan Poetry: Sources and Inspiration". Κρητικά Χρονικά 14 (1960), pp. 7-68, 203-270, 379-434. Also as a separately-paginated offprint: Heraclion, [Crete]: A.G. Kalokairinos, 1960. 194 p.

6.120 Morgan, Gareth. "The Emblems of *Erotocritos*". *The Texas Quarterly* 10, No. 4 (Winter 1967), pp. 241-268.

6.121 Morgan, Gareth. "French and Italian Elements in the *Erotokritos*". Κρητικά Χρονικά 7 (1953), pp. 201-228.

6.122 Morgan, Gareth. "The Model of Erotocritos—A Review". Κρητολογία 12-13 (1981), pp. 93-99.

6.123 Morgan, Gareth. "Three Cretan Manuscripts". Κρητικά Χρονικά 8 (1954), pp. 61-71.

6.124 *Pandelakis, Helene S. "The Erotokritos". *Crete* 470 (1969), p. 7; 475 (1969), pp. 5-6.

6.125 Philippides, Dia. "Computers and Modern Greek". Μαντατοφόρος 17 (June 1981), pp. 5-13.

6.126 Philippides, Dia M.L. Ἡ Θυσία τοῦ Ἀβραάμ στόν Ὑπολογιστή / The Sacrifice of Abraham *on the Computer*. Athens: Hermes Press, 1986. 240 p.

6.127 Puchner, Walter. "Scenic Space in Cretan Theatre". Μαντατοφόρος 21 (Apr. 1983), pp. 43-57.

6.128 Sherrard, Philip. "The Figure of Aretousa". Chapter 6 (Epilogue) of his *The Wound of Greece: Studies in Neo-Hellenism* (London: Rex Collings Ltd. with Athens: Anglo-Hellenic, 1978), pp. 118-124 {5.7}.

6.129 Sibbick, P.M. and A.L. Vincent. "Erofili". *TLS* (16 July 1970), p. 775.

6.130 Vincent, Alfred L. "A Manuscript of Chortatses' *Erophile* in Birmingham". *University of Birmingham Historical Journal* 12, No. 2 (1970), pp. 261-267.

6.131 Vincent, A.L. "A Production of Chortatsis' *Catzurbos* in England". Κρητικά Χρονικά 21 (1969), pp. 558-560.

D. THE EIGHTEENTH CENTURY: MODERN GREEK ENLIGHTENMENT

Texts

6.132 Cavarnos, Constantine, tr. and ed. *Modern Greek Philosophers on the Human Soul: Selections from the Writings of Five Representative Thinkers of Modern Greece on the Nature and Immortality of the Soul*. Belmont, Mass.: Institute for Byzantine and Modern Greek Studies, 1967. 111 p.
    Contains: Benjamin of Lesvos (pp. 13-28), Petros Vrailas Armenis (pp. 29-40), Ioannis Skaltsounis (pp. 41-54), St. Nectarios Kephalas (pp. 55-86), I.N. Theodorakopoulos (pp. 87-105).

6.133 Cavarnos, Constantine. *St. Cosmas Aitolos: Great Missionary, Awakener, Illuminator and Holy Martyr of Greece. An Account of his life, character and message, including his teaching on God, heaven and hell, and his prophecies, together with* *selections from his sermons*. 3rd ed., revised and considerably enlarged. Belmont, Mass.: Inst. for Byzantine and Modern Greek Studies, 1985. 118 p. The 1st ed. was published in 1971.

6.134 Clogg, Richard, ed., tr. and intro. *The Movement for Greek Independence 1770-1821: A Collection of Documents*. London and Basingstoke: The Macmillan Press Ltd., 1976. 232 p. Also *New York: Barnes & Noble, 1976. 232 p.

Includes excerpts from: the journal of Ioannis Pringos, documents of enlightenment and reaction, critics of society (the "Rossanglogallos", "The Greek Nomarchy"); the writings of Adamantios Korais, Count Ioannis Kapodistrias, Rigas Velestinlis, Theodoros Kolokotronis, and others.

6.135 Rallis, P., tr. and ed. *Korays's Letters Written from Paris, 1788-1792*. London: Hatchards, 1898. 108 p. Printed for private circulation.

Studies

6.136 Anton, John P. "Henderson's Treatment of the Neo-Hellenic Enlightenment". Review Article. *Neo-Hellenika* 2 (1975), pp. 299-305.

6.137 Chaconas, Stephen George. *Adamantios Korais. A Study in Greek Nationalism*. New York: Columbia University Press, 1942; London: P.S. King & Son, 1942. 181 p.

6.138 Chaconas, Stephen G. "The Jefferson-Korais Correspondance". *The Journal of Modern History* 14, No. 1 (Mar. 1942), pp. 64-70 and 14, No. 4 (Dec. 1942), pp. 593-596.

6.139 Clogg, Richard. "The Correspondence of Adhamantios Korais with the British and Foreign Bible Society (1808)". *The Greek Orthodox Theological Review* 14, No.1 (Spring 1969), pp. 65-84.

6.140 *Clogg, Richard. "Sense of the Past in Pre-Independence Greece". In *Culture and Nationalism in Nineteenth-Century Eastern Europe* (Roland Sussex and J.C. Eade, eds. Columbus, Ohio: Slavica Publishers, 1985), pp. 7-30.

6.141 Edmonds, Mrs. *Rhigas Pheraios: The Protomartyr of Greek Independence. A Biographical Sketch*. London and New York: Longmans, Green, and Co., 1890. 116 p.

6.142 Henderson, G.P. *The Revival of Greek Thought 1620-1830*. *Albany: State University of New York Press, 1970. Edinburgh & London: Scottish Academic Press, 1971. 216 p.

Includes: "Introduction: The Phases of Greek Reeducation" and essays on: Theophilos Korydaleus; the Mavrokordatos Family (Alexandros, Nikolaos, Konstantinos, and Alexander); Vikentios Damodos and Methodios Anthrakites; Eugenios Voulgaris; Nikephoros Theotokes and Demetrios Katartzes; Iosepos Moisiodax; Athanasios Psalidas; Benjamin Lesvios; Adamantios Koraes; *Greek Nomarchy*; Daniel Philippides; Gregorios Konstantas; Anthimos Gazes; Neophytos Doukas and Konstantinos Koumas.

6.143 Herrey, Maria Sagris. "Language Planning in the Greek Enlightenment: The Issue of a Literary Standard, 1790-1820". *Dissertation Abstracts International* 46, No. 8 (Feb. 1986), p. 2284A. Harvard University, 1985. 392 p.

6.144 Horton, Andrew S. "Jefferson and Korais: The American Revolution and the Greek Constitution". *Comparative Literature Studies* 13, No. 4 (Dec. 1976), pp. 323-329.

6.145 *Iatrides, G. El. *Coraes's Educational Message to Greece and the World*. New York, 1929. 64 p.

6.146 *Jeffreys, Michael. "Adamantios Korais: Language and Revolution". In *Culture and Nationalism in Nineteenth-Century Eastern Europe* (Roland Sussex and J.C. Eade, eds. Columbus, Ohio: Slavica Publishers, 1985), pp. 42-55.

6.147 Kitromilides, Paschalis M. "The Enlightenment and Womanhood: Cultural Change and the Politics of Exclusion". *JMGS* 1, No. 1 (May 1983), pp. 39-61.

6.148 *Kitromilides, Paschalis M. "Jeremy Bentham and Adamantios Korais". *The Bentham Newsletter,* No. 9 (June 1985), pp. 34-48.

6.149 Kitromilides, Paschalis M. "The Last Battle of the Ancients and Moderns: Ancient Greece and Modern Europe in the Neohellenic Revival". *MGSY* 1 (1985), pp. 79-91.

6.150 *Laourdas, Basil. "Greek Religious Texts During the Ottoman Period". In *Aspects of the Balkans: Continuity and Change. Contributions to the International Balkan Conference held at UCLA, Oct. 23-28, 1969* (Henrik Birnbaum and Speros Vryonis, Jr., eds. The Hague: Mouton, 1972), pp. 230-242.

6.151 Mackridge, Peter. "The Greek Intelligentsia 1780-1830: A Balkan Perspective". In *Balkan Society in the Age of Greek Independence* (Richard Clogg, ed. London: Macmillan, 1981), pp. 63-84.

6.152 Moles, Ian N. "Renaissance or *Anagenesis?*". In *Australasian Universities Language and Literature Association: Proceedings and Papers of the Thirteenth Congress Held at Monash University 12-18 August 1970* (J.R. Ellis, ed. [Melbourne: Aulla and Monash University, 1971]), pp. 395-397.

6.153 Motsios, Yannis. "The Anacreontian Poetry in Greek and Bulgarian Literature". *Balkan Studies* 25, No. 2 (1984), pp. 397-407.

6.154 Soulis, George Ch. "Adamantios Korais and Edward Everett". In *Mélanges offerts à Octave et Melpo Merlier,* Vol. 2 (Athènes: Collection de l' Institut Français d' Athènes, 93, 1956), pp. 397-407.

6.155 Vacalopoulos, Apostolos. "Byzantinism and Hellenism: Remarks on the Racial Origin and the Intellectual Continuity of the Greek Nation". *Balkan Studies* 9, No. 1 (1968), pp. 101-126.

6.156 Zakythinos, D.A. *The Making of Modern Greece: From Byzantium to Independence*. K.R. Johnstone, tr. and intro. Oxford: Blackwell, 1976. 235 p. Also Totowa, N.J.: Rowman and Littlefield, 1976. 235 p.

E. THE FOLK SONG

N.B. Books containing folk songs are listed with the anthologies (Chapter 4). For pages see entry "Folk Song" in the index.

Texts (within journals)

6.157 "Greek Demotic Love Songs and the Alphabet of Love". Theodore Stephanides, tr. *The Charioteer* 5 (1963), pp. 65-72.

6.158 "The Mourning Songs of Greece". Konstantinos Lardas, tr. *The Literary Review* 30, No. 1 (Fall 1986), pp. 81-83.
   Includes a brief introduction.

6.159 "Mourning Songs of Greece". Konstantinos Lardas, tr. *Translation* 2 (Winter 1974), pp. 18-21.

6.160 "Nine Poems from the Folksongs of Modern Greece". Konstantinos Lardas, tr. *Chicago Review* 21, No. 2 (Aug. 1969), pp. 106-108 {3.6}.

6.161 "Two Folksongs". George Economou, tr. *The Charioteer* 14 (1972), p. 10.

Studies

6.162 Alexander, John C. "The Klephts of the Morea: An Historiographic Essay". In *New Trends in Modern Greek Historiography* (A. Lily Macrakis and P. Nikiforos Diamandouros, eds. Occasional Papers, 1. [Thessaloniki]: The Modern Greek Studies Association in cooperation with Anatolia College, 1982), pp. 31-37 {5.11}.

6.163 Alexiou, Margaret. "Folklore: An Obituary?". *BMGS* 9 (1984/85), pp. 1-28.

6.164 Alexiou, Margaret. "The Lament of the Virgin in Byzantine Literature and Modern Greek Folksong". *BMGS* 1 (1975), pp. 111-140.

6.165 Alexiou, Margaret. "Modern Greek Folklore and its Relation to the Past: The Evolution of Charos in Greek Tradition". In *The "Past" in Medieval and Modern Greek Culture* (Speros Vryonis, Jr., ed. Malibu, [Calif.]: Undena Publications, 1978), pp. 221-236 {5.13}.

6.166 Alexiou, Margaret. *The Ritual Lament in Greek Tradition*. Cambridge: Cambridge University Press, 1974. 274 p.

6.167 Alexiou, Margaret. "Sons, Wives and Mothers: Reality and Fantasy in Some Modern Greek Ballads". *JMGS* 1, No. 1 (May 1983), pp. 73-111.

6.168 Baggally, John W. *The Klephtic Ballads in Relation to Greek History (1715-1821)*. Oxford: Basil Blackwell, 1936. 109 p. Reprinted as *Greek Historical Folksongs: The Klephtic Ballads in Relation to Greek History (1715-1821)*. Chicago Essays on World History and Politics, 12. Chicago: Argonaut Publishers, 1968. 109 p.

6.169 Beaton, Roderick. "The Art of Greek Folk Music". *JMH* 3 (Autumn 1986), pp. 47-55.

6.170 Beaton, Roderick. *Folk Poetry of Modern Greece*. Cambridge: Cambridge University Press, 1980. 229 p.

6.171 Beaton, Roderick. "Modern ΠΟΙΗΤΑΡΗΔΕΣ and Medieval Poetry in Vernacular Greek". In *Πρακτικά Β΄ Διεθνούς Κυπριολογικού Συνεδρίου, Τόμος Γ΄* (Λευκωσία, 1987), pp. 485-494.

6.172 Beaton, Roderick. "The Oral Traditions of Modern Greece: A Survey". *Oral Tradition* 1, No. 1 (Jan. 1986), pp. 110-133.

6.173 Boeschoten, Riki van. "Myth and History in Greek Folksongs Related to the War of Independence". *JHD* 13, Nos. 3 & 4 (Fall-Winter 1986), pp. 125-141.

6.174 Bourboulis, Photeine P. *Studies in the History of Modern Greek Story-Motives*. Thessaloniki: Ἑταιρεία Μακεδονικῶν Σπουδῶν, 1953. 108 p.

6.175 Caraveli, Anna. "The Song beyond the Song: Aesthetics and Social Interaction in Greek Folksong". *Journal of American Folklore* 95, No. 376 (Apr.-June 1982), pp. 129-158.

6.176 *Chaves, Anna C. "Love and Lamentation in Greek Oral Poetry". *Dissertation Abstracts International* 39 (1978), pp. 1531A-1532A.

6.177 Chouliaras, Yiorgos. "Modern Greek Culture: Some Critical Questions of Pedagogy and Research". *JMH* 3 (Autumn 1986), pp. 127-145.

6.178 Constantinides, Elizabeth. "Andreiomeni: The Female Warrior in Greek Folk Songs". *JMGS* 1, No. 1 (May 1983), pp. 63-72.

6.179 Constantinides, Elizabeth. "The Folk-Ballads of Crete: A Survey". *The Charioteer* 22 and 23 (1980/1981), pp. 130-140 {7.631}.

6.180 Dalven, Rae. "The Folk Song: Source of Modern Greek Poetry". In her *Modern Greek Poetry* (Second edition, revised and enlarged. New York: Russell & Russell, 1971), pp. 41-56 {4.26}.

6.181 Dawson, C.M. and A.E. Raubitschek. "A Greek Folksong Copied for Lord Byron". *Hesperia* 14 (1945), pp. 33-57.

6.182 Decavalles, Andonis. "The Demotic Songs of Greece: An Essay". *The Charioteer* 5 (1963), pp. 73-79.

6.183 Foley, John Miles. "The Traditional Oral Audience". *Balkan Studies* 18, No. 1 (1977), pp. 145-153.

6.184 Hadjioannou, Kyriakos. "Four Types of 'External Soul' in Greek and Other Folk-Narratives". Λαογραφία 22 (1965), pp. 140-150.

6.185 Herzfeld, Michael. "Social Borderers: Themes of Conflict and Ambiguity in Greek Folk-song". *BMGS* 6 (1980), pp. 61-80.

6.186 Holton, D.W. "*The Leprous Queen*—A Ballad from Lesbos". *BMGS* 1 (1975), pp. 97-109.

6.187 Ioannides, Costas D. "Folk Intonation Formulae". Ἐπετηρίς τοῦ Κέντρου Ἐπιστημονικῶν Ἐρευνῶν Κύπρου 6 (1972-1973), pp. 447-456.

6.188 Krikos-Davis, Katerina. "Moira at Birth in Greek Tradition". *Folia Neohellenica* 4 (1982), pp. 106-134.

6.189 Krikos-Davis, Katerina. "The Moires and Tyche in Modern Greek Folklore: A Critical Bibliography". Μαντατοφόρος 16 (July 1980), pp. 47-53.

6.190 Krikos, Katerina. "The 'Song of the Dead Brother': A Bibliography". Μαντατοφόρος 6 (May 1975), pp. 23-30.

6.191 Kyriakides, Stilpon P. *Two Studies on Modern Greek Folklore*. Robert A. Georges and Aristotle A. Katranides, trs. Ἑταιρεία Μακεδονικῶν Σπουδῶν, 97. Thessaloniki: Institute for Balkan Studies, 1968. 132 p. and 14 plates.
   Includes: "Modern Greek Folklore: Folk Poetry, Folk Religion, and Folk Art, with References to German Folklore" (pp. 15-43) and "The Language and Folk Culture of Modern Greece" (pp. 45-127).

6.192 Kyriakidou-Nestoros, Alki. "Modern Greek Ideology and Folklore". *JMH* 3 (Autumn 1986), pp. 35-46.

6.193 Kyriakidou-Nestoros, Maria-Alke. "Oral History and Folklore". In *New Trends in Modern Greek Historiography* (A. Lily Macrakis and P. Nikiforos Diamandouros, eds. Occasional Papers, 1. [Thessaloniki]: The Modern Greek Studies Association in cooperation with Anatolia College, 1982), pp. 1-5 {5.11}.

6.194 Lord, Albert B. "The Heroic Tradition of Greek Epic and Ballad: Continuity and Change". In *Hellenism and the First Greek War of Liberation (1821-1830): Continuity and Change* (Nikiforos P. Diamandouros et al., eds. Thessaloniki: Institute for Balkan Studies, No. 156, 1976), pp. 79-94.

6.195 MacAlister, Suzanne. "Greek Folksongs of the Human Cycle: Ideals and Values". Το Γιοφύρι 5 (Apr. 1979), pp. 38-47.

6.196 Mandel, Ruth. "Sacrifice at the Bridge of Arta: Sex Roles and the Manipulation of Power". *JMGS* 1, No. 1 (May 1983), pp. 173-183.

6.197 Megas, Georgios A. "Some Oral Greek Parallels to Aesop's Fables". Λαογραφία 25 (1967), pp. 284-297.

6.198 *Miller, Julia E. *Modern Greek Folklore: An Annotated Bibliography*. New York and London: Garland Publishing Inc., 1985. 141 p.

6.199 Mladenovic, Zivomir. "Some Common Symbols in Modern Greek, Macedonian and Serbo-Croat Folk Poetry". *Makedonski Folklor* 4, Nos. 7-8 (1971), pp. 85-92.

6.200 Morgan, Gareth. "The Laments of Mani". *Folklore* 84 (Winter 1973), pp. 265-298.

6.201 Notopoulos, James A. "Homer and Cretan Heroic Poetry: A Study in Comparative Oral Poetry". *American Journal of Philology* 73, No. 3 (July 1952), pp. 225-250.

6.202 Pallis, A.A. "The Ballad-Poetry of Modern Greece". In his *Greek Miscellany: A Collection of Essays on Mediaeval and Modern Greece* (Athens, 1964), pp. 164-187 {5.4}.

6.203 Parkhill, Peter. "Two Folk Epics from Melbourne". *Meanjin* 42, No. 1 (Mar. 1983), pp. 120-139.
   Contains "Today Black is the Sky" [composed and translated by George Tsourdalakis].

6.204 Schwartz, Benjamin and Apostolos N. Athanassakis. "The Greek-Jewish Songs of Yannina. A Unique Collection of Jewish Religious Poetry". *MGSY* 3 (1987), pp. 177-240.
   Contains an introduction, texts, a translation, and notes.

6.205 Seremetakis, Nadia C. "Introduction to Modern Greek Ideology and Folklore". *JMH* 3 (Autumn 1986), pp. 33-34.

6.206 Tuffin, Paul. "The Whitening Crow: Some ΑΔΥΝΑΤΑ in the Greek Tradition". Ἐπετηρίς τοῦ Κέντρου Ἐπιστημονικῶν Ἐρευνῶν Κύπρου 6 (1972-1973), pp. 79-92.

6.207 Verney, Lady F. "Songs and Legends of Modern Greece". *The Contemporary Review* 27 (Dec. 1875), pp. 96-113.

III. The Nineteenth and Twentieth Centuries

N.B. See also Collected Essays (Chapter 5).

6.208 Alexiou, Margaret. "Modern Greek Studies in the West: Between the Classics and the Orient". *JMGS* 4, No. 1 (May 1986), pp. 3-15.

6.209 Anghelaki-Rooke, Katerina. "The Greek Poetic Landscape: Recent Trends in Greek Poetry". *Review of National Literatures* 5, No. 2 (Fall 1974), pp. 13-26 {3.30}.

6.210 Anghelaki Rooke, Katerina. "A Note on Greek Poetry in the 1970's". *Modern Poetry in Translation* 34 (Summer 1978), pp. 3-4 {3.21}.

6.211 Anghelaki-Rooke, Katerina. "Sex Roles in Modern Greek Poetry". *JMGS* 1, No. 1 (May 1983), pp. 141-155.

6.212 Arghyriou, Alexandros. "The Style of a Language and the Language of a Style". Kevin Andrews, tr. In *Eighteen Texts* (Willis Barnstone, ed. Cambridge, Mass.: Harvard University Press, 1972), pp. 169-182 {4.1}.

6.213 Argyrakis, Minos. "Dream and Reality in Satire". Georgia Economou, tr. *The Charioteer* 3 (1961), pp. 23-27.

6.214 Avatanghelos, Henriette. "Modern Literary Forms and Currents in Greece". *Books Abroad* 28, No. 2 (Spring 1954), pp. 160-165.

6.215 Axelos, Loukas. "Publishing Activity and the Movement of Ideas in Greece". *JHD* 11, No. 2 (Summer 1984), pp. 5-46.

6.216 Bachtin, Nicholas. "English Poetry in Greek: Notes on the Comparative Study of Poetic Idioms". Part 1: *The Link*, No. 1 (June 1938), pp. 77-84. Part 2: *The Link,* No. 2 (June 1939), pp. 49-63. Republished in *Poetics Today* 6, No. 3 (1985), pp. 333-356.

6.217 Beaton, Roderick. "Myth and Text: Readings in the Modern Greek Novel". *BMGS* 9 (1984/85), pp. 29-53.
   Esp. re.: George Theotokas, *Argo;* Kosmas Politis, *Eroica;* Nikos Kazantzakis, *Christ Recrucified;* Stratis Tsirkas, *Drifting Cities.*

6.218 Beaton, Roderick. "Realism and Folklore in Nineteenth-Century Greek Fiction". *BMGS* 8 (1982/83), pp. 103-122.

6.219 Bien, Peter. "Arrogance and Intoxication: A Review of *Eighteen Texts*". *Boundary 2*, Vol. 1, No. 2 (Winter 1973), pp. 524-536 {3.5}.

6.220 Bien, Peter. "Hellenic Letters and the Language Question in Greece". In Ἑλληνικά Γράμματα / *(Essays in) Tribute to Hellenic Letters* (Fotios K. Litsas, ed.

Modern Greek Studies Series. Chicago, Ill.: University of Illinois at Chicago, 1985), pp. 174-178 {5.10}.

6.221 Bien, Peter. "The Predominance of Poetry in Greek Literature". *WLT* 59, No. 2 (Spring 1985), pp. 197-200.

6.222 Bien, Peter. "Some Modern Greek Responses to 'The Glory that Was Greece'". In *Classical Mythology in Twentieth-Century Thought and Literature* (Wendell M. Aycock and Theodore M. Klein, eds. Proceedings of the Comparative Literature Symposium, 11. Lubbock, Tex.: Texas Tech Press, 1980), pp. 21-44.

6.223 Brittain, Maryanne. "Some Greek Absurd Plays in their Literary Context". *Το Γιοφύρι* 5 (Apr. 1979), pp. 21-28.

6.224 Clark, Richard C. "Modern Greek Literature: Bibliographical Spectrum and Review Article". *Review of National Literatures* 5, No. 2 (Fall 1974), pp. 137-159 {3.30}.

6.225 Colakis, Marianthe. "Images of the Turk in Greek Fiction of the Asia Minor Disaster". *JMGS* 4, No. 2 (Oct. 1986), pp. 99-106.

6.226 Constantinides, Elizabeth. "Towards a Redefinition of Greek Romanticism". *JMGS* 3, No. 2 (Oct. 1985), pp. 121-136.

6.227 Constantinidis, Stratos E. "Classical Greek Drama in Modern Greece: Mission and Money". *JMGS* 5, No. 1 (1987), pp. 15-32.

6.228 Constantinidis, Stratos E. "Existential Protest in Greek Drama during the Junta". *JMGS* 3, No. 2 (Oct. 1985), pp. 137-143.

6.229 Constantinidis, Stratos E. "The Rebirth of Tragedy: Protest and Evolution in Modern Greek Drama". *Comparative Drama* 21, No. 2 (Summer 1987), pp. 156-181.

6.230 *Constantinidis, Stratos E. "Social Protest against Authoritarianism in Modern Greek Drama". In *Within the Dramatic Spectrum* (Karelisa V. Hartigan, ed. The University of Florida Department of Classics Comparative Drama Conference Papers, 6. Lanham, Md.: University Press of America, 1986), pp. 7-19.

6.231 Dalven, Rae. "The Growth of Modern Greek Poetry". In her *Modern Greek Poetry* (Second edition, revised and enlarged. New York: Russell & Russell, 1971), pp. 23-40.

6.232 Dancingsun, Kathryn. "Modern Greek Literature: Corle Contest Prize Essay". *Soundings: Collections of the University Library, University of California, Santa Barbara* 6, No. 1 (July 1974), pp. 29-34.

6.233 Danforth, Loring M. "Humour and Status Reversal in Greek Shadow Theatre". *BMGS* 2 (1976), pp. 99-111.

6.234 Danforth, Loring M. "The Ideological Context of the Search for Continuities in Greek Culture". *JMGS* 2, No. 1 (May 1984), pp. 53-85.

6.235 Danforth, Loring M. "Tradition and Change in Greek Shadow Theater". *Journal of American Folklore* 96, No. 381 (July-Sept. 1983), pp. 281-309.

6.236 *Davies, H.S. *Medieval Greek Imagery of the Instability of Life, Time and Human Fortunes, with particular reference to the wheel*. Unpublished doctoral dissertation. University of Oxford, 1973. 228 p.

6.237 Decavalles, Andonis. "The Development of Modern Greek Prose: An Essay". *The Charioteer* 4 (1962), pp. 74-82. {Cf. 4.17}.

6.238 Decavalles, Andonis. "Kimon Friar as Translator". *The Charioteer* 15 (1974), pp. 9-14 {4.75}.

6.239 Decavalles, Andonis. "Modernity: The Third Stage, The New Poets". *The Charioteer* 20 (1978), pp. 11-41.
    Accompanies anthology "Poems of the Post-War Poets" [Kimon Friar, tr.] {4.76}.

6.240 Decavalles, Andonis. "Poets of Two Decades". *The Charioteer* 15 (1974), pp. 15-27.
    Is prologue to {4.75}.

6.241 Dimaras, C.Th. "Literary Renaissance". *The Atlantic Monthly* 195, No. 6 (June 1955), pp. 142-146 {3.3}.

6.242 Doulis, Thomas. "The Asia Minor Disaster in Greek Fiction". In *The "Past" in Medieval and Modern Greek Culture* (Speros Vryonis, Jr., ed. Malibu, [Calif.]: Undena Publications, 1978), pp. 177-192 {5.13}.

6.243 Doulis, Th. *Disaster and Fiction: Modern Greek Fiction and the Impact of the Asia Minor Disaster of 1922*. Berkeley, Calif.: University of California Press, 1977. 313 p.

6.244 Fatouros, A.A. "Night without Moon: Aspects of the Rebetika". *JHD* 3, No. 4 (Dec. 1976), pp. 17-28.

6.245 Fletcher, Robin. "Cultural and Intellectual Development 1821-1911". In *Greece in Transition: Essays in the History of Modern Greece, 1821-1974* (John T.A. Koumoulides, ed. London: Zeno Booksellers & Publishers, 1977), pp. 153-172.

6.246 Fletcher, Robin. "The Literary-Historical Background of Modern Greek Literature". *Agenda* 7, No. 1 (Winter 1969), pp. 87-93 {3.1}.

6.247 Frangopoulos, Th.D. "Modern Greek Literature". *Greek Letters* 2 (1983), pp. 275-283.

6.248 Friar, Kimon. "Catching the Rhythm". *Aegean Review* 3 (Fall/Winter 1987), pp. 32-39.
Reminiscences from translating Modern Greek poets.

6.249 Friar, Kimon. "Contemporary Greek Poetry" and "A Note on the Prosody". *Poetry* 78, No. 3 (June 1951), pp. 145-153 {3.26}.

6.250 Friar, Kimon. "The Greek Tradition". *Wake* 12 (1953), pp. 52-57 {4.86}.

6.251 Friar, Kimon. "On Translation". *Comparative Literature Studies* 8, No. 3 (Sept. 1971), pp. 197-213.

6.252 Friar, Kimon. "On Translation". *Poetry Wales* 11, No. 3 (Winter 1976), pp. 17-20 {4.84}.

6.253 Friar, Kimon. "Post War Greek Poets". *Poetry* 139, No. 2 (Nov. 1981), pp. 99-107 {3.28}.

6.254 Gauntlett, Stathis. *Rebetika Carmina Graeciae Recentioris*. A Contribution to the Definition of the Term and the Genre *Rebetiko Tragoudi* through Detailed Analysis of its Verses and of the Evolution of its Performance. 2 vols. Athens: Denise Harvey & Company, 1985. 371 p.
A modified version of his doctoral dissertation. University of Oxford, 1978.

6.255 Gauntlett, Stathis. "*Rebetiko Tragoudi* as a Generic Term". *BMGS* 8 (1982/83), pp. 77-102.

6.256 Giannaris, George. "On Teaching Greek Literature in English". *Greek Letters* 1 (1982), pp. 324-333.

6.257 Gounelas, C.D. "Late Nineteenth-Century Views on Literature in Greece and the Periodical Ἡ Τέχνη". *SSMG* 6 (1982), pp. 43-68.

6.258 Gounelas, C.D. "The Literary and Cultural Periodicals in Athens between 1897 and 1910". Μαντατοφόρος 17 (June 1981), pp. 14-45.

6.259 Gounelas, G. "Neither Katharevousa nor Demotic: The Language of Greek Poetry in the Nineteenth Century". *BMGS* 6 (1980), pp. 81-107.

6.260 Gudas, Rom. *The Bitter-Sweet Art; Karaghiozis: The Greek Shadow Theater.* Athens: Gnosis, 1986. 263 p.

6.261 *Hadzopoulou-Caravia, Lia. "Instructive Animals in Greek Children's Literature". In *Triumphs of the Spirit in Children's Literature* (Francelia Butler, ed. and pref.; Richard

Rotert, ed. and pref.; Marcia Brown, foreword; Madeleine L'Engle, intro. Hamden, Conn.: Library Professional Publications, 1986), pp. 164-170.

6.262 *Halls, Aliki. "Greek Modern Theater: Roots and Blossoms". *Dissertation Abstracts International* 39 (1978), pp. 2918A-2919A.
   Cf. entry 6.1.

6.263 Hartigan, Karelisa. "Ancient Myth in Modern Poetry: Odysseus' Reappearance in Modern Greek Verse". *The Classical Outlook* 60, No. 3 (Mar.-Apr. 1983), pp. 69-74.

6.264 Hartigan, Karelisa V. "Helen So Fatefully Named: The Continuity of Her Myth in Modern Greek Poetry". *CML* 4, No. 1 (Fall 1983), pp. 17-24.

6.265 Hatzantonis, Emmanuel. "The Italian Influence on the Genesis of Modern Greek Literature". *Proceedings (of the) Pacific Northwest Council on Foreign Languages* 29, Part 1 (1978), pp. 85-90.

6.266 Hatzidimitriou, Costas. "From Paparrigopoulos to Vacalopoulos: Modern Greek Historiography on the Ottoman Period". In *New Trends in Modern Greek Historiography* (A. Lily Macrakis and P. Nikiforos Diamandouros, eds. Occasional Papers, 1. [Thessaloniki]: The Modern Greek Studies Association in cooperation with Anatolia College, 1982), pp. 13-23 {5.11}.

6.267 Herzfeld, Michael. *Ours Once More: Folklore, Ideology, and the Making of Modern Greece.* Austin: University of Texas Press, 1982. 197 p. Also New York: Pella Publishing Company, 1986. 197 p.

6.268 Holst, Gail. "Greek Urban Music: Rembetika". *The Coffeehouse* 1 (Fall 1975), pp. 58-66.

6.269 Holst, Gail. *Road to Rembetika: Music from a Greek Sub-Culture: Songs of Love, Sorrow and Hashish.* Athens: Anglo-Hellenic Publishing (Denise Harvey & Company), 1975. 176 p.

6.270 *Honig, Edwin. "Conversation with Two Translators". *Poetry Society of America Bulletin* 70 (Spring 1980), pp. 25-35. Also in his *The Poet's Other Voice: Conversations on Literary Translation* (Amherst: University of Massachusetts Press, 1985), pp. 133-149.
   Re. Edmund Keeley.

6.271 Horton, Andy. "The Many Masks of Kimon Friar". Part One: "The American Portrait". *The Athenian* (Oct. 1974), pp. 20-24. Part Two: "The Greek Portrait". *The Athenian* (Nov. 1974), pp. 19-24.

6.272 Jouanny, Robert. "Symbolism in Greece". Edouard Roditi, tr. from the French. In *The Symbolist Movement in the Literature of European Languages* (Anna Balakian, ed. Budapest: Akadémiai Kiadó, 1984), pp. 647-651.

6.273 Jusdanis, Gregory. "East is East—West is West: It's a Matter of Greek Literary History". *JMGS* 5, No. 1 (May 1987), pp. 1-14.

6.274 Jusdanis, Gregory. "Is Postmodernism Possible Outside the 'West'? The Case of Greece". *BMGS* 11 (1987), pp. 69-92.

6.275 Jusdanis, Gregory. "On the Impossibility of Greek Literary History". *JMH* 4 (Autumn 1987), pp. 25-35.

6.276 Jusdanis, Gregory. "The Politics of Criticism: Deconstruction, Kazantzakis, 'Literature'". *BMGS* 9 (1984/85), pp. 161-186.

6.277 Kanarakis, George. "Hellenic Letters and the Literature of the Greek Diaspora Since the Mid-Nineteenth Century". In Ἑλληνικά Γράμματα / *(Essays in) Tribute to Hellenic Letters* (Fotios K. Litsas, ed. Modern Greek Studies Series. Chicago, Ill.: University of Illinois at Chicago, 1985), pp. 84-109 {5.10}.

6.278 Kanarakis, George. "A Profile of Greek Australians through their Literature". *Études Helléniques* 1, No. 2 (Autumn 1983), pp. 55-62.

6.279 Karagiorgos, Panos. "The First Greek Translation of Shakespeare". *Shakespeare Translation* 2 (1975), pp. 65-73.

6.280 Karagiorgos, Panos. "The First Greek Translation of Shakespeare: *Macbeth* by Andreas Theotokis (1819)". Δωδώνη 5 (1976), pp. 223-241.

6.281 *Karagiorgos, Panagiotis. *Greek Translations of Shakespeare: A Comparative Study*. Unpublished doctoral dissertation. University of Birmingham, 1976. 291 p.

6.282 Karagiorgos, Panos. "Greek Translations of Shakespeare's Plays". In Ἀφιέρωμα στόν καθηγητή Λίνο Πολίτη (Θεσσαλονίκη, 1979), pp. 223-239.

6.283 Karampetsos, E.D. "Tyranny and Myth in the Plays of Four Contemporary Greek Dramatists". *WLT* 53, No. 2 (Spring 1979), pp. 210-214.

6.284 Karanikas, Alexander. "Greek-American Prose Writers". In Ἑλληνικά Γράμματα / *(Essays in) Tribute to Hellenic Letters* (Fotios K. Litsas, ed. Modern Greek Studies Series. Chicago, Ill.: University of Illinois at Chicago, 1985), pp. 200-205 {5.10}.

6.285 Keeley, Edmund. "Four Greek Poets". *Chicago Review* 14, No. 1 (Spring 1960), pp. 77-88.
    Re. George Seferis, D.I. Antoniou, Odysseus Elytis, and Nikos Gatsos.

6.286 Keeley, Edmund. "Literary Tradition as Burden and Resource: The Case of Greece". In *New Literary Continents: Selected Papers of the Fifth NDEA Seminar on Foreign Area Studies Sponsored by the School of International Affairs, Columbia University, and Council on National Literatures* (Caroline D. Eckhardt et al. Whitestone, N.Y.: Griffon House Publications, 1984), pp. 56-65.

6.287 Keeley, Edmund. "Problems in Rendering Modern Greek". In Μελετήματα στή μνήμη Βασιλείου Λαούρδα / *Essays in Memory of Basil Laourdas* (Thessaloniki, 1975), pp. 627-636.

6.288 Kehagioglou, George. "Modern Greek Orientalism: A Preliminary Survey of Literary Responses to the Arab World". *MGSY* 3 (1987), pp. 75-97.

6.289 Kitromilides, Paschalis M. "Collective Consciousness and Poetry: Three Moments in the Literary Tradition of Modern Cyprus". *Neo-Hellenika* 4 (1981), pp. 159-170.

6.290 Kitromilides, Paschalis M. "Historiographical Interpretations of Modern Greek Reality: An Exploratory Essay". In *New Trends in Modern Greek Historiography* (A. Lily Macrakis and P. Nikiforos Diamandouros, eds. [Thessaloniki]: The Modern Greek Studies Association in cooperation with Anatolia College, 1982), pp. 7-11 {5.11}.

6.291 Lambropoulos, Vassilis. "The Aesthetic Ideology of the Greek Quest for Identity". *JMH* 4 (Autumn 1987), pp. 19-24.

6.292 Lambropoulos, Vassilis. "Encountering the Epistemological Challenge or Beyond Humanism: Contemporary Greek Criticism and the Language of Theory". *BMGS* 9 (1984/85), pp. 225-246.

6.293 Lambropoulos, Vassilis. "Toward a Genealogy of Modern Greek Literature". In *The Text and its Margins* (Margaret Alexiou and Vassilis Lambropoulos, eds. New York: Pella Publishing Company, 1985), pp. 15-36 {5.8}.

6.294 Laourdas, Basil. "Ideas and Ideals in Contemporary Greek Literature". *Balkan Studies* 9, No. 1 (1968), pp. 155-166.
 Presents (mainly) three authors: Angelos Sikelianos, Nikos Kazantzakis, and Pandelis Prevelakis.

6.295 *Layoun, Mary Nicola. "The Non-Western Novel: Ideology and the Genre as Immigrant". *Dissertation Abstracts International* 46, No. 11 (May 1986), p. 3346A.

6.296 *Lekatsas, Barbara. "Toward a Mystical Geometry: The Influence of Surrealism on Modern Greek Poetry". *Dissertation Abstracts International* 46, No. 8 (Feb. 1986), pp. 2287A-2288A.

6.297 Leontis, Artemis. "'The Lost Center' and the Promised Land of Greek Criticism". *JMGS* 5, No. 2 (Oct. 1987), pp. 175-190.

6.298 Leuven, Jon Cloud van. "A Letter from Athens". *Prose* 1 (1970), pp. 153-159.
   Impressions of Modern Greece include *brief* mentions of Cavafy, Seferis, and Sikelianos.

6.299 Levitt, Morton P. "Modern Greek Poetry: 'Waiting for the Barbarians'". *Mosaic* 7, No. 4 (Summer 1974), pp. 171-178.
   Review article on Kimon Friar's anthology (*Modern Greek Poetry*, 1973) {4.33}.

6.300 Litsas, Fotios K. "Who's Who in Neo-Hellenic Letters: A Prosopography". In Ἑλληνικά Γράμματα / *(Essays in) Tribute to Hellenic Letters* (Fotios K. Litsas, ed. Modern Greek Studies Series. Chicago, Ill.: University of Illinois at Chicago, 1985), pp. 253-285 {5.10}.

6.301 Lorenzatos, Zissimos. "Freedom and Language". Edmund and Mary Keeley, trs. *Shenandoah* 27, No. 1 (Fall 1975), pp. 95-98 {3.32}.

6.302 Lord, Albert B. "Parallel Culture Traits in Ancient and Modern Greece". *BMGS* 3 (1977), pp. 71-80.

6.303 *Lucas, John and Andreas Angelakis. "The Greek Poetry Scene". *Poetry Review* 75, No. 1 (Apr. 1985), pp. 26-30.

6.304 Mackridge, Peter. "Brussels and the Greek Poetry Mountain: Some Thoughts on Greek Culture". In *Greece in the 1980s* (Richard Clogg, ed. London: Macmillan; New York: St. Martin's Press, 1983), pp. 245-265.

6.305 *Mackridge, Peter A. *The Development of the Greek Novel 1922-1940*. Unpublished doctoral dissertation. University of Oxford, 1972. 481 p.

6.306 Mackridge, Peter. "European Influences on the Greek Novel during the 1930s". *JMGS* 3, No. 1 (May 1985), pp. 1-20.

6.307 Marder, Brenda. "Edmund Keeley. Translation: A Creative Art". *The Athenian* (Oct. 1980), pp. 36-37.
   Interview with Edmund Keeley.

6.308 Maronitis, D.N. "Poetry and Politics: The First Postwar Generation of Greek Poets". *JMH* 3 (Autumn 1986), pp. 91-104.

6.309 *Menardos, Simos. "Modern Greek Poetry". *Poetry Review* 18 (1927), pp. 153-164, 247-258, 313-327, 385ff., 397ff. and 19 (1928), pp. 95-106, 169-178, 248-260, 347-355, 397-410.

6.310 Merchant, Paul. "Children of Homer: The Epic Strain in Modern Greek Literature". In *Aspects of the Epic* (Tom Winnifrith, Penelope Murray, and K.W. Gransden, eds. New York: St. Martin's, 1983 and London: Macmillan, 1983), pp. 92-108.

6.311 Michopoulos, Aristotle. "Hellenic Letters and the Greek Language: A Burden and Resource". In 'Ελληνικά Γράμματα / (Essays in) Tribute to Hellenic Letters (Fotios K. Litsas, ed. Modern Greek Studies Series. Chicago, Ill.: University of Illinois at Chicago, 1985), pp. 179-187 {5.10}.

6.312 Mira[m]bel, André. "General Characteristics of Modern Greek Literature". *Athene* 4, No. 5 (June 1943), pp. 42-48, 70.

6.313 Mira[m]bel, André. "Modern Greek Theatre". *Athene* 4, No. 9 (Dec. 1943), pp. 47-49; 75.

6.314 *Mistakidou, Aekaterina P. "Comparison of the Turkish and Greek Shadow Theatre". *Dissertation Abstracts International* 39 (1978), pp. 3232A-3233A. New York, 1978.

6.315 Mitsakis, Karolos. "Hellenic Letters in the Twentieth Century. In 'Ελληνικά Γράμματα / (Essays in) Tribute to Hellenic Letters (Fotios K. Litsas, ed. Modern Greek Studies Series. Chicago, Ill.: University of Illinois at Chicago, 1985), pp. 56-70 {5.10}.

6.316 *Myrsiades, Kostas. "Contemporary Greek Poetry of the Sixties and Seventies". *Grove* 5 (Winter 1979), pp. 1-2 {3.12}.

6.317 Myrsiades, Kostas. "A Theory of Resistance Poetry during the Greek Occupation, 1941-1944". *Folia Neohellenica* 4 (1982), pp. 135-146. Also *East European Quarterly* 17, No. 1 (Mar. 1983), pp. 79-88.

6.318 Myrsiades, Kostas and Linda Myrsiades. "Texts and Contexts: A Primer for Translating from the Oral Tradition". *Translation Review* 11 (1983), pp. 45-59.
 Re. Karangiozis.

6.319 Myrsiades, Linda. "The Alexander Play in Greek Shadow Puppet Theatre". *The Charioteer* 19 (1977), pp. 18-19.
 Followed by: Markos Xanthos, *The Seven Beasts and Karangiozis*. Kostas Myrsiades and Linda S. Myrsiades, trs. *The Charioteer* 19 (1977), pp. 20-49.

6.320 Myrsiades, Linda Suny. "Aristophanic Comedy and the Modern Greek Karagkiozis Performance". *CML* 7, No. 2 (Winter 1987), pp. 99-110.

6.321 Myrsiades, Linda Suny. "Greek Resistance Theatre in World War II". *The Drama Review* 21, No. 1 (Mar. 1977), pp. 99-106.

6.322 Myrsiades, Linda Suny. "Historical Source Material for the Karagkiozis Performance". *Theatre Research International* 10, No. 3 (Autumn 1985), pp. 213-225.

6.323 Myrsiades, Linda Suny. "Καραγκιόζης: A Bibliography of Primary Materials". Μαντατοφόρος 21 (Apr. 1983), pp. 15-42.

6.324 Myrsiades, Linda S. "The Karaghiozis Performance in Nineteenth-Century Greece". *BMGS* 2 (1976), pp. 83-97.

6.325 *Myrsiades, Linda S. *The Karaghiozis Tradition and Greek Shadow Puppet Theatre: History and Analysis*. Unpublished doctoral dissertation. Indiana, 1973.

6.326 Myrsiades, Linda Suny. "Legend in the Theatre: Alexander the Great and the Karaghiozis Text". *Educational Theatre Journal* 27, No. 3 (Oct. 1975), pp. 387-394.

6.327 Myrsiades, Linda Suny. "Nation and Class in the Karaghiozis History Performance". *Theatre Survey* 19, No. 1 (May 1978), pp. 49-62.

6.328 Myrsiades, Linda Suny. "Non-Theatrical Entertainments in Greece: Through the Eyes of Foreign Travellers, 1750-1850". *East European Quarterly* 16, No. 1 (Mar. 1982), pp. 45-58.

6.329 Myrsiades, Linda Suny. "Oral Composition and the Karaghiozis Performance". *Theatre Research International* 5, No. 2 (Spring 1980), pp. 107-121.

6.330 Myrsiades, Linda Suny. "The Struggle for Greek Theater in Post-Independence Greece". *JHD* 7, No. 1 (Spring 1980), pp. 33-52.

6.331 *Myrsiades, Linda S. "Theatre and Society: Social Content and Effect in the Karaghiozis Performance". In *To Hold a Mirror to Nature: Dramatic Images and Reflections* (Karelisa V. Hartigan, ed. The University of Florida Department of Classics Comparative Drama Conference Papers, 1. Washington, D.C.: University Press of America, 1982), pp. 61-76b. Also in *Folia Neohellenica* 4 (1982), pp. 145-159.

6.332 Myrsiades, Linda Suny. "Traditional History and Reality in the View of the Karaghiozis History Performance". *MGSY* 1 (1985), pp. 93-107.

6.333 Odysseus, George. "An Introduction to the Salonika Poets". *The Charioteer* 10 (1968), pp. 10-18.{4.100}.

6.334 Pallis, A.A. "Memoirs of the Greek War of Independence—and After". In his *Greek Miscellany: A Collection of Essays on Mediaeval and Modern Greece* (Athens, 1964), pp. 143-163 {5.4}.

6.335 Papadimitriou, Sakis. "Rebetika and Blues". In *Rebetika: Songs from the Old Greek Underworld* (Katharine Butterworth and Sara Schneider, eds. Athens: Komboloi, 1975), pp. 34-37 {4.24}.

6.336 Papanoutsos, E.P. "Poetry and Language". John P. Anton, tr. and adapt. *The Charioteer* 3 (1961), pp. 120-129.

6.337 Petropoulos, Elias. "Rebetika". In *Rebetika: Songs from the Old Greek Underworld* (Katharine Butterworth and Sara Schneider, eds. Athens: Komboloi, 1975), pp. 1-15 {4.24}.

6.338 Photiades, Marianthi. "The Translator's Voice: An Interview with Kimon Friar". *Translation Review* 2 (Fall 1978), pp. 2-8.

6.339 Politis, M.J. "Greek Literature Attains its Majority". *Books Abroad* 15, No. 1 (Winter 1941), pp. 11-16.

6.340 "Problems of Poetic Translation in Modern Greek: The Variants Considered from the Trot to the Imitation". *TLS* (2 Apr. 1970), pp. 349-350.
   Re. English-language translations of Palamas, Cavafy, Seferis.

6.341 Proussis, Costas. "The Literature and Art of Cyprus: An Introductory Note". *The Charioteer* 7 and 8 (1965), pp. 9-14 {4.95}.

6.342 Proussis, Costas M. "Modern Greek Poetry in America". *The Greek Orthodox Theological Review* 21, No. 4 (Winter 1976), pp. 385-397.

6.343 *Psichari, Jean. *The Language Question in Greece*. Three Essays by J.N. Psichari and one by H. Pernot translated into English by Chiensis. Calcutta, 1902.
   I. *The Literary Battle in Greece*. II. *The Gospel Riots in Greece*. III. *A Glance on Vulgar or Modern Greek Literature*.

6.344 Raizis, M. Byron. "The Emergence of Modern Greek Poetry". *JML* 4, No. 1 (Sept. 1974), pp. 159-163.
   Review article on Kimon Friar, *Modern Greek Poetry* (1973) {4.33}.

6.345 Raizis, M. Byron. "The Greek Poets Praise 'The Britannic Muse'". *Balkan Studies* 20, No. 2 (1979), pp. 275-307.

6.346 Raizis, M. Byron. "The Literary Renaissance in Post-War Greece". *The Literary Review* 16, No. 3 (Spring 1973), pp. 253-267 {3.15}.

6.347 Raizis, Marios Byron. "The Stream of Consciousness in Greek Fiction". *WLT* 60, No. 3 (Summer 1986), pp. 421-428.

6.348 Raizis, Marios Byron. "Suspended Souls: The Immigrant Experience in Greek-American Literature". *Greek Letters* 1 (1982), pp. 292-323.

6.349 Rexine, John E. "Recent Translations and Works of Modern Greek Poets". *MGSY* 1 (1985), pp. 198-206.
   Review article re. books of Kostas Kindinis, Yannis Ritsos, Manolis Anagnostakis, George Thaniel.

6.350 Robinson, Christopher. "The Comparison of Greek and French Women Poets: Myrtiotissa, Maria Polydoure, Anna de Noailles". *JMGS* 2, No. 1 (May 1984), pp. 23-38.

6.351 Robinson, Christopher. "The Greekness of Modern Greek Surrealism". *BMGS* 7 (1981), pp. 119-137.

6.352 Rodas, M. "The Theatre during the Occupation: Shakespeare under Ban". Ἀγγλο-ελληνική Ἐπιθεώρηση 1, No. 2 (Apr. 1945), pp. 14-16. Bilingual.

6.353 Santas, Constantine. "The Growth of Modern Greek Letters in the Nineteenth Century". In Ἑλληνικά Γράμματα / *(Essays in) Tribute to Hellenic Letters* (Fotios K. Litsas, ed. Modern Greek Studies Series. Chicago, Ill.: University of Illinois at Chicago, 1985), pp. 46-55 {5.10}.

6.354 Savidis, George P. "The Burden of the Past and the Greek Poet: From Aeschylus to the Present Day". *Grand Street* 5, No. 1 (Autumn 1985), pp. 164-190.
  Contains {entry 7.252}.

6.355 *Savvas, Minas. "Greek Spirit Seen Through Poetry". *Los Angeles Times* (28 May 1972), p. 48.

6.356 Sherrard, Philip. "The Poetry and the Myth". Chapter 6 of his *The Marble Threshing Floor: Studies in Modern Greek Poetry* (Freeport, N.Y.: Books for Libraries Press, 1956), pp. 233-255 {5.6}.
  This essay concerns the shared characteristics of the poetry of Solomos, Palamas, Sikelianos, Seferis.

6.357 Sideris, Yannis. "The Playwrights of the Modern Greek Theatre". *Thespis* 2-3 (May 1965), pp. 10-43.

6.358 *Sideris, Yannis. "Shakespeare in Greece". Mark Ogilvie-Grant, tr. *Theatre Research* 6 (1965), pp. 85-99.

6.359 Sophocleous, Andreas, ed. *Five Short Essays on Cypriot Literature*. John Vickers and Lana der Parthogh, trs. Nicosia, Cyprus: Cyprus PEN Publications, 1981. 71 p.
  Contains: Nicos Spanos, "A Brief Introduction to Cypriot Prose" (pp. 9-27); Kika Olymbiou, "Cypriot Poetry" (pp. 29-46); Dr. C.G. Yiangoullis, "Cypriot Folk Poetry" (pp. 47-53); Eleni Antoniadou, "The Theatre in Cyprus" (pp. 55-63); Kypros Chrysanthis, "Essay and Book Review" (pp. 65-70).

6.360 Spanias, Nikos. "'In Praise of Elytis, Yes, But ...'". *JHD* 3, No. 3 (1976), pp. 33-35.
  On the "War Generation".

6.361 Stone, James. "Greek Poetry since 1820". In *Critical Survey of Poetry*. Foreign Language Series, Vol. 5 (Frank N. Magill, ed. Englewood Cliffs, N.J.: Salem Press, 1984), pp. 1947-1973.

6.362 "A Survey of Greek American Poets". *The Amaranth* 9 (1985), pp. 2-11.
  Concerns poets who either are based in New York City or live in the vicinity. Discusses: Dionysis Maraveyas, Makis Tzilianos, Panos Vozikis, Christos Tsiamis, Manolis Polentas, Yorghos Veis, Anastasis Vistonitis.

6.363 Tannen, Deborah. "Introducing Constructed Dialogue in Greek and American Conversational and Literary Narrative". In *Direct and Indirect Speech* (Florian Coulmas, ed. Trends in Linguistics: Studies & Monographs, 31. Berlin: Mouton de Gruyter, 1986), pp. 311-332.

6.364 Terzakis, Angelos. "Contemporary Theatre in Greece". *Thespis* 6 (Dec. 1972), pp. 32-33.

6.365 Terzakis, Angelos. "Matesis' *Vassilikos:* The First Drama of Ideas". In *Modern Greek Writers* (Edmund Keeley and Peter Bien, eds. Princeton: Princeton University Press, 1972), pp. 93-107 {5.9}.

6.366 Terzakis, Angelos, et al. "The Greek Playwrights & their Problems: Notes". *Thespis* 2-3 (May 1965), pp. 45-50.
   Notes by Angelos Terzakis, GeorgeTheotokas, Alekos Lidorikis, Sotiris Patatzis, Notis Pergialis, Vangelis Goufas, Iakovos Kambanellis.

6.367 Tziovas, Dimitris. *The Nationism of the Demoticists and its Impact on their Literary Theory (1888-1930): An Analysis Based on Their Literary Criticism and Essays*. Amsterdam: A.M. Hakkert, 1986. 492 p.

6.368 Tziovas, Dimitris. "The Organic Discourse of Nationalistic Demoticism: A Tropological Approach". In *The Text and its Margins* (Margaret Alexiou and Vassilis Lambropoulos, eds. New York: Pella Publishing Company, 1985), pp. 253-277 {5.8}.

6.369 Valaoritis, Nanos. "Modern Greek Poetry". *Horizon* 13, No. 75 (Mar. 1946), pp. 205-216.

6.370 Vitti, M. "Family and Alienation in Contemporary Greek Fiction". In *Modern Greek Writers* (Edmund Keeley and Peter Bien, eds. Princeton: Princeton University Press, 1972), pp. 217-233 {5.9}.

6.371 Vitti, Mario. "Fiction Methods in Greece 1925-1965". *Eleutheria* 1, No. 4 (July 1970), pp. 17-18.
   Summary of paper given at the M.G.S.A. Symposium held at Princeton University, Oct. 30-Nov. 1, 1969.

6.372 Vitti, Mario. "Rural Greekness in Greek Prose Fiction". *Review of National Literatures* 5, No. 2 (Fall 1974), pp. 27-40 {3.30}.

6.373 Wallace, Warren. "The Translator's Voice: An Interview with Edmund Keeley". *Translation Review* 11 (1983), pp. 1-14.
   Re. translation from Greek.

6.374 Whitman, Cedric H. "Karaghiozes and Aristophanic Comedy". Appendix in his *Aristophanes and the Comic Hero* (Cambridge, Mass.: published for Oberlin College by Harvard University Press, 1964), pp. 281-293.

6.375 Xydias, Vassilis. "Notations: 'New' or 'Old': Orthodoxy in the Limelight". *JHD* 11, No. 2 (Summer 1984), pp. 69-72.
   Re. Makrygiannis.

6.376 Young, Kenneth. "The Contemporary Greek Influence on English Writers". *Life and Letters and the London Mercury* 64, No. 149 (Jan. 1950), pp. 53-64.

6.377 Zakythinos, Dionysios A. "Neo-Hellenic Letters and Comparative Literature and the Restoration of the Ionian Academy". *Neo-Hellenika* 2 (1975), pp. 9-20.

7. AUTHORS

In this chapter the (Greek) authors are listed under the heading of a standardized form of their name, following the transliteration scheme proposed by Linos Politis in his *History of Modern Greek Literature* (see introduction). The index provides a guide to the chosen spelling, and the alternate forms, of the names, i.e. a link between the heading and the actual spellings of the names used in publications.

Under the heading of each author the works are arranged in four categories:
  a. Translations in book form;
  b. Translations incorporated within larger works;
  c. Book-length studies about the author;
  d. Critical studies about the author incorporated within larger works.

Further information about this chapter is given under the heading "Authors (Chapter 7)" in the introduction.

Alexandrou, Aris (1922-1978)

b.

7.1 _____ "Poems". From *The Straightness of Ways* (1959). Peter Mackridge, tr. *Aegean Review* 1 (Fall/Winter 1986), pp. 16-19.

7.2 _____ "Three Poems". Peter Mackridge, tr. *Verse* 4 (1985), pp. 44-45.
  "Promotion"; "Make Sure"; "The First Anatomist".

7.3 _____ "Unsent Letters"; "The Book". Robert Crist, tr. *Raccoon* 24/25 (May 1987), pp. 162-169.

d.

7.4 C(h)rist, Robert L. "Translating *To Kivotio*: At Work with Aris Alexandrou". *Translation Review* 11 (1983), pp. 37-44.

Alexiou, Elli (1894-1988)

b.

7.5 _____ "The Fountain of Brahim-Baba". Theodore Sampson, tr. *Greek Letters* 2 (1983), pp. 249-256. Also in *Modern Greek Short Stories*. Vol. 2 (Kyr. Delopoulos, ed. Athens: Kathimerini Publications, 1981), pp. 105-115 {4.13}.

7.6 _____ "They Were All to be Pitied" [a short story]. Deborah Tannen, tr. *The Charioteer* 22 and 23 (1980/1981), pp. 147-151 {7.631}.

d.

7.7 Tannen, Deborah. "Elli Alexiou: An Informal Portrait". *The Charioteer* 22 and 23 (1980/1981), pp. 141-146 {7.631}.

Alexiou, Georgia

a.

7.8 _____ *Thorn / Ἀγκάθι*. Poems. Reginald Witt, tr. London: Zeno Booksellers and Publishers, 1977. 86 p. Bilingual edition.

Anagnostaki, Loula

b.

7.9 _____ "*The City*: A Trilogy of One-Act Plays". George Valamvanos and Kenneth MacKinnon, trs. *The Charioteer* 26 (1984), pp. 37-88 {4.18}.
The Overnight Visitor, The City, The Parade.

7.10 _____ "*The Town:* A Play in One Act". Aliki Halls, tr. *Chicago Review* 21, No. 2 (Aug. 1969), pp. 88-105 {3.6}.

d.

7.11 Doulis, Thomas. "Loula Anagnostaki and the New Theater of Greece". *Chicago Review* 21, No. 2 (Aug. 1969), pp. 83-87 {3.6}.

Anagnostakis, Manolis (b. 1925)

a.

7.12 _____ *The Target: Selected Poems*. Kimon Friar, tr. and intro. New York: Pella Publishing Company, 1980. 135 p. Bilingual edition.

b.

7.13 _____ "The Decision". Edmund and Mary Keeley, trs. *The New York Review of Books* (12 Aug. 1971), p. 10.

7.14 _____ "5 Poems". Martin McKinsey, tr. *Chelsea* 41 (1982), pp. 122-126.

7.15 _____ "Four Poems". James Stone, tr. *Translation* 14 (Spring 1985), pp. 51-53 {3.34}.
"The Betrayal"; "More and More Naked"; "The Sky"; "Now He is a Simple Spectator".

7.16 _____ "Poems by Manolis Anaghnostakis". Kimon Friar, tr. *Boundary 2,* Vol. 1, No. 2 (Winter 1973), pp. 419-432 {3.5}.

7.17 _____ "The Target". Edmund and Mary Keeley, tr. In *Eighteen Texts* (Willis Barnstone, ed. Cambridge, Mass.: Harvard University Press, 1972), pp. 103-116 {4.1}.

7.18 _____ "Two Poems". David Posner, tr. *The Charioteer* 14 (1972), pp. 18-19.
"The Decision"; "The Continuation".

Analytis, Panagiotis

a.

7.19 *_____ *Hymns to the Philosophy of Nature*. Poems. Athens, 1977.

Angelaki-Rooke, Katerina (b. 1939)

a.

7.20 _____ *Beings and Things on Their Own: Poems by Katerina Anghelaki-Rooke*. Katerina Anghelaki-Rooke and Jackie Willcox, trs. Brockport, N.Y.: Boa Editions, 1986. 47 p.

7.21 _____ *The Body is the Victory and the Defeat of Dreams*. Philip Ramp, tr. San Francisco: The Wire Press, 1975. 79 p. Bilingual edition.

b.

7.22 _____ "Diogenes". Philip Ramp, tr. *Omphalos* 1, No. 1 (Mar. 1972), pp. 74-77. Bilingual.

7.23 _____ "Four Poems". Gail Holst Warhaft, tr. *Translation* 14 (Spring 1985), pp. 66-70 {3.34}.
"Jealousy"; "The Heat"; "The Honey"; "At the Barber's".

7.24 _____ "The Greek Poetic Landscape". *The Iowa Review* 7, Nos. 2-3 (Spring-Summer 1976), pp. 213-221.

7.25 _____ "The Greek Poetic Landscape: Recent Trends in Greek Poetry". *Review of National Literatures* 5, No. 2 (Fall 1974), pp. 13-26 {3.30}.

7.26 _____ "Kazantzakis's *Buddha*: Phantasmagoria and Struggle". *JHD* 10, No. 4 (Winter 1983), pp. 69-72 {7.634}.

7.27 _____ "A Note on Greek Poetry in the 1970's". *Modern Poetry in Translation* 34 (Summer 1978), pp. 3-4 {3.21}.

7.28 _____ "Santa Cruz". Philip Ramp, tr. *The Coffeehouse* 1 (Fall 1975), pp. 14-17.

7.29 _____ "Sex Roles in Modern Greek Poetry". *JMGS* 1, No. 1 (May 1983), pp. 141-156.

Anthias, Tefkros (1903-1968)

a.

7.30 *_____ *Cyprus Village Tales*. Antoinette Diamantis, tr. Nicosia, 1942. 53 p.

7.31 *_____ *The Elegy of Haido*. A Theatrical Intermedium from *The Cyprus Tragedy*. Jack Lindsay, tr.; Daphne Mavrovouniotis, illustr. London: Anthias, 1966. 29 p.

7.32 *_____ *Greece, I Keep my Vigil over You*. Rhapsody. Jack Lindsay, tr.; Daphne Mavrovouniotis, illustr. London: Anthias, 1968. 39 p.

7.33 _____ *The Human Epic*. Epico-Lyric Poem. A. Raysson, tr. London: Flame, 1949. 30 p.

7.34 *_____ *The Song of the Earth*. Philip L. Nicolaides, tr. London: Union Publishers, 1952. 70 p. Also Johannesburg, 1952. 68 p.

7.35 *_____ *A Trip to the Sun*. Children's play in three acts with four songs. Rae Dalven, tr. London: Flame, 1954. 61 p.

Antoniou, D.I. (b. 1906)

b.
7.36 _____ "The Bad Businessmen". Peter Levi, tr. *Agenda* 7, No. 1 (Winter 1969), p. 78 {3.1}.

d.
7.37 Seferis, George. "Antoniou: Our Seafaring Friend". In his *On the Greek Style* (Boston and Toronto: Little, Brown and Company, 1966), pp. 67-71 {7.1342}.

Antoniou, Takis (b. 1932)

a.
7.38 _____ *First Trilogy, 1976-1979*. M.B. Raizis, tr. 2 vols. Athens: Epopteia Publications Ltd., 1980. Vol. A: 189 p.; Vol. B: 259 p.

7.39 _____ *Genesis und Tod / Genesis and Death*. M. Byron Raizis, tr. (from Greek into English) and intro. Athens, 1980. 107 p. Bilingual German/English.

b.
7.40 _____ "Epigrams". Th. Sampson, tr. *Greek Letters* 3 (1984-1985), pp. 217-225.

c.
7.41 Raizis, M.B., ed. and tr. Τάκης 'Αντωνίου. 'Απόψεις γιά τό ἔργο του. *Views on the Work of Takis Antoniou*. Athens: Epopteia Publications, 1980. 263 p. Bilingual edition.

Views of Dimitris Doukaris, M.B. Raizis, Kostas Kyrris, Angelos Fouriotis, Th.D. Frangopoulos, Kostas Gouliamos, Achilles Grigorogiannis, Pan. Efestios, Andreas Karandonis, Nikos Spanias. Essays by: Christos Korelas and Dimitris Poulakos. Bibliography and biography of T. Antoniou. Also Dimitris Doukaris, "My Friend the Poet", a poem (p. 135).

Aravantinou, Manto (b. 1926)

d.
7.42 Carroll, M.G. "The Geometric Poetry of Mando Aravandinou: Script A". *SSMG* 5 (1981), pp. 3-28.

Athanasiadis, Nikos (b. 1904)

a.
7.43 *_____ *A Naked Girl*. Stephanos Zotos, tr. New York: Orion Press, 1968. 217 p.

Averof-Tositsas, Evangelos (1910-1990)

a.
7.44 _____ *By Fire and Axe: The Communist Party and the Civil War in Greece, 1944-1949*. Sarah Arnold Rigos, tr. New Rochelle, N.Y.: Caratzas Brothers, 1978. 438 p.

7.45 _____ *The Call of the Earth*. A Novel. André Michalopoulos, tr. New Rochelle, N.Y.: Caratzas Brothers, Publishers, 1981. 305 p.

Avgeris, Markos (1884-1973)

b.
7.46 _____ "I Proclaim Good News". M. Byron Raizis, tr. *Journal of the Hellenic American Society* 1, No. 3 (1974), pp. 12-13.

Axioti, Melpo (1905-1973)

d.
7.47 Kakavoulia, Maria. "Telling, Speaking, Naming in Melpo Axioti's *Would you Like to Dance, Maria?*". In *The Text and its Margins* (Margaret Alexiou and Vassilis Lambropoulos, eds. New York: Pella Publishing Company, 1985), pp. 123-156 {5.8}.

Baras, Alexandros (1906-1990)

a.
7.48 _____ *The Yellow House and Other Poems (1933-1973)*. Yannis Goumas, tr. Winchester, Hampshire, England: Green Horse Publications, 1974. 80 p.

b.
7.49 *_____ "Eleven Poems by Alexandros Baras". Yannis Goumas, tr. and postscript. *Cave* 6, pp. 58-67.

Bastias, Kostis (1901-1972)

b.
7.50 _____ "Kavo-Malias. A Sea Story". Theodore Sampson, tr. In *Modern Greek Short Stories*. Vol. 2 (Kyr. Delopoulos, ed. Athens: Kathimerini Publications, 1981), pp. 205-221 {4.13}.

d.

7.51 Manning, Clarence A. "Kostis Bastias". *Books Abroad* 21, No. 1 (Winter 1947), pp. 18-20.

Bekatoros, Stefanos (b. 1946)

b.

7.52 _____ "Postscript or the Sky from the Window". Vito Orlando and Dino Siotis, trs. *The Coffeehouse* 1 (Fall 1975), pp. 45-48.

Beratis, Giannis (1904-1968)

d.

7.53 Doulis, Thomas. "Yiannis Beratis: Objectivity in Freedom". *Forum for Modern Language Studies* 8, No. 3 (July 1972), pp. 269-283.

Capetanakis, Demetrios (1912-1944)

a.

7.54 _____ *Demetrios Capetanakis: A Greek Poet in England*. John Lehmann, intro. London: John Lehmann, 1947. 183 p.

    This book contains all that he wrote in English during his stay in England. Also contains essays about the poet by Panayiotis Canellopoulos, William Plomer, and Edith Sitwell.

7.55 _____ *The Isles of Greece and Other Poems*. Edith Sitwell, intro. Athens: Denise Harvey & Company, 1981. 38 p.

    Original in English.

7.56 _____ *The Shores of Darkness: Poems and Essays by Demetrios Capetanakis*. John Lehmann, intro. New York: The Devin-Adair Company, 1949. 183 p.

    Contains the same material as *Demetrios Capetanakis: A Greek Poet in England* (John Lehmann, intro. London: John Lehmann, 1947) {7.54}.

b.

7.57 _____ "The Greeks are Human Beings". Ἀγγλο-ελληνική Ἐπιθεώρηση 1, No. 3 (May 1945), pp. 12-14. (Reprinted from "Daylight" 1941). Bilingual.

7.58 _____ "A Lecture on Proust". John Lehmann, tr. from the French. *New Writing and Daylight* 6 (1945), pp. 107-117.

Capri-Karka, Carmen

a.

7.59 *_____ *The Age of Antipoetry*. John Chioles, tr. New York: Athens Printing Co., 1969. 57 p. Bilingual edition.

7.60 *_____ *O Kaimos tis Romiosynis—The Sorrow of Hellenism*. Poems 1969-1971. Tr. by the author. New York: "Greek Voice" Publications, 1971. 76 p. Bilingual edition.

7.61 _____ *Love and the Symbolic Journey in the Poetry of Cavafy, Eliot and Seferis*. An interpretation with detailed poem-by-poem analysis. New York: Pella Publishing Company, 1982. 374 p.

7.62 _____ *War in the Poetry of George Seferis: A poem-by-poem analysis*. New York: Pella Publishing Company, 1985. 235 p.

Cavafy, C.P. (1863-1933)

a.

7.63 _____ *Collected Poems*. Edmund Keeley and Philip Sherrard, trs.; George Savidis, ed. Princeton, N.J.: Princeton University Press, 1975. 451 p. Bilingual edition. 6th printing with corrections, 1980; 3rd hardcover printing, with corrections, 1983. Also *London: The Hogarth Press, 1975.
   Collection organized chronologically; includes (some) "unpublished" poems.

7.64 _____ *Collected Poems*. Edmund Keeley and Philip Sherrard, trs.; George Savidis, ed. Princeton, N.J.: Princeton University Press, 1975. 261 p. Paperback. English only. Also London: The Hogarth Press, 1975 and 1984. 205 p. Reprinted, London: Chatto & Windus, 1978.

7.65 _____ *The Complete Poems of Cavafy*. Rae Dalven, tr.; W.H. Auden, intro. Expanded edition. New York and London: Harcourt, Brace, Jovanovich, 1976. 311 p. Original edition, New York: Harcourt, Brace & World, Inc., 1961. 234 p. Also *London: The Hogarth Press, 1961. 234 p.; London: Chatto and Windus, 1968.
   The poems are grouped: before 1911 and then on a yearly basis from 1911 to 1933. Also includes a collection of 33 early poems and 63 "unpublished" poems.

7.66 *_____ *Fourteen Poems by C.P. Cavafy*. Chosen and illustrated with twelve etchings by David Hockney; Nikos Stangos and Stephen Spender, trs. London: Alecto Ltd., 1967. Limited edition. 66 unnumbered loose pages.

7.67 *_____ *Passions and Ancient Days*. New Poems by C.P. Cavafy. Edmund Keeley and George Savidis, eds. and trs. New York: The Dial Press, 1971. 68 p. Bilingual edition. Also with subtitle *Twenty One New Poems by C.P. Cavafy*. London: The Hogarth Press, 1972. 64 p.
   Twenty one of the "unpublished" poems.

7.68 _____ *The Poems of C.P. Cavafy*. John Mavrogordato, tr.; Rex Warner, intro. New York: Grove Press, 1952. 199 p. Also as *Poems by C.P. Cavafy*. London: The Hogarth Press, 1951; reissued London: The Hogarth Press / Chatto & Windus, 1971
   Poems are grouped: before 1911 and then on a yearly basis from 1911 to 1933.

7.69 _____ *Poems of Constantine Cavafy.* George Khairallah, tr. Beirut: Heidelberg Press, 1979. 55 p.

7.70 _____ *Selected Poems.* Edmund Keeley and Philip Sherrard, trs. Princeton, N.J.: Princeton University Press, 1972. 98 p.
  Contains a selection of the 154 canonical poems along with five "unpublished" poems.

7.71 *_____ *Three Poems of Passion by C.P. Cavafy.* Edmund Keeley and George Savidis, trs.; Ger van Dijck, illustr. Verona, Italy: Plain Wrapper Press, 1975. 12 p.

b.
7.72 _____ "Absence". John Cavafy, tr. In Καβάφη Πεζά (Παρουσίαση, σχόλια Γ.Α. Παπουτσάκη. Ἀθήνα: Φέξης, 1963), p. 241.

7.73 _____ "Art Poetica: 1st and 2nd Parts". In his Ἀνέκδοτα Πεζά Κείμενα (Εἰσαγωγή καὶ μετάφραση Μιχάλη Πιερίδη. Ἀθήνα: Φέξης, 1963), pp. 36-69.

7.74 _____ "Ars Poetica". *The Charioteer* 10 (1968), pp. 72-80.
  Cf. Decavalles at {7.181}.

7.75 *_____ "The Bandaged Shoulder". Rae Dalven, tr. *The American Poetry Review* 3 (1974), p. 15.

7.76 *_____ "Candles". Edmund Keeley and Philip Sherrard, trs. In *Roots of Lyric: Primitive Poetry and Modern Poetics* (Andrew Welsh. Princeton, N.J.: Princeton University Press, 1978), p. 45.

7.77 *_____ "The City". Edmund Keeley and Philip Sherrard, trs. In *Cinderella After Midnight* (Fred Zackel. New York: Coward, McCann, and Geoghagan, Inc., 1980), p. 7.

7.78 *_____ "Days of 1896"; "In Despair"; "December 1903". Edmund Keeley and Philip Sherrard, trs. In *Gay Sunshine Anthology* (W. Leland, ed. San Francisco: Gay Sunshine Press, 1976).

7.79 _____ [Diary of the poet's first visit to Greece.] In his Πεζά (Παρουσίαση, σχόλια Γ.Α. Παπουτσάκη. Ἀθήνα: Φέξης, 1963), pp. 259-302.

7.80 _____ "The Early C.P. Cavafy". John Cavafy, tr.; Edmund Keeley, intro. *St. Andrews Review* 3, No. 1 (Fall and Winter 1974), pp. 37-47.
  The translations are selected from two unpublished typescripts dated 1916 and 1917. They include the poems: "Interruption"; "'Che Fece...Il Gran Rifiuto'"; "The Horses of Achilles"; "'This is He'"; "Walls"; "The Glory of the Ptolemies"; "The Place"; "Philhellene"; "Come Again"; "Of the Workshop"; "Sea of the Morning"; "In a Town of Osrhoene"; "At the Cafe Door"; "The Aemilian, Son of Monaes, of Alexandria. 628-655 A.D.".

7.81 _____ "Eight Parasyntheta after Cavafy". Minas Savvas, [tr.]. *Chicago Review* 21, No. 2 (Aug. 1969), pp. 5-13 {3.6}.

7.82 _____ "Eight Poems". Edmund Keeley and Philip Sherrard, trs. Introduced by a brief essay on C.P. Cavafy by Edmund Keeley. *Antaeus* 16 (Winter 1975), pp. 88-94.

7.83 _____ "Expecting the Barbarians". Marguerite Yourcenar and W.H. Auden, trs. *The Atlantic Monthly* 195, No. 6 (June 1955), p. 126 {3.3}.

7.84 _____ "Fifteen Poems by Kavafis". Philip Sherrard, tr. In *New Directions in Prose and Poetry* 14 (1953), pp. 268-280.

7.85 _____ "Five Poems". Alan Boegehold, tr. (under the initials BCJ). *Brown Classical Journal* 2 (1985), pp. 1-5.
  "Morning Sea"; "Epitaph of Antiochos, King of Commagene"; "Waiting for the Barbarians"; "Byzantine Official in Exile, Poetaster"; "Manuel Komnenos".

7.86 _____ "Five Poems". Edmund Keeley and Philip Sherrard, trs. *Boundary 2*, Vol. 1, No. 2 (Winter 1973), pp. 369-378 {3.5}.

7.87 _____ "Five Poems". Peter Mackridge, tr. *Omphalos* 1, No. 1 (Mar. 1972), pp. 28-33. Bilingual version.
  "The Pawn"; "Disgruntled Theatregoer"; "The Enemy"; "Characteristics"; "From the Drawer".

7.88 _____ "Five Poems: Alexandria, 34-30 B.C.". Edmund Keeley and Philip Sherrard, trs. *Shenandoah* 21, No. 3 (Spring 1970), pp. 77-81.

7.89 _____ "Five Poems by Cavafis". Philip Sherrard, tr. with a preface. *Encounter* 4, No. 1 (Jan. 1955), pp. 34-40.

7.90 _____ "Four Poems". Edmund Keeley and Philip Sherrard, trs. *The New Yorker* (17 June 1972), p. 31.
  "Exiles"; "From the School of the Renowned Philosopher"; "Half an Hour"; "To Have Taken the Trouble".

7.91 _____ "Four Poems by Constantine Cavafy". Alan L. Boegehold, tr. *Brown Classical Journal* 3 (1986), pp. 2-4.
  "Interruption"; "The Dangers"; "The Satrapy"; "Alexandrian Kings".

7.92 *_____ "Four Poems from Cavafy". Ian Scott-Kilvert, tr. In *The Penguin New Writing* 32 (John Lehmann, ed. Harmondsworth and New York: Penguin Books, 1947), pp. 63-64.

7.93 _____ "Give Back the Elgin Marbles". In his Πεζά (Παρουσίαση, σχόλια Γ.Α. Παπουτσάκη. Ἀθήνα: Ἴξης, 1963), pp. 9-12.

7.94 _____ "The God Abandons Antony". George Valassopoulos, tr. In *Pharos and Pharillon: An Evocation of Alexandria* (E.M. Forster. London: Michael Haag, 1983 [1923¹]), p. 55.

7.95 *_____ "The God Abandons Anthony"; "An Old Man"; "Che Fece...Il Gran Rifiuto"; "Longings"; "In the Same Space"; "Waiting for the Barbarians"; "Unfaithfulness"; "Things Ended"; "As Much as You Can". Edmund Keeley and Philip Sherrard, trs. In *Perfected Steel, Terrible Crystal* (Ned O' Gorman, ed. New York: The Seabury Press, 1981), pp. 33-34, 138-139, 190-193.

7.96 _____ "'Hellenes' and not 'Romaioi'". In his Ἀνέκδοτα Πεζά Κείμενα (Εἰσαγωγή καί μετάφραση Μιχάλη Πιερίδη. Ἀθήνα: ἑξῆς, 1963), pp. 76-81.

7.97 *____ "Hidden Things". Edmund Keeley and George Savidis, trs. In *By Her Own Admission: A Lesbian Mother's Fight to Keep her Son* (Gifford Guy Gibson, with the collaboration of Mary Jo Risher. Garden City, N.Y.: Doubleday, 1977), p. ix.

7.98 _____ "In Broad Daylight". James Merrill, tr. *Grand Street* 2, No. 3 (Spring 1983), pp. 99-107 {7.151}. Reprinted in *Aegean Review* 1 (Fall/Winter 1986), pp. 8-15.

7.99 _____ "In the Soul's House". John Cavafy, tr. In Καβάφη Πεζά (Παρουσίαση, σχόλια Γ.Α. Παπουτσάκη. Ἀθήνα: ἑξῆς, 1963), p. 249.
Autograph.

7.100 _____ "Ithaca". Alan L. Boegehold, tr. In *Brown: Guide to Liberal Learning* (Providence, R.I.: Brown University, 1985), p. 137.

7.101 *_____ "Ithaka". Edmund Keeley and Philip Sherrard, trs. *Athens College Bulletin* (Autumn 1961). *Also in *Homer: A Collection of Critical Essays* (George Steiner and Robert Fagles, eds. Englewood Cliffs, N.J.: Prentice-Hall, Inc., 1962), pp. 158-159; in *Gods and Heroes of the Greeks: The Library of Apollodorus* (Michael Simpson, ed. Amherst: University of Massachusetts Press, 1976), pp. 302-303; in "Real and Imaginary History in Borges and Cavafy". *Comparative Literature* 29, No. 1 (Winter 1977), p. 65; in *The Social Psychology of Organizing* (Karl E. Weick. Menlo Park, Calif.: Addison-Wesley Publishing Co., 1979), pp. 263-264; in *Feats and Seasons* 1, No. 1 (Jan.-Feb. 1980), pp. 1-2; in *Boston Latin School Register* 102 (May 1982), p. 32; in *In the Deep Heart's Core* (Craig Edward Clifford. College Station, Texas: Texas A. + M. University Press, 1985), pp. 127-128; and in *Critical Essays on Homer* (Kenneth Atchity, Ron Hogart, and Doug Price, eds. Boston: G.K. Hall and Co., 1987), pp. 223-224.

7.102 _____ "King Claudius". Edmund Keeley and George Savidis, trs. *The New York Review of Books* 14, No. 5 (12 Mar. 1970), p. 3.

7.103 _____ "Lovely White Flowers"; "The Horses of Achilles". Edmund Keeley and Philip Sherrard, trs. In *The Oxford Book of Death* (D.J. Enright, ed. Oxford and New York: Oxford University Press, 1983), pp. 111-112 and 308.

7.104 _____ "Masks". In his Πεζά (Παρουσίαση, σχόλια Γ.Α. Παπουτσάκη. Ἀθήνα: ἑξῆς, 1963), pp. 167-169.

7.105 _____ "Misplaced Tenderness". In his Πεζά (Παρουσίαση, σχόλια Γ.Α. Παπουτσάκη. 'Αθήνα: Φέξης, 1963), pp. 177-179.

7.106 *_____ "Monotony". Edmund Keeley and Philip Sherrard, trs. In *Feelings: Our Vital Signs* (Willard Gaylin. New York: Harper and Row, 1979), p. 117.

7.107 _____ "My Walls". From the Greek of Constantine Cavafy. John C. Cavafy, tr. Alexandria, 16 Jan. 1897. 4 p. In Κ.Π. Καβάφης, Πανομοιότυπα τῶν Πέντε Πρώτων Φυλλαδίων του (1891;-1904). Παρουσίαση-σχόλια Γ.Π. Σαββίδης. Athens: E.Λ.I.A., 1983. Bilingual version.

7.108 *_____ "Myris"; "Their Beginning"; "In the Evening"; "In the Tavernas"; "On Board Ship"; "Dareios". Edmund Keeley, sometimes in collaboration with Philip Sherrard, trs. *The Antaeus Anthology* (Daniel Halpern, ed. Toronto; New York: Bantam Books, 1986) {4.39}.

7.109 *_____ "Nero's Respite". Edmund Keeley and Philip Sherrard, trs. In *Hesitant Wolf and Scrupulous Fox: Fables Selected from World Literature* (Karen Kennedy, ed. New York, 1973), p. 44.

7.110 _____ "Notes on Poetics and Ethics". Martin McKinsey, tr. *Ploughshares* 11, No. 4 (June 1986), pp. 20-26 {3.25}.

7.111 _____ "Of the Ship". David Mason, tr. *Translation* 16 (Spring 1986), p. 142.

7.112 _____ "On C.P. Cavafy: Seven Poems". Edmund Keeley and Philip Sherrard, trs. *Antaeus* 6 (Summer 1972), pp. 38-47.

7.113 _____ "Persian Manners". In his Πεζά (Παρουσίαση, σχόλια Γ.Α. Παπουτσάκη. 'Αθήνα: Φέξης, 1963), pp. 174-176.

7.114 _____ "Poems". *The Transatlantic Review* 3 (Spring 1960), pp. 45-48.
 "Philhellene" [Edmund Keeley, tr.]; "From Nine O'Clock" [Willis Barnstone, tr.]; "Ithaka" [Philip Sherrard and Edmund Keeley, trs.].

7.115 _____ "Returning from Greece". Edmund Keeley and Philip Sherrard, trs. In: Diskin Clay, "The Silence of Hermippus: Greece in the Poetry of Cavafy". *BMGS* 3 (1977), pp. 107-108.

7.116 _____ "Romaïc Folk-Lore of Enchanted Animals". In his Πεζά (Παρουσίαση, σχόλια Γ.Α. Παπουτσάκη. 'Αθήνα: Φέξης, 1963), pp. 170-173.

7.117 _____ "The Satrapy". In his Ἀνέκδοτα Πεζά Κείμενα (Εἰσαγωγή καί μετάφραση Μιχάλη Πιερίδη. 'Αθήνα: Φέξης, 1963), pp. 86-89.
 Prose English version facing the Greek poem; must have been done by Cavafy himself after 1910; see p. 34 of the introduction.

7.118 *_____ "The Satrapy"; "Body, Remember...". Edmund Keeley and Philip Sherrard, trs. *The Nation* (13 Nov. 1972), p. 469.

7.119 _____ "September, 1903". Edmund Keeley and George Savidis, trs. *Evergreen Review* 15, No. 86 (Jan. 1971), p. 47.

7.120 *_____ "Seven Poems". Edmund Keeley and Philip Sherrard, trs. *The Nassau Literary Review* (Winter 1974), pp. 119-123.

7.121 _____ "Seventeen Poems". Edmund Keeley and Philip Sherrard, trs. *Arion's Dolphin* 3, Nos. 1-2 (Winter-Spring 1974), pp. 2-15.
   From C.P. Cavafy, *Collected Poems* to be published Dec. 1974 {7.63}.

7.122 _____ "Six Anaplases from the Greek of Cavafy". Konstantinos Lardas, [tr.]. *The Texas Quarterly* 10, No. 2 (Summer 1967), pp. 156-158.

7.123 *_____ "Steps". Alan Boegehold, tr. Stratford, Ontario: The Pasdeloup Press. A broadside. 18 x 25 inches. Limited edition, 100 copies. Also in *Margin* 5 (1987/88), p. 40.

7.124 _____ "Thirteen Erotic Poems". Edmund Keeley, tr. *The Malahat Review* 32 (Oct. 1974), pp. 121-128.

7.125 _____ "This Great, this Wonderful Saint" [=Symeon Stylites]. In his Ἀνέκδοτα Πεζά Κείμενα (Εἰσαγωγή καί μετάφραση Μιχάλη Πιερίδη. Ἀθήνα: ἕξης, 1963), pp. 70-75.

7.126 _____ "Three Cavafy Poems". James Merrill, [tr.]. *Grand Street* 6, No. 2 (Winter 1987), pp. 124-126.
   "The Afternoon Sun"; "On an Italian Shore"; "Days of 1908".

7.127 _____ "Three Poems by C.P. Cavafy". Rae Dalven, tr. *Poetry* 120, No. 5 (Aug. 1972), pp. 257-259.
   "The Pawn"; "The Mimiambi of Herodas"; "The Enemies".

7.128 *_____ "Three Poems by C.P. Cavafy". Edmund Keeley and George Savidis, trs. *The Dutton Review* 1 (1970), pp. 99-102.
   "At the Theatre"; "On the Stairs"; "The Bandaged Shoulder".

7.129 _____ "Three Poems by C.P. Cavafy". Edmund Keeley and Philip Sherrard, trs. *Poetry* 120, No. 5 (Aug. 1972), pp. 266-267.
   "The Footsteps"; "The Ides of March"; "Theodotos".

7.130 _____ "Three Poems by Constantine Cavafy". Edmund Keeley and Philip Sherrard, trs. *The New York Review of Books* 24, No. 2 (17 Feb. 1977), p. 33.
   "Ionic"; "The Bandaged Shoulder"; "Kaisarion".

7.131 _____ "Three Poems of Kavafis". Ian Scott-Kilvert, tr. *Nine* 2, No. 1 (Jan. 1950), pp. 22-28. Bilingual version.
"The God Leaves Antony"; "Resolutions"; "In the Year 200 B.C.".

7.132 _____ "Two Poems". Edmund Keeley and Philip Sherrard, trs. *New Letters* 38, No. 3 (Spring 1972), pp. 76-78.
"Julian and the Antiochians"; "On the Outskirts of Antioch".

7.133 *_____ "Two Poems by C.P. Cavafy". Edmund Keeley, tr. *The New York Review of Books* 18, No. 11 (15 June 1972), p. 13.
"In a Large Greek Colony, 200 B.C."; "A Prince from Western Libya".

7.134 _____ "Two Poems from the Modern Greek". Raphael Demos, tr. *The New Republic* (7 Feb. 1934), p. 355.
"In Expectation of the Barbarians"; "Thermopylae".

7.135 _____ "Understanding". Edmund Keeley and Philip Sherrard, trs. *Christopher Street* (Dec. 1978), p. 15.

7.136 *_____ "Waiting for the Barbarians"; "Half an Hour"; "One of Their Gods". Edmund Keeley and Philip Sherrard, trs. *University Publishing*, No. 4 (Spring 1978).

7.137 _____ "Waiting for the Barbarians"; "Thermopylae"; "Ithaka"; "One of Their Gods"; "Nero's Respite"; "For Ammonis, Who Died at 29, in 610"; "Very Seldom". Edmund Keeley and Philip Sherrard, trs. *Quarterly Review of Literature* 18, Nos. 1-2 (1972), pp. 38-43.

7.138 *_____ "Walls". Edmund Keeley and Philip Sherrard, trs. In *The Crowned Cannibals: Writings on Repression in Iran* (Reza Baraheni. New York: Vintage Books, 1977), p. 219.

c.

7.139 Bien, Peter. *Constantine Cavafy*. Columbia Essays on Modern Writers, No. 5. New York and London: Columbia University Press, 1964. 48 p.
Republished as "Cavafy" in his: *Three Generations of Greek Writers: Introductions to Cavafy, Kazantzakis, Ritsos*. Athens: Efstathiadis Group, 1983, pp. 9-54 {5.1}.

7.140 Capri-Karka, C. *Love and the Symbolic Journey in the Poetry of Cavafy, Eliot and Seferis*. An interpretation with detailed poem-by-poem analysis. New York: Pella Publishing Company, 1982. 374 p.
Esp. Part 1 (pp. 19-94) concerns Cavafy. See also Part 4, "Comparisons" (pp. 323-350).

7.141 Jusdanis, Gregory. *The Poetics of Cavafy: Textuality, Eroticism, History*. Princeton, N.J.: Princeton University Press, 1987. 193 p.

7.142 Keeley, Edmund. *Cavafy's Alexandria: Study of a Myth in Progress*. Cambridge, Mass.: Harvard University Press, 1976. 196 p. Also London: The Hogarth Press, 1977. 196 p.

7.143 *Keeley, Edmund. *Constantine Cavafy and George Seferis and their Relation to English and American Poetry*. Unpublished doctoral dissertation. University of Oxford, 1952.

7.144 Kolaitis, Memas. *Cavafy as I Knew Him*. With 12 annotated translations of his poems and a translation of *The Golden Verses of Pythagoras*. Santa Barbara, Calif.: Kolaitis Dictionaries, 1980. 129 p.

7.145 Liddell, Robert. *Cavafy: A Critical Biography*. London: Duckworth, 1974. 222 p. Also as *Cavafy*. A Quokka Book. New York: Pocket Books of Simon & Schuster, 1974. 223 p. and *Cavafy: A Biography*. New York: Schocken Books, 1976. 220 p.

7.146 Melissinos, Stavros. *Kavafy, the One String-Lyre Player*. [Nicholas Bassett, tr.]. Athens: Mangos Printers, 1979. 126 p.
   Includes: "Excerpts on the Poetry of K.P. Kavafy from the Diary of Stavros Melissinos" (pp. 7-50) and Melissinos, "Rubaiyat" (4th edition) (pp. 55-118).

7.147 *Michals, Duane. *Homage to Cavafy*. Ten Poems by Constantine Cavafy. Ten photographs by Duane Michals. Danbury, N.H.: Addison House, 1978. [48 p.]
   The poems are rendered in the translation of Edmund Keeley and Philip Sherrard.

7.148 *The Mind and Art of C.P. Cavafy: Essays on his Life and Work*. Athens: Denise Harvey & Company, 1983. 223 p.
   Includes: E.M. Forster, "The Poetry of C.P. Cavafy" (pp. 13-18); Robert Liddell, "Studies in Genius: Cavafy" (pp. 19-32); Patrick Leigh Fermor, "The Landmarks of Decline" (pp. 33-39); E.M. Forster, "The Complete Poems of C.P. Cavafy" (pp. 40-45); Edmund Keeley, "The 'New' Poems of Cavafy" (pp. 46-59); George Seferis, "Cavafy and Eliot—A Comparison" [Rex Warner and Th.D. Frangopoulos, trs.] (pp. 60-88); Stephen Spender, "Cavafy: The Historic and Erotic" (pp. 89-93); Philip Sherrard, "Cavafy's Sensual City: A Question" (pp. 94-99); Nasos Vayenas, "The Language of Irony (Towards a Definition of the Poetry of Cavafy)" (pp. 100-114); Francis Golffing, "The Alexandrian Mind: Notes Toward a Definition" (pp. 115-126); Renato Poggioli, "*Qualis Artifex Pereo!* or Barbarism and Decadence" (pp. 127-156); Diskin Clay, "The Silence of Hermippos: Greece in the Poetry of Cavafy" (pp. 157-181); I.A. Sarejannis, "Cavafy: The Man of the Crowd" [Sara Wheeler, tr.] (pp. 182-194); Constantine Melakopides, "Cavafy: The Philosophical Poetry" (pp. 195-223).

7.149 *Pieris, Michalis *The Inside and the Outside: Studies in Cavafy's Poetics*. Unpublished doctoral dissertation. University of Sydney, 1983.

7.150 Pinchin, Jane Lagoudis. *Alexandria Still: Forster, Durrell, and Cavafy*. Princeton, N.J.: Princeton University Press, 1977. 245 p.

Special issues of periodicals

7.151 *Grand Street*, Vol. 2, No. 3 (Spring 1983). Ben Sonnenberg, ed. New York: Grand Street Publications, Inc.
   Includes: C.P. Cavafy, "In Broad Daylight" [James Merrill, tr.] (pp. 99-107); J.A. Sareyannis, "'What Was Most Precious—His Form'" [Diana Haas, tr.] (pp. 108-126); George P. Savidis, "Photographs of C.P. Cavafy, his Family and Home" (pp. 127-142); C.Th. Dimaras, "Cavafy's Technique of Inspiration" [Diana Haas, tr.] (pp. 143-155); D[iana] H[aas], "Note" [to the preceding] (p. 156); Edmund Keeley, "Cavafy's Voice and Context" (pp. 157-177); Takis Sinopoulos, "Jacob" [James Stone, tr.] (pp. 178-179); G.W. Bowersock, "Cavafy and Apollonios" (pp. 180-189).
   Address: Grand Street, 50 Riverside Drive, New York, New York 10024.

7.152 *Journal of the Hellenic Diaspora,* Vol. 10, Nos. 1 & 2 (Spring-Summer 1983). Special Double Issue: C.P. Cavafy. Margaret Alexiou, guest ed. and intro. New York: Pella Publishing Co.
  Includes: Margaret Alexiou, "Introduction" (pp. 7-9); Alexander Kitroeff, "The Alexandria We Have Lost" (pp. 11-21); Roderick Beaton, "The History Man" (pp. 23-44); Margaret Alexiou, "Eroticism and Poetry" (pp. 45-65); S.D. Kapsalis, "'Privileged Moments': Cavafy's Autobiographical Inventions" (pp. 67-88); Dimitris Dimiroulis, "Cavafy's Imminent Threat: Still 'Waiting for the Barbarians'" (pp. 89-103); Helen Catsaouni, "Cavafy and the Theatrical Representation of History" (pp. 105-116); Peter Bien, "Cavafy's Three-Phase Development Into Detachment" (pp. 117-136); Gregory Jusdanis, "The Modes of Reading; Or Why Interpret? A Search for the Meaning of 'Imenos'" (pp. 137-148); Vassilis Lambropoulos, "The Violent Power of Knowledge: The Struggle of Critical Discourses for Domination over Cavafy's 'Young Men of Sidon, A.D. 400'" (pp. 149-166).
  Address: *JHD*, Pella Publishing Co., Inc., 337 W. 36th St., New York, N.Y. 10018.

d.

7.153 Alastos, Doros. "C.P. Cavafy. The Poet and the Man. 1863-1933". Κρίκος, 14th Year, No. 63 (154) (Oct. 1963), pp. 2-6.

7.154 Alexiou, Margaret. "C.P. Cavafy's 'Dangerous' Drugs: Poetry, Eros, and the Dissemination of Images". In *The Text and its Margins* (Margaret Alexiou and Vassilis Lambropoulos, eds. New York: Pella Publishing Company, 1985), pp. 157-196 {5.8}.

7.155 Alexiou, Margaret. "Eroticism and Poetry". *JHD* 10, Nos.1 & 2 (Spring-Summer 1983), pp. 45-65 {7.152}.

7.156 Anton, John P. "Alexandria: The History and Legend of a Cosmopolis". *Conspectus of History* 1, No. 4 (1977), pp. 13-23.

7.157 Anton, John P. "C.P. Cavafy's *Ars Poetica*". *Philosophy and Literature* 2, No. 1 (Spring 1978), pp. 85-109.

7.158 Barnstone, Willis. "Real and Imaginary History in Borges and Cavafy". *Comparative Literature* 29, No. 1 (Winter 1977), pp. 54-73.

7.159 Beaton, Roderick. "Against 'The Violent Power of Knowledge'". *JHD* 10, No. 3 (Fall 1983), pp. 59-63.

7.160 Beaton, Roderick. "Cavafy and Proust". *Grand Street* 6, No. 2 (Winter 1987), pp. 127-141.

7.161 Beaton, Roderick. "C.P. Cavafy: Irony and Hellenism". *The Slavonic and East European Review* 59, No. 4 (Oct. 1981), pp. 516-528.

7.162 Beaton, Roderick. "The History Man". *JHD* 10, Nos. 1 & 2 (Spring-Summer 1983), pp. 23-44 {7.152}.

7.163 Bien, Peter. "Cavafy". In his *Three Generations of Greek Writers: Introductions to Cavafy, Kazantzakis, Ritsos* (Athens: Efstathiadis Group, 1983), pp. 9-54 {5.1}.

7.164 Bien, Peter. "Cavafy's Three-Phase Development Into Detachment". *JHD* 10, Nos. 1 & 2 (Spring-Summer 1983), pp. 117-136 {7.152}.

7.165 Bowersock, G.W. "Cavafy and Apollonios". *Grand Street* 2, No. 3 (Spring 1983), pp. 180-189 {7.151}.

7.166 *Bowersock, Glen W. "Gibbon and Julian". In *Gibbon et Rome à la lumière de l' historiographie moderne* (Pierre Ducrey, F. Burkhalter, & R. Overmeer, eds. Publications de la Faculté des Lettres de l' Université de Lausanne, 22. Geneva: Droz, 1977), pp. 191-213.
　Re. Julian the Apostate. Discussion, pp. 214-217.

7.167 Bowersock, G.W. "The Julian Poems of C.P. Cavafy". *BMGS* 7 (1981), pp. 89-104.

7.168 Bowra, C.M. "Constantine Cavafy and the Greek Past". In his *The Creative Experiment* (London: Macmillan & Co. Ltd, 1949), pp. 29-60.

7.169 *Brodsky, Joseph. "On Cavafy's Side". *The New York Review of Books* 24, No. 2 (17 Feb. 1977), pp. 32-34.

7.170 *Brodsky, Joseph. "Pendulum's Song". In his *Less than One: Selected Essays* (New York: Farrar, Straus & Giroux, 1986), pp. 53-68.

7.171 Caires, Valerie A. "Originality and Eroticism: Constantine Cavafy and the Alexandrian Epigram". *BMGS* 6 (1980), pp. 131-155.

7.172 *Carroll, M.G. "A Matter of Style: Cavafy to Ritsos". *Antipodes* 2 (1975), pp. 19-23.

7.173 Catsaouni, Helen. "Cavafy and the Theatrical Representation of History". *JHD* 10, Nos. 1 & 2 (Spring-Summer 1983), pp. 105-116 {7.152}.

7.174 Chioles, John. "Eros and Revolution in the Poetry of Cavafy". *JMH* 1 (Apr. 1984), pp. 25-32.

7.175 Chioles, John. "On Poetics: The Ostensible / Real Dichotomy". *JMH* 4 (Autumn 1987), pp. 167-172.
　A "dialogue" with Gregory Jusdanis' book, *The Poetics of Cavafy: Textuality, Eroticism, History* (Princeton, 1987) {7.141}.

7.176 Chioles, John. "The Socratic Revolt and Cavafy". *JMH* 2 (Oct. 1985), pp. 21-30.

7.177 Clay, Diskin. "C.P. Cavafy: The Poet in the Reader". *JMGS* 5, No. 1 (May 1987), pp. 65-83.

7.178 Clay, Diskin. "The Silence of Hermippos: Greece in the Poetry of Cavafy". *BMGS* 3 (1977), pp. 95-116. Also in *The Mind and Art of C.P. Cavafy* (Athens: Denise Harvey & Company, 1983), pp. 157-181 {7.148}.

7.179 Colakis, Marianthe. "Cavafy and Lucian: Two Diaspora Hellenists". *CML* 6, No. 1 (Fall 1985), pp. 13-21.

7.180 *Corn, Alfred. "Cavafy and Alexandrianism". *Raritan* 5, No. 2 (Fall 1985), pp. 93-102.

7.181 Decavalles, Andonis. "The 'Poetics' of Cavafy". *The Charioteer* 10 (1968), pp. 69-71.
    Accompanies *Ars Poetica* {7.74}.

7.182 Dimaras, C.Th. "Cavafy's Technique of Inspiration". Diana Haas, tr. *Grand Street* 2, No. 3 (Spring 1983), pp. 143-155 {7.151}.

7.183 Dimiroulis, Dimitris. "Cavafy's Imminent Threat: Still 'Waiting for the Barbarians'". *JHD* 10, Nos. 1 & 2 (Spring-Summer 1983), pp. 89-103 {7.152}.

7.184 Durrell, Lawrence. "Cavafy". Poem in his *Selected Poems, 1935-1963* (London: Faber and Faber, 1964), pp. 62-63.

7.185 *Economou, George. "Eros, Memory, and Art". *The American Poetry Review* 10, No. 4 (July-Aug. 1981), pp. 30-31.

7.186 *Enright, D.J. "Too Many Caesars: The Poems of C.P. Cavafy". In his *Conspirators and Poets* (London: Chatto & Windus, 1966), pp. 160-166.

7.187 Fermor, Patrick Leigh. "The Landmarks of Decline". In *The Mind and Art of C.P. Cavafy* (Athens: Denise Harvey & Company, 1983), pp. 33-39 {7.148}. *Originally in *TLS* (11 Oct. 1977).

7.188 Fiedler, Theodore. "Brecht and Cavafy". *Comparative Literature* 25, No. 3 (Summer 1973), pp. 240-246.

7.189 Fontana, Ernest. "Browning's 'Protus' and Cavafy". *Studies in Browning and His Circle* 14 (1986), pp. 16-21.
    Re. "Kaisarion".

7.190 Forster, E.M. "The Complete Poems of C.P. Cavafy". In *The Mind and Art of C.P. Cavafy* (Athens: Denise Harvey & Company, 1983), pp. 40-45 {7.148}. Originally in his *Two Cheers for Democracy* (London: Edward Arnold & Co., 1951; New York: Harcourt, Brace & World, 1951), pp. 246-250.

7.191 *Forster, E.M. "In the Rue Lepsius". *The Listener* (5 July 1951).

7.192 Forster, E.M. "The Poetry of C.P. Cavafy". In *The Mind and Art of C.P. Cavafy* (Athens: Denise Harvey & Company, 1983), pp. 13-18 {7.148}. First published in *Athenaeum* (25 Apr. 1919), pp. 247-248. Reprinted in his *Pharos and Pharillon: An Evocation of Alexandria* (London: Michael Haag Limited, 1983 [1923¹]), pp. 91-97. Also in *Athene* 4, No. 5 (June 1943), pp. 52-53, 69.

7.193 Forster, E.M. et al. "C.P. Cavafy". In *Twentieth Century Literary Criticism 2: Excerpts from Criticism of the Works of Novelists, Poets, Playwrights, Short Story Writers, and Other Creative Writers, 1900-1960* (Detroit, Mich.: Gale Research Co., 1979), pp. 87-98.
    Excerpts from essays of E.M. Forster, C.M. Bowra, W.H. Auden, Peter Bien, Stephen Spender, Edmund Keeley, Jane Lagoudis Pinchin.

7.194 Fraser, P.M. "Cavafy and the Elgin Marbles". *The Modern Language Review* 58, No. 1 (Jan. 1963), pp. 66-68.

7.195 Friar, Kimon. "Cavafis and his Translators into English". *JHD* 5, No. 1 (Spring 1978), pp. 17-40.

7.196 Gifford, Henry. "Seferis and Cavafy". *Grand Street* 6, No. 4 (Summer 1987), pp. 245-256.

7.197 Golffing, Francis. "The Alexandrian Mind: Notes Toward a Definition". In *The Mind and Art of C.P. Cavafy* (Athens: Denise Harvey & Company, 1983), pp. 115-126 {7.148}. Originally in *Partisan Review* 22, No. 1 (Winter 1955), pp. 73-82.

7.198 Haas, Diana. "Cavafy's Reading Notes on Gibbon's 'Decline and Fall'". *Folia Neohellenica* 4 (1982), pp. 26-96.

7.199 Haas, Diana. "Early Cavafy and the European 'Esoteric' Movement". *JMGS* 2, No. 2 (Oct. 1984), pp. 209-224.

7.200 H[aas], D[iana]. "Note". *Grand Street* 2, No. 3 (Spring 1983), p. 156 {7.151}.
    Appended to: C.Th. Dimaras, "Cavafy's Technique of Inspiration" {7.182}.

7.201 Honig, Edwin. "Edmund Keeley". Chapter 8 in *The Poet's Other Voice: Conversations on Literary Translation* (Edwin Honig, ed. Amherst: The University of Massachusetts Press, 1985), pp. 133-149.
    Esp. re. Keeley's translations of Seferis and Cavafy.

7.202 Jakobson, Roman and Peter Colaclides. "Grammatical Imagery in Cavafy's Poem 'Θυμήσου, Σῶμα...'". *Linguistics* 20 (Mar. 1966), pp. 51-59.

7.203 Jusdanis, Gregory. "C.P. Cavafy and the Politics of Poetry". In *The Text and its Margins* (Margaret Alexiou and Vassilis Lambropoulos, eds. New York: Pella Publishing Company, 1985), pp. 37-57 {5.8}.

7.204 Jusdanis, Gregory. "Cavafy, Tennyson, and the Overcoming of Influence." *BMGS* 8 (1982/83), pp. 123-136.

7.205 Jusdanis, Gregory. "The Modes of Reading; Or Why Interpret? A Search for the Meaning of 'Imenos'". *JHD* 10, Nos. 1 & 2 (Spring-Summer 1983), pp. 137-148 {7.152}.

7.206 Kapsalis, S.D. "'Privileged Moments': Cavafy's Autobiographical Inventions". *JHD* 10, Nos. 1 & 2 (Spring-Summer 1983), pp. 67-88 {7.152}.

7.207 Katope, Christopher G. "Cavafy and Durrell's *The Alexandria Quartet*". *Comparative Literature* 21, No. 1 (Winter 1969), pp. 125-137.

7.208 Kazantzakis, Nikos. "Cavafy". Chapter in his *Journeying: Travels in Italy, Egypt, Sinai, Jerusalem and Cyprus* (Themi Vasils and Theodora Vasils, trs. San Francisco: Creative Arts Books Co. [Donald S. Ellis, Publisher], 1984), pp. 74-79 {7.586}.

7.209 Kazazis, J.N. "Studies in Kavafis: 1. A Commentary on T. Malanos' Theory of Hellenistic Influences in the Poetry of Kavafis". Ἑλληνικά 29, No. 1 (1976), pp. 132-154.

7.210 Keeley, Edmund. "Cavafy's Alexandria: Study of a Myth in Progress" (summary of research in progress). *Helios*, N.S. 4 (Fall 1976), pp. 42-43.

7.211 Keeley, Edmund. "Cavafy's Hellenism". *Review of National Literatures* 5, No. 2 (Fall 1974), pp. 66-89 {3.30}.

7.212 Keeley, Edmund. "Cavafy's Metaphoric City". *The Southern Review* 12, No. 1 (Winter 1976), pp. 83-109.

7.213 Keeley, Edmund. "Cavafy's Mythical Alexandria". *Boston University Journal* 23, No. 1 (Winter 1975), pp. 40-55.

7.214 Keeley, Edmund. "Cavafy's Sensual City". *Shenandoah* 26, No. 3 (Spring 1975), pp. 90-121 {3.31}.

7.215 Keeley, Edmund. "Cavafy's Universal Perspective". *Folia Neohellenica* 2 (1977), pp. 65-84.

7.216 Keeley, Edmund. "Cavafy's Voice and Context". *Grand Street* 2, No. 3 (Spring 1983), pp. 157-177 {7.151}. Also as "Voice, Perspective, and Context in Cavafy" in his

Modern Greek Poetry: Voice and Myth (Princeton, N.J.: Princeton University Press, 1983), pp. 3-30 {5.2}.

7.217 *Keeley, Edmund. "Edmund Keeley on C.P. Cavafy". *Envoy* 49 (1987), pp. 5-6.

7.218 Keeley, Edmund. "'Latest' Poems Increase Cavafy's Appeal to Students". *University* 48 (Spring 1971), pp. 25-29.

7.219 *Keeley, Edmund. "The 'New' Poems of Cavafy". In *The Mind and Art of C.P. Cavafy* (Athens: Denise Harvey & Company, 1983), pp. 46-59 {7.148}. Originally in *Modern Greek Writers* (Edmund Keeley and Peter Bien, eds. Princeton: Princeton University Press, 1972), pp. 123-143 {5.9}.

7.220 Keeley, Edmund. "On Translating Cavafy and Seferis". *Shenandoah* 23, No. 2 (Winter 1972), pp. 39-49.

7.221 Keeley, Edmund. "Voice, Perspective, and Context in Cavafy". In his *Modern Greek Poetry: Voice and Myth* (Princeton, N.J.: Princeton University Press, 1983), pp. 3-30 {5.2}. First published as "Cavafy's Voice and Context" {7.216}.

7.222 Kitroeff, Alexander. "The Alexandria We Have Lost". *JHD* 10, Nos.1 & 2 (Spring-Summer 1983), pp. 11-21 {7.152}.

7.223 *Klingopoulos, G.D. "E.M. Forster's Sense of History and Cavafy". *Essays in Criticism* 8 (Apr. 1958), pp. 156-165.

7.224 Lambropoulos, Vassilis. "Resisting on 'The Power of Knowledge' and the 'Knowledge of Power'". *JHD* 10, No. 3 (Fall 1983), pp. 65-69.

7.225 Lambropoulos, Vassilis. "The Violent Power of Knowledge: The Struggle of Critical Discourses for Domination over Cavafy's 'Young Men of Sidon, A.D. 400'". *JHD* 10, Nos. 1 & 2 (Spring-Summer 1983), pp. 149-166 {7.152}.

7.226 Lardas, Konstantinos. "Our Soul is Shaken, Paralyzed". *Ararat* 9, No. 3 (= Issue No. 35) (Summer 1968), pp. 24-33.
    On Cavafy and the Greek language, followed by translations of Cavafy's poetry.

7.227 Lavagnini, Renata. "The Unpublished Drafts of Five Poems on Julian the Apostate by C.P. Cavafy". David Sices, tr. *BMGS* 7 (1981), pp. 55-88.

7.228 Liddell, Robert. "Studies in Genius: Cavafy". In *The Mind and Art of C.P. Cavafy* (Athens: Denise Harvey & Company, 1983), pp. 19-32 {7.148}. Originally in *Horizon* 18, No. 105 (Sept. 1948), pp. 187-202.

7.229 MacAlister, Suzanne. "Cavafy and the Greek Past". *Το Γιοφύρι* 3-4 (Nov. 1978), pp. 36-39.

7.230 Malanos, Timos. "Letter to the Editor" (July 30, 1983). *JHD* 10, No. 3 (Fall 1983), pp. 95-96.
   Concerns M. Alexiou article "Eroticism and Poetry" (*JHD* 10, Nos. 1 & 2 [1983], pp. 45-65) {7.152}.

7.231 Malkoff, Karl. "Varieties of Illusion in the Poetry of C.P. Cavafy". *JMGS* 5, No. 2 (Oct. 1987), pp. 191-205.

7.232 Maronitis, D.N. "Arrogance and Intoxication: The Poet and History in Cavafy". A.A. Fatouros, tr. In *Eighteen Texts* (Willis Barnstone, ed. Cambridge, Mass.: Harvard University Press, 1972), pp. 117-134 {4.1}.

7.233 *McCarthy, Shaun. "Lost Alexandria: Cavafy, Durrell and the City of God". *Journal of English* 14 (Sept. 1986), pp. 21-39.

7.234 Melakopides, Constantine. "Cavafy: The Philosophical Poetry". In *The Mind and Art of C.P. Cavafy* (Athens: Denise Harvey & Company, 1983), pp. 195-223 {7.148}.

7.235 Merrill, James. "Marvelous Poet". *The New York Review of Books* 22, No. 12 (17 July 1975), pp. 12-17. Republished as *"Unreal Citizen" in his *Recitative: Prose by James Merrill* (San Francisco: North Point Press, 1986), pp. 96-108.

7.236 Nehamas, Alexander. "Memory, Pleasure and Poetry: The Grammar of the Self in the Writing of Cavafy". *JMGS* 1, No. 2 (Oct. 1983), pp. 295-319.

7.237 Pinchin, Jane A.L. "It Goes on Being Alexandria Still: C.P. Cavafy and the English Alexandrians". *Dissertation Abstracts International* 35 (1975), p. 4546A {See 7.150}.

7.238 Poggioli, Renato. *"Qualis Artifex Pereo!* or Barbarism and Decadence". In *The Mind and Art of C.P. Cavafy* (Athens: Denise Harvey & Company, 1983), pp. 127-156 {7.148}. First published in *The Harvard Library Bulletin* 13, No. 1 (Winter 1959), pp. 135-159.

7.239 *Raffel, Burton. [A reading of Cavafy's "Ἡ Πόλη"]. In his *How to Read a Poem* (A Meridian Book. New York and Scarborough, Ontario: New American Library, 1984), pp. 108-109.
   The poem, "The City", is given in Rae Dalven's translation.

7.240 Raizis, M. Byron. "Cavafy and His English Translators". *Balkan Studies* 18, No. 1 (1977), pp. 91-97. *Also *Greek World* 1 (July-Aug. 1976), pp. 47-49; *Yearbook of Comparative and General Literature* 25 (1976), pp. 90-93; in his *Essays and Studies from Professional Journals*. Panhellenic Association of University Graduates in English (Athens, 1980), pp. 169-175.

7.241 Raizis, M. Byron. "More Cavafiana" (or "C.P. Cavafy"). *JML* 6, No. 4 (1977 Supplement), pp. 581-584. Also in his *Essays and Studies from Professional Journals*. Panhellenic Association of University Graduates in English (Athens, 1980), pp. 176-178.

Review of Dalven's 1976 translation, Keeley's *Cavafy's Alexandria* and Liddell's *Cavafy: A Biography* {7.65, 7.142, 7.145}.

7.242 *Robillard, Douglas, Jr. "In the Capital of Memory: The Alexandria of Durrell and Cavafy". *Deus Loci* 5, No. 1 (Fall 1981), pp. 78-87.

7.243 Roditi, Edouard. "Cavafis and the Permanence of Greek History". *Poetry* 81, No. 6 (Mar. 1953), pp. 389-392.

7.244 Roditi, Edouard. "Remembrance of the Greek Past in the Poetry of Constantinos Cavafy". *Brown Classical Journal* 4 (1987), pp. 2-6.

7.245 Ruehlen, Petroula Kephala. "Constantine Cavafy: A European Poet". In *Nine Essays in Modern Literature* (Donald E. Stanford, ed. Baton Rouge, La.: Louisiana State University Press, 1965), pp. 36-62.

7.246 Sarejannis, I.A. "Cavafy: The Man of the Crowd". Sara Wheeler, tr. In *The Mind and Art of C.P. Cavafy* (Athens: Denise Harvey & Company, 1983), pp. 182-194 {7.148}.

7.247 Sareyannis, J.A. "'What Was Most Precious—His Form'". Diana Haas, tr. *Grand Street* 2, No. 3 (Spring 1983), pp. 108-126 {7.151}.

7.248 Savidis, George P. "The Burden of the Past and the Greek Poet". *Grand Street* 5, No. 1 (Autumn 1985), pp. 164-190.
  This essay contains {7.252}.

7.249 Savidis, George. "Cavafy and Forster". *TLS* (14 Nov. 1975), p. 1356.
  The same issue contains: "Modern Greece: Ten Pages of Articles and Reviews".

7.250 Savidis, G.P. "Cavafy and Forster". In his Μικρά Καβαφικά Α' ('Αθήνα: Ἑρμῆς, 1985), pp. 167-178.

7.251 Savidis, G.P. "Cavafy, Gibbon and Byzantium". In his Μικρά Καβαφικά Α' ('Αθήνα: Ἑρμῆς, 1985), pp. 91-99.

7.252 Savidis, G.P. "Cavafy versus Aeschylus". In his Μικρά Καβαφικά Α' ('Αθήνα: Ἑρμῆς, 1985), pp. 359-379.
  Also contained in {7.248}.

7.253 Savidis, G.P. "A Greek Citizen of the Eternal City". Is Appendix 5 in his Μικρά Καβαφικά Β' ('Αθήνα: Ἑρμῆς, 1987), pp. 421-425.

7.254 Savidis, G.P. "Photographs of C.P. Cavafy, his Family and Home". *Grand Street* 2, No. 3 (Spring 1983), pp. 127-142 {7.151}.

7.255 Schartau, Bjarne. "A New Translation of Cavafy". *SSMG* 2 (1978), pp. 65-77.

Re. K.P. Kaváfis, *Verzamelde Gedichten,* vertaald en ingeleid door G.H. Blanken. I. De 154 gedichten. Amsterdam, 1977.

7.256 Scodel, Ruth. "Apollo's Perfidy: *Iliad* Ω 59-63". *Harvard Studies in Classical Philology* 81 (1977), pp. 55-57.

7.257 Seferis, George. "Cavafy and Eliot—A Comparison". Rex Warner and Th.D. Frangopoulos, trs. In *The Mind and Art of C.P. Cavafy* (Athens: Denise Harvey & Company, 1983), pp. 60-88 {7.148}. Originally in his *On the Greek Style: Selected Essays on Poetry and Hellenism.* (Athens: Denise Harvey & Company, 1982), pp. 119-161 {7.1342}.

7.258 Sherrard, Philip. "Cavafy's Sensual City: A Question". *BMGS* 4 (1978), pp. 133-137. Also in *The Mind and Art of C.P. Cavafy* (Athens: Denise Harvey & Company, 1983), pp. 94-99 {7.148}.

7.259 Sherrard, Philip. "Constantine Cavafis". In his *The Marble Threshing Floor* (London: Valentine, Mitchell & Co. Ltd., 1956), pp. 83-123 {5.6}.

7.260 Spender, Stephen. "Cavafy: The Historic and the Erotic". In *The Mind and Art of C.P. Cavafy* (Athens: Denise Harvey & Company, 1983), pp. 89-93 {7.148}. Originally in *The New York Review of Books* 18, No. 11 (15 June 1972), pp. 12-13.
  Re. *Passions and Ancient Days* {7.67}.

7.261 Tarelli, C.G. "Cavafis". *The Link*, No. 2 (June 1939), pp. 30-35. Also in *Athene* 5, No. 2 (June 1944), pp. 38-40.

7.262 Tsiovas, Dimitris. "Cavafy's Barbarians and their Western Genealogy". *BMGS* 10 (1986), pp. 161-178.

7.263 Vayenas, Nasos. "The Language of Irony (Towards a Definition of the Poetry of Cavafy)". *BMGS* 5 (1979), pp. 43-56. Also in *The Mind and Art of C.P. Cavafy* (Athens: Denise Harvey & Company, 1983), pp. 100-114 {7.148}.

7.264 Xenopoulos, Gregorios. "C.P. Cavafy: A Greek Poet". Th. Sampson, tr. *Greek Letters* 2 (1983), pp. 317-327.

7.265 *Yourcenar, Marguerite. "A Critical Introduction to Cavafy". Richard Howard, tr. *Shenandoah* 32, No. 1 (1980), pp. 3-37. Also in her *The Dark Brain of Piranesi and Other Essays* (Richard Howard in collaboration with the author, trs. New York: Farrar, Straus, Giroux, 1980 [second printing 1985]), pp. 154-198.

Chakkas, Marios (1931-1972)

b.
7.266 ____ "The Bidet". Kay Cicellis, tr. *Shenandoah* 27, No. 1 (Fall 1975), pp. 3-5 {3.32}.

7.267 _____ "Of His Own Will". Thanasis Maskaleris, tr. *The Coffeehouse* 3 (Fall 1976), pp. 3-6.

7.268 _____ "The Other Face". Kay Cicellis, tr. *The Athenian* (July 1975), pp. 24-25.

Charis, Petros (b. 1902)

a.

7.269 _____ *The Longest Night: Chronicle of a Dead City*. Theodore Sampson, tr. A Nostos Book. Minneapolis, Minn.: North Central Publishing Company, 1985. 128 p.

b.

7.270 _____ "Lights in the Sea". Theodore Sampson, tr. In *Modern Greek Short Stories*. Vol. 2 (Kyr. Delopoulos, ed. Athens: Kathimerini Publications, 1981), pp. 223-232 {4.13}.

Charkianakis, Stylianos (b. 1938)

b.

7.271 _____ "Six Poems". Peter Bien, tr. *Translation* 14 (Spring 1985), pp. 38-42 {3.34}.

7.272 _____ [10 Poems]. Peter Bien, tr. *Paintbrush* 10, Nos. 19 & 20 (Spring & Autumn 1983), pp. 32-41.

d.

7.273 Bien, Peter. "Stylianos Harkianakis". *Paintbrush* 10, Nos. 19 & 20 (Spring & Autumn 1983), pp. 30-31.

Chatzidaki, Natasa (b. 1946)

b.

7.274 _____ "Dark Red"; "Self-Portrait"; "Continuing Sexual Reports". Dino Siotis, tr. *The Coffeehouse* 2 (Spring 1976), pp. 21-23.

Chatzis, Dimitris (1913-1981)

b.

7.275 _____ "The Detective" [from *The End of Our Little Town*]. Theodore Sampson, tr. *Greek Letters* 1 (1982), pp. 242-254.

7.276 _____ "From Fifty-fifty to Love" [from *The Double Book*]. Edward Fenton, tr. *Descant XVIII,* Vol. 8, No. 2 (1977), pp. 89-97 {3.8}.

7.277 _____ "Outworn Symbols". Roderick Beaton, tr. *Shenandoah* 27, No. 1 (Fall 1975), pp. 118-124 {3.32}.

7.278 _____ "Sioulas the Tanner". Theodore Sampson, tr. *The Athenian* (Apr. 1975), pp. 29-32.

7.279 _____ "Sioulas the Tanner". Theodore Sampson, tr. *Greek Letters* 4 (1986-1989), pp. 169-178.

Chatzopoulou-Karavia, Lia (b. 1932)

a.
7.280 _____ *The Silent Piano Keys; Le Lion; Riki*. Athens: Editions Bilateral, 1984. 92 p.
The first story is the only one in English in this volume; it occupies pp. 11-28 and has been translated by the author.

b.
7.281 *_____ "Instructive Animals in Greek Children's Literature". In *Triumphs of the Spirit in Children's Literature* (Francelia Butler, ed. and pref.; Richard Rotert, ed. and pref.; Marcia Brown, foreword; Madeleine L'Engle, intro. Hamden, Conn.: Library Professional Publications, 1986), pp. 164-170.

Chimonas, Giorgos (b. 1936)

b.
7.282 _____ "Dr. Ineotis". Willis Barnstone, tr. In *Eighteen Texts* (Willis Barnstone, ed. Cambridge, Mass.: Harvard University Press, 1972), pp. 83-87 {4.1}.

7.283 _____ "from *The Wedding*". Kay Cicellis, tr. *Descant XVIII,* Vol. 8, No. 2 (1977), pp. 81-84 {3.8}.

c.
7.284 Crist, Robert L. *Man in the Midst of Immensities: The Works of Georgos Heimonas*. Athens: Kedros, 1983. 74 p.

Chioles, John (b. 1940)

b.
7.285 _____ "Five Poems". *The Coffeehouse* 9 (Winter 1979), pp. 27-31.
No translator mentioned.

Chionis, Argyris (b. 1943)

b.
7.286 _____ "I", "IX", "XIV" (from *Transformations*) [Stavros Deligiorgis, tr.]; "7" (from *The Containing Content);* "12", "15" (from *Shadows*) [Yannis Goumas, tr.]. *The Coffeehouse* 10 (Summer 1981), pp. 25-29.

7.287 _____ "Prose Poems". Fred A. Reed, tr. *Aegean Review* 3 (Fall/Winter 1987), pp. 30-31.

Christianopoulos, Dinos (b. 1931)

b.

7.288 _____ "Hilyos". Robert Wright, tr. *The Coffeehouse* 5 (Winter 1977), pp. 55-59.

7.289 _____ "Ithaca". Kimon Friar, tr. *The Literary Review* 16, No. 3 (Spring 1973), p. 387 {3.15}.

7.290 _____ "The Poetry of Dinos Christianopoulos: A Selection". Kimon Friar, tr. *JHD* 6, No. 1 (Spring 1979), pp. 68-83.

d.

7.291 Friar, Kimon. "The Poetry of Dinos Christianopoulos: An Introduction". *JHD* 6, No. 1 (Spring 1979), pp. 59-67.

7.292 *Taylor, John. "A Note on Dinos Christianopoulos's *I rebetes tou dounia*". *International Fiction Review* 14, No. 1 (Winter 1987), pp. 36-38.

Christodoulou, Dimitra (b. 1953)

b.

7.293 *_____ [Two Poems]. Yannis Goumas, tr. *Prism International* 23, No. 2 (Winter 1984), p. 134.

Christodoulou, Dimitris (b. 1924)

a.

7.294 _____ *Aegeans, and Other Poems*. John A. Goumas, tr. [Athens: J. Makris, 1965]. 67 p.

b.

7.295 _____ "Two Poems: 'From Aegeans'; 'Hydra'". John A. Goumas, tr. *Eleutheria* 1, No. 4 (July 1970), pp. 10-12.

Chronas, Giorgos (b. 1948)

b.

7.296 _____ "A Dry Yellow Color"; "Ode to the Oxyacetylene-Welder from Beirut"; "From the Mythology of Saturday". Robert Rowe, tr. *The Coffeehouse* 3 (Fall 1976), pp. 37-40.

7.297 *_____ "Ode to Marilyn Monroe"; "A Dry Yellow Colour"; "Lament for Initiated Travellers". Robert Lowe, tr. *Panjandrum* 5 (1977), pp. 125-127 (pages not numbered).

Chrysanthis, Kypros (b. 1915)

a.

7.298 _____ *The Betrayal:* A One-Act Play. Christos Cameris, tr. Nicosia, Cyprus, 1964. 8 p.

7.299 _____ *The Wanderer Ballad* [poetry]. Claude Légagneux, tr. [Nicosia, Cyprus: printed by Zavallis Press, 1953]. 23 p.

Cicellis, Kay (b. 1926)

a.

7.300 _____ *The Road to Colonus: A Greek Triptych.* London: Secker & Warburg, 1960. 156 p.

Subsequently published in Greek as Ὁ Δρόμος πρός τόν Κολωνό: Νουβέλες. Ἀθήνα: Ἑρμῆς, 1979. 190 p.

b.

7.301 _____ "Brief Dialogue". Kay Cicellis, tr. In *Eighteen Texts* (Willis Barnstone, ed. Cambridge, Mass.: Harvard University Press, 1972), pp. 5-9 {4.1}.

7.302 _____ "Cephalonia the First". *Descant XVIII,* Vol. 8, No. 2 (1977), pp. 64-68 {3.8}.

Originally published in *Die Griechischen Inseln* (Evi Mylonas, ed. Köln, 1976).

7.303 _____ "The Exile". *The Charioteer* 1, No. 2 (Autumn 1960), pp. 11-45.

7.304 _____ "The Home Companion". *Aegean Review* 1 (Fall/Winter 1986), pp. 34-38.

7.305 _____ "The Mark". *Mundus Artium* 4, No. 1 (Winter 1970), pp. 14-18 {4.82}.

7.306 _____ "Orpheus in Hades". *The Atlantic Monthly* 195, No. 6 (June 1955), pp. 149-152 {3.3}.

7.307 _____ "Proportions". *Shenandoah* 27, No. 1 (Fall 1975), pp. 26-34 {3.32}.

7.308 _____ "Puppet Show" [a short story]. Kay Cicellis, tr. *Translation* 14 (Spring 1985), pp. 54-62 {3.34}.

d.

7.309 Boatwright, James. "Are You Tourists?". *Shenandoah* 26, No. 3 (Spring 1975), pp. 156-171 {3.31}.

A journal/review dated June 5-Aug. 16, 1974; especially re. Stratis Tsirkas and Kay Cicellis.

Dalakoura, Veroniki (b. 1948)

b.

7.310 _____ "December" [Dinos Siotis, tr.]; "Let Me Twist the Blade"; "Mysterious Barricades"; "Excessive Aestheticism" [Nikos Spanias, tr.]. *The Coffeehouse* 3 (Fall 1976), pp. 44-47.

Daraki, Zefi (b. 1939)

b.

7.311 _____ "Dark on Dark"; "Freedom"; "The Hanging Kites"; "Suicide". Kimon Friar, tr. *The Coffeehouse* 5 (Winter 1977), pp. 38-41.

Decavalles, Andonis (b. 1920)

a.

7.312 _____ *Pandelis Prevelakis and the Value of a Heritage*. A Talk. Theofanis G. Stavrou, ed. and intro. The Second Annual Public Lecture in Modern Greek Studies, Special Collections, University of Minnesota Libraries, Minneapolis. With a supplement "Rhethymno as a Style of Life" by Pandelis Prevelakis [Jean H. Woodhead, tr.] (pp. 37-52). Minneapolis, Minn.: North Central Publishing Company, 1981. 52 p.

7.313 _____ *Ransoms to Time: Selected Poems*. Kimon Friar, tr. with introduction and notes. Rutherford; Madison; Teaneck, N.J.: Fairleigh Dickinson University Press; London and Toronto: Associated University Presses, 1984. 142 p.

b.

7.314 _____ "Cycles". Kimon Friar, tr. *The Literary Review* 16, No. 3 (Spring 1973), p. 252 {3.15}.

7.315 _____ "A Poet's Novel". *Poetry* 105, No. 1 (Oct. 1964), pp. 65-67 {3.27}.
　Re. translation by Edmund and Mary Keeley of *The Plant, The Well, The Angel: A Trilogy* by Vassilis Vassilikos {7.1770}.

7.316 _____ "Resurrection". George Economou, tr. *The Charioteer* 14 (1972), p. 15.

7.317 _____ "Three Poems". Kimon Friar, tr. *The Literary Review* 21, No. 4 (Summer 1978), pp. 389-393.
　"To the Master Builder"; "Zoophoros"; "The Third Year".

7.318 _____ "Three Poems in Greek and English". Kimon Friar and author, trs. *The Literary Review* 28, No. 4 (Summer 1985), pp. 538-543. Bilingual version.
　"Waterdrops and Drummer"; "The Fingers"; "Crimes or Genesis II".

d.

7.319 Bien, Peter. "Andonis Decavalles's Busy Fingers". *The Literary Review* 28, No. 4 (Summer 1985), pp. 533-537.

7.320 Keyishan, Marjorie. "Links, Joints and Vessels: An Interview with Andonis Decavalles". *The Literary Review* 21, No. 4 (Summer 1978), pp. 394-412.

7.321 Thaniel, George. "The Poetry of Andonis Decavalles". *The Charioteer* 28 (1986), pp. 143-151.

Denegris, Tasos (b. 1935)

b.

7.322 _____ "Perversion"; "The Spies"; "The Mayor of Tulsa"; "Greece, the Land of Marvels"; "The Death of an Old Nun who Lived as a Recluse". Kimon Friar, tr. *The Coffeehouse* 4 (Summer 1976), pp. 58-62.

7.323 _____ "Poems". Dino Siotis, tr. *Aegean Review* 1 (Fall/Winter 1986), pp. 39-41.

Dimoula, Kiki (b. 1931)

b.

7.324 _____ "Jungle"; "Dialogue Between Me and Myself"; "Incompatible Things". Kimon Friar, tr. *The Coffeehouse* 4 (Summer 1976), pp. 39-42.

Doxas, Takis (1913-1976)

a.

7.325 _____ *Light of Olympia*. Athan Anagnostopoulos, tr.; George Varlamos, illustr. Athens: privately printed, 1968. 12 unnumbered p. Bilingual edition.

Dragoumi, Julia D. (1858-1937)

a.

7.326 *_____ *A Man of Athens*. Boston, [Mass.]: Houghton, Mifflin Co., 1917.

7.327 *_____ *Tales of a Greek Island*. Freeport, N.Y.: Books for Libs. Reprint. Originally: Boston, [Mass.]: Houghton, Mifflin Co., 1912. Second edition, 1925.
   First published in English, then in Greek.

7.328 *_____ *Under Greek Skies*. New York: Dutton and Co., 1913.

Drosinis, Georgios (1859-1951)

a.

7.329 _____ *Amaryllis*. E.M. Edmonds, tr. London: T. Fisher Unwin, 1891. 163 p.

7.330 _____ *The Herb of Love*. Eliz. M. Edmonds, tr. London: T. Fisher Unwin; New York: Tait, Sons and Company, 1892. 223 p.

7.331 _____ *Stories from Fairyland by George Drosines and The Cup of Tears and Other Tales by Aristotle Kourtidos.* Translated from the Greek by Mrs. Edmonds. The Children's Library, Vol. 3. London: T. Fisher Unwin, 1892. 153 p.

b.
7.332 _____ "The God-Father". In *Modern Greek Stories* (Demetra Vaka and Aristides Phoutrides, trs. New York: Duffield and Company, 1920), pp. 91-101 {4.16}.

7.333 _____ "Scenes in Greek Life. Chrysoula: After the Greek of George Drosines. A Sketch". E.M. Edmonds, [tr.]. *The Eastern and Western Review* (Apr. 1893), pp. 291-295.

Eftaliotis, Argyris (1849-1923)

a.
7.334 _____ *Tales from the Isles of Greece, being Sketches of Modern Greek Peasant Life*. W.H.D. Rouse, tr. from the Greek of Argyris Ephtaliotis. London: J.M. Dent & Co., 1897. 231 p.

b.
7.335 _____ "Angelica". In *Modern Greek Stories* (Demetra Vaka and Aristides Phoutrides, trs. New York: Duffield and Company, 1920), pp. 155-170 {4.16}.

7.336 _____ "Angelica". Theodore Sampson, tr. In *Modern Greek Short Stories*. Vol. 1 (Kyr. Delopoulos, ed. Athens: Kathimerini Publications, 1980), pp. 85-97 {4.12}.

Eligia, Giosef (1901-1931)

a.
7.337 _____ *Poems by Joseph Eliyia*. Rae Dalven, tr. New York: Anatolia Press, 1944. 205 p. Bilingual.

Elytis, Odysseas (b. 1911)

a.
7.338 _____ Τό Ἄξιον Ἐστί / *The Axion Esti*. Edmund Keeley and George Savidis, trs. and notes. An International Poetry Forum Selection. Pittsburgh, Pa.: University of Pittsburgh Press, 1974. 159 p. Bilingual edition.
  Out of print in 1986.

7.339 _____ Τό Ἄξιον Ἐστί / *The Axion Esti*. Edmund Keeley and George Savidis, trs. Pittsburgh: University of Pittsburgh Press, 1974. 159 p. Second printing: 1979. 87 p. English only. Also London: Anvil Press Poetry, 1980. 102 p. English only.

7.340 *_____ *Clear Days*. Poems by Palamas and Elytis in versions by Nikos Tselepides. Portland, Oreg.: Press-22, 1972. [54 p.] Unpaged.

7.341 _____ *Maria Nephele: A Poem in Two Voices*. Athan Anagnostopoulos, tr. Boston, [Mass.]: Houghton Mifflin Company, 1981. 74 p.

7.342 _____ ’Ωδή στή Σαντορίνη. Μέ ἕνα σχέδιο τοῦ Γεράσιμου Στέρη. ’Αθήνα: ’Αρχεῖο Θηραϊκῶν Μελετῶν—Συλλογή Δημήτρη Τσίτουρα, 1984. *Ode to Santorini*. Edmund Keeley and Philip Sherrard, trs. With a Drawing by Gerassimos Steris. Athens: Archive of Santorini Studies—Dimitris Tsitouras Collection, 1984. A folio edition of 8 loose sheets. Bilingual edition.
    Translation is on pp. 6-7.

7.343 *_____ *Poems*. Nanos Valaoritis, tr. with an intro. San Francisco: Wire Press, 1982.

7.344 _____ *Selected Poems*. Edmund Keeley and Philip Sherrard, eds. and intro.; Edmund Keeley, George Savidis, Philip Sherrard, John Stathatos, Nanos Valaoritis, trs. New York: The Viking Press and Penguin Books, 1981. 114 p. Also London: The Anvil Press, 1981.

7.345 _____ *The Sovereign Sun: Selected Poems*. Kimon Friar, tr., intro. and notes. Philadelphia: Temple University Press, 1974. 200 p. Reissued in 1980.

7.346 _____ *What I Love: Selected poems of Odysseus Elytis*. Olga Broumas, tr. Port Townsend, Washington: Copper Canyon Press, 1986. 96 p. Bilingual edition.

b.
7.347 _____ "Aegean Melancholy". Edmund Keeley and Philip Sherrard, trs. *University* 82 (Winter 1980), p. 26.

7.348 _____ "Art-Chance-Risk". *Greek Letters* 1 (1982), pp. 203-227.

7.349 _____ "Axion Esti" [Part 2: The Passion, VII]. Edmund Keeley and George Savvides, trs. In *Cyprus '74: Aphrodite's Other Face* (Emmanuel C. Casdaglis, ed. Athens: National Bank of Greece, 1976), p. 118 {4.87}.

7.350 _____ "Axion Esti. Part III: The Gloria". Edmund Keeley and George Savidis, trs. *Agenda* 7, No. 1 (Winter 1969), pp. 60-68 {3.1}. Also in **The Contemporary World Poets* (Donald Junkins, ed. New York: Harcourt Brace Jovanovich, 1976), pp. 115-118 {4.41}.

7.351 _____ "from *Axion Esti*: 'The Genesis'". Edmund Keeley and George Savidis, trs. *Poetry* 105, No. 1 (Oct. 1964), pp. 1-15 {3.27}.

7.352 _____ "from *Axion Esti*: This Then is I" and "from *Six and One Regrets for the Sky*: The Sleep of the Brave". Ruth Whitman, tr. *Poetry* 105, No. 1 (Oct. 1964), pp. 21-23 {3.27}.

7.353 *_____ "from *The Axion Esti*". Edmund Keeley and George Savidis, trs. *Greece* (Jan.-Mar. 1975), pp. 21-24.

7.354 *_____ "Drinking the Sun of Corinth". Edmund Keeley, tr. *The Christian Science Monitor* (10 Apr. 1980), p. 20.

7.355 _____ "Drinking the Sun of Corinth"; "The Mad Pomegranate Tree". Edmund Keeley, tr. *The Beloit Poetry Journal* 7, No. 3 (Spring 1957), pp. 13-15.
   Part of "Four Greek Poets" {4.73}.

7.356 _____ "Eight Poems". *The Coffeehouse* 9 (Winter 1979), pp. 2-7.
   "Epigram" (from *Second Nature);* "III" (from *Seven Nocturnal Heptastichs);* "XVI", "XIX" (from *Sun-Bright Days);* "VI" (from *Hourglasses of the Unknown)* [Thanasis Maskaleris, tr.]; "Marina of the Rocks" [John Chioles, tr.] (the latter is a bilingual version).

7.357 *_____ "An Elytis Sampler". Edmund Keeley and Philip Sherrard, trs. *The New York Times* (19 Oct. 1979), p. A12.
   "The Autopsy"; "Drinking the Sun of Corinth".

7.358 _____ [Four Poems]. Kimon Friar, tr. *Kayak* 34 (1974), pp. 47-49.
   "Delos"; "Archetype; "Palm Sunday"; "Little Green Sea".

7.359 _____ "Heroic and Elegiac Song for the Lost Second Lieutenant of the Albanian Campaign". Kimon Friar, tr. *Accent* 14, No. 3 (Summer 1954), pp. 163-173.
   This is followed by a brief essay, "Odysseus Elytis", by Kimon Friar (pp. 174-175) and "Two Letters from Odysseus Elytis" (pp. 175-179).

7.360 *_____ "I Brought My Life this Far" (from "Commemoration"). Edmund Keeley and Philip Sherrard, trs. *Miami Herald* (19 Oct. 1979).

7.361 _____ "I Know the Night No Longer". Kimon Friar, tr. *The Atlantic Monthly* 195, No. 6 (June 1955), p. 141 {3.3}.

7.362 _____ "'Ο Κῆπος Βλέπει / The Garden Sees: Ποίημα-Θεωρία / A Poem Theory". Athan Anagnostopoulos, tr. *Chicago Review* 30, No. 2 (Autumn 1978), pp. 20-39.

7.363 *_____ "The Mad Pomegranate Tree". Edmund Keeley, tr. In *The Guinness Book of Poetry* 5 (London: Putnam, 1962), pp. 72-73.

7.364 _____ "The Mad Pomegranate-Tree". Nanos Valaoritis and Bernard Spencer, trs. In *New Writing and Daylight* 7 (John Lehmann, ed. London: John Lehmann, 1946), pp. 48-49.

7.365 _____ "from *Maria Nefeli*". Kimon Friar and Andonis Decavalles, trs. *The Charioteer* 24 and 25 (1982/1983), pp. 59-78 {7.392}.

7.366 _____ "from *Maria Nephele*". Athan Anagnostopoulos, tr. *The Paris Review* 78 (1980), pp. 62-78.

7.367 _____ "from *The Monogram*". Edward Morin and Lefteris Pavlides, trs. *New Letters* 51, No. 4 (Summer 1985), p. 13.

7.368 _____ "Odysseus Elytis on His Poetry—From an Interview with Ivar Ivask". Ivar and Astrid Ivask, trs. from the French. *Books Abroad* 49, No. 4 (Autumn 1975), pp. 631-645 {7.391}. Also in *Odysseus Elytis: Analogies of Light* (Ivar Ivask, ed. Norman, Okla.: University of Oklahoma Press, 1981), pp. 7-15 {7.389}.

7.369 _____ "Odyssey". John Chioles and Edmund Keeley, trs. *Translation* 14 (Spring 1985), pp. 10-14 {3.34}.

7.370 _____ "From *Open Book:* Equivalences Chez Picasso". Joyce Miller, tr. from the French. *The Charioteer* 24 and 25 (1982/1983), pp. 97-100 {7.392}.

7.371 _____ "Poems". Edmund Keeley and Philip Sherrard, trs. *The Malahat Review* 57 (Jan. 1981), pp. 141-147.

7.372 _____ "Poems by Odysseus Elytis". Kimon Friar, tr. *Boundary 2,* Vol. 1, No. 2 (Winter 1973), pp. 401-418 {3.5}.

7.373 _____ "Poems by Odysseus Elytis". Kimon Friar, tr. *The Charioteer* 1, No. 2 (Autumn 1960), pp. 69-83.

7.374 _____ "Seagull". Alan L. Boegehold, tr. *Brown Classical Journal* 4 (1987), p. 7.

7.375 _____ "Selections from the Poetry of Odysseus Elytes". Edmund Keeley, tr. *The Antioch Review* 17, No. 3 (Fall 1957), pp. 291-296.

7.376 _____ "A Short Anthology of Translations from Elytis's Works". *Books Abroad* 49, No. 4 (Autumn 1975), pp. 646-659 {7.391}.
   Four Poems from *Stepchildren* (1974) ["Small Analogon for Nikos Hadjikyriakos-Ghika"; "Mozart: Romance"; "Event in August"; "The Leaf Diviner"] [Kimon Friar, tr.]; "Picasso's Equivalences" (essay) [Ivar and Astrid Ivask, trs. from the French]; Selections from the *Open Book* [Theofanis G. Stavrou, tr.]; from the *Book of Signs* (aphorisms) [Kimon Friar, tr.].

7.377 _____ "Six and a Single Remorses for the Sky". Stuart Montgomery, tr. *Agenda* 7, No. 1 (Winter 1969), pp. 69-77 {3.1}.

7.378 _____ "Sleep of the Valiant"; "Seven Days for Eternity". Kimon Friar, tr. *Mundus Artium* 4, No. 1 (Winter 1970), pp. 12-13 {4.82}.

7.379 _____ "Spring". George Económou, tr. *The Charioteer* 14 (1972), p. 11.

7.380 _____ "Three Poems". Kimon Friar, tr. *Accent* 10, No. 4 (Autumn 1950), pp. 219-222.
"The Body of Summer"; "The Age of Blue Memory"; "Marina of the Rocks".

7.381 _____ "Three Poems". Kimon Friar, tr. *Books Abroad* 45, No. 2 (Spring 1971), pp. 230-231.
"Shape of Boeotia"; "Laconic"; "Psalm II".

7.382 _____ "Three Poems". Martin McKinsey, tr. *Ploughshares* 11, No. 4 (June 1986), pp. 16-19 {3.25}.

7.383 _____ "Two Poems". Edmund Keeley, tr. *Western Humanities Review* 14, No. 1 (Winter 1960), pp. 38-39.
"The Autopsy"; "Beauty and the Illiterate".

7.384 *_____ "Two Poems". Edmund Keeley and Philip Sherrard, trs. *Imprint* 3 (1980), pp. 7-9.
"The Autopsy"; "The Mad Pomegranate Tree".

7.385 _____ "Two Poems". Nanos Valaoritis, tr. *The Literary Review* 16, No. 3 (Spring 1973), pp. 354-356 {3.15}.
"Ode VII"; "Ode X".

7.386 _____ "Two Poems". Nanos Valaoritis, tr. *New Writing and Daylight* 6 (1945), pp. 65-67.
"The Age of Blue Memory"; "Helen".

7.387 _____ "Two Poems". Nanos Valaoritis, tr. *Orpheus* 1 (1948), pp. 56-58.
"Body of Summer"; "Sadness of the Aegean".

c.

7.388 Carson, Jeffrey. *49 σχόλια στήν ποίηση τοῦ 'Οδυσσέα 'Ελύτη / 49 Scholia on the Poems of Odysseus Elytis*. Ἀπόδοση: Στρατῆς Πασχάλης. Athens: Ypsilon, 1983. 139 p.

7.389 Ivask, Ivar, ed. *Odysseus Elytis: Analogies of Light*. Critical Studies on the Nobel Prize Winner. Norman, Okla.: University of Oklahoma Press, 1981. 116 p.
Includes: Preface; Ivar Ivask, "Analogies of Light: The Greek Poet Odysseus Elytis" (pp. 3-6); "Odysseus Elytis on His Poetry—From an Interview with Ivar Ivask" [Ivar and Astrid Ivask, trs. from the French] (pp. 7-15). A short anthology of translations from Elytis's works: "Four poems from *Stepchildren* (1974)" [Kimon Friar, tr.] (pp. 21-23); "Picasso's Equivalences" [Ivar and Astrid Ivask, trs. from the French] (pp. 24-26); "Selections from the *Open Book*" [Theofanis G. Stavrou, tr.] (pp. 27-33); "from the *Book of Signs*" [Kimon Friar, tr.] (pp. 34-35). Critical perspectives: Lawrence Durrell, "The Poetry of Elytis" (p. 43); Andonis Decavalles, "Eros: His Power, Forms and Tranformations in the Poetry of Odysseus Elytis" (pp. 45-58); Hans Rudolph Hilty, "Odysseus Elytis: A Contemporary Greek Poet" (pp. 59-63); Christopher Robinson, "Elytis and French Poetry 1935-1945" (pp. 64-69); Robert Jouanny, "Aspects of Surrealism in the Works of Odysseus Elytis" (pp. 70-74); Vincenzo Rotolo, "The *Heroic and Elegiac Song for the Lost Second Lieutenant of the Albanian Campaign*: The Transition from the Early to the Later Elytis" (pp. 75-80); Edmund Keeley, "The Voices of Elytis's *The Axion Esti*" (pp. 81-86); M. Byron Raizis, "1979 Nobel Laureate Odysseus Elytis: From *The Axion Esti* to *Maria Nefeli*" (pp. 87-95);

Theofanis G. Stavrou, "Notes on the *Open Book* of Odysseus Elytis" (pp. 96-98); Kimon Friar, "The Imagery and Collages of Odysseus Elytis" (pp. 99-107). "Chronology" (pp. 109-111). "Selected Bibliography (1939-1979)" (pp. 113-116).

This volume is a reproduction of the Autumn 1975 special issue of *Books Abroad* {entry 7.391} with an updated chronology and an updated bibliography (both up to 1979). Also new herein is the study by M. Byron Raizis on pp. 87-95.

7.390 Savidis, George P. *Odysseus Elytis: Roes, Esa, Nus, & Miroltamity*. A lecture delivered for the Department of Comparative Literature of Harvard University on Tuesday 4th December 1979. Athens: Λέσχη, 1980. 38 p.

Special issues of periodicals

7.391 *Books Abroad* 49, No. 4 (Autumn 1975). The Greek Poet Odysseus Elytis and World Literature in Review.

"Analogies of Light: The Greek Poet Odysseus Elytis" (pp. 627-716) contains: Ivar Ivask, "Introduction" (pp. 627-630); "Odysseus Elytis on His Poetry—From an Interview with Ivar Ivask" [Ivar and Astrid Ivask, trs. from the French] (pp. 631-643); "A Short Anthology of Translations from Elytis's Works" (pp. 646-659): Four Poems from *Stepchildren* (1974) ["Small Analogon for Nikos Hadjikyriakos-Ghika"; "Mozart: Romance"; "Event in August"; "The Leaf Diviner"] [Kimon Friar, tr.]; "Picasso's Equivalences" (essay) [Ivar and Astrid Ivask, trs. from the French]; Selections from the *Open Book* [Theofanis G. Stavrou, tr.]; from the *Book of Signs* (aphorisms) [Kimon Friar, tr.]. "Critical Perspectives": Lawrence Durrell, "The Poetry of Elytis" (p. 660); Andonis Decavalles, "Eros: His Power, Forms and Transformations in the Poetry of Odysseus Elytis" (pp. 661-674); Hans Rudolf Hilty, "Odysseus Elytis: A Contemporary Greek Poet" (pp. 674-678); Christopher Robinson, "Elytis and French Poetry 1935-1945" (pp. 679-684); Robert Jouanny, "Aspects of Surrealism in the Works of Odysseus Elytis" (pp. 685-689); Vincenzo Rotolo, "The *Heroic and Elegiac Song for the Lost Second Lieutenant of the Albanian Campaign*: The Transition from the Early to the Later Elytis" (pp. 690-695); Edmund Keeley, "The Voices of Elytis's *The Axion Esti*" (pp. 695-700); Theophanis G. Stavrou, "Notes on the *Open Book* of Odysseus Elytis" (pp. 701-703); Kimon Friar, "The Imagery and Collages of Odysseus Elytis" (pp. 703-711). "Chronology" (pp. 712-713); "Selected Bibliography" (1939-1974) (pp. 714-716); "Odysseus Elytis in *Books Abroad* (1962-1975)" (p. 716). Photographs.

Address: Kraus Reprint Co., 16 East 46th St., New York, N.Y. 10017.

Also available in a slightly updated form: see *Odysseus Elytis: Analogies of Light* {7.389}.

7.392 *The Charioteer* 24 and 25 (1982/1983). Special issue: Odysseus Elytis.

Includes: Moralis, "Odysseus Elytis: Portrait 1980" (p. 5); Despoina Spanos Ikaris, "Editorial" (pp. 6-22); Andonis Decavalles, "*Maria Nefeli* and the Changeful Sameness of Elytis. Variations on a Theme: An essay" (pp. 23-57); Odysseus Elytis, "From *Maria Nefeli*" (poem) [Kimon Friar and Andonis Decavalles, trs.] (pp. 59-78); Edmund Keeley, "Elytis and the Greek Tradition: an essay" (pp. 79-96); Odysseus Elytis, "From *Open Book*: Equivalencies Chez Picasso" [Joyce Miller, tr. from the original French] (pp. 97-100); Dionysios Solomos, "*The Woman of Zakynthos*: Narrative Poem" [Marianthe Colakis, tr.] (pp. 118-136).

Address: Pella Publishing Co., Inc., 337 W. 36th St., New York, N.Y. 10018.

d.

7.393 Anghelidis-Spinedi, Nina. "Odysseus Elytis's *Calendar of an Invisible April*". *WLT* 60, No. 1 (Winter 1986), pp. 54-56.

7.394 Beaton, Roderick. "The Sign of the Dolphin". *TLS* (23 May 1980), p. 580.

Re. Odysseas Elytis, *Eklogi* (Selection), *1935-1977*.

7.395 Decavalles, Andonis. "Elytis's Sappho, His Distant Cousin". *WLT* 59, No. 2 (Spring 1985), pp. 226-229.

7.396 Decavalles, Andonis. "Eros: His Power, Forms and Transformations in the Poetry of Odysseus Elytis". *Books Abroad* 49, No. 4 (Autumn 1975), pp. 661-674 {7.391}.

7.397 Decavalles, Andonis. "*Maria Nefeli* and the Changeful Sameness of Elytis: Variations on a Theme". *The Charioteer* 24 and 25 (1982/1983), pp. 23-58 {7.392}.

7.398 Decavalles, Andonis. "Three Poets: Notes in Passing". *The Charioteer* 22 and 23 (1980/1981), pp. 16-22 {7.631}.
    Re. Kazantzakis, Seferis and Elytis.

7.399 Decavalles, Andonis. "Time versus Eternity: Odysseus Elytis in the 1980s". *WLT* 62, No. 1 (Winter 1988), pp. 22-32.

7.400 Deligiorgis, Stavros. "Elytis' Brecht and Hatzidakis' Pirandello. In *Modern Greek Writers* (Edmund Keeley and Peter Bien, eds. Princeton: Princeton University Press, 1972), pp. 191-215 {5.9}.

7.401 Durrell, Lawrence. "The Poetry of Elytis". *Books Abroad* 49, No. 4 (Autumn 1975), p. 660 {7.391}.

7.402 Friar, Kimon. "Between the Baltic and the Mediterranean: Five Modern Poets, Odysseus Elytis". *Books Abroad* 45, No. 2 (Spring 1971), pp. 225-230.

7.403 Friar, Kimon. "The Imagery and Collages of Odysseus Elytis". *Books Abroad* 49, No. 4 (Autumn 1975), pp. 703-711 {7.391}.

7.404 *Green, Peter. "The Poet's Greece". *The New York Review of Books* (26 June 1980), pp. 40-44.

7.405 Hilty, Hans Rudolf. "Odysseus Elytis: A Contemporary Greek Poet". *Books Abroad* 49, No. 4 (Autumn 1975), pp. 674-678 {7.391}.

7.406 Ivask, Ivar. "Greek Poet Odysseus Elytis, Nobel 1979, and Czech Novelist Josef Skvorecky, Neustadt 1980: Reflections on Two Laureates". *WLT* 54, No. 2 (Spring 1980), pp. 189-191.

7.407 Jouanny, Robert. "Aspects of Surrealism in the Works of Odysseus Elytis". *Books Abroad* 49, No. 4 (Autumn 1975), pp. 685-689 {7.391}.

7.408 Keeley, Edmund. "Elytis and the Greek Tradition". In his *Modern Greek Poetry: Voice and Myth* (Princeton, N.J.: Princeton University Press, 1983), pp. 130-148 {5.2}.
    Also in *The Charioteer* 24 and 25 (1982/1983), pp. 79-96 {7.392}.

7.409 *Keeley, Edmund. "The Genesis: A Commentary". *Poetry* 105, No. 1 (Oct. 1964), pp. 16-20 {3.27}.
    {Cf. entry 7.351}.

7.410 Keeley, Edmund. "Literary Tradition as Burden and Resource: The Case of Greece". In *New Literary Continents: Selected Papers of the Fifth NDEA Seminar on Foreign Area Studies Sponsored by the School of International Affairs, Columbia University, and Council on National Literatures* (Caroline D. Eckhardt et al. Whitestone, N.Y.: Griffon House Publications, 1984), pp. 56-65.

7.411 *Keeley, Edmund. "A Lyric, Poetic Greek Voice that Has a Special Texture". *The New York Times* (19 Oct. 1979), p. A12.

7.412 Keeley, Edmund. "The Vision of Odysseus Elytis". *University* 82 (Winter 1980), pp. 21-23. Also in *Princeton Alumni Weekly* (11 Feb. 1980), pp. 11-13.

7.413 Keeley, Edmund. "The Voices of Elytis's *The Axion Esti*". In his *Modern Greek Poetry: Voice and Myth* (Princeton, N.J.: Princeton University Press, 1983), pp. 119-129 {5.2}. First published in *Books Abroad* 49, No. 4 (Autumn 1975), pp. 695-700 {7.391}. Also in *Odysseus Elytis: Analogies of Light* (Ivar Ivask, ed. Norman, Okla.: University of Oklahoma Press, 1981), pp. 81-86 {7.389}.

7.414 *Keeley, Edmund and Philip Sherrard. "Introduction". In *Odysseus Elytis: Selected Poems*. Nobel Prize Library. Helvetica Press, 1984.

7.415 Levitt, Morton P. "Odysseus Elytis and Modern Greek Poetry". *The Charioteer* 19 (1977), pp. 8-17.
  Also includes some poems by Elytis from *Sun the First*.

7.416 Malkoff, Karl. "Eliot and Elytis: Poet of Time, Poet of Space". *Comparative Literature* 36, No. 3 (Summer 1984), pp. 238-257.

7.417 *Niketas, George. *The 'Axion Esti' of Odysseus Elytis*. Translated and annotated with an introduction. *Dissertation Abstracts International* 28 (1967), p. 2216A.

7.418 Noonan, J.D. "Notes on the *Axion Esti* of Elytis and the Vitality of Some Greek Compounds". *CML* 3, No. 1 (Fall 1982), pp. 25-31.

7.419 Papanikolaou, Mitsos, Andreas Karandonis, Samuel Baud-Bovy, Nanos Valaoritis, Kimon Friar, and Nikos Gatsos. "Odysseus Elytis: A Critical Mosaic". Andonis Decavalles and Beebe Spanos, trs. *The Charioteer* 1, No. 2 (Autumn 1960), pp. 63-68.

7.420 *Pastras, Philip James. "A Clear Field: The Idea of Improvisation in Modern Poetry". *Dissertation Abstracts International* 42, No. 4 (Oct. 1981), p. 1626A.
  Comparison with Walt Whitman, Giannes Ritsos, William Carlos Williams.

7.421 Petropoulos, Elias. *Elytis, Moralis, Tsarouchis*. 2nd edition. Athens: Pleias, 1974. 156 p.

7.422 Raizis, M. Byron. "1979 Nobel Laureate Odysseus Elytis: From *The Axion Esti* to *Maria Nefeli*". *WLT* 54, No. 2 (Spring 1980), pp. 196-201.

7.423 *Raizis, M. Byron. "The Poetry of the Aegean: Glimpses into the Work of Odysseus Elytis". *Greek World* (Mar.-Apr. 1976). Also in *Balkan Studies* 17 (1976), pp. 164-165.

7.424 Robinson, Christopher. "Elytis and French Poetry 1935-1945". *Books Abroad* 49, No. 4 (Autumn 1975), pp. 679-684 {7.391}.

7.425 Rotolo, Vincenzo. "The *Heroic and Elegiac Song for the Lost Second Lieutenant of the Albanian Campaign:* The Transition from the Early to the Later Elytis". *Books Abroad* 49, No. 4 (Autumn 1975), pp. 690-695 {7.391}.

7.426 Sherrard, Philip. "Odysseus Elytis and the Discovery of Greece". *JMGS* 1, No. 2 (Oct. 1983), pp. 271-293.

7.427 Spanias, Nikos. "'In Praise of Elytis, Yes, But ...'". *JHD* 3, No. 3 (Aug. 1976), pp. 33-35.

7.428 Stavrou, Theophanis G. "Notes on the *Open Book* of Odysseus Elytis". *Books Abroad* 49, No. 4 (Autumn 1975), pp. 701-703 {7.391}.

7.429 *Strouse, Jean. "Nobel Laureates. Literature: Poet of the Aegean". *Newsweek* (29 Oct. 1979), pp. 48 and 53.

Embirikos, Andreas (1901-1975)

a.

7.430 _____ *Amour, Amour: Writings or Personal Mythology*. Nanos Valaoritis, intro.; Nikos Stangos and Alan Ross, trs. Drawings by Minos Argyrakis. London: Alan Ross, 1966. 167 p.

7.431 _____ *Two Stories: Argo, or the Voyage of a Balloon* by Andreas Embiricos. Nikos Stangos and David Plante, trs. *We Killed Mangy-Dog* by Luis Bernado Honwana. Dorothy Guedes, tr. from the Portuguese. London Magazine Editions, 12. London: Alan Ross, 1967. 106 p.
  The Embiricos story is on pp. 5-50.

b.

7.432 _____ "Amour Amour". Nikos Stangos and Alan Ross, trs. *The London Magazine* 6, No. 5 (Aug. 1966), pp. 36-44.

7.433 _____ "A Blending of Seasons". C. Tachtsis and Kay Cicellis, trs. *The London Magazine,* N.S. 5, No. 7 (Oct. 1965), pp. 6-7.

7.434 _____ "Daybreak". Kimon Friar, tr. *The Atlantic Monthly* 195, No. 6 (June 1955), p. 146 {3.3}.

7.435 _____ "Echo"; "Suckling of Forage"; "Time"; "Dawn"; "Ram". Soteroula Syka-Karampetsou, tr. *The Coffeehouse* 10 (Summer 1981), pp. 2-6.

7.436 _____ "The Great Bleating or Pan-Jesus Christ"; "The Words". Kimon Friar, tr. *Contemporary Literature in Translation* 9 (Winter 1970), p. 19.

7.437 _____ "Instead of a Teacup"; "Light on a Whale". Yannis Goumas, tr. *Contemporary Literature in Translation* 14 (Fall/Winter 1972/73), p. 20.

7.438 _____ "The Silence"; "High Plateau of Passage". Kimon Friar, tr. *The Athenian* (Sept. 1975), p. 41.

7.439 _____ "Two Stories". Nikos Stangos, tr. *The London Magazine*, N.S. 5, No. 8 (Nov. 1965), pp. 37-44.
"The Texts"; "Samuel Harding".

d.
7.440 Friar, Kimon. "How a Poem Was Translated". *Translation Review* 11 (1983), pp. 15-19.
Re. "The Eyelids".

7.441 Karandonis, Andreas. "Two Greek Surrealist Poets. A. Embiricos-N. Engonopoulos". Theodore Sampson, tr. *Greek Letters* 1 (1982), pp. 255-271.

Engonopoulos, Nikos (1910-1985)

a.
7.442 *_____ *Bolivar*. James Laughlin, tr. New York: New Directions, 1960.

b.
7.443 _____ [11 Poems]. Kimon Friar, tr. *Contemporary Literature in Translation* 9 (Winter 1970), pp. 13-18.
"Ballad of the Tall Ladder" or "An Episode from the Life of the Painter Theofilos"; "Supplication"; "On Boeotian Lands"; "Memory"; "The Lover"; "The Kindness of Man"; "Orpheus Xenophobe"; "Reality"; "Nocturnal Maria"; "Ten and Four Themes for a Painting"; "Eleonora".

7.444 _____ "Four Poems". Martin McKinsey tr. *The Paris Review* 69 (1977), pp. 124-128.

7.445 _____ "Gardens in the Blazing Sun" [Nanos Valaoritis, tr.]; "News about the Death of the Spanish Poet Federico Garcia Lorca on the 19th of August 1936 in a Ditch of Caminonte La Fuente" [Thanasis Maskaleris, tr.]; "For Rent" [Kimon Friar, tr.]. *The Coffeehouse* 5 (Winter 1977), pp. 8-13.

7.446 _____ "News about the Death of the Spanish Poet Federico Garcia Lorca on the 19th of August 1936 in a Ditch of Caminonte La Fuente". Thanasis Maskaleris, tr. *The Coffeehouse* 6 (Summer 1978), p. 47.
    Reprinted from *The Coffeehouse* 5, p. 9, because the last stanza was missing.

7.447 _____ "Poetry 1948". Kimon Friar, tr. *The Atlantic Monthly* 195, No. 6 (June 1955), pp. 148 {3.3}.
    Andreas Embirikos, "Daybreak" [Kimon Friar, tr.] (p. 146); Henry Miller, "Coming into Poros Harbor" (pp. 147-148);

7.448 _____ "Vulture and Guard"; "Mercurius Bouas"; "Psychoanalysis of Phantoms". Yannis Goumas, tr. *Contemporary Literature in Translation* 14 (Fall/Winter 1972/73), pp. 18-19.

d.
7.449 Karandonis, Andreas. "Two Greek Surrealist Poets. A. Embiricos-N. Engonopoulos". Theodore Sampson, tr. *Greek Letters* 1 (1982), pp. 255-271.

7.450 Karavidas, Yannis. "Surrealism and the Early Poetry of Nikos Engonopoulos". *JMGS* 5, No. 1 (May 1987), pp. 33-46.

7.451 'Manna'. "An Interview with Nikos Engonopoulos". Lorne Shirinian, tr. from the French. *Manna* 5 (1974), pp. 34-38 {3.18}.

Evangelou, Anestis (b. 1937)
b.
7.452 _____ "The Heavy Knife"; "The Poet"; "The First Steps". M. Byron Raizis, tr. *The Coffeehouse* 3 (Fall 1976), pp. 23-26.

Fakinos, Aris (b. 1935)
a.
7.453 *_____ *The Marked Men*. Jacqueline Lapidus, tr. from the French; Helen Kazantzakis, foreword. New York: Liveright, 1971. 249 p.

Fokas, Angelos
b.
7.454 _____ "Two Poems". Amy Mims, tr. *Sumac* 1 (Winter 1969), pp. 63-66.
  "Rectilinear"; "Sound of Death".

Fokas, Nikos (b. 1927)
b.
7.455 _____ "The Poetry of Nicos Phocas: A Selection". Kimon Friar, tr. *JHD* 10, No. 3 (Fall 1983), pp. 35-57. Bilingual version.

7.456 _____ "The Three Knocks". Kimon Friar, tr. *The Literary Review* 16, No. 3 (Spring 1973), pp. 290-292 {3.15}.

Fostieris, Antonis (b. 1953)
a.
7.457 _____ *The Devil Sang in Tune* and *Dark Eros* (and *Poetry within Poetry*). Kimon Friar, tr. Contemporary Poets Series, 3. San Jose, Calif.: Realities Library, 1984. 30 p. + 30 p. (The two works are bound back to back in the same volume.)

Ganas, Michalis (b. 1944)
a.
7.458 *_____ *Concerning the Ascension*. John Stathatos, tr. Somerset: Bran's Head Books, 1984.

b.
7.459 _____ "Four Poems". John Stathatos, tr. *Translation* 14 (Spring 1985), pp. 73-75 {3.34}.
   "Concerning the Ascension"; "Persistence"; "Shipwreck"; "The Dog".

7.460 _____ "Poems". John Stathatos, tr. *Aegean Review* 2 (Spring/Summer 1987), pp. 66-68.

Gatsos, Nikos (b. 1915)
a.
7.461 *_____ *Amorgos*. Sally Purcell, tr. London: Other Poetry Editions, 1980. 8 p.

7.462 _____ *Amorgos*. Sally Purcell, tr. Athens: Zodion Press, 1986. 17 p.

b.
7.463 _____ "Amorgos". Edmund Keeley, tr. *Poetry* 105, No. 1 (Oct. 1964), pp. 24-32 {3.27}.

7.464 _____ "Death and the Knight (1513)". Edmund Keeley, tr. *The Colorado Quarterly* 8, No. 4 (Spring 1960), pp. 321-322 {4.78}.

7.465 *_____ "In the Courtyard of the Afflicted". Agnes Sotiracopoulou, tr. *Poetry* (Madras) 9, No. 2 (1968), p. 18 {3.29}.

7.466 _____ "In the Griever's Courtyard". Edmund Keeley, tr. *The Beloit Poetry Journal* 7, No. 3 (Spring 1957), p. 16.
   Part of anthology "Four Greek Poets" {4.73}.

7.467 _____ "Song of the Old Days". Peter Levi, tr. *Agenda* 7, No. 1 (Winter 1969), pp. 58-59 {3.1}.

7.468 _____ "They Say the Mountain Fell". Edmund Keeley, and Philip Sherrard, trs. *The Western Humanities Review* 22, No. 2 (Winter 1958), pp. 95-96.

d.

7.469 Keeley, Edmund. "*Amorgos:* A Commentary". *Poetry* 105, No. 1 (Oct. 1964), pp. 33-35 {3.27}.

7.470 *Lardas, Konstantinos Nick. "*Amorgos:* Studies of a Poem by Nikos Gatsos". *Dissertation Abstracts International* 28 (1967), p. 234A.

Georgakas, Dan (b. 1938)
b.

7.471 _____ "The Coup". *The Coffeehouse* 1 (Fall 1975), pp. 8-12.
   No translator mentioned.

Germanacos, N.C. (b. 1940)
b.

7.472 _____ "Two Poems". *Omphalos* 1, No. 3 (Winter 1973), pp. 54-55.
   "The Second Burial Mound at Marathon"; "Bell-Tongues". No translator is mentioned.

Giannopoulos, Alkiviadis (1896-1981)
b.

7.473 _____ "The Buddha's Tooth". Theodore Sampson, tr. In *Modern Greek Short Stories*. Vol. 2 (Kyr. Delopoulos ed. Athens: Kathimerini Publications, 1981), pp. 127-135 {4.13}.

7.474 _____ "The Burden of the Whole World". Liza Constantinides, tr. *The Charioteer* 9 (1967), pp. 71-78.

Gogou, Katerina (b. 1947)
b.

7.475 _____ "Five Poems". Jack Hirschman, tr. *The Coffeehouse* 10 (Summer 1981), pp. 40-45.
   "7" [bilingual version]; "14"; "Misty"; "19".

7.476 _____ "Katerina Gogou". Jack Hirschman, tr. *Third Rail* 5 (1982), pp. 68-74.

d.

7.477 Robbins, Doren. "The Furious Outcry of Katerina Gogou". *Third Rail* 5 (1982), pp. 65-67.

Gonatas, E.C. (b. 1924)

a.
7.478 *_____ *Some Prose Works*. J.C. Stathatos, tr. Montréal: Anthelion Press, 1968. 20 p.

Goudelis, Giannis (b. 1921)

a.
7.479 *_____ *Nero the Sensitive: A Play*. Taki Votoras, tr.; Athens: Difros, 1977. 86 p.

b.
7.480 *_____ "Borinage". Agnes Sotiracopoulou, tr. *Poetry* (Madras), Vol. 9, No. 2 (1968), pp. 17-18.

Goulimi, Alki

a.
7.481 *_____ *The Mystery of the Golden Lily*. Peter Megann, tr.; David Smee, illustr. Leicester: Brockhampton Press, 1971. 152 p.

b.
7.482 *_____ "Spyridoula's Gift" (from *The Two Anchors and Other Stories*). In *The Children Everywhere* (Childcraft Annual Supplement for 1970. Chicago: Field Enterprises Educational Corporation, 1970), pp. 246-253.
 In the chapter on Greece.

Goumas, Giannis (b. 1940)

a.
7.483 _____ *Athenians Go to Work*. Knotting, Bedfordshire: The Sceptre Press, 1978. 41 p.
 No translator mentioned.

7.484 _____ *Signing on and Other Poems 1974-1977*. Knotting, Bedfordshire: The Sceptre Press, 1977. 48 p.
 No translator mentioned.

b.
7.485 _____ "If I am Elected, When I am Elected..." [a poem]. *The Malahat Review* 61 (Feb. 1982), pp. 14-15.

Haviaras, Stratis (b. 1935)

a.
7.486 _____ *The Heroic Age*. New York: Simon and Schuster, 1984. 352 p. Also: [Great Britain]: Methuen, 1985; A King Penguin. Harmondsworth, Middlesex, England: Penguin Books, 1986. 352 p.
 Originally written in English. Translated into Greek as Τά Ἡρωικά Χρόνια by Nestoras Chounos. Athens: Ἐκδόσεις Bell, 1985. 398 p.

7.487 _____ *When the Tree Sings.* Drawings by Fred Marcellino. New York: Simon and Schuster, 1979. 219 p.
  Subsequently published in Greek as Ὅταν τραγουδοῦσαν τά δέντρα. Athens: Hermes, 1980. 259 p.

b.
7.488 _____ "Advertisement (Or, Sr. Calvino's Shaving Brush)". *Ploughshares* 11, No. 4 [June 1986], pp. 11-14 {3.25}.

7.489 _____ "First Exile". *Aegean Review* 3 (Fall/Winter 1987), pp. 27-29.
  Excerpt from *The House of Sleep*, a novel-in-progress. Original is English.

7.490 _____ "Tree"; "Graveyard Shift"; "Break"; "Gray on Gray". *The Coffeehouse* 4 (Summer 1977), pp. 10-13.

d.
7.491 Georgakas, Dan. "An Interview with Stratis Haviaras". *JHD* 8, No. 4 (Winter 1981), pp. 73-82.

Iatridi, Julia (b. 1914)
b.
7.492 _____ "The Corporal's Goodbye". Costas Taktsis, tr. *Greek Letters* 4 (1986-1989), pp. 179-183.

Ioannou, Giorgos (1927-1985)
b.
7.493 _____ "The Bed". M. Byron Raizis, tr. *The Literary Review* 16, No. 3 (Spring 1973), pp. 303-308 {3.15}.

7.494 _____ "The Butchers". Thomas Doulis, tr. *The Coffeehouse* 1 (Fall 1975), pp. 30-33.

7.495 _____ "Chickens" [a story]. Theodore Sampson, tr. *The Athenian* (Feb. 1975), pp. 23-24.

7.496 _____ "The Dogs of Seikh-Sou" (a story). Calliope Doxiadis, tr. *Boundary 2*, Vol. 1, No. 2 (Winter 1973), pp. 349-355 {3.5}.

7.497 _____ "The Fleas". Thomas Doulis, tr. *The Charioteer* 19 (1977), pp. 83-85.

7.498 _____ "Lazarina". Thomas Doulis, tr. *The Charioteer* 19 (1977), pp. 86-87.

7.499 _____ "Life and Deeds of Alexis Zorbas: A Novel of Lived Experience". Elli Marmara and George Thaniel, trs. *The Amaranth* 3 (1982), pp. 5-11.

7.500 _____ "Οὐκ ἠπίστατο φεύγειν...". Peter Mackridge and P.R. Dreyer, trs. *Omphalos* 1, No. 2 (Summer 1972), pp. 19-28.

7.501 _____ "Ten Short Stories" [from *Out of Self-Respect* and *The Sole Inheritance*]. Rick M. Newton, tr. *The Charioteer* 28 (1986), pp. 102-142.

7.502 _____ "Thessaly Once Was a Sea". K. Mitsakis, tr. *Greek Letters* 3 (1984-1985), pp. 81-84.

7.503 _____ "Three Short Pieces in Prose". Theodore Sampson, tr. *Greek Letters* 1 (1982), pp. 282-286.
   "Foul Birds"; "The Heads"; "Do What You Will".

7.504 _____ "'Voungari'". Roderick Beaton, tr. *Shenandoah* 27, No. 1 (Fall 1975), pp. 104-117 {3.32}.

d.
7.505 Doulis, Thomas. "About George Ioannou". *The Charioteer* 19 (1977), p. 82.

7.506 Germanacos, N.C. "An Interview with Three Contemporary Greek Prose Writers (May 1972): Stratis Tsirkas, Thanassis Valtinos, George Ioannou". *Boundary 2*, Vol. 1, No. 2 (Winter 1973), pp. 266-313 {3.5}.

Isaïa, Nana (b. 1934)

b.
7.507 _____ "Black and White Faces"; "The God". Thanasis Maskaleris, tr. *The Coffeehouse* 1 (Fall 1975), pp. 34-37.

7.508 _____ "Poem: Excursion to the Sky". *Omphalos* 1, No. 3 (Winter 1973), pp. 16-21. Bilingual version.

Kachtitsis, Nikos (1926-1970)

b.
7.509 _____ "A Letter". Minas Savvas, tr. *The Coffeehouse* 5 (Winter 1977), pp. 18-20.

d.
7.510 Thaniel, George. "The Prefaces of Nikos Kachtitsis". *Études Helléniques* 2, No. 1 (Spring 1984), pp. 63-68.

Kakavelakis, Dimitris (b. 1927)

a.
7.511 *_____ *Massa Confusa or A Vision for America*. Athan Anagnostopoulos, tr. Contemporary Poetry. Brookline, Mass.: Hellenic College Press, 1982. 50 p.

b.
7.512 _____ "Breast Onion"; "Massa Confusa"; "The Apple and the Panic"; "Breakfast of Detonations"; "Mechanized Boss". Philip J. Ramp, tr. *The Coffeehouse* 6 (Summer 1978), pp. 38-42.

Kakoulidis, Giannis (b. 1946)

b.
7.513 _____ "Thinvoiced"; "The Proceeding of Deliverance". Dino Siotis and D. Constantaras, trs. *The Coffeehouse* 3 (Fall 1976), pp. 53-56.

Kalamaras, Vasso (b. 1932)

a.
7.514 *_____ *Bitterness*. Six short stories. Reg Durack and the author, trs. Perth, Western Australia: Artlook, 1983. 150 p.

7.515 *_____ *Landscape and Soul*. Greek-Australian Poems. June Kingdom and the author, trs.; Leonidas Kalamaras, sculptures. Claremont: Claremont Print, 1980. 90 p.

7.516 _____ *Other Earth*. Four Greek-Australian Stories. Reg Durack and the author, trs.; Ian Wroth, drawings. Fremantle, Western Australia: Fremantle Arts Centre Press, 1977. 116 p. Bilingual edition.

7.517 *_____ *Twenty Two Poems*. Reg Durack and the author, trs. Daglish, Western Australia, 1977. 56 p.

d.
7.518 Castan, Con. "Vasso Kalamaras: A Tale of Two Countries". *Meanjin* 44, No. 1 (Mar. 1985), pp. 87-92.

Kalvos, Andreas (1792-1869)

d.
7.519 Bouvier, Bertrand. "Calvos in Geneva". In *Modern Greek Writers* (Edmund Keeley and Peter Bien, eds. Princeton, N.J.: Princeton University Press, 1972), pp. 67-91 {5.9}.

7.520 Constantinides, Elizabeth. "Language and Meaning in Kalvos' Ode to Parga". *JMH* 1 (Apr. 1984), pp. 1-14.

7.521 Rexine, John E. "From Lincolnshire to Zakynthos; Two Greek Poets in England: Andreas Kalvos and George Seferis". *JHD* 7, No. 2 (Summer 1980), pp. 51-64.

7.522 Sherrard, Philip. "Andreas Kalvos and the Eighteenth-Century Ethos". *BMGS* 1 (1975), pp. 175-206. Also in his *The Wound of Greece* (London: Rex Collings Ltd. with Athens: Anglo-Hellenic, 1978), pp. 17-50 {5.7}.

7.523 Topping, Eva Catafygiotu. "Thalassa, Thalassa: An Essay on Kalvos". *Neo-Hellenika* 2 (1975), pp. 259-279.

7.524 Tsatsos, Constantinos. "Andreas Calvos: Poet of Ideas". *Greek Letters* 1 (1982), pp. 135-174.

Kambanellis, Iakovos (b. 1922)

b.

7.525 _____ "*Courtyard of Miracles,* a play in four acts". I.T. Murdoch, tr. *Thespis* 2-3 (May 1965), pp. 127-151.

7.526 _____ *He and his Pants.* George Valamvanos and Kenneth MacKinnon, trs. *The Charioteer* 26 (1984), pp. 9-15 {4.18}.

7.527 _____ *The Woman and the Wrong Man.* George Valamvanos and Kenneth MacKinnon, trs. *The Charioteer* 26 (1984), pp. 17-35 {4.18}.

Kambouroglou, Christos

d.

7.528 _____ "Simply". Kostas Myrsiades, tr. *JHD* 4, No. 1 (Mar. 1977), p. 62.

Kanellopoulos, Panagiotis (1902-1986)

a.

7.529 _____ *Ascent to Faith: Essays on Death, Suffering and Faith.* Mary P. Gianos, tr. and intro. An Exposition-University Book. New York: Exposition Press, 1966. 101 p.

Revision and expansion of three chapters of the author's *Christianity and Our Times* (1953), published in Greece.

Karapanou, Margarita (b. 1946)

a.

7.530 _____ *Kassandra and the Wolf.* A Novel. N.C. Germanacos, tr. New York and London: Harcourt, Brace, Jovanovich, 1976. 115 p.

b.

7.531 _____ "Four Stories". N.C. Germanacos, tr. *Antaeus* 16 (Winter 1975), pp. 72-78.

"My Friend France"; "Alberto"; "The Marbles"; "The Word".

7.532 _____ "Hour of the Wolf". N.C. Germanacos, tr. *Antaeus* 13/14 (Spring/Summer 1974), pp. 162-175.

7.533 _____ "from *Kassandra and the Wolf*". N.C. Germanacos, tr. *Shenandoah* 27, No. 1 (Fall 1975), pp. 6-19 {3.32}.

Karatza, Maria G.

a.

7.534 _____ *Mirror of the Past: Sketches from King Otho's Greece*. Athens: Mavridis, 1979. 263 p.

Karelli, Zoi (b. 1901)

b.

7.535 *_____ "As Beautiful Naked Women". Agnes Sotiracopoulou, tr. *Poetry* (Madras) 9, No. 2 (1968), pp. 5-6 {3.29}.

7.536 _____ "Poet". Kimon Friar, tr. *The Literary Review* 16, No. 3 (Spring 1973), pp. 388-389 {3.15}.

7.537 _____ "Two Poems". David Posner, tr. *The Charioteer* 14 (1972), pp. 16-17.
 "Aspects of the Moon"; "Elegies for the Moon".

Karkavitsas, Andreas (1865-1922)

a.

7.538 _____ *The Beggar*. A Novel. William F. Wyatt, Jr, tr. With an Appendix on Andreas Karkavitsas and Nineteenth Century Greek Literature (pp. 157-187) by P.D. Mastrodemetres. New Rochelle, N.Y.: Caratzas Brothers, Publishers, 1982. 191 p.

b.

7.539 _____ "The Black Coral". Theodore Sampson, tr. In *Modern Greek Short Stories*. Vol. 1 (Kyr. Delopoulos, ed. Athens: Kathimerini Publications, 1980), pp. 183-195 {4.12}.

7.540 _____ "Évythos". A Short Story. Solon Tsiaperas and Theony Condos, trs. *The Charioteer* 14 (1972), pp. 88-92.

7.541 _____ "Scenes from Greek Life: Chrysanthos. From the Greek of Andreas Karkavitsas". E.M. Edmonds, tr. *The Eastern and Western Review* 2, No. 3 (Aug. 1892), pp. 235-240.

7.542 _____ "The Sea". Christina Pappas and staff, trs. *The Charioteer* 4 (1962), pp. 123-137 {4.17}.

7.543 _____ "Sea". In *Modern Greek Stories* (Demetra Vaka and Aristides Phoutrides, trs. New York: Duffield and Company, 1920), pp. 21-53 {4.16}.

7.544 _____ "The Yousouri". Fotine Nicholas, tr. *The Charioteer* 4 (1962), pp. 138-145 {4.17}.

d.
7.545 Wyatt, William. "Andreas Karkavitsas's *The Beggar* and *The Archaeologist*". *MGSY* 1 (1985), pp. 115-130.

Karoussou, Despo
a.
7.546 *_____ Ἀντίλαλοι τῆς Ἀβύσσου: Ποιήματα. *Echoes of the Abyss: Poems*. Philip Ramp, tr. Athens, 1985.

Karouzos, Nikos (b. 1926)
b.
7.547 _____ "Lindos". Maria Kotzamanidou and N.C. Germanacos, trs. *Translation* 14 (Spring 1985), pp. 98-102 {3.34}.

7.548 _____ "Poems by Nikos Karouzos". Philip Ramp and Katerina Angelaki-Rooke, trs. *Boundary 2*, Vol. 1, No. 2 (Winter 1973), pp. 433-438 {3.5}.

7.549 _____ "Terrifying Joy". Kimon Friar, tr. *The Literary Review* 16, No. 3 (Spring 1973), p. 289 {3.15}.

Karyotakis, K.G. (1896-1928)
b.
7.550 _____ "Four Poems". Kostas Myrsiades, tr. *The Charioteer* 14 (1972), pp. 20-25.
"Ideal Suicides"; "Repulsion"; "Preveza"; "Mihalios". With a biographical note.

d.
7.551 Hadas, Rachel. "Enjoying the Funeral: Constantine Caryotakis". *Grand Street* 3, No. 1 (Autumn 1983), pp. 153-160.

7.552 Hadas, Rachel. "Spleen à la Grecque: Karyotakis and Baudelaire". *JMGS* 3, No. 1 (May 1985), pp. 21-27.

7.553 Hokwerda, Hero. "Karyotakis and Katharevousa". *BMGS* 6 (1980), pp. 109-130.

Kasdagli, Lina (b. 1921)
b.
7.554 _____ "Traffic Lights". Edmund and Mary Keeley, trs. In *Eighteen Texts* (Willis Barnstone, ed. Cambridge, Mass.: Harvard University Press, 1972), pp. 167-168 {4.1}.
*Also in *A Book of Women Poets from Antiquity to Now* (Aliki Barnstone and Willis Barnstone, eds. New York: Schocken Books, 1980), pp. 52-55 {4.22}.

Kasdaglis, Nikos (b. 1928)

b.

7.555 _____ "Athos". N.C. Germanakos, tr. In *Eighteen Texts* (Willis Barnstone, ed. Cambridge, Mass.: Harvard University Press, 1972), pp. 135-151 {4.1}.

7.556 _____ "Blessed Are the Merciful: For They Shall Obtain Mercy" [a story]. N.C. Germanacos, tr. *Boundary 2*, Vol. 1, No. 2 (Winter 1973), pp. 470-505 {3.5}.
   With a note to the English translation by the author.

7.557 _____ "Shave Heads" [excerpts]. Thomas Doulis, tr. *The Coffeehouse* 6 (Summer 1978), pp. 12-16.

7.558 _____ *Shaved Heads*. Novel. Thomas Doulis, tr. *The Charioteer* 21 (1979), pp. 38-107.

7.559 _____ "The Sponge-Diver". Roderick Beaton, tr. *Shenandoah* 27, No. 1 (Fall 1975), pp. 125-142 {3.32}.

d.

7.560 Doulis, Thomas. "Nikos Kasdaglis and the Regimented State". *The Charioteer* 21 (1979), pp. 35-37.

Katsanis, Vangelis

b.

7.561 _____ *"The Successors"* [a play]. George Valamvanos and Kenneth MacKinnon, trs. *JHD* 6, No. 4 (Winter 1979), pp. 31-83.
   Ὅταν οἱ Ἀτρεῖδες...

Katsaros, Michalis (b. 1920)

b.

7.562 _____ "In the Dead Forest" [Thanasis Maskaleris, tr.]; "My Testament" [Stratis Haviaras, tr.]. *The Coffeehouse* 2 (Spring 1976), pp. 12-15.

7.563 _____ "Three Poems". John Stathatos, tr. *Translation* 14 (Spring 1985), pp. 71-72 {3.34}.
   "In Contrast"; "I Shall Expect You"; "The Deserted Street".

Katselli, Rina (b. 1938)

a.

7.564 _____ *Blue Whale*. Mary Ioannides, tr. Nicosia, Cyprus: Kyrenia Municipality Edition, 1983. 81 p.

7.565 _____ *Refugee in my Homeland: Cyprus 1974*. David Bailey, tr. Lucy MacLaurin, ed. Nicosia, Cyprus: Printed for the Kyrenia Flower Show, 1979. 66 p.

Katsimbalis, George C. (1899-1978)

c.

7.566 Miller, Henry. *The Colossus of Maroussi*. [New York]: New Directions, 1941. 244 p. Reprinted as a paperback in 1958. London: Heinemann, 1960. 248 p.

d.

7.567 *Levesque, Robert. "Katsimbalis". Philip Sherrard, tr. from the French. In *G.C. Katsimbalis*. Athens, 1955. 20 p.
   The volume contains articles by M. Politis, Robert Levesque and Costas Proussis, all in English.

7.568 Politis, M.J. "In Understanding of Greece: The Colossus of Maroussi". Reprinted from *The New York Times Book Review* (29 Mar. 1942), p. 24. *Also a separatum. 7 p.
   Re. Henry Miller's *The Colossus of Maroussi* {7.566}.

7.569 Proussis, Costas. "George C. Katsimbalis". *Athene* 13, No. 1 (Spring 1952), p. 34.

Kavvadias, Nikos (1910-1975)

a.

7.570 _____ *The Collected Poems of Nikos Kavadias*. Gail Holst Warhaft, tr. Amsterdam: Adolf M. Hakkert, 1987. 256 p. Bilingual edition.

b.

7.571 *_____ "Excerpts from *The Watch* by Nikos Kavadias". Alec Kitroeff, tr. *JHD* 7, Nos. 3-4 (Fall-Winter 1980), pp. 99-123.

7.572 _____ "Marabou". Kimon Friar, tr. *The Athenian* (Mar. 1975), p. 35.

7.573 _____ "Seven Poems". Gail Holst Warhaft, tr. *Translation* 12 (Spring 1984), pp. 127-135.

7.574 _____ "Vardia" (from 'The Sixth Watch'). Thanasis Maskaleris, tr. *The Coffeehouse* 6 (Summer 1978), pp. 48-49.

Kazantzakis, Nikos (1883-1957)

a.

7.575 _____ *Alexander the Great. A Novel*. Theodora Vasils, tr. Virgil Burnett, illustr. Athens, Ohio and London: Ohio University Press, 1982. 222 p.

7.576 _____ *Buddha*. Kimon Friar and Athena Dallas-Damis, trs.; Michael Tobias, pref.; Peter Bien, intro. San Diego, [Calif.]: Avant Books, 1983. 172 p.

7.577 _____ *Christ Recrucified*. See *The Greek Passion*.

7.578 *_____ *Christopher Columbus*. A play. Athena Gianakas-Dallas, tr. Kentfield, Calif.: Allen Press, 1972. 79 p. Limited ed.: 140 copies.

7.579 _____ *England.* A Travel Journal. Amy Mims, tr. New York: Simon and Schuster, 1965. 284 p. Also Oxford: Bruno Cassirer, 1971.

7.580 _____ *The Fratricides.* A Novel. Athena Gianakas-Dallas, tr. New York: Simon and Schuster, 1964. 254 p. Also Oxford: Bruno Cassirer, 1967. London: Faber and Faber, 1974. 254 p.

7.581 _____ *Freedom or Death.* A Novel. Jonathan Griffin, tr.; A. den Doolaard, pref. New York: Simon and Schuster, 1956. 433 p. Published in England as *Freedom and Death.* Oxford: Bruno Cassirer; London: Faber and Faber, 1956. 472 p. Also London: Faber and Faber, 1966. 472 p.

7.582 _____ *God's Pauper, St. Francis of Assisi.* See *Saint Francis.*

7.583 _____ *The Greek Passion.* A Novel. Jonathan Griffin, tr. New York: Simon and Schuster, 1954. 432 p. Second printing, 1959. Also New York: Ballantine Books, 1965. 511 p. Published in England as *Christ Recrucified.* A Novel. Jonathan Griffin, tr. *Oxford: Bruno Cassirer; London: Faber and Faber, 1954. 470 p. 2nd edition, Oxford: Bruno Cassirer, 1960. 470 p. Also London: Faber and Faber, 1962. 470 p. Reprinted 1963, 1966.

7.584 _____ *Japan, China.* A Journal of Two Voyages to the Far East: 1935 and 1957. George C. Pappageotes, tr.; Helen Kazantzakis, epilogue. New York: Simon and Schuster, 1963. 382 p. Published in England as *Travels in China & Japan.* Oxford: Bruno Cassirer, 1964. 382 p.; London: Faber and Faber, 1964.

7.585 _____ *Journey to the Morea.* F.A. Reed, tr.; Alexander Artemakis, photographs. New York: Simon and Schuster, 1965. 190 p. Published in England as *Travels in Greece, Journey to the Morea.* Oxford: Bruno Cassirer, 1966.

7.586 _____ *Journeying: Travels in Italy, Egypt, Sinai, Jerusalem and Cyprus.* Themi Vasils and Theodora Vasils, trs. Boston and Toronto: Little, Brown and Company, 1975. 201 p. Also San Francisco: Creative Arts Books Co. (Donald S. Ellis, Publisher), 1984.

7.587 _____ *The Last Temptation of Christ.* A Novel. Peter A. Bien, tr. New York: Simon and Schuster, 1960. 506 p. Also New York: Bantam Books, 1961. 496 p. Published in England as *The Last Temptation.* With a Translator's Note on the Author and his Language (pp. 509-518). Oxford: Bruno Cassirer, 1961. 519 p.; *Oxford: Bruno Cassirer; London: Faber and Faber, 1975.

7.588 _____ *The Odyssey: A Modern Sequel.* Kimon Friar, tr. into English verse, intro., synopsis, and notes. Illustrations by Ghika. New York: Simon and Schuster, 1958. 824 p. Also London: Secker and Warburg, 1958.

7.589 _____ *Report to Greco*. Peter A. Bien, tr. New York: Simon and Schuster, 1965. 512 p. Also, Oxford: Bruno Cassirer; London: Faber and Faber, 1965. New York: Bantam Books, 1971. 495 p. London: Faber and Faber, 1973.

7.590 _____ *The Rock Garden*. A Novel. Richard Howard, tr. from the French. Passages from *The Saviors of God*. Kimon Friar, tr. New York: Simon and Schuster, 1963. 251 p.

7.591 _____ *Saint Francis*. A Novel. Peter A. Bien, tr. New York: Simon and Schuster, 1962. 379 p. Published in England as *God's Pauper: Saint Francis of Assisi*. A Novel. Oxford: Bruno Cassirer, 1962. 390 p. Oxford: Cassirer; London: Faber and Faber, 1975.

7.592 _____ *The Saviors of God: Spiritual Exercises*. Kimon Friar, tr. and intro. New York: Simon and Schuster, 1960. 143 p.

7.593 _____ *Serpent and Lily*. A Novella, with a Manifesto, "The Sickness of the Age". Theodora Vasils, tr., intro. and notes. Berkeley; Los Angeles; London: University of California Press, 1980. 117 p.

7.594 _____ *Spain*. Amy Mims, tr. New York: Simon and Schuster, 1963. 254 p.

7.595 _____ *The Suffering God: Selected Letters to Galatea and to Papastephanou*. Philip Ramp and Katerina Anghelaki Rooke, trs.; Katerina Anghelaki Rooke, intro. New Rochelle, N.Y.: Caratzas Brothers, 1979. 114 p.

7.596 _____ *Symposium*. Theodora Vasils and Themi Vasils, trs. New York: Thomas Y. Crowell Company, 1974. 97 p. Also New York: Minerva Press, 1974. 97 p.

7.597 _____ *Three Plays*. Athena Gianakas-Dallas, tr. New York: Simon and Schuster, 1969. 285 p.
    Χριστόφορος Κολόμβος, Μέλισσα, Κοῦρος.

7.598 _____ *Toda Raba*. Amy Mims, tr. from the French. New York: Simon and Schuster, 1964. 220 p.

7.599 _____ *Travels in China & Japan*. See *Japan, China*.

7.600 _____ *Travels in Greece, Journey to the Morea*. See *Journey to the Morea*.

7.601 _____ *Two Plays: Sodom and Gomorrah* and *Comedy: A Tragedy in One Act*. Kimon Friar, tr. and intro., with an introduction to *Comedy: A Tragedy in One Act* by Karl Kerényi [Peter Bien, tr.] (pp. 93-97). A Nostos Book. [Minneapolis, Minn.]: North Central Publishing Co., 1982. 120 p.
  Reprinted from *The Literary Review* 18, No. 4 (Summer 1975) and 19, No. 2 (Winter 1976) {7.635, 7.636}. The translation of the plays has been slightly revised for this edition.

7.602 _____ *Zorba the Greek*. Carl Wildman, tr.; Ian Scott-Kilvert, intro. London: John Lehmann, 1952. Also New York: Simon and Schuster, 1953. 319 p. Oxford: Bruno Cassirer, 1959. London and Boston: Faber and Faber, 1961. 311 p. New York: Ballantine Books, 1964. 346 p.
   Only the first edition has the introduction.

b.
7.603 _____ "The Angels of Cyprus". Amy Mims, tr. In *Cyprus '74: Aphrodite's Other Face* (Emmanuel C. Casdaglis, ed. Athens: National Bank of Greece, 1976), pp. 148-150 {4.87}.

7.604 _____ "*Burn Me to Ashes:* An Excerpt". Kimon Friar, tr. *Greek Heritage* 1, No. 2 (Spring 1964), pp. 61-64 {7.1441}.

7.605 _____ "Christ" (poetry). Kimon Friar, tr. *JHD* 10, No. 4 (Winter 1983), pp. 47-51 {7.634}.

7.606 _____ "*Comedy: A Tragedy in One Act*". Kimon Friar, tr. *The Literary Review* 18, No. 4 (Summer 1975), pp. 417-454 {7.635}.

7.607 _____ "Death, the Ant". From *The Odyssey: A Modern Sequel,* Book XV, 829-63. Kimon Friar, tr. *The Charioteer* 1, No. 1 (Summer 1960), p. 39.

7.608 _____ "Drama and Contemporary Man", an essay. Peter Bien, tr. *The Literary Review* 19, No. 2 (Winter 1976), pp. 115-121 {7.636}.

7.609 _____ "Father Yanaros" [from his novel: *The Fratricides*]. Theodore Sampson, tr. In *Modern Greek Short Stories*. Vol. 1 (Kyr. Delopoulos, ed. Athens: Kathimerini Publications, 1980), pp. 307-333 {4.12}.

7.610 _____ "He Wants to be Free—Kill Him!". A Story. Athena G. Dallas, tr. *Greek Heritage* 1, No. 1 (Winter 1963), pp. 78-82.

7.611 _____ "The Homeric G.B.S.". *The Shaw Review* 18, No. 3 (Sept. 1975), pp. 91-92.
   The tribute to G.B.S. was originally a broadcast in Greek, aired in 1946 on Shaw's ninetieth birthday by the B.B.C. Overseas Service. This text is a translation of the broadcast.

7.612 _____ "Hymn (Allegorical)". M. Byron Raizis, tr. *Spirit* 37, No. 3 (Fall 1970), pp. 16-17.

7.613 _____ "from *Odysseus*, A Drama". M. Byron Raizis, tr. *The Literary Review* 16, No. 3 (Spring 1973), p. 352 {3.15}.

7.614 _____ [Selections from] "The Odyssey". Kimon Friar, prose tr. *Wake* 12 (1953), pp. 58-65 {4.86}.

7.615 _____ "The Return of Odysseus". Kimon Friar, tr. *The Atlantic Monthly* 195, No. 6 (June 1955), pp. 110-112 {3.3}.

7.616 _____ "from *The Saviors of God: Spiritual Exercises*". Kimon Friar, tr. *The Charioteer* 1, No. 1 (Summer 1960), pp. 40-51.
   Reprinted in *The Charioteer* 22 and 23 (1980/1981), pp. 116-129 {7.631}.

7.617 _____ "*Sodom and Gomorrah*, a play". Kimon Friar, tr. *The Literary Review* 19, No. 2 (Winter 1976), pp. 122-256 {7.636}.

7.618 _____ "A Tiny Anthology of Kazantzakis' Remarks on the Drama, 1910-1957". Compiled by Peter Bien. *The Literary Review* 18, No. 4 (Summer 1975), pp. 455-459 {7.635}.

7.619 _____ "Two Dreams". Peter Mackridge, tr. *Omphalos* 1, No. 2 (Summer 1972), p. 3.

c.

7.620 Anapliotes, John. *The Real Zorbas and Nikos Kazantzakis*. Lewis A. Richards, tr. Chicago: Argonaut, 1967. 163 p. Also Amsterdam: Adolf M. Hakkert, 1978. 163 p.

7.621 Bien, Peter. *Kazantzakis and the Linguistic Revolution in Greek Literature*. Princeton Essays in European and Comparative Literature, 6. Princeton, N.J.: Princeton University Press, 1972. 291 p.

7.622 Bien, Peter. *Nikos Kazantzakis*. Columbia Essays on Modern Writers, 62. New York: Columbia University Press, 1972. 48 p.
   Republished as "Kazantzakis" in his *Three Generations of Greek Writers* (Athens: Efstathiadis Group, 1983), pp. 55-94 {5.1}.

7.623 *Bien, Peter A. *Tempted by Happiness: Kazantzakis' Post-Christian Christ*. Pendle Hill Pamphlet, 253. Wallingford, Pa.: Pendle Hill Publications, 1984. 21 p.
   A theological interpretation of *The Last Temptation*.

7.624 Friar, Kimon. *The Spiritual Odyssey of Nikos Kazantzakis: A Talk*. Edited with an introduction by Theofanis G. Stavrou. With a Supplement: "A Few Letters from Nikos Kazantzakis to Kimon Friar" (pp. 33-38) and "Critical Comment on *The Odyssey: A Modern Sequel*" (pp. 39-51). Minneapolis, Minn.: North Central Publishing Co., 1979. 51 p.

7.625 Kazantzakis, Helen. *Nikos Kazantzakis: A Biography Based on his Letters*. Amy Mims, tr. from the French. New York: Simon and Schuster, 1968. 589 p. Also Oxford: Bruno Cassirer, 1968. Reprinted 1975 and 1979. *Berkeley, [Calif.]: Creative Arts Book Co., 1983.

7.626 Lea, James F. *Kazantzakis: The Politics of Salvation*. Helen Kazantzakis, foreword. Alabama: University of Alabama Press, 1979. 207 p.

7.627 Levitt, Morton P. *The Cretan Glance: The World and Art of Nikos Kazantzakis.* Columbus, Ohio: Ohio State University Press, 1980. 187 p.

7.628 *McDonough, B.T. *Nietzsche and Kazantzakis.* Washington D.C.: University Press of America, 1978. 91 p.

7.629 *Prevelakis, Pandelis. *Nikos Kazantzakis and His Odyssey: A Study of the Poet and the Poem.* Philip Sherrard, tr.; Kimon Friar, pref. New York: Simon and Schuster, 1961. 192 p.

7.630 *Wessman, Robert Leo. *Beyond the Abyss: The Concept of God in the Writings of Nikos Kazantzakis and Its Application to Preaching.* Doctor of Ministry Thesis, School of Theology at Claremont, 1978.
    Available from University Microfilms, Ann Arbor, No. 7815349.

Special issues of periodicals
7.631 *The Charioteer* 22 and 23 (1980/1981). Special Issue: Kazantzakis.
    Contains: Takis Kalmouchos, "Nikos Kazantzakis: Sketch" (p. 5); Despoina Spanos Ikaris, "Editorial" (pp. 6-15); Andonis Decavalles "Three Poets: Notes in Passing" [Nikos Kazantzakis, Seferis and Elytis] (pp. 16-22); Pandelis Prevelakis, "Kazantzakis: Life and Works" [Peter Bien, tr.] (pp. 23-65); George Manousakis, "The Characters in *Freedom or Death*: A Kazantzakean Anthropological Scale" [Marios Philippides, tr.] (pp. 66-102); Kostas Mihailidis, "Ascent, the Interpretive Figure of Being in Nikos Kazantzakis" [Edward Phinney, tr.] (pp. 103-115); Nikos Kazantzakis, from *The Saviors of God: Spiritual Exercises* [Kimon Friar, tr.] (pp. 116-129); Elizabeth Constantinides, "The Folk Ballads of Crete: A Survey" (pp. 130-140); Deborah Tannen, "Elli Alexiou: An Informal Portrait" (pp. 141-146); Elli Alexiou, "They were All to be Pitied", a short story [Deborah Tannen, tr.] (pp. 147-151).
    Address: Pella Publishing Co., Inc., 337 W. 36th St., New York, N.Y. 10018.

7.632 *Folia Neohellenica* 5 (1983). Festschrift Nikos Kasantzakis 1883-1983.
    Includes: Eleni N. Kazantzaki, "Nikos Kazantzakis and the Freedom" (pp. 50-64); Patroclos Stavrou, "Nikos Kazantzakis and Cyprus" (pp. 65-70); Andreas K. Poulakidas, "The Operatic Aspects of Kazantzakis' 'Broken Souls'" (pp. 157-173).
    Address: Prof. Dr. Isidora Rosenthal-Kamarinea, Am Dornbusch 28, Bochum, West Germany.

7.633 *Journal of Modern Literature* 2, No. 2 (Second Issue 1971-1972). Nikos Kazantzakis Special Number.
    Contains: Morton P. Levitt, "The Cretan Glance: The World and Art of Nikos Kazantzakis" (pp. 163-188); Adèle Bloch, "The Dual Masks of Nikos Kazantzakis" (pp. 189-198); M. Byron Raizis, "Kazantzakis' Ur-Odysseus, Homer, and Gerhart Hauptmann" (pp. 199-214); Kimon Friar, "A Unique Collaboration: Translating *The Odyssey: A Modern Sequel*" (pp. 215-244); Peter Bien, "Kazantzakis' Nietzschianism" (pp. 245-266); Andreas K. Poulakidas, "Kazantzakis and Bergson: Metaphysic Aestheticians" (pp. 267-283); Minas Savvas, "Kazantzakis and Marxism" (pp. 284-292); Joseph C. Flay, "The Erotic Stoicism of Nikos Kazantzakis" (pp. 293-302); A. Owen Aldridge, "The Modern Spirit: Kazantzakis and Some of His Contemporaries" (pp. 303-313); Donald Falconio, "Critics of Kazantzakis: Selected Checklist of Writings in English" (pp. 314-326.).
    Address: Journal of Modern Literature, Temple University, Room 1241, Humanities Building, Philadelphia, Pa. 19122.

7.634 *Journal of the Hellenic Diaspora* 10, No. 4 (Winter 1983). Special issue: Nikos Kazantzakis. Kimon Friar, guest editor. New York: Pella Publishing Co.
    Includes: Pandelis Prevelakis, "Kazantzakis-Sikelianos: The Chronicle of a Friendship" (pp. 5-20); Peter Bien, "*Christopher Columbus*: Kazantzakis's Final Play" (pp. 21-30); Roger Green, "A Frank Says

'Thank You' to Nikos Kazantzakis" (pp. 31-39); Morton P. Levitt, "Homer, Joyce, Kazantzakis: Modernism and the Epic Tradition" (pp. 41-45); Nikos Kazantzakis, "Christ" (poetry) [Kimon Friar, tr.] (pp. 47-51); John P. Anton, "Kazantzakis and the Tradition of the Tragic" (pp. 53-67); Katerina Angelaki-Rooke, "Kazantzakis's *Buddha:* Phantasmagoria and Struggle" (pp. 69-72); J. Moatti-Fine, "Odysseus-Moses, or God's Presence in History" [Jocelyn M. Phelps, tr. from the French] (pp. 73-78); John G. Papaioannou, "Kazantzakis and Music" (pp. 79-83); Peter Colaclides, "Homer and Kazantzakis: Masters of Wordcraft" (pp. 85-98).
   Address: Pella Publishing Co., Inc., 337 W. 36th St., New York, N.Y. 10018.

7.635 *The Literary Review* 18, No. 4 (Summer 1975). *Kazantzakis.*
   Includes: Kimon Friar, "Nikos Kazantzakis in the United States" (pp. 381-397); Peter Bien, "Kazantzakis' *The Masterbuilder,* with an additional note on *Capodhistrias"* (pp. 398-411); Karl Kerenyi, "Prologue to *Comedy: A Tragedy in One Act"* [Peter Bien, tr.] (pp. 412-416); Nikos Kazantzakis, "*Comedy: A Tragedy in One Act"* [Kimon Friar, tr.] (pp. 417-454); [Nikos Kazantzakis], "A Tiny Anthology of Kazantzakis' Remarks on the Drama, 1910-1957" [compiled by Peter Bien] (pp. 455-459).
   Address: The Literary Review, Fairleigh Dickinson University, Madison, N.J. 07940.

7.636 *The Literary Review* 19, No. 2 (Winter 1976). *Kazantzakis.*
   Contains: Nikos Kazantzakis, "Drama and Contemporary Man", an essay [Peter Bien, tr.] (pp. 115-121); Nikos Kazantzakis, "*Sodom and Gomorrah,* a play" [Kimon Friar, tr.]. (pp. 122-256).
   Address: The Literary Review, Fairleigh Dickinson University, Madison, N.J. 07940.

7.637 Μαντατοφόρος 5 (Nov. 1974). Special issue: Kazantzakis Check List.
   Contains: Peter Bien, "Nikos Kazantzakis: A Check List of Primary and Secondary Works Supplementing the Katsimbalis Bibliography" (pp. 7-53).
   Address: *Mantatoforos,* Universiteit van Amsterdam, Byzantijns-Nieuwgrieks Seminarium, Nieuwe Doelenstraat 16, 1012 CP Amsterdam, Holland. Out of print in 1990. Not expected to be reissued.

d.

7.638 Aldridge, A. Owen. "The Modern Spirit: Kazantzakis and Some of His Contemporaries". *JML* 2, No. 2 (1971-1972), pp. 303-313 {7.633}.

7.639 Andriopoulos, Dimitri Z. "A Note on Kazantzakis' Platonic References". Κρητικά Χρονικά 23 (1971), pp. 231-238.

7.640 Anghelaki-Rooke, K. "Kazantzakis's *Buddha:* Phantasmagoria and Struggle". *JHD* 10, No. 4 (Winter 1983), pp. 69-72 {7.634}.

7.641 Anton, J.P. "Kazantzakis and the Tradition of the Tragic". *JHD* 10, No. 4 (Winter 1983), pp. 53-67 {7.634}.

7.642 *Antonakes, Michael. "Christ as Hero and Kazantzakis." *English Review of Salem State College* 1, No. 1 (1973), pp. 55-65.

7.643 *Ant(h)onakes, Michael A. "Christ, Freedom and Kazantzakis". *Dissertation Abstracts International* 27 (1966), p. 1331A.

7.644 Banks, Arthur C. and Finley C. Campbell. "The Vision of the Negro in the Kazantzakian Universe". *Phylon* 25, No. 3 (Fall 1964), pp. 254-262.

7.645 Beaton, Roderick. "Myth and Text: Readings in the Modern Greek Novel". *BMGS* 9 (1984/85), pp. 29-53 {6.217}.
   Re. *Christ Recrucified* on pp. 45-48.

7.646 Bessa, Maria. "Nikos Kazantzakis and *The Saviors of God*". *Michigan Academician* 5, No. 4 (Spring 1973), pp. 441-447.

7.647 Beukas, Anthony S. "Structure and Meaning in the Plays of Kazantzakis". *Dissertation Abstracts International* 35 (1975), p. 7436A.

7.648 Bien, Peter. "*Buddha*, Kazantzakis' Most Ambitious and Most Neglected Play". *Comparative Drama* 11, No. 3 (Fall 1977), pp. 252-272.

7.649 Bien, Peter. "*Christopher Columbus:* Kazantzakis's Final Play". *JHD* 10, No. 4 (Winter 1983), pp. 21-30 {7.634}.

7.650 Bien, Peter. "The Demoticism of Kazantzakis". In *Modern Greek Writers* (Edmund Keeley and Peter Bien, eds. Princeton, N.J.: Princeton University Press, 1972), pp. 145-169 {5.9}.

7.651 Bien, Peter. "*Fratricides:* Interesting Document, Defective Work of Art". *JMGS* 2, No. 1 (May 1984), pp. 1-21.

7.652 Bien, Peter. "O Kapetán Mihális, an Epic (Romance?) Manqué". *JMGS* 5, No. 2 (Oct. 1987), pp. 153-173.

7.653 Bien, Peter. "Kazantzakis". In his *Three Generations of Greek Writers. Introductions to Cavafy, Kazantzakis, Ritsos*. Athens: Efstathiadis Group, 1983, pp. 55-94 {5.1}. Reprinted from {7.622}.

7.654 Bien, Peter. "Kazantzakis' *Kapodistrias*, a (Rejected) Offering to Divided Greece, 1944-1946". *BMGS* 3 (1977), pp. 141-173.

7.655 Bien, Peter. "Kazantzakis' Nietzschianism". *JML* 2, No. 2 (1971-1972), pp. 245-266 {7.633}.

7.656 Bien, Peter. "Kazantzakis' *The Masterbuilder* with an Additional Note on *Capodhistrias*". *The Literary Review* 18, No. 4 (Summer 1975), pp. 398-411 {7.635}.

7.657 Bien, Peter. "The Mellowed Nationalism of Kazantzakis' *Zorba the Greek*". *Review of National Literatures* 5, No. 2 (Fall 1974), pp. 113-136 {3.30}.

7.658 Bien, Peter. "Nikos Kazantzakis". In *The Politics of Twentieth-Century Novelists* (George A. Panichas, ed. New York: Hawthorn Books, 1971), pp. 137-159.

7.659 Bien, Peter. "*Zorba the Greek,* Nietzsche, and the Perennial Greek Predicament". *The Antioch Review* 25, No. 1 (Spring 1965), pp. 147-163.

7.660 Bloch, Adèle. "The Dual Masks of Nikos Kazantzakis". *JML* 2, No. 2 (1971-1972), pp. 189-198 {7.633}.

7.661 Bloch, Adèle. "Kazantsakis and the Image of Christ". *Literature and Psychology* 15, No. 1 (Winter 1965), pp. 2-11.

7.662 Caro, F.A. de. "Kazantzakis, Folklore, and the Politics of Reaction". *Journal of Popular Culture* 8, No. 4 (1974), pp. 792-804.

7.663 Chilson, Richard W. "The Christ of Nikos Kazantzakis". *Thought* 47, No. 184 (Spring 1972), pp. 69-89.

7.664 Colaclides, Peter. "Homer and Kazantzakis: Masters of Wordcraft". *JHD* 10, No. 4 (Winter 1983), pp. 85-98 {7.634}.

7.665 Constantinides, Elizabeth. "Kazantzakis and the Cretan Hero". *JMH* 2 (Oct. 1985), pp. 31-41.

7.666 Coxe, Louis O. "A Romantic Failure". Comment. *Poetry* 95, No. 3 (Dec. 1959), pp. 179-181.

7.667 Decavalles, Andonis C. "Kazantzakis and Prevelakis: Two Cretan Voices". *JMH* 2 (Oct. 1985), pp. 43-63.

7.668 Decavalles, Andonis. "Three Poets: Notes in Passing". *The Charioteer* 22 and 23 (1980/1981), pp. 16-22 {7.631}.
   Re. Kazantzakis, Seferis, and Elytis.

7.669 Decavalles, Andonis. "The Torrent and the Sun". Comment. *Poetry* 95, No. 3 (Dec. 1959), pp. 175-178.

7.670 Demetrius, James K. "Nikos Kazantzakis in Spain". In *Studies in Honor of M.J. Benardete* (Izaak A. Langnas and Barton Sholod, eds. Essays in Hispanic and Sephardic Culture. New York: Las Americas Publishing Company, 1965), pp. 215-225.

7.671 Dillistone, F.W. "The Shepherd is Smitten". In his *The Novelist and the Passion Story* (New York: Sheed and Ward, 1960; also St. James's Place, London: Collins, 1960), pp. 69-91.
   Re. *The Greek Passion.*

7.672 Dombrowski, Daniel A. "Eating and Spiritual Exercises: Food for Thought from Saint Ignatius and Nikos Kazantzakis". *Christianity and Literature* 32, No. 4 (Summer 1983), pp. 25-32.

7.673 Doulis, Tom. "Kazantzakis and the Meaning of Suffering". *Northwest Review* 6, No. 1 (Winter 1963), pp. 33-57.

7.674 Elsman, Kenneth R. and John V. Knapp. "Life-Span Development in Kazantzakis's *Zorba the Greek*". *International Fiction Review* 11, No. 1 (Winter 1984), pp. 37-44.

7.675 Falconio, Donald. "Critics of Kazantzakis: Selected Checklist of Writings in English". *JML* 2, No. 2 (1971-1972), pp. 314-326 {7.633}.

7.676 Flay, Joseph C. "The Erotic Stoicism of Nikos Kazantzakis". *JML* 2, No. 2 (1971-1972), pp. 293-302 {7.633}.

7.677 Friar, Kimon. "George Seferis: The Greek Poet Who Won the Nobel Prize". *Saturday Review* 46 (30 Nov.1963), pp. 16-20.
   Compares Seferis and Kazantzakis.

7.678 Friar, Kimon. "Nikos Kazantzakis in the United States". *The Literary Review* 18, No. 4 (Summer 1975) pp. 381-397 {7.635}.

7.679 Friar, Kimon. "A Unique Collaboration: Translating *The Odyssey: A Modern Sequel*". *JML* 2, No. 2 (1971-1972), pp. 215-244 {7.633}.

7.680 Friar, Kimon et al. "Nikos Kazantzakis". In *Twentieth Century Literary Criticism 2: Excerpts from Criticism of the Works of Novelists, Poets, Playwrights, Short Story Writers, and Other Creative Writers, 1900-1960* (Detroit, Mich.: Gale Research Co., 1979), pp. 311-324.
   Excerpts from essays of Kimon Friar, Pandelis Prevelakis, W.B. Stanford, Peter Bien, Colin Wilson, Morton P. Levitt, Adèle Bloch, Joseph C. Flay, Andreas K. Poulakidas.

7.681 Georgopoulos, N. "Kazantzakis, Bergson, Lenin and the 'Russian Experiment'". *JHD* 5, No. 4 (Winter 1979), pp. 33-44.

7.682 Georgopoulos, N. "Marxism and Kazantzakis". *BMGS* 3 (1977), pp. 175-200. Reprinted in *Varieties of Twentieth Century Socialism* (Jack Thomas, ed. Chicago, Ill.: Nelson Hall, 1977).

7.683 Green, Peter. "Odysseus Translated". *TLS* (15 May 1959), p. 288. Reprinted in his *Essays in Antiquity* (London: John Murray, 1960; New York: World Publishing Co., 1960).

7.684 Green, Roger. "A Frank Says 'Thank You' to Nikos Kazantzakis". *JHD* 10, No. 4 (Winter 1983), pp. 31-39 {7.634}.

7.685 Green, Roger. "Kazantzakis in Iraklion: 'A Worthy Pioneer'". *The Cornhill Magazine,* No. 1053 (Autumn 1967), pp. 189-216.

7.686 Gregory, Dorothy M.-T. "Kazantzakis and Sikelianos: Complementary Spirits". *JMH* 2 (Oct. 1985), pp. 65-73.

7.687 Hadgopoulos, Saralyn Poole. "Odysseus' Choice: A Comparison and Contrast of Works by Albert Camus and Nikos Kazantzakis". *Dissertation Abstracts International* 27 (July-Oct. 1966), p. 204A.

7.688 Hartocollis, Peter. "Mysticism and Violence: The Case of Nikos Kazantzakis". *The International Journal of Psycho-Analysis* 55, Part 2 (1974), pp. 205-210.
   Followed by P. Sakellaropoulos, "A Discussion of the Paper by Peter Hartocollis on 'Mysticism and Violence': The Case of Nikos Kazantzakis", ibid. pp. 211-213.

7.689 Hatzantonis, Emmanuel. "Captain Sole: Don Quijote's After-Image in Kazantzakis' *Odyssey*". *Hispania* 46, No. 2 (May 1963), pp. 283-286.

7.690 Hatzantonis, Emmanuel. "Kazantzakis' Spiritual Itinerary through Spain". *Hispania* 49, No. 4 (Dec. 1966), pp. 787-792.

7.691 Hoffman, Frederick J. "The Friends of God: Dostoevsky and Kazantzakis". In his *The Imagination's New Beginning: Theology and Modern Literature* (University of Notre Dame Ward-Phillips Lectures in English Language and Literature, 1. Notre Dame & London: University of Notre Dame Press, 1967), pp. 49-72.

7.692 Holliday, Vivian L. "The Feminine Melody in Kazantzakis' *Odyssey*". *Neo-Hellenika* 3 (1978), pp. 56-67.

7.693 Ikaris, Despoina Spanos. "Editorial". *The Charioteer* 22 and 23 (1980/1981), pp. 6-15 {7.631}.

7.694 Ioannou, Yorghos. "Life and Deeds of Alexis Zorbas: A Novel of Lived Experience". Elli Marmara and George Thaniel, trs. *The Amaranth* 3 (1982), pp. 5-11.

7.695 Jusdanis, Gregory. "The Politics of Criticism: Deconstruction, Kazantzakis, 'Literature'". *BMGS* 9 (1984/85), pp. 161-186.

7.696 Karanikas, Alexander. "Kazantzakis and his Heroes". *Athene* 18, No. 1 (Spring 1957), pp. 4-9.

7.697 Karnezis, George T. "*Zorba the Greek*: The Artist and Experience". In *A Modern Miscellany* (Carnegie Series in English, No. 11. Pittsburgh, [Pa.]: Carnegie-Mellon University, 1970), pp. 43-52.

7.698 Kazantzaki, Eleni N. "Nikos Kazantzakis and the Freedom". *Folia Neohellenica* 5 (1983), pp. 50-64 {7.632}.

7.699 Kazantzakis, Helen. "Kazantzakis and Freedom". *Journal of the Hellenic American Society* 1, No. 3 (1974), pp. 1-12.

7.700 Kerényi, Karl. "Prologue to *Comedy: A Tragedy in One Act*". Peter Bien, tr. *The Literary Review* 18, No. 4 (Summer 1975), pp. 412-416 {7.635}.

7.701 Laourdas, Basil. "Ideas and Ideals in Contemporary Greek Literature". *Balkan Studies* 9, No. 1 (1968), pp. 155-166.
   On Angelos Sikelianos, Nikos Kazantzakis, and Pandelis Prevelakis.

7.702 Levitt, Morton P. "The Cretan Glance: The World and Art of Nikos Kazantzakis". *JML* 2, No. 2 (1971-1972), pp. 163-188 {7.633}.

7.703 Levitt, Morton P. "Homer, Joyce, Kazantzakis; Modernism and the Epic Tradition". *JHD* 10, No. 4 (Winter 1983), pp. 41-45 {7.634}.

7.704 Levitt, Morton P. "Kazantzakis' *Odyssey:* A Modern Rival to Homer". *JHD* 5, No. 2 (Summer 1978), pp. 19-45.

7.705 Levitt, Morton. "A Modern Byzantine Mosaic: *The Greek Passion* of Nikos Kazantzakis". *Neo-Hellenika* 3 (1978), pp. 7-36.

7.706 Levitt, Morton P. "The Modernist Kazantzakis and *The Last Temptation of Christ*". *Mosaic* 6, No. 2 (Winter 1973), pp. 103-124.

7.707 Littlewood, A.R. "The Apple in the Sexual Imagery of Kazantzakis: A Study in the Continuity of a Greek Tradition". *Neo-Hellenika* 3 (1978), pp. 37-55.

7.708 Manousakis, George. "The Characters in *Freedom or Death:* A Kazantzakean Anthropological Scale". Marios Philippides, tr. *The Charioteer* 22 and 23 (1980/1981), pp. 66-102 {7.631}.

7.709 McKeever, Clare. "Man's Response to a Functional World Echoed in *The Waste Land* and *Zorba the Greek*". *Humanitas* 6, No. 3 (Winter 1971), pp. 325-350. Republished in *Creative Formation of Life and World* (Adrian Van Kaam and Susan A. Muto, eds. Washington, D.C.: UP of America, 1982), pp. 177-202.

7.710 Merrill, Reed B. *"Zorba the Greek* and Nietzschean Nihilism". *Mosaic* 8, No. 2 (1975), pp. 99-113.

7.711 Mihailides, Kostas. "Ascent, the Interpretive Figure of Being in Nikos Kazantzakis". Edward Phinney, tr. *The Charioteer* 22 and 23 (1980/1981), pp. 103-115 {7.631}.

7.712 Moatti-Fine, J. "Odysseus-Moses, or God's Presence in History". Jocelyn M. Phelps, tr. from the French. *JHD* 10, No. 4 (Winter 1983), pp. 73-78 {7.634}.

7.713 *Notopoulos, James A. "Kazantzakis' Golden Extremes". *The Virginia Quarterly Review* 35 (1959), pp. 320-326.
   On Kazantzakis' *Odyssey* and the mythical method.

7.714 Papaioannou, John G. "Kazantzakis and Music". *JHD* 10, No. 4 (Winter 1983), pp. 79-83 {7.634}.

7.715 *Parker, Sandra A. "Kazantzakis in America: A Bibliography of Translations and Comment". *Bulletin of Bibliography* 25 (Sept.-Dec. 1968), pp. 166-170.

7.716 Poulakidas, Andreas K. "Dostoevsky, Kazantzakis' Unacknowledged Mentor". *Comparative Literature* 21, No. 4 (Fall 1969), pp. 307-318.

7.717 Poulakidas, Andreas K. "Kazantzakis and Bergson: Metaphysic Aestheticians". *JML* 2, No. 2 (1971-1972), pp. 267-283 {7.633}.

7.718 Poulakidas, Andreas K. "Kazantzakis as a Symbolist Poet". *Folia Neohellenica* 4 (1982), pp. 160-181.

7.719 Poulakidas, Andreas K. "Kazantzakis' Recurrent Victim: Woman". *Southern Humanities Review* 6, No. 2 (Spring 1972), pp. 177-189.

7.720 Poulakidas, Andreas K. "Kazantzakis' *Spiritual Exercises* and Buddhism". *Comparative Literature* 27, No. 3 (Summer 1975), pp. 208-217.

7.721 Poulakidas, Andreas K. "Kazantzakis' *Zorba the Greek* and Nietzsche's *Thus Spake Zarathustra*". *Philological Quarterly* 49, No. 2 (Apr. 1970), pp. 234-244.

7.722 Poulakidas, Andreas K. "Nikos Kazantzakis: 'Odysseus as a Symbol'". *Filologia Moderna* 9, No. 37 (Nov. 1969), pp. 3-22. Also Κρητικά Χρονικά 21 (1969), pp. 256-272.

7.723 Poulakidas, Andreas K. "Nikos Kazantzakis: Odysseus as Phenomenon". *Comparative Literature Studies* 6, No. 2 (June 1969), pp. 126-140.

7.724 Poulakidas, Andreas K. "The Novels of Kazantzakis and their Existential Sources". *Dissertation Abstracts International* 28 (1967), p. 2260A.

7.725 Poulakidas, Andreas K. "The Operatic Aspects of Kazantzakis' 'Broken Souls'". *Folia Neohellenica* 5 (1983), pp. 157-173 {7.632}.

7.726 Poulakidas, Andreas K. "Steinbeck, Kazantzakis, and Socialism". *Steinbeck Quarterly* 3, No. 3 (Summer 1970), pp. 62-72.

7.727 Presley, Del E. "Buddha and the Butterfly: Unifying Motifs in Kazantzakis' *Zorba*". *Notes on Contemporary Literature* 2, No. 1 (Jan. 1972), pp. 2-4.

7.728 Prevelakis, Pandelis. "Kazantzakis: Life and Works". Peter Bien, tr. *The Charioteer* 22 and 23 (1980/1981), pp. 23-65 {7.631}.

7.729 Prevelakis, Pandelis. "Kazantzakis-Sikelianos: The Chronicle of a Friendship". Kimon Friar, tr. *JHD* 10, No. 4 (Winter 1983), pp. 5-20 {7.634}.

7.730 Prevelakis, Pandelis. "from *Nikos Kazantzakis and his Odyssey*". Philip Sherrard, tr. *The Charioteer* 1, No. 1 (Summer 1960), pp. 10-36.

7.731 Raizis, M. Byron. "Kazantzakis' Ur-Odysseus, Homer, and Gerhart Hauptmann". *JML* 2, No. 2 (1971-1972), pp. 199-214 {7.633}.

7.732 Raizis, M. Byron. "Nikos Kazantzakis and Chaucer". *Comparative Literature Studies* 6, No. 2 (June 1969), pp. 141-147.

7.733 Raizis, M. Byron. "Symbolism and Meaning in Kazantzakis' *The Greek Passion*". *Ball State University Forum* 11, No. 3 (Summer 1970), pp. 57-66.

7.734 Rexine, John E. "Kazantzakis's 'Cretan Glance' and his 'Politics of Salvation'". *JHD* 9, No. 1 (Spring 1982), pp. 91-97.
   Re. Levitt and Lea books {7.626, 7.627}.

7.735 Richards, Lewis A. "Christianity in the Novels of Kazantzakis". *Western Humanities Review* 21, No. 1 (Winter 1967), pp. 49-55.

7.736 Richards, Lewis A. "Fact and Fiction in Nikos Kazantzakis' *Alexis Zorbas*". *Western Humanities Review* 18, No. 4 (Autumn 1964), pp. 353-359.

7.737 Savvas, Minas. "Kazantzakis and Marxism". *JML* 2, No. 2 (1971-1972), pp. 284-292 {7.633}.

7.738 Scouffas, George. "Kazantzakis: Odysseus and the 'Cage of Freedom'". *Accent* 19, No. 4 (Autumn 1959), pp. 234-246.

7.739 Stanford, W.B. "No Rest for Ulysses: From Homer to Kazantzakis". *Encounter* 13, No. 1 (July 1959), pp. 44-50.

7.740 Stanford, W.B. "The Re-integrated Hero". Is Chapter 15 in his *The Ulysses Theme: A Study in the Adaptability of a Traditional Hero* (Oxford: Basil Blackwell, 1954. Second edition, 1963. Also Ann Arbor, Mich.: University of Michigan Press, 1968), pp. 211-240.

7.741 Stavrou, C.N. "The Limits of the Possible: Nikos Kazantzakis's Arduous Odyssey". *Southwest Review* 57, No. 1 (Winter 1972), pp. 54-65.

7.742 Stavrou, C.N. "Mr. Bloom and Nikos' Odysseus". *The South Atlantic Quarterly* 62, No. 1 (Winter 1963), pp. 107-118.

7.743 Stavrou, C.N. "Some Notes on Nikos Kazantzakis". *The Colorado Quarterly* 12, No. 4 (Spring 1964), pp. 317-334.

7.744 Stavrou, Patroclos. "Nikos Kazantzakis and Cyprus". *Folia Neohellenica* 5 (1983), pp. 65-70 {7.632}.

7.745 Szabó, Kálmán. "Zorbas: A New Model of Unalienated Man". *Folia Neohellenica* 3 (1981), pp. 130-150.

7.746 Taylor, Timothy W. "Kazantzakis and the Cinema". *BMGS* 6 (1980), pp. 157-168.

7.747 Thaniel, George. "Odysseus and Death: A Study of Kazantzakis' *Odyssey*". *Neo-Hellenika* 3 (1978), pp. 68-80.

7.748 Theroux, Paul. "'You Orientals!': Kazantzakis' *England*". *Encounter* 39, No. 6 (Dec. 1972), pp. 71-74. Review Article.

7.749 Will, Frederic. "Kazantzakis' Making of God: A Study in Literature and Philosophy". *The Iowa Review* 3, No. 4 (Fall 1972), pp. 109-124.

7.750 Will, Frederic. "Kazantzakis' *Odyssey*". In *Hereditas: Seven Essays on the Modern Experience of the Classical* (Frederic Will, ed. Austin: University of Texas Press, 1964), pp. 55-73.

7.751 Wilson, Colin. "Kazantzakis". Appendix II in his *The Strength to Dream: Literature and the Imagination* (London: Victor Gollancz Ltd., 1962), pp. 203-211. Also *Boston, Mass.: Houghton Mifflin, 1962, pp. 239-249.

7.752 Wilson, Colin. "Nikos Kazantzakis". *Mediterranean Review* 1, No. 1 (Fall 1970), pp. 33-47.

7.753 Ziolkowski, Theodore. [Treats *The Greek Passion* and also *The Last Temptation.*] In his *Fictional Transfigurations of Jesus* (Princeton, N.J.: Princeton University Press, 1972), pp. 16-17, 124-140, 270-298.

Kechaïdis, Dimitris (b. 1933)

b.

7.754 _____ "Backgammon". George Valamvanos and Kenneth MacKinnon, trs. *The Charioteer* 26 (1984), pp. 89-121 {4.18}.

7.755 _____ "The Wedding Band" (A One-Act Play). John Chioles, tr. *Translation* 14 (Spring 1985), pp. 110-166 {3.34}.

Kindynis, Kostas (b. 1932)

a.

7.756 _____ *Poems: Reinvestigations* and *Descent from the Cross*. Kimon Friar, tr. and pref. A Nostos Book. [Minneapolis, Minn.]: North Central Publishing Company, 1980. 58 p.

Kolokotronis, Theodoros (1770-1843)

a.

7.757 _____ *Kolokotrones, the Klepht and the Warrior: Sixty Years of Peril and Daring: An Autobiography*. Mrs. Edmonds, tr. with intro. and notes. With a preface by Monsieur J. Gennadius, Greek envoy to the Court of St. James. London: T. Fisher Unwin, 1892. 317 p.

7.758 _____ *Memoirs from the Greek War of Independence, 1821-1833*. Tr. from the Greek text of G. Tertzetis. E.M. Edmonds, tr. with intro. and notes; John Gennadius, pref. New enlarged American edition with preface, bibliography and, for the first time, completely indexed by George J. Koutris. Chicago: Argonaut Publishers, 1969. 353 p.

Kondylakis, Ioannis (1861-1920)

b.

7.759 _____ "The Funeral Oration". Alice-Mary Maffry, tr. *The Charioteer* 4 (1962), pp. 117-123 {4.17}.

7.760 _____ "The Funeral Oration". Theodore Sampson, tr. In *Modern Greek Short Stories*. Vol. 1 (Kyr. Delopoulos, ed. Athens: Kathimerini Publications, 1980), pp. 171-181 {4.12}.

Konstantinidou, Loula D. (b. 1917)

a.

7.761 _____ *The Anthologized Poetry of Loula D. Constantinidou*. Maria P. Hogan, tr. Hicksville, N.Y.: Exposition Press, 1979. 31 p.

7.762 _____ *Hellenic Hours; or, It All Happened in Greece: Essays on Free Thought*. Maria Papazoglou Hogan, tr. and adapted. New York and Washington: Vantage Press, 1982. 53 p.

Kontoglou, Fotis (1895-1965)

b.

7.763 _____ "Captain Ikon-Painter": A Story. Fotine Nicholas, tr. *The Charioteer* 5 (1963), pp. 119-122.

7.764 _____ "Preface"; "Palamidi"; "Mystra". From *Journeys*. JoAnne Cacoullos and Katherine Hortis, trs. *The Charioteer* 5 (1963), pp. 86-103.

7.765 _____ "Stringaros". Theodore Sampson, tr. In *Modern Greek Short Stories*. Vol. 2 (Kyr. Delopoulos, ed. Athens: Kathimerini Publications, 1981), pp. 117-126 {4.13}.

d.
7.766 Panayotopoulos, I.M. "From Writers and Texts". Staff, tr. *The Charioteer* 5 (1963), pp. 80-85.
   Re. Photis Kontoglou.

Kontos, Giannis (b. 1943)

a.
7.767 _____ *The Bones: Selected Poems 1972-1982*. James Stone, tr. Cleveland, Ohio; New York: The Globe Press, 1985. 58 p.

7.768 *_____ *Danger in the Streets*. John Stathatos, tr. London: Oxus Press, 1979. 16 p.

7.769 _____ *Mercurial Time and Other Poems*. Yannis Goumas, tr. Knotting, Bedfordshire, England: The Sceptre Press, 1978. 43 p.

b.
7.770 _____ "Five Poems". Kostas Myrsiades, tr. *The Coffeehouse* 2 (Fall 1976), pp. 15-19.
   "The Chronometer"; "The New Year"; "Rain and the Present"; "Without Temporal Duration"; "The Essence of Matter".

7.771 _____ "Four Poems". Kostas Myrsiades, tr. *Panjandrum* 5 (1977), pp. 128-131 (pages not numbered).
   "The Essence of Matter"; "Without Temporal Duration"; "Monologue or my Hand in April"; "Words and Lock-Jaw".

7.772 _____ "In the Dialect of the Desert: Selected Poems of Yannis Kondos". James Stone, tr. and intro. *JHD* 9, No. 2 (Summer 1982), pp. 105-117. Bilingual version.

7.773 _____ "Reportage"; "Polish Periodicals". Kostas Myrsiades, tr. *Translation* 9 (Fall 1982), pp. 247-248.

7.774 *_____ "Seven Poems". Kostas Myrsiades, tr. *Grove* 5 (Winter 1979), pp. 3-9 {3.12}.

7.775 _____ "Three Poems". Kimon Friar and Kostas Myrsiades, trs. *Chelsea* 38 (1979), pp. 80-83.
   "Lightless"; "The Earth's Attraction"; "Secret Audience".

7.776 _____ "Three Poems". James Stone, tr. *Translation* 14 (Spring 1985), pp. 43-44 {3.34}.
   "23"; "45"; "65".

7.777 _____ "Two Poems". Edmund Keeley, tr. *Translation* 14 (Spring 1985), pp. 45-46 {3.34}.
"In the Half Dark"; "Photo Duplication".

Kontou, Nana P.

a.

7.778 _____ *Voices from Greece.* Poems. Anthula Zolder, tr.; supervised by Dr. Herbert Stern. [Greece]: Editions D.O., 1967. 63 p.

Korovesis, Periklis

a.

7.779 _____ *The Method: A Personal Account of the Tortures in Greece.* Les Nightingale and Catherine Patrakis, trs. London: Allison & Busby, 1970. 87 p.
Tr. from the French.

Korres, Manolis (b. 1922)

a.

7.780 *_____ *The "Happy Sunset" Rest Home.* A satire in three acts. Amy Mims, tr. Athens, n.d. 126 p.
Mimeographed. Not on the market. Available only at the Theatrical Museum in Athens.

7.781 *_____ *The Seedy Ward.* A satire in two parts and ten scenes. Amy Mims, tr. Athens, 1979. 150 p.
Mimeographed. Not on the market. Available only at the Theatrical Museum in Athens.

Kotzias, Alexandros (b. 1926)

b.

7.782 _____ "from *Brave Telemachus*".John Stathatos, tr. *Descant XVIII,* Vol. 8, No. 2 (1977), pp. 69-72 {3.8}.

7.783 _____ "Going Home". Sarah Kafatou, tr. In *Eighteen Texts* (Willis Barnstone, ed. Cambridge, Mass.: Harvard University Press, 1972), pp. 37-51 {4.1}.

c.

7.784 Romanos, Christos S. *Poetics of a Fictional Historian.* American University Studies, Series III, Comparative Literature, Vol. 7. New York: Peter Lang, 1985. 267 p.

d.

7.785 Romanos, Christos S. "Alexandros Kotzias: *Antipoiesis Archis* and the Poetics of an Antihistorian". *JHD* 9, No. 1 (Spring 1982), pp. 17-29.

7.786 Romanos, Christos S. "Alexandros Kotzias: *Brave Telemachos* and Expressionist Art". *JHD* 8, No. 3 (Fall 1981), pp. 77-92.

7.787 *Romanos, Christos S. "Poetics of a Fictional Historian: A Synchronic/Diachronic Approach with a Focus on Alexandros Kotzias in the Context of European Fiction". *Dissertation Abstracts International* 44, No. 7 (Jan. 1984), p. 2141A.

Koulis, Vasilis (b. 1928)

a.

7.788 *_____ *Selected Poems*. Nikos Spanias, tr. and pref. Athens: [V. Koulis], 1985. 45 p.

Koumantareas, Menis (b. 1931)

b.

7.789 _____ "The Bath", a story. Amy Mims, tr. *Greek Heritage* 1, No. 2 (Spring 1964), pp. 30-35 {7.1441}.

7.790 _____ "The Burnt Ones". Stavros Deligiorgis, tr. *The Literary Review* 16, No. 3 (Spring 1973), pp. 357-386 {3.15}.

7.791 _____ "Holy Sunday on the Rock". Stavros Deligiorgis, tr. In *Eighteen Texts* (Willis Barnstone, ed. Cambridge, Mass.: Harvard University Press, 1972), pp. 161-166 {4.1}.

7.792 _____ "In a Place Where the Sun is Mute". John Taylor, tr. *Aegean Review* 2 (Spring/Summer 1987), pp. 27-32.

Kountouri, Eleftheria

a.

7.793 *_____ *Futile Songs on the River-banks of the World*. Poems. Amy Mims, tr. Athens: I.G. Vasiliu, 1984. 61 p.

Kourtidis, Aristotelis (1858-1928)

a.

7.794 _____ *Stories from Fairyland by George Drosines and The Cup of Tears and Other Tales by Aristotle Kourtidos* (sic). Translated from the Greek by Mrs. Edmonds. The Children's Library, Vol. 3. London: T. Fisher Unwin, 1892. 153 p.

Koutsocheras, John (b. 1904)

a.

7.795 *_____ *The March of the Lilies*. A Poem. Philip Sherrard, tr. London and Colchester: Hutchinson, 1966. 50 p.

7.796 _____ *Men for the Rights of Man Rise*. A poetic manifesto. Antigone Kefala, tr. Sydney: Alfa Books, 1974. 80 p. Bilingual edition.

c.

7.797 *Cochrane, P.N. *John Coutsoheras Today: A Profile of the Greek Poet*. Sydney, 1976. 23 p.

Ladaki-Filippou, Niki (1937)

a.

7.798 *_____ *The Virgin of the Steps*. A Modern Poem. Nicosia, Cyprus, [1967]. 32 p.

Laïna, Maria (b. 1947)

b.

7.799 _____ "Indian"; "Triumphant"; "That Which Comes Before". Dino Siotis, tr. *The Coffeehouse* 3 (Fall 1976), pp. 62-64.

7.800 _____ "Landscapes". Yannis Goumas, tr. *Prism International* 23, No. 2 (Winter 1984), pp. 128-129.

7.801 _____ "Two Poems". Yannis Goumas, tr. *Prism International* 24, No. 1 (Fall 1985), pp. 60-61.
"Death in a Hospital"; "Unexpected".

Lidorikis, Alekos (1906-1988)

b.

7.802 _____ *The Uprooted,* a play in three acts. (Second title used by the translator: "California Here I Am".) Leslie Finer, tr. *Thespis* 2-3 (May 1965), pp. 101-125.

Lotris, Konstantinos (1912-1989)

a.

7.803 *_____ *The Thief of the Museums*. A Novel. Andreas Mavromatis, tr. Athens, 1978. 116 p.

Lymberaki, Margarita (b. 1919)

a.

7.804 _____ *The Other Alexander*. Willis and Halle Tzalopoulou Barnstone, trs. New York: The Noonday Press, 1959. 146 p.

Makris, Giorgos (1923-1968)

b.

7.805 _____ "Lifedeath"; "Desire that All Other Men Should Die". Nanos Valaoritis, tr. *The Coffeehouse* 9 (Winter 1979), pp. 48-50.

Makrygiannis, Ioannis (1797-1864)

a.

7.806 ____ *The Memoirs of General Makrygiannis, 1797-1864*. Harold A. Lidderdale, ed. and tr.; C.M. Woodhouse, intro. London: Oxford University Press, 1966. 234 p.

b.

7.807 ____ "General Makriyannis: Excerpts from his *Memoirs*". Rick M. Newton. *The Charioteer* 28 (1986), pp. 15-34.

7.808 ____ "The Siege of the Acropolis". C.M. Woodhouse, tr. *Greek Heritage* 1, No. 1 (Winter 1963), pp. 65-69.

d.

7.809 Holton, David. "Ethnic Identity and Patriotic Idealism in the Writings of General Makriyannis". *BMGS* 9 (1984/85), pp. 133-160.

7.810 Kazazis, J.N. "Constructing a Computer-assisted Complete Index to Makriyannis' Memoirs". Μαντατοφόρος 22 (Nov. 1983), pp. 27-33.

7.811 Pavlopoulos, Georgis. "The Cellar: Remembrance of Makriyannis" [a poem]. Peter Dreyer, tr. *Omphalos* 1, No. 1 (Mar. 1972), pp. 40-41. Bilingual version.

7.812 Proussis, Costas M. "The *Memoirs* of Makrygiannis". *Neo-Hellenika* 3 (1978), pp. 135-147.

7.813 Seferis, George. "Makrygiannis". In his *On the Greek Style: Selected Essays in Poetry and Hellenism* (Rex Warner and Th.D. Frangopoulos, trs. Athens: Denise Harvey & Company, 1982), pp. 23-65 {7.1342}.

7.814 Seferis, George. "Memory of Makriyannis". Athan Anagnostopoulos, tr. *The Charioteer* 28 (1986), pp. 9-10.
   Poem from the *Journals: Days C*, August 1939.

7.815 Sherrard, Philip. "General Makrygiannis: The Portrait of a Greek". In his *The Wound of Greece: Studies in Neo-Hellenism* (London: Rex Collings Ltd. with Athens: Anglo-Hellenic, 1978), pp. 51-71 {5.7}.

7.816 Woodhouse, C.M. "Two Greek Primitives". *Greek Heritage* 1, No. 1 (Winter 1963), pp. 55-63.

7.817 Xydias, Vassilis. "Notations: 'New' or 'Old': Orthodoxy in the Limelight". *JHD* 11, No. 2 (Summer 1984), pp. 69-72.

Mangakis, Georgios-Alexandros (b. 1922)

b.

7.818 ____ "My Greece": Essay. Rachel Hadas, tr. *The Charioteer* 19 (1977), pp. 65-81.

Manglis, Giannis (b. 1909)

a.

7.819 *_____ *Smugglers in the Aegean*. Thanasis Maskaleris, tr. New York: Greek Cultural Society, 1967.

b.

7.820 _____ "The Secret of Captain Tony the Bear". Th. Stephanidis, tr. *Greek Letters* 4 (1986-1989), pp. 153-167.

7.821 _____ "from *Smugglers of the Aegean*". Thanasis G. Maskaleris and Claire B. Oleson, trs. *The Charioteer* 9 (1967), pp. 51-70.

c.

7.822 Hionides, Harry T. *Yannis Manglis*. Twayne's World Authors Series, No. 350. Boston, Mass.: Twayne Publishers, 1975. 162 p.

d.

7.823 Maskaleris, Thanasis G. "Yannis Manglis and his Work". *The Charioteer* 9 (1967), pp. 49-50.

Maniotis, Giorgos (b. 1951)

b.

7.824 _____ *The Match*. George Valamvanos and Kenneth MacKinnon, trs. *The Charioteer* 26 (1984), pp. 123-148 {4.18}.

7.825 _____ "Three Dramatic Monologues". George Valamvanos and Kenneth MacKinnon, trs. *The Charioteer* 26 (1984), pp. 149-154 {4.18}.
　The Little Wooden Man ; *The Electric Lamp*; *The Snow.*

Markopoulos, Giorgos (b. 1947)

b.

7.826 _____ "As You Will Be Leaving"; "On Sunday Afternoons"; "Well". Makis Moraitis, tr. *The Coffeehouse* 5 (Winter 1977), pp. 60-62.

Mastoraki, Jenny (b. 1949)

b.

7.827 _____ "Four Poems". Yannis Chioles, tr. *The Coffeehouse* 2 (Spring 1976), pp. 48-51.
　"1."; "2."; "3. Byzantine Fresco: Brave Man, Dawn of Palm Sunday"; "4.".

7.828 _____ "Four Poems". John Stathatos, tr. *Translation* 14 (Spring 1985), pp. 23-25 {3.34}.
　"The Battle Fought and Won"; "The Joys of Motherhood"; "Scheherazade"; "Résumé".

7.829 _____ "Three Poems". Karen Van Dyck, tr. *Translation* 14 (Spring 1985), pp. 26-27 {3.34}.
"Of the Underworld"; "The Unfaithful"; "'They Sang a Song all their Own'".

7.830 _____ "Three Young Poets: Jenny Mastoraki, Haris Megalinos, and Lefteris Poulios". N.C. Germanacos et al., trs. *Boundary 2*, Vol. 1, No. 2 (Winter 1973), pp. 507-518 {3.5}.

Matesis, Antonios (1794-1875)
d.
7.831 Terzakis, Angelos. "Matesis' *Vassilikos:* The First Drama of Ideas". In *Modern Greek Writers* (Edmund Keeley and Peter Bien, eds. Princeton: Princeton University Press, 1972), pp. 93-107 {5.9}.

Matsas, Alexander (1911-1969)
b.
7.832 _____ "Poems". Kimon Friar, tr. *Greek Heritage* 1, No. 1 (Winter 1963), pp. 90-92.
"Of Sleep"; "The Tree"; "Sleep at Delos"; "Landscape"; "Aubade".

Matsas, Nestor (b. 1932)
a.
7.833 *_____ *The Memoirs of Alexander the Great According to the Babylon Manuscript*. Fotios K. Litsas, tr. and intro.; Helen Kazantzakis, foreword. Modern Greek Studies Program Series. Chicago, Ill.: University of Illinois at Chicago, 1984. 166 p.

Mavroidi-Panteleskou, Afroditi
b.
7.834 _____ "Makronisos Journal". Eleni Fourtouni, tr. *JHD* 5, No. 3 (Fall 1978), pp. 115-128.

7.835 _____ "The Makronisos Journal". In *Greek Women in Resistance. Journals—Oral Histories* (Eleni Fourtouni, sel., tr., and intro. [New Haven, Conn.]: Thelphini Press, 1986), pp. 144-183 {4.2}.

Megalynos, Charis
d.
7.836 _____ "Three Young Poets: Jenny Mastoraki, Haris Megalinos and Lefteris Poulios". N.C. Germanacos et al., trs. *Boundary 2*, Vol. 1, No. 2 (Winter 1973), pp. 507-518 {3.5}.

Melissanthi (b. 1910)

a.

7.837 _____ *Hailing the Ascending Morn: Selected Poems*. Maria Voelker-Kamarinea, tr. and intro. Athens: Prosperos, 1987. 118 p.

b.

7.838 *_____ "Lyric Confession". Agnes Sotiracopoulou, tr. *Poetry* (Madras) 9, No. 2 (1968), p. 2 {3.29}.

Melissinos, Stavros (b. 1929)

a.

7.839 _____ *Kavafy, the One String-Lyre Player*. [Nicholas Bassett, tr.]. Athens: Mangos Printers, 1979. 126 p.
   Includes: "Excerpts on the Poetry of K.P. Kavafy from the Diary of Stavros Melissinos" (pp. 7-50) and Melissinos, "Rubaiyat" (4th edition) (pp. 55-118).

7.840 *_____ *The Lady and the Gamekeeper*. A stage play based on the story "Lady Chatterley's Lover" by D.H. Lawrence. Stavros Melissinos, tr. with the assistance of Carola Matthews. Athens, 1969. 94 p.

7.841 *_____ *Persian Rubaiyat*. F. Ragovin, tr. Athens: Pergamali, 1965. 85 p. Bilingual edition.

7.842 _____ *Persian Rubaiyat*. Nicholas Bassett, tr. Athens: The Author, 1959. 3rd edition, 1968. 95 p. Bilingual version. 5th edition in English as *Rubaiyat,* 1981. 111 p.; 6th edition as *Athenian 'Rubaiyat'*, 1986. 112 p. The left pages contain the Greek written in the Latin alphabet.

Mitras, Michael (b. 1944)

a.

7.843 *_____ *Discretive Transitions*. Nottingham: Zenos Publications, 1983. 16 p.

d.

7.844 _____ "Comment". Dino Siotis, tr. (To which is appended a sample of Michael Mitras' work, a page from his book *Alibi of the Description*.) *The Coffeehouse* 3 (Fall 1976), pp. 27-28.

Mitropoulou, Kostoula

b.

7.845 _____ "The Fire" from *Life on the Periphery. Short Stories*. Dimitri Spilios, tr. *Greek Letters* 1 (1982), pp. 287-291.

Mitropoulou, Mona (b. 1926)

a.

7.846 *_____ *From 'Yellow' to 'Nostos'*. David Phillip, tr. London: Narcis, 1974. 46 p.

Montis, Kostas (b. 1914)

a.

7.847 *_____ *Moments*. Translations from the work of a Cypriot Poet by Amaranth Sitas & Charles Dodd. Nicosia, Cyprus: Zavallis Press, 1965. 56 p.

Moraïtidis, Alexandros (1851-1929)

b.

7.848 _____ "The Saint of the Seas". Theodore Sampson, tr. In *Modern Greek Short Stories*. Vol. 1 (Kyr. Delopoulos, ed. Athens: Kathimerini Publications, 1980), pp. 99-114 {4.12}.

7.849 _____ "The Upside-Down Man". Merella Psarakis Assmus, tr. *The Charioteer* 4 (1962), pp. 108-117 {4.17}.

Moskof, Kostis (b. 1939)

d.

7.850 _____ "An Interview with Kostis Moskoff". *JHD* 14, Nos. 3 & 4 (Fall-Winter 1987), pp. 77-89.
This interview was taken by Alexandros Kitroeff and Vasias Tsokopoulos in Sept. 1985, in Thessaloniki.

Mourselas, Kostas (b. 1930)

a.

7.851 _____ *The Ear of Alexander*. Mary A. Nickles, tr. Athens: Anglo-Hellenic Publishing, 1975. 70 p.

7.852 _____ *Selected Short Plays*. Andrew Horton, tr. and intro. Athens: Anglo-Hellenic Publishing, 1975. 123 p.
Contains: *This One and ... That One* (an original theatrical series of one act sketches); *The Lady Doesn't Mourn*.

b.

7.853 _____ "A Dialogue from Mourselas". Andy Horton, tr. From the one-act sketch *The Egg* from the theatrical series *This One...That One*. *The Athenian* (Jan. 1975), p. 36.

7.854 _____ "The Wheel" [a one act play]. Andrew Horton, tr. *The Coffeehouse* 2 (Spring 1976), pp. 3-11.

d.

7.855 Horton, Andy. "The Bitter Satire of Kostas Mourselas". *The Athenian* (Jan. 1975), pp. 35-36.

7.856 *Nickels (sic), Mary A. "Alexander's Ear". *The Athenian* (Jan. 1975), pp. 36-37.

Mylona, Eva (b. 1938)

b.

7.857 _____ "Ectoplasm"; "Bright Noon"; "To Me"; "Biography". Kimon Friar, tr. *The Coffeehouse* 6 (Summer 1978), pp. 57-60.

Myrivilis, Stratis (1890-1969)

a.

7.858 _____ *Life in the Tomb*. Peter Bien, tr. Hanover, N.H.: University Press of New England for Dartmouth College, 1977. 329 p. Reprinted with a new introduction by Peter Levi. Hanover, N.H.: University Press of New England, 1987; London and New York: Quartet Books, 1987. 328 p.

7.859 _____ *The Mermaid Madonna*. Abbott Rick, tr. New York: Thomas Y. Crowell Press, 1959. 310 p. Also *London: Hutchinson, 1959. 287 p. Reprinted: Athens, Greece: Efstathiadis Group, 1981. 244 p.

7.860 _____ *The Schoolmistress with the Golden Eyes*. Philip Sherrard, tr. *London: Hutchinson, 1964. 288 p. Athens, Greece: Efstathiadis Group, 1981. 261 p.

7.861 _____ *Vasilis Arvanitis*. Pavlos Andronikos, tr. Armidale, N.S.W., Australia: The University of New England Publishing Unit, 1983. 112 p.

7.862 *_____ *Vasilis Arvanitis. Pan. The Goblins and Other Short Stories*. Abbott Rick, tr. New York: The American Library, 1959.

7.863 Myrivilis, S., C. Ouranis, and Z. Papantoniou. *Travels in Greece*. Peter Andreou, sel. and tr. 1980. 155 p.

b.

7.864 _____ "A Small Anthology of Stratis Myrivilis". Abbott Rick and Harry Nickles, trs. *The Charioteer* 1, No. 1 (Summer 1960), pp. 98-137.

From *Pan;* from *Vasilis Arvanitis;* "The Two Hoaxers"; "The Loneliness of God" from *The Song of the Earth.*

7.865 _____ "The Step-Daughter". Theodore Sampson, tr. In *Modern Greek Short Stories*. Vol. 2 (Kyr. Delopoulos ed. Athens: Kathimerini Publications, 1981), pp. 65-83 {4.13}.

7.866 _____ "To the Country of Statues". Robert Liddell, tr. *The Atlantic Monthly* 195, No. 6 (June 1955), pp. 160-164 {3.3}.

d.

7.867 Andronikos, Pavlos. "The Narrator of Stratis Myrivilis' *Vasilis Arvanitis:* An Exploration into Emotional Response to the Reading of Fiction". In *The Text and its Margins* (Margaret Alexiou and Vassilis Lambropoulos, eds. New York: Pella Publishing Company, 1985), pp. 85-122 {5.8}.

7.868 Karandonis, Andreas. "The Prose of Stratis Myrivilis". Jacques A. Case-Kessissoglou, tr. *The Charioteer* 1, No. 1 (Summer 1960), pp. 89-97.

7.869 Mason, Hugh J. "'Generations of Our Lesvian Ancestors'. Myrivilis' Use of Sappho and Longus". *The Amaranth* 10 (1987), pp. 11-23.

Myrtiotissa (1885-1968)

d.

7.870 Robinson, Christopher. "The Comparison of Greek and French Women Poets: Myrtiotissa, Maria Polydoure, Anna de Noailles". *JMGS* 2, No. 1 (May 1984), pp. 23-38.

Nakou, Lilika (1903-1989)

a.

7.871 *_____ *The Children's Inferno*. Stories of the Great Famine in Greece. Alan Ross Macdougall, tr. from the French; Bessie Breuer, intro. Hollywood: Gateway Books, 1946. 234 p.

b.

7.872 _____ "The Companions". Theodore Sampson, tr. In *Modern Greek Short Stories*. Vol. 2 (Kyr. Delopoulos ed. Athens: Kathimerini Publications, 1981), pp. 233-244 {4.13}.

7.873 _____ "Lilika Nakos Writes about Her Mother". Deborah Tannen, tr. *Women's Studies* 6, No. 2 (1979), pp. 218-221.

c.

7.874 *Tannen, Deborah. *Lilika Nakos*. Twayne's World Authors Series, No. 677. Boston, Mass.: Twayne Publishers, 1983. 191 p.

d.

7.875 Tannen, Deborah. "Coming of Age in the Modern Greek Prose of Lilika Nakos". *Regionalism and the Female Imagination* 4, No. 1 (Spring 1978), pp. 37-50.

7.876 Tannen, Deborah. "Mothers and Daughters in the Modern Greek Novels of Lilika Nakos". *Women's Studies* 6, No. 2 (1979), pp. 204-217.

Niarchos, Thanasis (b. 1945)

b.

7.877 _____ "Four Poems" (from *Eros Erotas*). Dino Siotis, tr. *The Coffeehouse* 9 (Winter 1979), pp. 15-18.

Nollas, Dimitris (b. 1940)

b.

7.878 _____ "Tender Skin" [a short story]. Mary Keeley, tr. *Translation* 14 (Spring 1985), pp. 47-50 {3.34}.

7.879 _____ "The Wedding". Anna Lillios, tr. *The Coffeehouse* 10 (Summer 1981), pp. 7-12.

Ouranis, Kostas (1890-1953)

a.

7.880 Myrivilis, S., C. Ouranis, and Z. Papantoniou. *Travels in Greece*. Peter Andreou, sel. and tr. 1980. 155 p.

b.

7.881 _____ "The Landscape of Attica". Ἀγγλο-ελληνική Ἐπιθεώρηση 1, No. 3 (May 1945), pp. 17-19. Bilingual.

7.882 _____ "The Picturesque and Peaceful Ayassos". George Thaniel, tr. *Greek Letters* 3 (1984-1985), pp. 75- 80.

7.883 _____ "Rudyard Kipling: The Poet of the British Empire". Ἀγγλο-ελληνική Ἐπιθεώρηση 1, No. 2 (Apr. 1945), pp. 10-12. Bilingual.

7.884 _____ "What We Feel for England". Ἀγγλο-ελληνική Ἐπιθεώρηση 1, No. 1 (Mar. 1945), pp. 4-5. Bilingual.

Pagoulatou, Regina

a.

7.885 *_____ *Motherhood*. Kali Loverdos-Streichler, tr.; Yanni Posnakoff, cover and drawings. New York: Pella Publishing Company, 1985. 87 p. Bilingual edition.

7.886 _____ *Pyrrhichios*. Poems by Regina Pagoulatou. Apostolos N. Athanassakis, tr.; George Fokas, cover and drawings. New York: Pella Publishing Company, 1979. 111 p. Bilingual edition.

7.887 _____ *Transplants*. Poems. Apostolos N. Athanassakis, tr.; Despina Magoni, cover and drawings. New York: Pella Publishing Company, 1982. 63 p. Bilingual edition.

Palamas, Kostis (1859-1943)

a.

7.888 *_____ Byron, 1824-1924.* Translated from the Greek of Costis Palamas by Ph. Michalopoulos. Athens, 1924. A broadside. 4 p.

7.889 *_____ Clear Days.* Poems by Palamas and Elytis in versions by Nikos Tselepides. Portland, Oreg.: Press-22, 1972. [54 p.] Unpaged.

7.890 *_____ The Grave.* Demetrios A. Michalaros, tr. into verse; Louis Roussel, intro. Chicago, Ill.: The American Hellenic Book Publ. Co., 1930. 92 p.

7.891 _____ *A Hundred Voices.* Theodore Ph. Stephanides and George C. Katsimbalis, trs. London: The Translators, 1976. 110 p.

7.892 _____ *A Hundred Voices and Other Poems from the Second Part of 'Life Immovable' by Kostes Palamas.* Aristides E. Phoutrides, tr., intro., notes. Cambridge, Mass.: Harvard University Press, 1921. Also *London: Humphrey Milford, Oxford University Press, 1921. 227 p.

7.893 _____ *The King's Flute.* Theodore P. Stephanides and George C. Katsimbalis, trs.; Charles Diehl, pref.; E.P. Papanoutsos, intro. Athens, Greece: The Kostes Palamas Institute, 1982. 335 p. Bilingual edition.

7.894 _____ *The King's Flute.* Frederic Will, tr. and intro. Lincoln, Nebr.: University of Nebraska Press, 1967. 226 p.

7.895 _____ *Life Immovable (First Part).* Aristides E. Phoutrides, tr., intro., notes. Cambridge, Mass.: Harvard University Press, 1919. 237 p.

7.896 _____ *A Man's Death.* A Story. A.E. Phoutrides, tr.; D.C. Hesseling, foreword. Athens: Printing Office "Hestia", 1934. 59 p.

7.897 _____ *Poems by Kostes Palamas.* Theodore Ph. Stephanides and George C. Katsimbalis, eds. and trs. London: Hazell, Watson & Viney, 1925. 143 p.

7.898 _____ *Royal Blossom or Trisevyene.* A play. Aristides E. Phoutrides, tr. and intro. New Haven: Yale University Press, 1923. 163 p. Also *London: Humphrey Milford, Oxford University Press, 1923. 163 p.

7.899 _____ *Three Poems.* Theodore Ph. Stephanides and George C. Katsimbalis, trs. London, published privately, 1969. Printed in Athens: F. Constantinidis & C. Mihalas. 38 p.
   Contains: "The Palm Tree"; "The Chains"; "The Satyr or The Song of Nakedness".

7.900 _____ *The Twelve Lays of the Gipsy.* George Thomson, tr. and intro. London: Lawrence & Wishart, 1969. 146 p.

7.901 _____ *The Twelve Words of the Gypsy*. Theodore Ph. Stephanides and George C. Katsimbalis, trs. London: [published privately], 1974. Printed in Greece by F. Constantinidis and C. Michalas. 194 p.

7.902 _____ *The Twelve Words of the Gypsy*. Theodore Ph. Stephanides and George C. Katsimbalis, trs. New edition. Memphis, Tenn.: Memphis State University Press, 1975. 314 p. Bilingual edition.

7.903 _____ *The Twelve Words of the Gypsy by Kostes Palamas*. Frederic Will, tr. and intro. Lincoln, Nebr.: University of Nebraska Press, 1964. 205 p.

b.

7.904 _____ "*Ascraeus*". Theodore Ph. Stephanides and George C. Katsimbalis, trs. In *Kostis Palamas: A Portrait and an Appreciation* (Theofanis G. Stavrou and Constantine A. Trypanis. A Nostos Book. Minneapolis, Minn.: North Central Publishing Company, 1985), pp. 79-126 {7.934}.

7.905 _____ "Attic Morn" (from the 'King's Flute'). Th.P. Stephanides, and G.C. Katsimbalis, trs. Ἀγγλο-ελληνική Ἐπιθεώρηση 1, No. 3 (May 1945), p. 9. Bilingual.

7.906 _____ "Death of a Young Man". Theodore Sampson, tr. In *Modern Greek Short Stories*. Vol. 1 (Kyr. Delopoulos, ed. Athens: Kathimerini Publications, 1980), pp. 135-169 {4.12}.

7.907 _____ "The Death of Digenis Akritas" and "The Woodman". D. Michalaros, tr. *Athene* 4, No. 5 (June 1943), p. 41 {7.936}.

7.908 _____ "The Eyes of the Prince". X.C. Panopoulos-Payne, tr. *Athene* 20, No. 2 (Summer 1959), pp. 54 and 55 {7.937}.

7.909 _____ "Five Poems from 'Farewells and Greetings'". Catherine Karamagianis, tr. *Athene* 20, No. 2 (Summer 1959), p. 10 {7.937}.

7.910 _____ "The Grave". D. Michalaros, tr. *Athene* 4, No. 5 (June 1943), pp. 11-15. Bilingual {7.936}.

7.911 _____ "The Grave". D. Michalaros, tr. *Athene* 20, No. 2 (Summer 1959), pp. 35-43 {7.937}.

7.912 _____ "*Iambs and Anapaests*". Theodore Ph. Stephanides and George C. Katsimbalis, trs. In *Kostis Palamas: A Portrait and an Appreciation* (Theofanis G. Stavrou and Constantine A. Trypanis. A Nostos Book. Minneapolis, Minn.: North Central Publishing Company, 1985), pp. 59-78 {7.934}.

7.913 _____ "Life Immovable"; "Emerson, Poe, Whitman"; "Aristides Phoutrides". Theodore Giannakoulis, tr. *Athene* 20, No. 2 (Summer 1959), p. 23 {7.937}.

7.914 _____ "A Man's Death". In *Modern Greek Stories* (Demetra Vaka and Aristides Phoutrides, trs. New York: Duffield & Co., 1920), pp. 171-218 {4.16}.

7.915 _____ "Olympic Hymn". Theofanis G. Stavrou and Soterios G. Stavrou, trs. In *Kostis Palamas: A Portrait and an Appreciation* (Theofanis G. Stavrou and Constantine A. Trypanis. A Nostos Book. Minneapolis, Minn.: North Central Publishing Company, 1985), pp. 127-129 {7.934}.

7.916 _____ "Palamas' Masterpiece *The Twelve Lays of the Gypsy*: An Analysis of the Poem and Translation of 'Lay the Seventh'". Theodore Ph. Stephanides and George C. Katsimbalis, trs. *Athene* 20, No. 2 (Summer 1959), pp. 12-17 {7.937}.

7.917 _____ "Rose Fragrance". D. Michalaros, tr. *Athene* 4, No. 5 (June 1943), p. 9 {7.936}.

7.918 _____ "*Royal Blossom* or *Trisevyene*" (a play in four acts), Part 1. Aristides E. Phoutrides, tr. *Athene* 20, No. 2 (Summer 1959), pp. 44-53 {7.937}.

7.919 _____ "Selections from 'Life Immovable': Part II: A Hundred Voices". Aristides E. Phoutrides, tr. *Athene* 20, No. 2 (Summer 1959), pp. 7-9 {7.937}.

7.920 _____ "The Twelve Lays of the Gipsy", an analysis of the poem and tr. of "Lay the Seventh" by Theodore Ph. Stephanides and George C. Katsimbalis. *Athene* 4, No. 5 (June 1943), pp. 22-27 {7.936}.

7.921 _____ "3 Palamas Poems". Theodore Giannakoulis, tr. *Athene* 20, No. 2 (Summer 1959), p. 53 {7.937}.
  "Life Immovable"; "The Oak"; "Brotherhood".

7.922 _____ "Two Octaves". Kimon Friar, tr. *The Atlantic Monthly* 195, No. 6 (June 1955), p. 152 {3.3}.

7.923 _____ "Who Knows in Other Stars". Rae Dalven, tr. *Poetry* 120, No. 5 (Aug. 1972), pp. 264-265.

c.

7.924 Diehl, Charles, A. Embiricos, and André Therive. *The King's Flute of Kostes Palamas*. Articles. [Philip Sherrard, tr.]. Athens: Printing Office P. Sergiades, 1956. 21 p.

7.925 Eklund, Bo-Lennart. *The Ideal and the Real: A Study of the Ideas in Kostis Palamas'* Ὁ Δωδεκάλογος τοῦ Γύφτου. Göteborg: Avhandling for filosofie doktorsexamen, 1972. 147 p.
  Re. the *Dodecalogue of the Gypsy*.

7.926 Fletcher, Robin A. *Kostes Palamas: A Great Modern Greek Poet (1859-1943); His Life, his Work and his Struggle for Demoticism.* Athens: The Kostes Palamas Institute, 1984. 229 p.

7.927 Jenkins, R.J.H. *Palamas.* An Inaugural Lecture Delivered at King's College London, on 30th January, 1947. [1947]. 28 p.

7.928 Lebesgue, Philéas. "The New Hellenism and the Poetic Work of Kostis Palamas". *The New World* (Sept. 1920), pp. 363-368. Detached copy.

7.929 Maskaleris, Thanassis. *Kostis Palamas.* Twayne's World Authors Series, No. 197. New York: Twayne Publishers, Inc., 1972. 156 p.

7.930 Palamas, Leandros. *A Study on the Palm-Tree of Kostes Palamas.* Theodore Ph. Stephanides and George C. Katsimbalis, trs. Athens: Printing Office "Hestia", 1931. 27 p.

7.931 *Proussis, Costas M. *Platonic Elements in Palamas: Lucretius and Palamas.* Lefkosia, Cyprus: Stasinos, 1973. 12 p.
  Also in serial publication. See below {7.948, 7.949}.

7.932 *Proussis, Costas M. *Kostis Palamas, 1859-1943.* Brookline, Mass., 1974. 26 p.

7.933 Stavrou, Theophanis G. *Kostis Palamas / 1859-1943 / ΚΩΣΤΗΣ ΠΑΛΑΜΑΣ.* An exhibit. May 14-July 14, 1982. Modern Greek Collection. Special Collections. 466 Wilson Library. University of Minnnesota, 309 Nineteenth Avenue, South. Minneapolis, Minn. 55455. 33p. Pamphlet.

7.934 Stavrou, Theofanis G. and Constantine A. Trypanis. *Kostis Palamas: A Portrait and an Appreciation.* Including *Iambs and Anapaests* and *Ascraeus* translated by Theodore Ph. Stephanides and George C. Katsimbalis. A Nostos Book. Minneapolis, Minn.: North Central Publishing Company, 1985. 129 p.
  Includes: Theofanis G. Stavrou, "Kostes Palamas: A Literary Profile" (pp. 1-27); Constantine A. Trypanis, "The Poetry of Kostis Palamas" (pp. 28-46); Supplement I: Kostes Palamas, *Iambs and Anapaests* [Theodore Ph. Stephanides and George C. Katsimbalis, trs.] (pp. 59-78) prefaced by Kostis Palamas, "How I Remember the *Iambs and Anapaests*" (pp. 49-58); Supplement II: Kostis Palamas, *Ascraeus* [Theodore Ph. Stephanides and George C. Katsimbalis, trs.] (pp. 104-126) prefaced by Andreas Karandonis, "Introduction to Palamas' *Ascraeus*" (pp. 81-103); Supplement III: Kostis Palamas, "Olympic Hymn" [Theofanis G. Stavrou and Soterios G. Stavrou, trs.] (pp. 127-129).

7.935 *Tagore, Rabindranath, Aristides Phoutrides, Benjamin de Casseres, Leonard Lanson Cline, and others. *Kostes Palamas: A Living Poet of Greece.* Athens: Printing Office "Hestia", 1933. 22 p.

Special issues of periodicals
7.936 *Athene* 4, No. 5 (June 1943). Contains "Kostes Palamas and his Period".
  Includes: Eugene Clement, "Life and Works of Kostes Palamas" (pp. 7-8 and 66); Kostes Palamas, "Rose Fragrance" [D. Michalaros, tr.] (p. 9); "The Grave" [D. Michalaros, tr.] (pp. 11-15) [bilingual]; David Harrison Stevens, "Palamas and the Western World" (pp. 16-17 and 64); Kostes Palamas, "Life Immovable" [Aristides Phoutrides, tr.] (pp. 19-20 and 68); Kostes Palamas, "The Twelve Lays of the

Gipsy", an analysis of the poem and tr. of "Lay the Seventh" by Theodore Ph. Stephanides and George C. Katsimbalis (pp. 22-27); D. Michalaros, "Palamas as Philosopher" (pp. 28-32 and 68); George E. Mylonas, "The Critical Essays of Kostes Palamas" (pp. 33-37); David M. Robinson, "Palamas and Phoutrides" (pp. 38-39); T. Leslie Shear, "The Greek Academy" (pp. 40-41); Kostes Palamas, "The Death of Digenis Akritas" and "The Woodman" [D. Michalaros, tr.] (p. 41).

Original address: Athene, The American Magazine of Hellenic Thought Publication Office, 919 Wellington Avenue, Chicago, Ill.

7.937 *Athene* 20, No. 2 (Summer 1959). "The 100th Anniversary of the Birth of Kostes Palamas, Poet and Patriot".

Includes: "The 100 Years of Kostes Palamas" [essay] (pp. 3-5 and 24); Kostes Palamas, "Selections from 'Life Immovable': Part II: A Hundred Voices" [Aristides E. Phoutrides, tr.] (pp. 7-9); Kostes Palamas, "Five Poems from 'Farewells and Greetings'" [Catherine Karamagianis, tr.] (p. 10); Theodore Ph. Stephanides and George C. Katsimbalis, "Palamas' Masterpiece *The Twelve Lays of the Gypsy*: An Analysis of the Poem and Translation of 'Lay the Seventh'" (pp. 12-17); D. Michalaros, "Palamas as Philosopher: Vezanis' Much Discussed Volume on the Philosophical Aspects of the Greek Poet's Works" (pp. 18-22); Kostes Palamas, "Life Immovable", "Emerson, Poe, Whitman", "Aristides Phoutrides" [Theodore Giannakoulis, tr.] (p. 23); Alkis Thrylos, "On Palamas" [X.C. Panopoulos-Payne, tr.] (p. 24); Aristides Phoutrides, "Hesiodic Reminiscences in the 'Ascraean' of Kostes Palamas" (pp. 25-29); Kostis T. Argoe, "Kostes Palamas, 1859-1943" (pp. 30-32); Christian X. Palamas, "Palamas and Peace" (pp. 33-34); Kostes Palamas, "The Grave" [D. Michalaros, tr.] (pp. 35-43), "*Royal Blossom* or *Trisevyene*" (a play in four acts), Part 1 [Aristides E. Phoutrides, tr.] (pp. 44-53); "3 Palamas Poems" ["Life Immovable"; "The Oak"; "Brotherhood"] [Theodore Giannakoulis, tr.] (p. 53); "The Eyes of the Prince" [X.C. Panopoulos-Payne, tr.] (pp. 54 and 55).

Original address: Athene, The American Magazine of Hellenic Thought Publication Office, 919 Wellington Avenue, Chicago, Illinois.

d.

7.938 Argoe, Kostis T. "Kostes Palamas, 1859-1943". *Athene* 20, No. 2 (Summer 1959), pp. 30-32 {7.937}.

7.939 Carroll, Margaret. "Images of Encirclement and Enchantment in the Poetry of Palamas". *BMGS* 3 (1977), pp. 117-140.

7.940 Carroll, Margaret G. "Meter and Mood in Palamas' *Dodecalogue of the Gypsy*". *Neo-Hellenika* 3 (1978), pp. 81-101.

7.941 *Constantinidis, Stratos E. "The New Dionysus of Modern Greek Poetic Drama: Crucifix or Grapevine?". In *From the Bard to Broadway* (Karelisa V. Hartigan, ed. University of Florida Department of Classics Comparative Drama Conference Papers, 7. Lanham, Md.: University Presses of America, 1987), pp. 21-31.

Re. *Trisevgeni*. Treatment of myth of Dionysus compared to Angelos Sikelianos and Nikos Kazantzakis.

7.942 Maskaleris, Thanasis. "Palamas and World Literature". In *Modern Greek Writers* (Edmund Keeley and Peter Bien, eds. Princeton: Princeton University Press, 1972), pp. 109-122 {5.9}.

7.943 Michalaros, D. "Palamas as Philosopher". *Athene* 4, No. 5 (June 1943), pp. 28-32 and 68 {7.936}.

7.944 Michalaros, D. "Palamas as Philosopher: Vezanis' Much Discussed Volume on the Philosophical Aspects of the Greek Poet's Works". *Athene* 20, No. 2 (Summer 1959), pp. 18-22 {7.937}.

7.945 Mylonas, George E. "The Critical Essays of Kostes Palamas". *Athene* 4, No. 5 (June 1943), pp. 33-37 {7.936}.

7.946 Palamas, Christian X. "Palamas and Peace". *Athene* 20, No. 2 (Summer 1959), pp. 33-34 {7.937}.

7.947 Phoutrides, Aristides. "Hesiodic Reminiscences in the 'Ascraean' of Kostes Palamas". *Athene* 20, No. 2 (Summer 1959), pp. 25-29 {7.937}.

7.948 Proussis, Costas M. "Lucretius and Palamas". *Στασῖνος* 4 (1968-1972), pp. 9-12.

7.949 Proussis, Costas M. "Platonic Elements in Palamas". *Στασῖνος* 4 (1968-1972), pp. 1-8.

7.950 Raizis, M. Byron. "Palamas and his English Translators". *Neo-Hellenika* 4 (1981), pp. 201-210.

7.951 Robinson, Christopher. "Greece in the Poetry of Costis Palamas". *Review of National Literatures* 5, No. 2 (Fall 1974), pp. 41-65 {3.30}.

7.952 Robinson, David M. "Palamas and Phoutrides". *Athene* 4, No. 5 (June 1943), pp. 38-39 {7.936}.

7.953 Roussel, Louis. "The Romaic Decapentesyllabic and the Versification of Costis Palamas". Part 1: *The Link*, No. 1 (June 1938), pp. 61-65; Part 2: *The Link*, No. 2 (June 1939), pp. 36-48.
　Re. *The King's Flute.*

7.954 Shear, T. Leslie. "The Greek Academy". *Athene* 4, No. 5 (June 1943), pp. 40-41 {7.936}.

7.955 Sherrard, Philip. "Costis Palamas". In his *The Marble Threshing Floor* (Freeport, N.Y.: Books for Libraries Press, 1956), pp. 39-82 {5.6}.

7.956 Stevens, David Harrison. "Palamas and the Western World". Aristides Phoutrides, tr. *Athene* 4, No. 5 (June 1943), pp. 19-20 and 68 {7.936}.

7.957 Thrylos, Alkis. "On Palamas". X.C. Panopoulos-Payne, tr. *Athene* 20, No. 2 (Summer 1959), p. 24. {7.937}.

Palamas, Leandros K. (1891-1969)

a.

7.958 _____ *A Study on the Palm-Tree of Kostes Palamas*. Theodore Ph. Stephanides and George C. Katsimbalis, trs. Athens: Printing Office "Hestia", 1931. 27 p.

Pamboudi, Pavlina (b. 1948)

b.

7.959 _____ "Autobiographical"; "The Relationship"; "The Alibi"; "Wednesday 3". Kimon Friar, tr. *The Coffeehouse* 4 (Summer 1977), pp. 19-22.

Panagiotopoulos, I.M. (1901-1982)

a.

7.960 _____ *The Contemporary Man: An Essay on Free Thought*. Maria P. Hogan, tr. New York; Washington; Hollywood: Vantage Press, 1970. 101 p.

7.961 _____ *The New Barbarians & the Downfall of Authenticity*. Maria P. Hogan, tr. New York; Washington; Atlanta; Hollywood: Vantage Press, 1977. 94 p.

b.

7.962 _____ "The Englishwoman on the Pier". Theodore Sampson, tr. In *Modern Greek Short Stories*. Vol. 2 (Kyr. Delopoulos, ed. Athens: Kathimerini Publications, 1981), pp. 193-204 {4.13}.

7.963 _____ "I.M. Panayotopoulos: A Selection". Mary Gianos, Amy Mims, and Kimon Friar, trs. *The Charioteer* 3 (1961), pp. 67-113.
   From *Humble Life;* from *Starlight;* "Downfall of the Geometric Mind"; "Five Poems"; from *The Seven Sleepers.*

7.964 _____ "From *Writers and Texts*". Staff, tr. *The Charioteer* 5 (1963), pp. 80-85.
   Re. Photis Kontoglou.

d.

7.965 Dimakis, Minas. "I.M. Panayotopoulos: Man of Letters". Beebe Spanos and Tedd Athas, trs. *The Charioteer* 3 (1961), pp. 61-66.

7.966 Mitsakis, Karolos. "The River of Time". In Memory of I.M. Panagiotopoulos. *Greek Letters* 1 (1982), pp. 334-340.

Panagiotounis, Panos N. (b. 1930)

a.

7.967 *_____ *A Greek Poet. Panos N. Panayotounis*. June Kingdon, Vasso Kalamara, Goula Smyrniotis, trs. [Athens?]: Editions D.O., n.d. 15 p.

Papadiamantis, Alexandros (1851-1911)

a.

7.968 _____ *The Murderess*. George X. Xanthopoulides, tr., intro. and notes. London; Athens: Doric Publications Ltd. / "Kathimerini", 1977. 167 p.
   Out of print in 1986.

7.969 _____ *The Murderess*. Peter Levi, tr. New York and London: Writers and Readers, 1983. 127 p.

7.970 _____ *Tales from a Greek Island*. Elizabeth Constantinides, tr., intro. and notes. Baltimore and London: The Johns Hopkins University Press, 1987. 176 p.

b.

7.971 _____ "Love in the Snow". Theodore Sampson, tr. In *Modern Greek Short Stories*. Vol. 1 (Kyr. Delopoulos, ed. Athens: Kathimerini Publications, 1980), pp. 115-122 {4.12}.

7.972 _____ "She That was Homesick". Demetra Vaka, tr. In *Modern Greek Stories* (Demetra Vaka and Aristides Phoutrides, trs. New York: Duffield & Co., 1920), pp. 236-270 {4.16}.

7.973 _____ "The Yearly Victim". JoAnne Cacoullos, tr. *The Charioteer* 4 (1962), pp. 100-107 {4.17}.

c.

7.974 Coutelle, Louis, Theofanis G. Stavrou and David R. Weinberg. *A Greek Diptych: Dionysios Solomos and Alexandros Papadiamantis*. A Nostos Book. Minneapolis, Minn.: North Central Publishing Company, 1986. 113 p.

7.975 *Meranaios, Kostis. *Papadiamantis-Kierkegaard*. Athens, 1974. 16 p.

d.

7.976 Proussis, Costas M. "Papadiamantis and his National Literary Conscience". *JMH* 1 (Apr. 1984), pp. 15-23.

7.977 *Weinberg, David Robert. "The Nature, Style, and Aesthetics of Papadhiamandian Prose". *Dissertation Abstracts International* 39 (1977), p. 1537A.

Papadimitrakopoulos, Ilias (b. 1930)

b.

7.978 _____ "The Execution"; "Glykeria"; "Dancing Lesson". Yannis Goumas, tr. *Contemporary Literature in Translation* 27 (1977), pp. 4-6 {3.7}.

7.979 _____ "Toothpaste with Clorophyll". Dino Siotis, tr. *The Coffeehouse* 3 (Fall 1976), pp. 20-22.

d.
7.980 *Taylor, John. "A Note on Elias Papadimitrakopoulos's *Toothpaste with Chlorophyll* and *Maritime Hot Baths*". *International Fiction Review* 13, No. 2 (Summer 1986), pp. 94-96.

Papadimitriou, Sakis (b. 1940)

a.
7.981 _____ *The Lift: Prose Writings*. Gillian Tweed, tr. Thessaloniki: Diagonios, 1972. 93 p.

7.982 *_____ *The "Other" Piano*. Aris Georgiou, photographs. Thessaloniki: "Plus and Minus" Editions, 1983.

b.
7.983 _____ "The Lift". Gillian Tweed, tr. *Contemporary Literature in Translation* 27 (Summer 1977), pp. 21-23 {3.7}.

7.984 _____ "A Walk". Gillian Tweed, tr. *The Coffeehouse* 4 (Summer 1976), pp. 43-46.

Papanoutsos, E.P. (1900-1982)

b.
7.985 _____ "Poetry and Language". John P. Anton, tr. and adapt. *The Charioteer* 3 (1961), pp. 120-129.

c.
7.986 Anton, John. *Critical Humanism as a Philosophy of Culture: The Case of E.P. Papanoutsos*. A Talk. Theofanis G. Stavrou, ed. and intro. The Third Annual Public Lecture in Modern Greek Studies, Special Collections, University of Minnesota Libraries, Minneapolis. St. Paul, Minn.: The North Central Publishing Company, 1981. 45 p. With a Supplement (pp. 42-45): "The Major Works of E.P. Papanoutsos: A Chronological Record".

7.987 *Henderson, G.P. *E.P. Papanoutsos*. Twayne's World Authors Series, No. 678. Boston, Mass.: Twayne Publishers, 1983.

Papantoniou, Zacharias (1877-1940)

a.
7.988 Myrivilis, S., C. Ouranis, and Z. Papantoniou. *Travels in Greece*. Peter Andreou, sel. and tr. 1980. 155 p.

b.
7.989 _____ "The Good Wife of Malis". Theodore Sampson, tr. In *Modern Greek Short Stories*. Vol. 1 (Kyr. Delopoulos, ed. Athens: Kathimerini Publications, 1980), pp. 273-280 {4.12}.

Papapetros, Anastos (b. 1919)

b.

7.990 _____ "The Miracle" [a short story]. Robert and Despina Crist, trs. *The Athenian* (May 1975), pp. 31-32.

Papastamou, Olga

a.

7.991 *_____ *Ancestral Dynamo*. D. Carion, Cali Orfanidi, Ascreo, and Gaston-Henri Aufrère, trs. Athens, 1959. 43 p.

7.992 *_____ *The Apotheosis of the Mind*. Daniel Carion, André Hammel, Ascreo, Cali Orfanidi, and Gaston-Henri Aufrère, trs. Athens, 1959. 45 p.

7.993 *_____ *Awakened Daffodil*. Gaston-Henri Aufrère and André Hammel, trs. [Athens?], 1956. 24 p.

7.994 *_____ *Beauty of Life*. Gaston-Henri Aufrère and André Hammel, trs. Alexandria, Egypt, [1960]. 22 p.

7.995 *_____ *Deep Flames*. Henri Boissin, tr. Athens, 1957. 43 p.

7.996 *_____ *Far Beyond Countries*. Gaston-Henri Aufrère, André Hammel, and Henri Boissin, trs. Athens, 1958. 45 p.

7.997 *_____ *Process of People*. Gaston-Henri Aufrère, André Hammel, and Ascreo, trs. Athens, 1961. 41 p.

7.998 *_____ *Shady Eyelids*. Gaston-Henri Aufrère, André Hammel, and Henri Boissin, trs. Athens, 1958. 45 p.

7.999 *_____ *Sun's Fate*. André Hammel and Henri Boissin, trs. Athens, 1958. 48 p.

7.1000 *_____ *Velvety Breaths* [poems]. Gaston-Henri Aufrère, André Hammel, Cali Orfanidi, and George Papadimas, trs. Alexandria, Egypt, 1961. 20 p.

Papatsonis, Takis (1895-1976)

a.

7.1001 *_____ *Ursa Minor and Other Poems*. Kimon Friar and Kostas Myrsiades, trs. A Nostos Book. Minneapolis, Minn.: North Central Publishing Company, 1987? 103 p.

b.

7.1002 _____ "Before the First Coming". Kimon Friar, tr. *The Atlantic Monthly* 195, No. 6 (June 1955), p. 105 {3.3}.

7.1003 _____ "Poems by Takis Papatzonis". Kimon Friar, tr. *The Charioteer* 3 (1961), pp. 33-47.

7.1004 _____ "*Ursa Minor:* Poem". Kostas Myrsiades, tr. *The Charioteer* 18 (1976), pp. 12-48.

c.
7.1005 Myrsiades, Kostas. *Takis Papatsonis*. Twayne's World Authors Series, No. 313. New York: Twayne Publishers, Inc., 1974. 166 p.

d.
7.1006 Myrsiades, Kostas. "A Fusion of Christianity and Myth: The Woman-Goddess Figure in the Poetry of Takis Papatsonis with Special Reference to *Ursa Minor*". *MGSY* 1 (1985), pp. 131-143.

7.1007 Myrsiades, Kostas. "The Poetry of Takis Papatsonis: A Note on *Ursa Minor*". *The Charioteer* 18 (1976), pp. 10-11.

7.1008 Myrsiades, Kostas J. "The *Ursa Minor* of Takis Papatsonis and Its Dantean Parallels". *Dissertation Abstracts International* 33 (1973), p. 6321A.

7.1009 Paraschos, Cleon. "The Poetry of Takis Papatzonis". Thomasina Alexander and John Karkas, trs. *The Charioteer* 3 (1961), pp. 28-32.

Pappas, Angelos
a.
7.1010 *_____ *In the Path of the Beast*. Stavroula Will, tr. Cleveland, 1952. 238 p.

Parnis, Alexis (b. 1924)
a.
7.1011 *_____ Τό νησί τῆς Ἀφροδίτης. *The Island of Aphrodite, an International Theatrical Success* [a play]. Athens, 1968. 164 p. Illustrated.
   Text in Greek, English, French, and German.

7.1012 *_____ *Pasternak Highway: The Play*. Sophia Ladas, tr. Westlake Village, Calif.: F. & J. Publishing Co., 1977. 97 p.

7.1013 _____ *The Proofreader*. A Novel. Thomas Hatton and Byron Raizis, trs. London: André Deutsch, 1980. 221 p. Also Athens: Efstathiadis Group, 1986. 221 p.

Paschos, Vasilis Th. (b. 1924)
a.
7.1014 _____ *Atlantes, Not the "Gods"*. John N. Karadelis and Zanettos Tofallis, trs. Athens: Editions "Museum of Atlantis", 1983. 80 p.

Patrikios, Titos (b. 1928)

b.

7.1015 _____ "Four Poems". Peter Mackridge, tr. *Verse* 5 (1986), pp. 57-58.

7.1016 _____ "A Selection of his Poems". C. Capri-Karka, tr. *The Charioteer* 28 (1986), pp. 42-101.
From *Poems,* 1: 1948-1954; from *Apprenticeship;* from *Optional Stop.*

d.

7.1017 Maronitis, D.N. "Excerpts from *Poetics and Political Ethics*". C. Capri-Karka, tr. *The Charioteer* 28 (1986), pp. 35-41.
The two chapters from his book that deal with the poetry of Patrikios.

Pavlopoulos, George (b. 1924)

a.

7.1018 _____ *The Cellar.* Peter Levi, tr. with an intro. London: Anvil Press Poetry in association with Rex Collings, 1977. 47 p.

b.

7.1019 _____ "The Cellar: Remembrance of Makriyannis" [a poem]. Peter Dreyer, tr. *Omphalos* 1, No. 1 (Mar. 1972), pp. 40-41. Bilingual version.

7.1020 _____ "Three Greek Poets: Yannis Ritsos, Takis Sinopoulos, George Pavlopoulos". Translated respectively by: Peter Levi & Nikos Stangos; Ian Scott-Kilvert; and Peter Levi. *TLS* (14 Nov. 1975), p. 1365.

Pentzikis, Nikos Gavriil (b. 1909)

b.

7.1021 _____ "from 'The Dead and the Resurrection'". Stavros Deligiorgis, tr. *The Literary Review* 16, No. 3 (Spring 1973), pp. 268-272 {3.15}.

c.

7.1022 Thaniel, George. *Homage to Byzantium: The Life and Work of Nikos Gabriel Pentzikis.* A Nostos Book. Minneapolis, Minn.: North Central Publishing Company, 1983. 156 p.

Petropoulos, Ilias (b. 1937)

a.

7.1023 _____ *A Macabre Song. Testimony of the Goy. Concerning Anti-Jewish Sentiments in Greece.* With a Postscriptum by Pierre Vidal-Naquet. Texts translated from the Greek and from the French by John Taylor. Paris, 1985. 32 p.
Loose pages in a folder. The Gennadius Library has No. 6 of 333 numbered copies.

d.

7.1024 Taylor, John. "Elias Petropoulos: A Presentation". *JHD* 8, No. 4 (Winter 1981), pp. 7-39.
    Includes a translation of excerpts of Petropoulos. Preceded by a "Statement" by the editors, pp. 5-6.

Petsalis, Thanasis (b. 1904)

b.

7.1025 _____ "Contrasts". Theodore Sampson, tr. In *Modern Greek Short Stories*. Vol. 2 (Kyr. Delopoulos, ed. Athens: Kathimerini Publications, 1981), pp. 257-277 {4.13}.

7.1026 _____ "Exaltation of the Sweet Land of Cyprus" [Chronicle of the 12th century]. Amy Mims, tr. In *Cyprus '74: Aphrodite's Other Face* (Emmanuel C. Casdaglis, ed. Athens: National Bank of Greece, 1976), pp. 151-160 {4.87}.

7.1027 _____ "Thanassis Petsalis: Excerpts from Three Novels" [from *The Bell of the Holy Trinity, The Mavrolykoi, The Greek Dawn*]. Katherine Hortis, Fotine Nicholas, and Tula Lewnes, trs. *The Charioteer* 6 (Spring 1964), pp. 24-70.

d.

7.1028 Decavalles, Andonis. "An Introduction to Thanassis Petsalis". *The Charioteer* 6 (Spring 1964), pp. 71-78.

Pieridis, Giorgos Filippou (b. 1904)

b.

7.1029 _____ "George Philippou Pierides: A Selection". Jack Gaist, tr. *JHD* 5, No. 2 (Summer 1978), pp. 47-58.
    Selection from his collection of short stories entitled Ὁ καιρός τῶν Ὀλβίων (The Time of the Blissful).

Pikkolos, Nikolaos S. (1792-1866)

a.

7.1030 _____ *The Death of Demosthenes*. A tragedy in four acts; in prose. Gregorius Palaeologus of Constantinople, tr. Cambridge: Printed for the Author, and sold by Richard Newby, Trinity Street, 1824. 63 p.

Pittas, Triantafyllos (b. 1927)

b.

7.1031 _____ "The Monsters are Coming". Theodora Vasils, tr. *The Literary Review* 16, No. 3 (Spring 1973), pp. 274-289 {3.15}.

7.1032 _____ "The Vespa", a short story. Kimon Friar, tr. *The Charioteer* 15 (1973), pp. 102-113.

Plaskovitis, Spyros (b. 1917)

b.

7.1033 _____ "The Last Visit", a short story. Themi Vasils, tr. *The Charioteer* 18 (1976), pp. 87-95.

7.1034 _____ "My Father's Kepi" from *Brought to the Knees* and *The Radar*. Theodore Sampson, tr. *Greek Letters* 1 (1982), pp. 272-281.

7.1035 _____ "The Radar". N.C. Germanakos, tr. In *Eighteen Texts* (Willis Barnstone, ed. Cambridge, Mass.: Harvard University Press, 1972), pp. 19-36 {4.1}.

Politis, Kosmas (1888-1974)

b.

7.1036 _____ "Anthology of Kosmas Politis". *The Charioteer* 11 and 12 (1969/1970), pp. 22-128.
    Contains: "from *Eroica*" [Thanasis Maskaleris, tr.]; *"Julia"* [Mary P. Gianos, tr.]; "from *At Hadzifrangos*" [Katherine Hortis, Fotine Nicholas, Alice-Mary Maffry, and Penelope Black, trs.].

7.1037 _____ "The Funeral Games". Robert Liddell and Andreas Cambas, trs. *The Atlantic Monthly* 195, No. 6 (June 1955), pp. 139-141 {3.3}.

7.1038 _____ "Julia". Theodore Sampson, tr. In *Modern Greek Short Stories*. Vol. 2 (Kyr. Delopoulos, ed. Athens: Kathimerini Publications, 1981), pp. 35-64 {4.13}.

d.

7.1039 Decavalles, Andonis. "Kosmas Politis: The Quest for Love". *The Charioteer* 11 and 12 (1969/1970), pp. 8-21.

7.1040 Mackridge, Peter. "Bibliography of George Theotokas and Kosmas Politis". Μαντατοφόρος 3 (Nov. 1973), pp. 17-21.

7.1041 Mackridge, Peter. "Symbolism and Irony in Three Novels by Kosmas Politis". *BMGS* 5 (1979), pp. 77-93.

7.1042 Mackridge, Peter. "The Two-Fold Nostalgia: Lost Homeland and Lost Time in the Work of G. Theotokas, E. Venezis and K. Politis". *JMGS* 4, No. 2 (Oct. 1986), pp. 75-83.

Polydouri, Maria (1902-1930)

b.

7.1043 _____ "Because You Loved Me". Jack Gaist, tr. Πνευματική Κύπρος 181 (Oct. 1975), pp. 30-31.

7.1044 _____ "The Poetry of Maria Polydouri: A Selection". Various translators under the direction of Athan Anagnostopoulos. *JHD* 5, No. 1 (Spring 1978), pp. 41-67.

d.

7.1045 Robinson, Christopher. "The Comparison of Greek and French Women Poets: Myrtiotissa, Maria Polydoure, Anna de Noailles". *JMGS* 2, No. 1 (May 1984), pp. 23-38.

Polylas, Iakovos (1826-1898)

b.

7.1046 _____ "The Error". Theodore Sampson, tr. In *Modern Greek Short Stories*. Vol. 1 (Kyr. Delopoulos, ed. Athens: Kathimerini Publications, 1980), pp. 11-28 {4.12}.

7.1047 _____ "Forgiveness". In *Modern Greek Stories* (Demetra Vaka and Aristides Phoutrides, trs. New York: Duffield and Company, 1920), pp. 131-154 {4.16}.

7.1048 _____ "Prolegomena to Dionysios Solomos". *Greek Letters* 2 (1983), pp. 196-228.
  Translator not named.

Pontikas, Marios (b. 1942)

b.

7.1049 _____ "An Arbitrary Act During the Lawful Transaction of the Butcher Trade". Minas Savvas. tr. *The Coffeehouse* 2 (Spring 1976), pp. 36-38.

7.1050 _____ "Civil War". Yannis Goumas, tr. *Contemporary Literature in Translation* 27 (Summer 1977), pp. 15-16 {3.7}.

Porfyras, Lambros (1879-1932)

b.

7.1051 _____ "The Poetry of Lambros Porphyras: A Selection". Tr. under the direction of Athan Anagnostopoulos. *JHD* 7, Nos. 3-4 (Fall-Winter 1980), pp. 47-71. Bilingual version.

Poulios, Lefteris (b. 1944)

b.

7.1052 _____ "The Box"; "At a Trolley Stop"; "An American Bar in Athens". Philip Ramp and Katerina Anghelaki-Rooke, trs. *The Coffeehouse* 1 (Fall 1975), pp. 54-57.

7.1053 _____ "Three Young Poets: Jenny Mastoraki, Haris Megalinos and Lefteris Poulios". N.C. Germanacos et al., trs. *Boundary 2*, Vol. 1, No. 2 (Winter 1973), pp. 507-518 {3.5}.

7.1054 *_____ "Two Poems". Kostas Myrsiades, tr. *Grove* 5 (Winter 1979), pp. 12-13 {3.12}.

Prevelakis, Pantelis (1909-1986)

a.

7.1055 *_____ *Fire in Painting and in Poetry*. Philip Sherrard, tr. Athens: Greek Insurance Company "Ethniki", 1963. 54 p.

7.1056 *_____ *Nikos Kazantzakis and His Odyssey: A Study of the Poet and the Poem*. Philip Sherrard, tr.; Kimon Friar, pref. New York: Simon and Schuster, 1961. 192 p.

7.1057 _____ *The Sun of Death*. Abbott Rick, tr.; Henry Miller, pref. New York: Simon and Schuster, 1964. 255 p.

7.1058 *_____ *The Sun of Death*. Philip Sherrard, tr. Toronto: Macmillan, 1965. 206 p. Also *London: John Murray, 1965. 206 p.

7.1059 _____ *The Tale of a Town*. Kenneth Johnstone, tr. London; Athens: Doric Publications, 1976. 119 p.

b.

7.1060 _____ "The Angel in the Well: A Nouvelle". Peter Mackridge, tr. *The Charioteer* 16 and 17 (1974/1975), pp. 46-121.

7.1061 _____ "Crete and Cyprus". Kevin Andrews, tr. In *Cyprus '74: Aphrodite's Other Face* (Emmanuel C. Casdaglis, ed. Athens: National Bank of Greece, 1976), pp. 115-117 {4.87}.

7.1062 _____ "The Death of Giuliano De' Medici". Abbott Rick, tr. *Greek Letters* 3 (1984-1985), pp. 17-34.

7.1063 _____ "The Hand of the Slain: Drama in Three Days". Peter Mackridge, tr. *The Charioteer* 16 and 17 (1974/1975), pp. 127-146.

7.1064 _____ "Kazantzakis: Life and Works". Peter Bien, tr. *The Charioteer* 22 and 23 (1980/1981), pp. 23-65 {7.631}.

7.1065 _____ "Kazantzakis-Sikelianos: The Chronicle of a Friendship". Kimon Friar, tr. *JHD* 10, No. 4 (Winter 1983), pp. 5-20 {7.634}.

7.1066 _____ "'The Light-Shadowed' of Angelos Sikelianos". Ted Sampson, tr. *Greek Letters* 4 (1986-1989), pp. 123-146.

7.1067 _____ "from *Nikos Kazantzakis and his Odyssey*". Philip Sherrard, tr. *The Charioteer* 1, No. 1 (Summer 1960), pp. 10-36.

7.1068 _____ "Poems". Kimon Friar, tr. *The Charioteer* 16 and 17 (1974/1975), pp. 42-45.

7.1069 _____ "Rhethymno as a Style of Life". Jean H. Woodhead, tr. In *Pandelis Prevelakis and the Value of a Heritage. A Talk* (Andonis Decavalles. Minneapolis, Minn.: North Central Publishing Company, 1981), pp. 37-52 {7.1073}.

7.1070 _____ "The Smile of Maya" [from his novel: *The Bread of Angels*]. Theodore Sampson, tr. In *Modern Greek Short Stories*. Vol. 2 (Kyr. Delopoulos, ed. Athens: Kathimerini Publications, 1981), pp. 323-337 {4.13}.

7.1071 _____ "A Summer's Seminar" (from P. Prevelakis, Ὁ Ποιητής Γιάννης Ρίτσος). Edward Phinney, tr. *The Amaranth* 6 (1983), pp. 23-27.

7.1072 _____ "From *The Sun of Death*". Translated excerpt and preface by Henry Miller. *Greek Heritage* 2, No. 5 (1965), pp. 125-128.

c.
7.1073 Decavalles, Andonis. *Pandelis Prevelakis and the Value of a Heritage: A Talk*. Theofanis G. Stavrou, ed. and intro. The Second Annual Public Lecture in Modern Greek Studies, Special Collections, University of Minnesota Libraries, Minneapolis. With a supplement "Rhethymno as a Style of Life" by Pandelis Prevelakis [Jean H. Woodhead, tr.] (pp. 37-52). Minneapolis, Minn.: The North Central Publishing Company, 1981. 52 p.

d.
7.1074 Decavalles, Andonis C. "Kazantzakis and Prevelakis: Two Cretan Voices". *JMH* 2 (Oct. 1985), pp. 43-63.

7.1075 Decavalles, Andonis. "Pandelis Prevelakis: An Introduction". *The Charioteer* 16 and 17 (1974/1975), pp. 10-40.

7.1076 Decavalles, Andonis. "Prevelakis Reveals Ritsos". *MGSY* 1 (1985), pp. 207-217. A review article.

7.1077 Grammatopoulos, Kostas. "Pandelis Prevelakis (A Woodcut)". *The Charioteer* 16 and 17 (1974/1975), p. 41.

7.1078 Mackridge, Peter. "A Glossary of Unusual Words and Phrases in Ὁ Ἥλιος τοῦ Θανάτου by Pandelis Prevelakis". *Greek Letters* 3 (1984-1985), pp. 99-147.

7.1079 Mackridge, Peter. "A Matter of Light and Death: Symbolism in *The Sun of Death* by P. Prevelakis". *Folia Neohellenica* 6 (1984), pp. 61-70.

7.1080 Mackridge, Peter. "Popular Tradition and Individual Creativity: Pandelis Prevelakis (1909-1986)". *MGSY* 2 (1986), pp. 143-152.

7.1081 Mackridge, Peter A. "Prevelakis' *The Angel in the Well* and the Weight of the Orthodox Tradition". *Balkan Studies* 11, No. 2 (1970), pp. 305-311.

7.1082 Mitsakis, K. "Pandelis Prevelakis: The Myth of 'Romiosyni' as an Instructive Value in the Modern World". Th. Sampson, tr. *Greek Letters* 2 (1983), pp. 285-299.

7.1083 "Pandelis Prevelakis Talks to Peter Mackridge". Peter Mackridge, tr. *Omphalos* 1, No. 1 (Mar. 1972), pp. 34-39.

7.1084 Raizis, M. Byron. "The Early Poetry of Pandelis Prevelakis". *Greek Letters* 3 (1984-1985), pp. 201-216.

Psycharis, Giannis (1854-1929)

b.

7.1085 _____ "The Earrings". Alice-Mary Maffry, tr. *The Charioteer* 4 (1962), pp. 93-100 {4.17}.

7.1086 _____ "The Earrings". Theodore Sampson, tr. In *Modern Greek Short Stories*. Vol. 1 (Kyr. Delopoulos, ed. Athens: Kathimerini Publications, 1980), pp. 123-134 {4.12}.

Psychountakis, Giorgos

a.

7.1087 _____ *The Cretan Runner: His Story of the German Occupation*. Patrick Leigh Fermor, tr. and intro. Annotated by the translator and Xan Fielding. London: John Murray; Athens: Efstathiadis Group, n.d. 242 p.

Rangavis, A.R. (1809-1892)

d.

7.1088 Ricks, D.B. "A.R. Rangavis, 'The Voyage of Dionysus'". Ἑλληνικά 38, No. 1 (1987), pp. 89-97.

Ritsos, Giannis (b. 1909)

a.

7.1089 *Aeschylus and Yannis Ritsos. *Trojan Women*. The *Trojan Women* by Aeschylus, and *Helen* and *Orestes* by Ritsos. Gwendolyn MacEwen and Nikos Tsingos, trs. Toronto: Exile Editions, 1980.

7.1090 Amichai[, Yehuda] and Yannis Ritsos: *Two Long Poems. Travels of a Latter Day Benjamin of Tudela* [Ruth Nevo, tr.]; *Helen* [Nikos and Gwendolyn Tsingos, trs.]. Toronto: The House of Exile, 1976. 114 unnumbered p.

7.1091 *_____ *Ashy and White*. Kimon Friar, tr. San Jose, Calif.: Realities Library, 1983. A card.

7.1092 _____ *Chronicle of Exile*. Minas Savvas, tr. and intro.; Louis Aragon, foreword. Illustrated by the poet. San Francisco: Wire Press, 1977. 93 p.

7.1093 *_____ *Contradictions*. John Stathatos, tr. Rushden, Northamptonshire: Sceptre Press, 1973. 4 p.

7.1094 _____ *Corridor and Stairs*. Nikos Germanacos, tr.; Desmond Egan, intro. The Curragh, Ireland: The Goldsmith Press, 1976. 63 p. Bilingual edition.

7.1095 _____ *Eighteen Short Songs of the Bitter Motherland*. Amy Mims, tr. Illustrated by the poet. Theofanis G. Stavrou, ed. and intro. Minneapolis, Minn.: North Central Publishing Company, 1974. 60 p. Bilingual edition.

7.1096 _____ *Erotica: "Small Suite in Red Major"; "Naked Body"; "Carnal Word"*. Kimon Friar, tr. Old Chatham, N.Y.: Sachem Press, 1982. 96 p.

7.1097 _____ *Exile and Return: Selected Poems 1967-1974*. Edmund Keeley, tr. New York: The Ecco Press, 1985. 200 p. Paperback edition, 1987.

7.1098 *_____ *The Faraway*. Ninos Chryssopoulos, tr. Ottawa, 1978. 40 p.

7.1099 *_____ *14 Poems*. Illustrated by Claudia Lemay; Athan Anagnostopoulos, tr. Boston, Mass.: printed privately, 1977. 16 leaves. Limited edition.

7.1100 _____ *The Fourth Dimension. Selected Poems of Yannis Ritsos*. Rae Dalven, tr. Boston, Mass.: David R. Godine, 1977. 156 p.
    Selections from various poetry collections (not just the Τέταρτη Διάσταση).

7.1101 _____ *Gestures and Other Poems 1968-1970*. Nikos Stangos, tr. Illustrated by the poet. London and New York: Cape Goliard Press in association with Grossman Publishers, 1971. 88 p.

7.1102 _____ *The Lady of the Vineyards*. Apostolos N. Athanassakis, tr. New York: Pella Publishing Company, 1978. 77 p. Bilingual edition.

7.1103 _____ *Manifestation of Emptiness*. Martin McKinsey, tr. North Cambridge, Mass.: Pomegranate Press, 1979. A broadside. Limited edition.

7.1104 _____ *Monovasia and The Women of Monemvasia*. Kimon Friar, and Kostas Myrsiades, trs. A Nostos Book. Minneapolis, Minn.: North Central Publishing Company, 1987. 67 p.

7.1105 _____ *The Moonlight Sonata*. John Stathatos, tr. New Malden, Surrey: Tangent Books, 1975. 13 p.

7.1106 *_____ *Philoctetes*. Ninos Chryssopoulos, tr. Toronto, 1975. 26 p.

7.1107 *_____ *Respectful Comparison*. Paul Merchant, tr. and printed at the Windmill Hill Press to honour Yannis Ritsos. Birmingham, 8 July 1978. 4 p.

7.1108 *_____ *Return and Other Poems.* Edmund Keeley, tr.; Sidney Chafetz, woodcuts. Birmingham, Ala.: Parallel Editions, Graduate School of Library Science, University of Alabama, 1983. 36 p. Bilingual edition.

7.1109 _____ *Ritsos in Parentheses.* Edmund Keeley, tr. and intro. Princeton, N.J.: Princeton University Press, 1979. 175 p. Bilingual edition.
   Poems from *Parentheses* (in two groups), written 1946-47 and 1950-61, and *The Distant,* 1975.

7.1110 _____ *Romiossini: The Story of the Greeks.* O. Laos, tr.; Dan Georgakas, intro.; Gary Elder, ink drawings. Paradise, Calif.: Dust Books, 1969. 39 unnumbered p.

7.1111 _____ *Romiossini and Other Poems.* Dan Georgakas and Heleni Paidoussi, trs. with assistance on individual poems by John Chioles and others. Madison, Wisc.: Quixote Press, 1969. 24 p. Bilingual edition.

7.1112 *_____ *Romiosyne.* Elefterios K. Parianos, tr. Designed and bound by M.C. Caine. London, 1981. 12 p.

7.1113 _____ *Scripture of the Blind.* Kimon Friar and Kostas Myrsiades, trs. and intro. Columbus, Ohio: Ohio State University Press, 1979. 251 p. Bilingual edition.

7.1114 _____ *Selected Poems.* Nikos Stangos, tr.; Peter Bien, intro. Athens: Efstathiadis Group, 1981. 207 p. Originally Harmondsworth, Middlesex, England and Baltimore, Md.: Penguin Books, 1974. The original edition was out of print in 1986.
   The introduction by Peter Bien can also be found in his *Three Generations of Greek Writers. Introductions to Cavafy, Kazantzakis, Ritsos* (Athens: Efstathiadis Group, 1983), pp. 95-125 {5.1}.

7.1115 *_____ *Smudged Pot.* Ninos Chryssopoulos, tr. Toronto, 1975. 22 p.

7.1116 _____ *Subterranean Horses.* Illustrated by the author. Minas Savvas, tr.; Vassilis Vassilikos, intro. Athens, Ohio: Ohio University Press, 1980. 63 p. Also *Chicago: International Poetry Forum, 1980. 63 p.

7.1117 *_____ *Twelve for Cavafis.* Kimon Friar, tr. San Jose, Calif.: Realities Library, 1985. 12 p.

b.
7.1118 _____ "Agamemnon". Philip Pastras and George Pilitsis, trs. *JHD* 11, No. 4 (Winter 1984), pp. 47-67. Bilingual version.

7.1119 _____ "The Annihilation of Melos". Rick M. Newton, tr. *The Charioteer* 29/30 (1987-88), pp. 168-193 {7.1260}.

7.1120 _____ "Appearances"; "Small Trail"; "In the Rain"; "Invigorating". Kostas Myrsiades, tr. *Translation* 9 (Fall 1982), pp. 249-251.

7.1121 *____ "Belfry". Kimon Friar and Kostas Myrsiades, trs. *Durak* 5 (1980), pp. 34-44.

7.1122 ____ "Blockade"; "The Most Precious Things". Edmund Keeley, tr. *New England Review and Bread Loaf Quarterly* 8, No. 1 (Autumn 1985), p. 23.
   Is part of E. Keeley, *Exile and Return: Selected Poems 1967-74*. New York: The Ecco Press, 1985 {7.1097}.

7.1123 ____ "The Body and the Blood". C. Capri-Karka and Ilona Karka, trs. *The Charioteer* 29/30 (1987-88), pp. 217-236 {7.1260}.

7.1124 ____ "By Way of Introduction to the *Testimonies*". Rick M. Newton, tr. *The Charioteer* 29/30 (1987-88), pp. 111-116 {7.1260}.

7.1125 ____ "Chile". Thanasis Maskaleris, tr. *The Falcon* 9, No. 16 (Spring 1978), p. 12 {7.1261}.

7.1126 ____ "Chile" (for Alliende and Neruda). Kostas Myrsiades, tr. *JHD* 4, No. 1 (Mar. 1977), p. 56.

7.1127 ____ "from *Corridor and Stairs* (1970): Seven Poems". N.C. Germanacos, tr. *The Falcon* 9, No. 16 (Spring 1978), pp. 42-49 {7.1261}.

7.1128 *____ "Danger"; "On Returning"; "Greece"; "With Slow Unfolding". Edmund Keeley and Mary Keeley, trs. *The Pacific Review* 2 (Spring 1984), pp. 8-11.

7.1129 *____ "'The Dead' and 'In the Center'". Kimon Friar and Kostas Myrsiades, trs. *Footprint Magazine* 5 (Autumn 1980), pp. 92-93.

7.1130 *____ "Disfigurement"; "Penelope's Despair"; "Philomela"; "Marpessa's Choice"; "Our Land". Edmund Keeley, sometimes in collaboration with Philip Sherrard, trs. In *The Antaeus Anthology* (Daniel Halpern, ed. Toronto; New York: Bantam Books, 1986) {4.39}.

7.1131 ____ "The Disjunctive 'OR'" (from *Repetitions*); "Pardon"; "Nausica"; "Eurylokhos"; "Non-Hero". G.P. Savidis, tr. *The Coffeehouse* 10 (Summer 1978), pp. 14-18.

7.1132 ____ "from *The Distant*: Six Poems". Kostas Myrsiades, tr. *The Falcon* 9, No. 16 (Spring 1978), pp. 8-11 {7.1261}.

7.1133 ____ "from *Doorman's Booth*". C. Capri-Karka, tr. and intro. *The Charioteer* 29/30 (1987-88), pp. 196-216 {7.1260}.

7.1134 ____ "Eight Paper Poems". Edmund Keeley, tr. *Ploughshares* 11, No. 4 (1985), pp. 27-30 {3.25}.

7.1135 *_____ "Eight Poems". Edmund Keeley, tr. *Graham House Review* 9 (Fall 1985), pp. 45-53.

7.1136 _____ "Eight Poems". Edmund Keeley, tr. *Grand Street* 5, No. 1 (Autumn 1985), pp. 191-196.

7.1137 *_____ "Eight Poems from *The Wall Inside the Mirror*". Edmund Keeley, tr. *The American Poetry Review* 10, No. 4 (July/Aug. 1981), p. 22.

7.1138 *_____ "8 Poems, Including *Orestes*". Martin McKinsey, tr. *The American Poetry Review* 10, No. 4 (July/Aug. 1981).

7.1139 _____ "Eighteen Short Songs of the Bitter Motherland". C. Capri-Karka, tr. *The Charioteer* 29/30 (1987-88), pp. 155-167 {7.1260}.

7.1140 _____ "The Eleni". Amy Mims, tr. *Boundary 2,* Vol. 3, No. 3 (Spring 1975), pp. 797-823.

7.1141 _____ "Eleven Poems" (Poems from *Muted Poems*). Edmund Keeley, tr. *Chelsea* 40 (Winter 1981), pp. 38-45.

7.1142 *_____ "from *Eleven Poems*". Edmund Keeley, tr. *Chelsea Retrospective 1958-1983* (1984), pp. 413-417.

7.1143 _____ "The *Epitaphios* of Yannis Ritsos". Rick M. Newton, tr. *JHD* 13, Nos. 1 & 2 (Spring & Summer 1986), pp. 12-51. Bilingual version. With an introduction by the translator, "The *Epitaphios* of Yannis Ritsos", pp. 5-11.

7.1144 _____ "from *Exercises* (1950-1960): Twelve Poems". Minas Savvas, tr. *The Falcon* 9, No. 16 (Spring 1978), pp. 86-98 {7.1261}.

7.1145 _____ "'False Discoveries' by Yannis Ritsos". Kimon Friar and Kostas Myrsiades, trs. *Arizona Quarterly* 37, No. 3 (Autumn 1981), p. 244.

7.1146 _____ "The Five". Kimon Friar and Kostas Myrsiades, trs. *The Beloit Poetry Journal* 30, No. 4 (Summer 1980), p. 39.

7.1147 _____ [5 Poems]. Kimon Friar, tr. *Mundus Artium* 4, No. 1 (Winter 1970), pp. 6-7 {4.82}.
  "Afternoon"; "Moment"; "Danger Outstripped"; "Interchanges"; "Morning".

7.1148 _____ "Five Poems". Kimon Friar and Kostas Myrsiades, trs. *The Literary Review* 21, No. 4 (Summer 1978), pp. 457-459.
  "Way of Life"; "Liturgical"; "Simultaneously"; "Small Sonata"; "Stages of Ignorance".

7.1149 _____ "Five Poems". Edmund Keeley, tr. *The New Yorker* (23 Oct. 1978), p. 42.

7.1150 _____ "Five Poems of Yannis Ritsos". Kimon Friar and Kostas Myrsiades, trs. *Field* 22 (Spring 1980), pp. 75-81.
   "Sea Stroke"; "The Journey"; "Irresolute"; "White"; "This Darkness".

7.1151 *_____ "For a Little Summer: Yannis Ritsos' *Chrysothemis* and a Letter for Us". C. Capri-Karka, tr. *The Charioteer* 29/30 (1987-88), pp. 133-154 {7.1260}.

7.1152 *_____ "Four Poems". Edmund Keeley, tr. *The American Poetry Review* 8, No. 2 (Mar./Apr. 1979), p. 33.

7.1153 *_____ "Four Poems". Edmund Keeley, tr. *The Athenian* (Mar. 1981), p. 30.

7.1154 _____ "Four Poems". L.T. Manousakas, tr. *Eleutheria* 1, No. 2 (May 1970), pp. 18-19.
   "Summer"; "A Person"; "The Thank You"; "Conclusion".

7.1155 _____ "Four Poems and a Triptych". Edmund Keeley, tr. *Translation* 6 (Winter 1978-79), pp. 160-162.

7.1156 _____ "Four Poems of Yannis Ritsos". Kimon Friar and Kostas Myrsiades, trs. *Ploughshares* 6, No. 4 (1981), pp. 196-199.
   "The Iron Mosaic"; "The Scarecrow"; "Dilettantism"; "Improvised Achievement".

7.1157 _____ "Fourteen Poems". Edmund Keeley, tr. *Scripsi* 4, No. 2 (Nov. 1986), pp. 116-122.

7.1158 _____ "from *Gestures* (1969-1970): Four Poems". Minas Savvas, tr. *The Falcon* 9, No. 16 (Spring 1978), pp. 50-54 {7.1261}.

7.1159 *_____ "The Hill". Agnes Sotiracopoulou, tr. *Poetry* (Madras) 9, No. 2 (1968), pp. 16-17 {3.29}.

7.1160 _____ "Hymn and Lament for Cyprus". Amy Mims, tr. In *Cyprus '74: Aphrodite's Other Face* (Emmanuel C. Casdaglis, ed. Athens: National Bank of Greece, 1976), pp. 161-162 {4.87}.

7.1161 *_____ "In Nausicaa's House"; "Nausicaa". Edmund and Mary Keeley, trs. In *Literary Olympians II* (Crosscurrents Anthologies. Westlake Village, Calif., 1987), pp. 299-301.

7.1162 _____ "from *Lady of the Vineyards*". Sarah Kafatou, tr. *Arion's Dolphin* 1, No. 1 (Autumn 1971), pp. 2-3.

7.1163 _____ "The March of the Ocean". Marjorie Chambers, tr. *The Charioteer* 29/30 (1987-88), pp. 44-73 {7.1260}.

7.1164 *_____ "Modern Greek Poetry in Translation". Kimon Friar and Kostas Myrsiades, trs. *Ohio Journal* 4, No. 2 (Winter 1978), pp. 56-65.

7.1165 *_____ "Monovasia". Kimon Friar and Kostas Myrsiades, trs. *Baltic Avenue Poetry Journal* 5 (1981).

7.1166 _____ "The Moonlight Sonata". Rae Dalven, tr. In *New Directions in Prose and Poetry* 23 (J. Laughlin, ed. A New Directions Book. New York: New Directions, 1971), pp. 167-177.

7.1167 _____ "Moving". Edmund Keeley, tr. *The Missouri Review* 8, No. 3 (1985), p. 62.

7.1168 _____ "My Sister's Song". Marjorie Chambers, tr. *The Charioteer* 29/30 (1987-88), pp. 19-43 {7.1260}.

7.1169 _____ "News Bulletin"; "Sources". Edmund Keeley, tr. *Ironwood* 25 (Spring 1985), pp. 20-21.

7.1170 *_____ "Nine Poems". Kimon Friar and Kostas Myrsiades, trs. *Grove* 4 (Spring 1978), pp. 23-31.
   "Hesitation"; "Extinction"; "Midnight Cry"; "Gradually Stripped Bare"; "Unfulfilled Promise"; "Symbolical"; "St. Nicholas Station"; "Liter"; "Portioning Out".

7.1171 _____ "Nine Poems". N.C. Germanacos, tr. *Omphalos* 1, No. 1 (Mar. 1972), pp. 14-21. Bilingual version.
   "The Chair-Maker and the Blind Man"; "The Fundamentals"; "Mindlessness"; "Memorial Services"; "Disturbance"; "Dislocation"; "Disconnection"; "Whitewash". All the poems are dated 1970.

7.1172 _____ "Nine Poems". Edmund Keeley, tr. *New Letters* 51, No. 4 (Summer 1985), pp. 9-13.

7.1173 _____ "Nineteen Poems". Kimon Friar and Kostas Myrsiades, trs. *Grove* 3 (Winter 1977), pp. 44-62.
   "Unburied"; "Doubtful Therapy"; "Without a Mirror Now"; "Monologue with Someone Hidden"; "Demolished Shelters"; "At the Harbor's End"; "Nightly Performance"; "Spasmodically"; "The Third Poem"; "Transposition"; "Habitual Surprise"; "Outline of a Nightmare"; "The Meaning of Art"; "Resistance to the Indefinite"; "Common Miracles"; "The Dissonant Chord"; "Anonymous Street"; "Reticence"; "Limits".

7.1174 _____ "from *Notes on the Margins of Time* (1938-1941): Six Poems". Kimon Friar, tr. *The Falcon* 9, No. 16 (Spring 1978), pp. 123-129 {7.1261}.

7.1175 _____ "On Rereading the Poetic Collections *The Wall in the Mirror* and *Porter's Lodge* (1972)". Kostas Myrsiades, tr. *The Falcon* 9, No. 16 (Spring 1978), pp. 130-132 {7.1261}.

7.1176 _____ "Orestes". Philip Pastras and George Pilitsis, trs. *JHD* 12, No. 1 (Spring 1985), pp. 53-81.

7.1177 *_____ "Our Land". Edmund Keeley, tr. In *Ecco Pocket Poetry* (New York: Ecco Press, 1984).

7.1178 _____ "from *Parenthesis* (1946-1947): Twelve Poems". Edmund Keeley, tr. *The Falcon* 9, No. 16 (Spring 1978), pp. 106-118 {7.1261}.

7.1179 _____ "Peace (1953)". Kimon Friar, tr. *The Falcon* 9, No. 16 (Spring 1978), pp. 99-101 {7.1261}.

7.1180 _____ "Penelope's Despair". Kostas Myrsiades, tr. *College Literature* 3, No. 3 (Fall 1976), p. 256.

7.1181 _____ "Penelope's Despair". Kostas Myrsiades, tr. *New Orleans Review* 8, No. 1 (Winter 1981), p. 14.

7.1182 _____ "Persephone" (a poem). Peter Green and Beverly Bardsley, trs. *Grand Street* 6, No. 4 (Summer 1987), pp. 143-156.

7.1183 _____ "from *Petrified Time* (1949): Two Poems". Martin McKinsey, tr. *The Falcon* 9, No. 16 (Spring 1978), pp. 102-105 {7.1261}.

7.1184 _____ "Philoctetes (The Ultimate Mask)". Peter Bien, tr. *Shenandoah* 27, No. 1 (Fall 1975), pp. 68-87 {3.32}.

7.1185 _____ "Poems from *Corridors and Stairs*". N.C. Germanakos, tr. *Boundary 2*, Vol. 1, No. 1 (Fall 1972), pp. 169-207. Includes "A Biographical Note" by William V. Spanos and Robert Kroetsch, pp. 171-173.
   Continued, as "Poems from the Unpublished Collection *Corridors and Stairs* by Yannis Ritsos". N.C. Germanacos, tr. *Boundary 2*, Vol. 1, No. 2 (Winter 1973), pp. 379-399 {3.5}.

7.1186 *_____ "Poems from Exile". N.C. Germanacos, tr. *The American Poetry Review* 2, No. 5 (1973), pp. 23-26.

7.1187 *_____ "Poems from *The Wall Inside the Mirror* by Yannis Ritsos". Edmund Keeley, tr. *Milkweed Chronicle* 2, No. 2 (Spring/Summer 1981), p. 7.
   "Transgression"; "Changing Habits".

7.1188 *_____ "Poems from *The World is One* ". Kostas Myrsiades, tr. *Durak* 5 (1980), pp. 45-48.
   "Doubtful Encounters"; "Freedom of Travel"; "Vatican Museum"; "Encounters".

7.1189 _____ "Poems of Yannis Ritsos". Edmund Keeley, tr. *The Iowa Review* 9, No. 2 (Spring 1978), pp. 103-105.

7.1190 *_____ "Poems of Yannis Ritsos". Alan Page, tr. *The Review* (Oxford) (1969). 24 p.

7.1191 _____ "Poetry by Yannis Ritsos". Minas Savvas, tr. *JHD* 2, No. 3 (July 1975), pp. 63-65.
"Nevertheless"; "Old-Comrade-Mitsos".

7.1192 _____ "Poetry Feature: Poems by Yannis Ritsos". Kimon Friar and Kostas Myrsiades, trs. *Antaeus* 28 (Winter 1978), pp. 56-65.
Preceded by an essay by Edmund Keeley: "A Preface to Selections from *Scripture of the Blind* by Yannis Ritsos" (pp. 52-55).

7.1193 _____ "Poetry of Yannis Ritsos". Edmund Keeley, tr. *The Charioteer* 21 (1979), pp. 11-17.
Selections from *Ritsos in Parentheses*. With biographical data. Preceded by a brief essay by Edmund Keeley: "Selections from *Ritsos in Parentheses*" (p. 10).

7.1194 _____ "A Portfolio". *Shenandoah* 27, No. 1 (Fall 1975), pp. 49-87 {3.32}.
Including: "from *The Wall in the Mirror*" [N.C. Germanacos, tr.] (pp. 51-52); "from *The Paper Poems*" [N.C. Germanacos, tr.] (pp. 53-55); "Stones, Bones, Roots" [Kay Cicellis, tr.] (pp. 56-67); and "Philoctetes" (The Ultimate Mask) [Peter Bien, tr.] (pp. 68-87).

7.1195 _____ "*The Prison Tree and the Women (1962)*". Kimon Friar, tr. *The Falcon* 9, No. 16 (Spring 1978), pp. 59-67 {7.1261}.

7.1196 *_____ "Reconstruction"; "Preparing the Ceremony". Edmund Keeley, tr. *The Hellenic Journal* (4 Oct. 1979), p. 7.

7.1197 *_____ "Romiosini". *The American Poetry Review* 2, No. 5 (1973), pp. 13-17.

7.1198 _____ "Romiosini". N.C. Germanakos, tr. *Chelsea* 30/31 (June 1972), pp. 64-79.
With "A Biographical and Critical Note on Yannis Ritsos" by William V. Spanos (pp. 79-81).

7.1199 _____ "Romiosini". Philip Pastras and George Pilitsis, trs. *The Charioteer* 29/30 (1987-88), pp. 74-87 {7.1260}.

7.1200 *_____ "Romiosyne". Eleftherios K. Parianos, tr. In the *Penguin Book of Socialist Verse* (Alan Bold, ed. and intro. Harmondsworth, Middlesex, England: Penguin Books, 1970), pp. 312-329.

7.1201 _____ "from *Scripture of the Blind*: Twenty Poems". Kimon Friar and Kostas Myrsiades, trs. *The Falcon* 9, No. 16 (Spring 1978), pp. 13-31 {7.1261}.

7.1202 _____ "A Selection from the Forties". Athan Anagnostopoulos, tr. *JHD* 5, No. 3 (Fall 1978), pp. 57-87. Bilingual version.

7.1203 _____ "A Selection of Short Poems". C. Capri-Karka, George Pilitsis, Martin McKinsey, and Marjorie Chambers, trs. *The Charioteer* 29/30 (1987-88), pp. 237-250 {7.1260}.

7.1204 _____ "Septeria and Daphnephoria" (from *Repetitions*). Nikos Stangos, tr. In *Greece Old and New* (Tom Winnifrith and Penelope Murray, eds. London and Basingstoke: The Macmillan Press, Ltd., 1983), pp. 175-176.

7.1205 _____ "Seven from Samos". Poems by Yannis Ritsos from the unpublished collection *Replacements* (Karlovasi, Samos, Aug. 1978). Minas Savvas, tr. *Aegean Review* 1 (Fall/Winter 1986), pp. 31-33.

7.1206 _____ [7 Poems]. Kimon Friar and Kostas Myrsiades, trs. *The Hudson Review* 34, No. 2 (Summer 1981), pp. 169-172.

7.1207 _____ [Seven Poems]. Edmund Keeley, tr. *Antaeus* 30/31 (Spring 1978), pp. 188-191.

7.1208 _____ "Seven Poems". Edmund Keeley, tr. *Antaeus* 40/41 (Winter/Spring 1981), pp. 375-378.

7.1209 _____ [7 poems]. Edmund Keeley, tr. *Pequod* 3, No. 1 (1979), pp. 80-81.

7.1210 _____ "Seven Poems". Edmund Keeley, tr. *Translation* 14 (Spring 1985), pp. 3-9 {3.34}.

7.1211 _____ "Seven Poems by Yannis Ritsos". Rae Dalven, tr. *Poetry* 116, Nos. 5-6 (Aug.-Sept. 1970), pp. 292-298.
  "The Meaning of Simplicity"; "In the Barracks"; "Absence"; "Suspicious Sleep"; "Not Unsuspecting"; "Achievement"; "A Minimum Delay".

7.1212 _____ [7 Poems from *Repetitions*]. Martin McKinsey, tr. *International Poetry Review* 9, No. 2 (Fall 1983), pp. 60-63.

7.1213 *_____ "Seventeen Poems". Kimon Friar and Kostas Myrsiades, trs. *The American Poetry Review* 7, No. 4 (July-Aug. 1978), pp. 23-26.

7.1214 *_____ "A Short Tale"; "Time"; "The Mirror". Rita Taylor, tr. *Contemporary Literature in Translation* 11 (Fall 1971), pp. 28-29.

7.1215 _____ "Silent Message". Edmund Keeley, tr. *Seneca Review* 12, Nos. 1-2 (1981), pp. 20-21. Bilingual.

7.1216 _____ "Six Poems". Edmund Keeley, tr. *Antaeus* 55 (Autumn 1985), pp. 314-318.

7.1217 _____ "Six Poems". Edmund Keeley, tr. *Boston University Journal* 25, No. 3 (1978), pp. 62-64.

7.1218 _____ "[Six Poems]". Edmund Keeley, tr. *Field* 19 (Fall 1978), pp. 17-22.
  "Toward Saturday"; "Slowly"; "Red-Handed"; "The Same Thorn"; "Autumn Expression"; "Marking".

7.1219 _____ "Six Poems". Edmund Keeley, tr. *The Iowa Review* 15, No. 2 (Spring-Summer 1985), pp. 96-98.

7.1220 _____ [6 Poems]. John Constantine Stathatos, tr. *Mundus Artium* 4, No. 1 (Winter 1970), pp. 8-9 {4.82}.

7.1221 _____ "Six Poems from *Scripture of the Blind* ". Kimon Friar and Kostas Myrsiades, trs. *Poet Lore* 72, No. 4 (Winter 1978), pp. 154-157.

7.1222 *_____ "Special Section: Yannis Ritsos. [8 Poems]". Kostas Myrsiades, tr. *Durak* 4 (1980), pp. 55-62.

7.1223 *_____ "The Statues in the Cemetery and The Nights and the Statues". Edmund Keeley, tr. *Footprint Magazine* 2 (Autumn 1978), p. 15.

7.1224 *_____ "Suddenly"; "Circus"; "Insomnia". Edmund Keeley, tr. In *Nightwalks: A Bedside Companion* (Joyce Carol Oates, comp. Princeton, N.J.: The Ontario Review Press, 1982), pp. 174-176.

7.1225 _____ "Surveillance". Kimon Friar and Kostas Myrsiades, trs. *The Antioch Review* 35, No. 4 (Fall 1977), p. 407.

7.1226 _____ "from *The Swaying of the Scale* (1943): Two Poems". Martin McKinsey, tr. *The Falcon* 9, No. 16 (Spring 1978), pp. 119-122 {7.1261}.

7.1227 _____ "Ten Poems". Rae Dalven, tr. *The Noiseless Spider* 2, No. 2 (Spring 1973), pp. 7-15.
    "Special Supplement: The Greek Reality", also including: Kostis Palamas, "Egypt"; "Athens" [Mary Gregory, tr.] (pp. 20-21); Lili Bita, "Love in the Genitals of Kronos"; "I am a Greek" [Robert Zaller, tr.] (pp. 24-26).

7.1228 _____ "Ten Poems". Minas Savvas, tr. *Antaeus* 15 (Autumn 1974), pp. 37-40.

7.1229 _____ "from *Testimonies A*". Rick M. Newton, tr. *The Charioteer* 29/30 (1987-88), pp. 117-123 {7.1260}.

7.1230 _____ "from *Testimonies B*". Martin McKinsey, tr. *The Charioteer* 29/30 (1987-88), pp. 124-125 {7.1260}.

7.1231 _____ "from *Testimonies I* (1957-1963): Seventeen Poems". Kimon Friar and George Thaniel, trs. *The Falcon* 9, No. 16 (Spring 1978), pp. 68-85 {7.1261}.

7.1232 _____ "from *Testimonies II* (1964-1965): Six Poems". Kimon Friar, tr. *The Falcon* 9, No. 16 (Spring 1978), pp. 55-58 {7.1261}.

7.1233 _____ "Three Greek Poets: Yannis Ritsos, Takis Sinopoulos, George Pavlopoulos". Translated respectively by Peter Levi & Nikos Stangos; Ian Scott-Kilvert; and Peter Levi. *TLS* (14 Nov. 1975), p. 1365.

7.1234 _____ "Three Poems". Edmund Keeley, tr. *Columbia* 8 (1983), pp. 177-179.
From *The Wall inside the Mirror*.

7.1235 _____ "Three Poems". Edmund Keeley, tr. *The New Republic,* Issue 3714 (24 Mar. 1986), p. 40.
"Apollo's First Altar"; "The Decay of the Argo"; "Requiem on Poros".

7.1236 *_____ "Three Poems". Edmund and Mary Keeley, trs. *Crosscurrents* 4, No. 4 and 5, No. 1 (1985), pp. 27-29.

7.1237 _____ "Three Poems". Martin McKinsey, tr. *The Paris Review* 91 (1984), pp. 122-123.
"Wavering Decisions"; "Provincial Spring"; "Small Composition".

7.1238 _____ [3 Poems]. Rita Taylor, tr. *Contemporary Literature in Translation* 11 (Fall 1971), pp. 28-29.
"A Short Tale"; "Time"; "The Mirror".

7.1239 _____ "Three Poems by Yannis Ritsos". Rae Dalven, tr. *Poetry* 120, No. 5 (Aug. 1972), pp. 260-261.
"Injustice"; "Without Position"; "Security".

7.1240 _____ "Three Poems by Yannis Ritsos". Minas Savvas, tr. *Boundary 2,* Vol. 4, No. 3 (Spring 1976), pp. 807-814.
"Change"; "Night"; "Nevertheless"

7.1241 _____ "Twelve Poems for Louis Aragon". Kimon Friar and Kostas Myrsiades, trs. *The Falcon,* No. 15 (Fall 1977), pp. 4-18.
"Meaningless Exception"; "The Mute"; "Demolished Shelters"; "At the Harbor's End"; "Relapse"; "Vulnerability"; "Eyewitness"; "Night Arrests"; "Real Hands"; "Habitual Surprise"; "The Dissonant Chord"; "Silent Praise".

7.1242 _____ "Twelve Poems from *Parenthesis* (1946-1947)". Edmund Keeley, tr. *The Falcon* 9, No. 16 (Spring 1978), pp. 106-118 {7.1261}.

7.1243 _____ "Two Poems". Kimon Friar and Kostas Myrsiades, trs. *Epoch* 27, No. 1 (Fall 1977), p. 82.
"The Earthen Adolescent"; "Hyalography of the Bath".

7.1244 _____ "Two Poems". Edmund Keeley, tr. *The Ontario Review* 23 (Fall-Winter 1985-86), pp. 93-94.
"After the Fact"; "Precisely Now".

7.1245 _____ "Two Poems". Thanasis Maskaleris, tr. *The Literary Review* 16, No. 3 (Spring 1973), p. 353 {3.15}.
"If I Had the Water of Immortality"; "My Sweet One, You Did Not Vanish".

7.1246 _____ "Two Poems". Martin McKinsey, tr. *The Kenyon Review*, N.S. 5, No. 1 (Winter 1983), pp. 86-87.
"Achilles after Death"; "Penelope's Despair".

7.1247 _____ "Two Poems". Martin McKinsey, tr. *The Yale Review* 74, No. 3 (Spring 1985), pp. 452-453.
"The Choice"; "Our Life in Phares".

7.1248 _____ "Two Poems: 'The Laugh'; 'Multidimensional'". Kostas Myrsiades, tr. *Seneca Review* 12, Nos. 1-2 (1981), pp. 22-25. Bilingual.

7.1249 _____ "Two Unpublished Poems". Kimon Friar and Kostas Myrsiades, trs. *The Denver Quarterly* 12, No. 2 (Summer 1977), p. 268.
"On the Television Screen"; "Opposition".

7.1250 *_____ "The Unhinged Shutter". Edmund and Mary Keeley, trs. *Crosscurrents* 4, No. 2 (1984), p. 41.

7.1251 _____ "Upon Reading Again the Collections *The Wall in the Mirror* and *Doorman's Booth*". C. Capri-Karka, tr. *The Charioteer* 29/30 (1987-88), pp. 194-195 {7.1260}.

7.1252 _____ "from *The Wall in the Mirror* (1971): Eleven Poems". Andonis Decavalles, tr. *The Falcon* 9, No. 16 (Spring 1978), pp. 32-41 {7.1261}.

7.1253 _____ "from *The Wall Inside the Mirror*". Edmund Keeley, tr. *The Ontario Review* 14 (Spring-Summer 1981), pp. 47-50.
"Elegy"; "Narrowness"; "Elation"; "Enlightenment".

7.1254 _____ "Wax Images". Edmund Keeley, tr. *Willow Springs Magazine* 8 (Spring 1981), p. 29.

7.1255 _____ "We Wait"; "Secret Ritual"; "Dusk"; "A Sick Man's Reward"; "Wonder"; "Night". Minas Savvas, tr. With illustrations by the poet. *The Coffeehouse* 1 (Fall 1975), pp. 2-7.

7.1256 *_____ "Wind". Edmund Keeley, tr. Santa Cruz, Calif.: Greenhouse Review Press, [1985]. A broadsheet, limited publication.

7.1257 _____ "The Window". Rae Dalven, tr. In *New Directions in Prose and Poetry* 26 (J. Laughlin, ed., with Peter Glassgold and Frederick R. Martin. New York: New Directions, 1973), pp. 126-138.

7.1258 _____ "With a Distant Lightning"; "After the Rain". Martin McKinsey, tr. *The Massachusetts Review* 24, No. 4 (Winter 1983), pp. 721-722.

7.1259 _____ "Yannis Ritsos". Translated by Paul Merchant, with the exceptions noted: "The Poet's Place"; "Putting out the Lamp"; "Final Hair"; "Dusk"; "Alone with His Work"; "Miniature" [Edmund Keeley, tr.]; "Beauty" [Minas Savvas, tr.]; "Insignificant Needs" [Minas Savvas, tr.]. In *Another Republic: 17 European & South American Writers* (Charles Simic and Mark Strand eds. New York: The Ecco Press, 1976), pp. 201-209.

c.
Special issues of periodicals

7.1260 *The Charioteer* 29/30 (1987-88). Special Double Issue: Yannis Ritsos.
Contains: "My Sister's Song" [Marjorie Chambers, tr.] (pp. 19-43); "The March of the Ocean" [Marjorie Chambers, tr.] (pp. 44-73); "Romiosini" [Philip Pastras and George Pilitsis, trs.] (pp. 74-87); William Spanos, "Yannis Ritsos' *Romiosini*: Style as Historical Memory" (pp. 88-110); [Yannis Ritsos,] "By Way of Introduction to the *Testimonies*" [Rick M. Newton, tr.] (pp. 111-116); "from *Testimonies A*" [Rick M. Newton, tr.] (pp. 117-123); "from *Testimonies B*" [Martin McKinsey, tr.] (pp. 124-125); Peter Bien, "Orestes' Cow" (pp. 126-132); "For a Little Summer: Yannis Ritsos' *Chrysothemis* and a Letter for Us" [C. Capri-Karka, tr.] (pp. 133-154); "Eighteen Short Songs of the Bitter Motherland" [C. Capri-Karka, tr.] (pp. 155-167); "The Annihilation of Melos" [Rick M. Newton, tr.] (pp. 168-193); "Upon Reading Again the Collections *The Wall in the Mirror* and *Doorman's Booth*" [C. Capri-Karka, tr.] (pp. 194-195); "from *Doorman's Booth*" [C. Capri-Karka, tr. and intro.] (pp. 196-216); "The Body and the Blood" [C. Capri-Karka and Ilona Karka, trs.] (pp. 217-236); "A Selection of Short Poems" [C. Capri-Karka, George Pilitsis, Martin McKinsey, and Marjorie Chambers, trs.] (pp. 237-250); "Short Biographical Note" (p. 251); "Works by Yannis Ritsos" (p. 252).
Address: Pella Publishing Co., Inc., 337 W. 36th St., New York, N.Y. 10018.

7.1261 *The Falcon* (Mansfield State College, Pa.), Vol. 9, No. 16 (Spring 1978). *Yannis Ritsos: Selected Poems 1938-1975*. Kimon Friar and Kostas Myrsiades, eds. 137 p.
Contains: Kostas Myrsiades, "Yannis Ritsos: The Man and the Poet" (pp. 4-7); Yannis Ritsos, "from *The Distant* (1975): Six Poems" [Kostas Myrsiades, tr.] (pp. 8-11); "Chile" [Thanasis Maskaleris, tr.] (p. 12); "from *Scripture of the Blind* (1972): Twenty Poems" [Kimon Friar and Kostas Myrsiades, trs.] (pp. 13-31); "from *The Wall in the Mirror* (1971): Eleven Poems" [Andonis Decavalles, tr.] (pp. 32-41); "From *Corridor and Stairs* (1970): Seven Poems" [N.C. Germanacos, tr.] (pp. 42-49); "from *Gestures* (1969-1970): Four Poems" [Minas Savvas, tr.] (pp. 50-54); "from *Testimonies II* (1964-1965): Six Poems" [Kimon Friar, tr.] (pp. 55-58); *The Prison Tree and the Women* (1962) [Kimon Friar, tr.] (pp. 59-67); "from *Testimonies I* (1957-1963): Seventeen Poems" [Kimon Friar and George Thaniel, trs.] (pp. 68-85); "from *Exercises* (1950-1960): Twelve Poems" [Minas Savvas, tr.] (pp. 86-98); "Peace" (1953) [Kimon Friar, tr.] (pp. 99-101); "from *Petrified Time* (1949): Two Poems" [Martin McKinsey, tr.] (pp. 102-105); "from *Parenthesis* (1946-1947): Twelve Poems" [Edmund Keeley, tr.] (pp. 106-118); "from *The Swaying of the Scale* (1943): Two Poems" [Martin McKinsey, tr.] (pp. 119-122); "from *Notes on the Margins of Time* (1938-1941): Six Poems" [Kimon Friar, tr.] (pp. 123-129); "On Rereading the Poetic Collections *The Wall in the Mirror* and *Porter's Lodge* (1972)" [Kostas Myrsiades, tr.] (pp. 130-132); "The Published Works of Yannis Ritsos" (pp. 133-135).
Address: Mansfield State College, Mansfield, Pa. 16933. Back issues are available on microfilm from University Microfilms, 300 North Zeeb Road, Ann Arbor, Mich. 48106.

7.1262 Μαντατοφόρος 12 (May 1978), pp. 1-95 (the entire issue). *Ritsos Bibliography*. Contains: Μακρυνικόλα, Αἰκατερίνη (Ninetta Makrynikola), "Συνοπτική Βιβλιογραφία Γιάννη Ρίτσου" (Comprehensive Ritsos Bibliography).
See especially translations into English (pp. 25-27).

Address: *Mantatoforos*, Universiteit van Amsterdam, Byzantijns-Nieuwgrieks Seminarium, Nieuwe Doelenstraat 16, 1012 CP Amsterdam, Holland. Out of print in 1990. Not expected to be reissued.

d.

7.1263 Bien, Peter. "Myth in Modern Greek Letters, with Special Attention to Yannis Ritsos's *Philoctetes*". *Books Abroad* 48, No. 1 (Winter 1974), pp. 15-20.

7.1264 Bien, Peter. "Orestes' Cow". *The Charioteer* 29/30 (1987-88), pp. 126-132 {7.1260}.

7.1265 Bien, Peter. "Ritsos". In his *Three Generations of Greek Writers: Introductions to Cavafy, Kazantzakis, Ritsos* (Athens: Efstathiadis Group, 1983), pp. 95-125 {5.1}.
Reprinted from his introduction to {7.1114}.

7.1266 Brittain, Maryanne. "'The Moonlight Sonata' by Yannis Ritsos: An Analysis". Το Γιοφύρι 3-4 (Nov. 1978), pp. 18-21.

7.1267 *Carroll, M.G. "A Matter of Style: Cavafy to Ritsos". *Antipodes* 2 (1975), pp. 19-23.

7.1268 Colakis, Marianthe. "Classical Mythology in Yannis Ritsos' Dramatic Monologues". *CML* 4, No. 3 (Spring 1984), pp. 117-130.

7.1269 Decavalles, Andonis. "Prevelakis Reveals Ritsos". *MGSY* 1 (1985), pp. 207-217. A review article.

7.1270 *Economou, George. "Eros, Memory, and Art". *The American Poetry Review* 10, No. 4 (July-Aug. 1981), pp. 30-31.

7.1271 Hadas, Rachel. "Two Worlds According to Ritsos". *Parnassus* 9, No. 1 (Spring/Summer 1981), pp. 342-355.
Is a review of Keeley's translation *Ritsos in Parentheses* and Friar & Myrsiades' *Scripture of the Blind* {7.1109, 7.1113}.

7.1272 Hadas, Rachel. "Voice from an Empty House". *Parnassus* 6, No. 2 (Spring/Summer 1978), pp. 26-29.
Is a review of Rae Dalven's translation *The Fourth Dimension* {7.1100}.

7.1273 Keeley, Edmund. "Ritsos: Voice and Vision in the Shorter Poems". In his *Modern Greek Poetry: Voice and Myth* (Princeton, N.J.: Princeton University Press, 1983), pp. 149-179 {5.2}. First published as "Yannis Ritsos in Parentheses". *Boston University Journal* 25, No. 3 (1978), pp. 53-61 {7.1274}.

7.1274 Keeley, Edmund. "Yannis Ritsos in Parentheses". *Boston University Journal* 25, No. 3 (1978), pp. 53-61.
Subsequently included, as "Ritsos: Voice and Vision in the Shorter Poems", in his *Modern Greek Poetry: Voice and Myth* (Princeton, N.J.: Princeton University Press, 1983), pp. 149-179 {5.2}.

7.1275 *Myrsiades, Kostas. "By Way of an Introduction to *Testimonies*". *Durak* 5 (1980), pp. 29-33.

7.1276 Myrsiades, Kostas. "The Classical Past in Yannis Ritsos' Dramatic Monologues". *Papers on Language and Literature* 14, No. 4 (Fall 1978), pp. 450-458.

7.1277 *Myrsiades, Kostas. "A Conversation with Yannis Ritsos" (introduction and interview). *Durak* 5 (1980), pp. 23-28.

7.1278 Myrsiades, Kostas. "The Poetry of Oppression: Yannis Ritsos' *Scripture of the Blind*". *The Literary Review* 21, No. 4 (Summer 1978), pp. 460-464.

7.1279 Myrsiades, Kostas. "Yannis Ritsos and Greek Resistance Poetry". *JHD* 5, No. 3 (Fall 1978), pp. 47-56.
 Is linked with "A Selection from the Forties" {7.1202}.

7.1280 Myrsiades, Kostas. "Yannis Ritsos: The Man and the Poet". *The Falcon* 9, No. 16 (Spring 1978), pp. 4-7 {7.1261}.

7.1281 Pandiri, Thalia. "Ritsos Old and New: Some Recent Translations". *Translation Review* 11 (1983), pp. 20-30.
 Review article. On the following English-language translations of Ritsos: Minas Savvas, *Chronicle of Exile;* Edmund Keeley, *Ritsos in Parentheses;* Kimon Friar and Kostas Myrsiades, *Scripture of the Blind* {7.1092, 7.1109, 7.1113}.

7.1282 *Pastras, Philip J. "A Clear Field: The Idea of Improvisation in Modern Poetry". *Dissertation Abstracts International* 42, No. 4 (Oct. 1981), p. 1626A.
 Comparison of O. Elytis with Walt Whitman, Giannes Ritsos, and William Carlos Williams.

7.1283 Plassara, Katerina. "Yiannis Ritsos: The Path towards the Myth". Grace Edwards, tr. *The Athenian* (Nov. 1979), pp. 24-29.

7.1284 Prevelakis, Pandelis. "A Summer's Seminar" (from his Ὁ Ποιητής Γιάννης Ρίτσος). Edward Phinney, tr. *The Amaranth* 6 (1983), pp. 23-27.

7.1285 Raizis, M. Byron. "Yannis Ritsos: Four New Collections". Review article. *WLT* 57, No. 3 (Summer 1983), pp. 416-418.

7.1286 Siotis, Dino. "Yannis Ritsos: A Voyage with No End" [interview]. *Aegean Review* 1 (Fall/Winter 1986), pp. 20-30.

7.1287 Spanos, William. "Yannis Ritsos' *Romiosini*: Style as Historical Memory". *The Charioteer* 29/30 (1987-88), pp. 88-110 {7.1260}.

7.1288 Vincent, Alfred. "Note on Ritsos' Ρωμιοσύνη". Το Γιοφύρι 2 (June 1978), pp. 24-29.

7.1289 Vincent, Alfred. "Notes on Ritsos' Δεκαοχτώ λιανοτράγουδα". Το Γιοφύρι 6 (Aug. 1979), pp. 10-23.

7.1290 Wallace, Warren. "The Writer's Situation Here and Abroad: Toward a Literary Community—On Yannis Ritsos". *PEN American Center Newsletter,* No. 45 (Dec. 1980), pp. 3-5.
Interview by Warren Wallace with Edmund Keeley.

Rodokanaki, C.P.
a.
7.1291 *_____ *Forever Ulysses.* A Novel. Patrick Leigh Fermor, tr. New York: The Viking Press, 1938. 315 p.

Roïdis, Emmanouil (1836-1904)
a.
7.1292 *_____ *Papissa Joanna.* T.D. Kriton, tr. Athenai: Govostis, [1935]. 179 p.

7.1293 Durrell, Lawrence. *Pope Joan.* Translated and adapted from the Greek of Emmanuel Royidis. Woodstock, N.Y.: The Overlook Press, 1960. 157 p. Reprinted 1984. Also a revised edition: New York: Dutton, 1961. 157 p.

7.1294 _____ *Pope Joan: A Romantic Biography by Emmanuel Royidis.* Lawrence Durrell tr. London: Derek Verschoyle, 1954. 163 p. *Also a revised edition: London: André Deutsch, 1960. 163 p. London: World Distributors, 1962. London: Mayflower, 1965. London: Sphere, 1971. London: Owen, 1981. Reissued, London: Overlook Press, 1984.

7.1295 _____ *Pope Joan. An Historical Romance by Emmanuel Roides.* J.H. Freese, tr. London: H.J. Cook, 1900. 171 p.

7.1296 _____ *Pope Joan, the Female Pope: A Historical Study.* Translated from the Greek of Emmanuel Rhoidis, with preface by Charles Hastings Collette. London: George Redway, 1886. 102 p.
A translation of the introduction to the novel.

b.
7.1297 _____ "from *Pope Joan*". Lawrence Durrell, tr. *The Charioteer* 3 (1961), pp. 11-19.

7.1298 _____ "The Story of a Dog". Theodore Sampson, tr. In *Modern Greek Short Stories.* Vol. 1 (Kyr. Delopoulos, ed. Athens: Kathimerini Publications, 1980), pp. 43-51 {4.12}.

d.
7.1299 Durrell, Lawrence. "Preface to *Pope Joan*". *The Charioteer* 3 (1961), pp. 7-11.

Roufos, Rodis (1924-1972)

a.

7.1300 *_____ *The Age of Bronze*. London; Melbourne; Toronto: Heinemann, [1960]. 285 p.

7.1301 'Athenian' [=Rodis Roufos]. *Inside the Colonel's Greece*. Richard Clogg, tr. and intro. London: Chatto & Windus, 1972. 215 p.

b.

7.1302 _____ "The Candidate". Rodis Roufos and Sarah Kafatou, trs. In *Eighteen Texts* (Willis Barnstone, ed. Cambridge, Mass.: Harvard University Press, 1972), pp. 69-81 {4.1}.

Roumbanis, Theodoros

a.

7.1303 *Ρουμπάνης, Θεόδωρος. Τό ταξίδι συνεχίζεται. Kimon Friar, tr. into English. Athens, 1970. Privately printed. Bilingual edition.

Roussou, Maya-Maria (1937-1989)

a.

7.1304 *_____ Ἀντίψαλμος. Translations into many languages including English by Thomas Tumberg. Athènes, 1985.

7.1305 *_____ *To the Unknown Student and the Massacre of Kalavrita*. Thomas Tumberg, tr. Athens: Anglo-Hellenic Agency, n.d. 30 p.

Sachtouris, Miltos (b. 1919)

a.

7.1306 _____ *Quicklime*. John Stathatos, tr. London: Oasis Books, 1974. 20 p.

7.1307 _____ *Selected Poems*. Kimon Friar, tr. and intro. Old Chatham, N.Y.: Sachem Press, 1982. 127 p.

7.1308 *_____ *Strange Sunday: Selected Poems 1952-1971*. John Stathatos, tr. Frome, Somerset: Hunting Raven Press (Bran's Head Books?), 1984. 47 p.

7.1309 _____ *With Face to the Wall: Selected Poems of Miltos Sahtouris*. Kimon Friar, tr. and intro. Washington, D.C.: The Charioteer Press, 1968. 40 p.

b.

7.1310 _____ "Four Poems". John Stathatos, tr. *Translation* 14 (Spring 1985), pp. 63-65 {3.34}.
"The Poet's Head"; "Chronicle"; "The Inspector"; "The Watch".

7.1311 _____ "The Lord"; "The Stigmata"; "The Inspector"; "The Dog"; "The Watch". John Stathatos, tr. *The Coffeehouse* 6 (Summer 1978), pp. 2-6.

7.1312 _____ "Poems". Margaret Leedis and Dino Siotis, trs. *Aegean Review* 1 (Fall/Winter 1986), pp. 58-60.
"Orange Tree"; "A Little Story"; "When"; "The Visit"; "October".

d.
7.1313 Georgakas, Dan. "Two Greek Commentaries". *Chicago Review* 21, No. 2 (Aug. 1969), pp. 109-114 {3.6}.
Refers respectively to the translations of Vassilis Vassilikos, *Z* and Miltos Sahtouris, *With Face to the Wall* {7.1771, 7.1309}.

Samarakis, Antonis (b. 1919)

a.
7.1314 _____ *The Flaw*. A Novel. Peter Mansfield and Richard Burns, trs. New York: Weybright and Talley, 1969. 208 p. Also *London: Hutchinson, 1969.

7.1315 _____ *The Passport and Other Stories*. Gavin Betts, tr. [and intro.]. Melbourne, Australia: Longman Cheshire, 1980. 112 p.

b.
7.1316 _____ "An Anthology of Antonis Samarakis". *The Charioteer* 13 (1971), pp. 26-97.
Includes: "The Blond Cavalier", "The River", "War Story" [Edwin Jahiel, tr.]; from *Danger Signal*, a novel [Katherine Hortis, tr.]; "Post Office Street" [Michael Antonakes, tr.]; "Ideas, Inc.", "The Jungle" [Edwin Jahiel, tr.]; "The Mother" [Katherine Hortis, tr.].

7.1317 _____ "Christmas Eve" [a short story]. Kimon Friar, tr. *The Athenian* (Dec. 1974), pp. 27-30.

7.1318 _____ "50 Kilos of Mothballs". Catherine Raizis, tr. *The Literary Review* 16, No. 3 (Spring 1973), pp. 325-337 {3.15}.

7.1319 _____ "The Mother" [a short story]. Robert and Despina Crist, trs. *The Athenian* (Aug. 1975), pp. 23-25.

7.1320 _____ "The Passport". Andrew Horton, tr. *JHD* 6, No. 3 (Fall 1979), pp. 73-93.

7.1321 _____ "The River". Minas Savvas, tr. *The Coffeehouse* 2 (Spring 1976), pp. 61-64.

d.
7.1322 Brittain, Maryanne. "'Αρνοῦμαι: Some Themes". *Τo Γιοφύρι* 9 (Aug. 1980), pp. 35-40.

7.1323 Decavalles, Andonis. "Antonis Samarakis". *The Charioteer* 13 (1971), pp. 8-11.

7.1324 Horton, Andrew. "The Craft and Reality of Antonis Samarakis's *The Passport*". *JHD* 6, No. 3 (Fall 1979), pp. 65-71.

7.1325 Horton, Andy. "Samarakis". *The Athenian* (Mar. 1975), pp. 18-21.
Esp. re. *The Flaw.*

7.1326 Jahiel, Edwin. "Antonis Samarakis: Fiction as Scenario". *Books Abroad* 42, No. 4 (Autumn 1968), pp. 531-534.

7.1327 Jahiel, Edwin. "Antonis Samarakis's *To Diavatirio*". *Books Abroad* 49, No. 1 (Winter 1975), pp. 58-61.

7.1328 Jahiel, Edwin. "The Cinematic World of Antonis Samarakis". *The Charioteer* 13 (1971), pp. 12-23.

7.1329 Jeffreys, Michael. "Andonis Samarakis and His Literary Style: Message and Technique". Τὸ Γιοφύρι 9 (Aug. 1980), pp. 41-53.

7.1330 Koestler, Arthur et al. "Comments on Samarakis' Novel *The Flaw*". *The Charioteer* 13 (1971), pp. 23-25.

7.1331 Palmer, Laura. "An Analysis of Samarakis' Ἡ ἐφεύρεση, Τὸ δέντρο, Ἡ ζούγκλα, Ἀρνοῦμαι". Τὸ Γιοφύρι 9 (Aug. 1980), pp. 25-34.

Saranti, Galatia (b. 1920)

b.

7.1332 _____ "Sunlight" [a story]. Katherine Hortis, tr. *The Charioteer* 9 (1967), pp. 79-83.

Savina, Zoi

a.

7.1333 *_____ *Enchantresses. Haiku. Tanka.* Betty Simos, tr. Athens, 1985. 237 p. Bilingual edition.

Seferis, George (1900-1971)

a.

7.1334 _____ *Collected Poems.* Edmund Keeley and Philip Sherrard, trs., eds., and intro. Princeton, N.J.: Princeton University Press, 1981. 550 p. Expanded bilingual edition. Also *London: Anvil Poetry Press, 1982.
Is expanded edition of their *Collected Poems (1924-1955)* {7.1335}.

7.1335 _____ *Collected Poems (1924-1955)*. Edmund Keeley and Philip Sherrard, trs., eds., and intro. Princeton, N.J.: Princeton University Press, 1967. 490 p. Bilingual edition. *Supplemented edition, 1969. 502 p. Also London: Routledge and Kegan Paul, 1967; London: Jonathan Cape Ltd., 1969 and 1973. 490 p.

7.1336 _____ *Collected Poems (1924-1955)*. Edmund Keeley and Philip Sherrard, trs. Princeton, N.J.: Princeton University Press, 1971. 277 p. English only.

7.1337 _____ *Delphi*. Philip Sherrard, tr.; illustrations by Herbert Kreft and others. Munich and Ahrbeck/Hannover: Knorr & Hirth Verlag GMBH, 1963. 24 p. and 36 plates.

7.1338 *_____ Γράμμα στόν *Rex Warner* πάροικο τοῦ *Storrs, Connecticut, U.S.A.* γιά τά ἑξῆντα του χρόνια. Ἀθήνα, 20 Νοεμβρίου 1972. *Letter to Rex Warner*. Edmund Keeley, tr. 9 p. Bilingual edition.
    Προσφορά τῆς Μαρῶς Σεφέρη καί τῶν Ἐκδόσεων "Ἑρμῆς". Ἐκτός ἐμπορίου. Not on the market.

7.1339 _____ *The King of Asine and Other Poems*. Bernard Spencer, Nanos Valaoritis and Lawrence Durrell, trs.; Rex Warner, intro. London: John Lehmann, 1948. 82 p.

7.1340 *_____ *The Land Within a Wall; A Poem, and Towards a Precipice; A Declaration*. John Richmond, tr. Echoes from Greece, 2. Montreal: Anthelion Press, 1969. 39 p.

7.1341 _____ *Mythistorima and Gymnopaidia*. Mary Cooper Walton, tr. Athens: Lycabettus Press, 1977. 69 p. Bilingual edition.

7.1342 _____ *On the Greek Style: Selected Essays in Poetry and Hellenism*. Rex Warner and Th.D. Frangopoulos, trs.; Rex Warner, intro. Boston and Toronto: Little, Brown and Company, 1966. 196 p. Also *London; Sydney; Toronto: The Bodley Head, [1967]. Athens: Denise Harvey & Company, 1982. 196 p.
    Includes: I. "Theophilos" (pp. 1-11); II. "Sikelianos" (pp. 13-21); III. "Makryannis" (pp. 23-65); IV. "Antoniou: Our Seafaring Friend" (pp. 67-71); V. "Dialogue on Poetry: What is Meant by Hellenism?" (pp. 73-97); VI. "Letter on 'The *Thrush*'" (pp. 99-105); VII. "The *Thrush*" (pp. 107-117); VIII. "Cavafy and Eliot—A Comparison" (pp. 119-161); IX. "Letter to a Foreign Friend" [Edmund Keeley and Nanos Valaoritis, trs.] (pp. 163-181); X. "On a Phrase of Pirandello" (pp. 183-190); XI. "Art in Our Times" (pp. 191-196).

7.1343 _____ *Poems*. Rex Warner, tr. London; Sydney; Toronto: The Bodley Head, 1960. 127 p. *Also An Atlantic Monthly Press Book. Boston and Toronto: Little, Brown and Company, 1960. 127 p. Reprinted, with a new introduction, 1964. Boston: David R. Godine, 1979. Boston: Nonpareil Books, 1981.

7.1344 _____ *A Poet's Journal: Days of 1945-1951*. Athan Anagnostopoulos, tr.; Walter Kaiser, intro. Cambridge, Mass.: The Belknap Press of Harvard University Press, 1974. 206 p. Also London: Harvard University Press, 1975.

7.1345 *_____ *Postscript* [a poem]. Minas Savvas, tr. Santa Barbara, Calif.: Unicorn Press, 1967. 1 card.

7.1346 _____ Σαντορίνη. Μέ ἕνα Σχέδιο τοῦ Χατζηκυριάκου-Γκίκα. Ἀθήνα: Ἀρχεῖο Θηραϊκῶν Μελετῶν—Συλλογή Δημήτρη Τσίτουρα, 1984. *Santorini*. Edmund Keeley and Philip Sherrard, trs. With a drawing by N. Hatjikyriakos-Ghikas. Athens: Archive of Santorini Studies—Dimitris Tsitouras Collection, 1984. A folio edition.
   The translation is on pp. 7-8.

7.1347 *Six Poems from the Greek of Sikelianos and Seferis*. Lawrence Durrell, [tr.] Rhodes: [published privately], 1946. 18 p.

7.1348 _____ Τρία Κρυφά Ποιήματα. *Three Secret Poems*. Walter Kaiser, tr. Cambridge, Mass.: Harvard University Press, 1969. 71 p. Bilingual edition. Also *London: Oxford University Press, 1969.

7.1349 Seferis, George and Rex Warner. *Calligram*. For Max Reinhardt. Richmond: Miniature Press. 10 November 1960. 8 unnumbered pages folded as a card. English only [Rex Warner, tr.].

b.
7.1350 _____ "Across Gorse...". Walter Kaiser, tr. *Boundary* 2, Vol. 1, No. 2 (Winter 1973), pp. 264-265. Bilingual version {3.5}.

7.1351 _____ "Against Whitethorns...". M. Byron Raizis, tr. *The Southern Review*, N.S. 9, No. 3 (July 1973), pp. 680-681.

7.1352 _____ "All Things are Full of Gods", an essay. Peter Bien, tr. *The Charioteer* 27 (1985), pp. 15-23 {7.1440}.

7.1353 _____ "Argo"; "The Last Chorus". Edmund Keeley, tr. *The Charioteer* 27 (1985), pp. 10-13. Bilingual version {7.1440}.

7.1354 _____ "By the Name of Orestes". Kimon Friar, tr. *Greek Heritage* 1, No. 2 (Spring 1964), p. 11 {7.1441}.

7.1355 _____ "The Cats of St. Nicholas". Edmund Keeley, tr. *Eleutheria* 1, No. 5 (Aug. 1970), pp. 18-19.
   Reprinted from *The Greek Report*.

7.1356 _____ "The Cats of St. Nicholas". Edmund Keeley, tr. *Encounter* 33, No. 1 (July 1969), pp. 3-4.

7.1357 _____ "The Cats of St. Nicholas". Edmund Keeley, tr. In *Eighteen Texts* (Willis Barnstone, ed. Cambridge, Mass.: Harvard University Press, 1972), pp. 1-3 {4.1}.

7.1358 _____ "Conversation with Fabrice". *Agenda* 7, No. 1 (Winter 1969), pp. 50-57 {3.1}.

7.1359 _____ "from *Days 'B'*". Athan Anagnostopoulos, tr. *The Charioteer* 27 (1985), pp. 41-54 {7.1440}.

7.1360 _____ (Declaration of 1969 against the Junta). *Eleutheria* 1, No. 3 (June 1970), pp. 9-10.

7.1361 _____ "Denial". Edmund Keeley and Philip Sherrard, trs. *Boston University Journal* 22, No. 1 (Winter 1974), p. 19.

7.1362 _____ "Discourse of Love". Edmund Keeley, tr. *The Virginia Quarterly Review* 42, No. 1 (Winter 1966), pp. 58-61.

7.1363 _____ "Foreword". In *Dimitri Mitropoulos—Katy Katsoyanis. A Correspondence 1930-1960* (Louis Biancolli and Katy Katsoyanis, intro. New York: A Martin Dale Book, 1973), pp. 1-3.

7.1364 _____ "Four Poems". Edmund Keeley, tr. *Accent* 16, No. 3 (Summer 1956), pp. 147-152.
    All refer to Stratis the Mariner: "Stratis the Mariner on the Dead Sea"; "Hampstead"; "Monday"; "Thursday".

7.1365 _____ "Four Poems by George Seferis". Edmund Keeley and Philip Sherrard, trs. *Quarterly Review of Literature* 15, Nos. 1/2 (1967), pp. 205-208.
    "Interlude of Joy"; "Memory I"; "The Last Day"; "Morning".

7.1366 _____ "Haiku"; "Mythistorima 6". Edmund Keeley and Philip Sherrard, trs. In *The Limits of Imagination: Wordsworth, Yeats, and Stevens* (Helen Regueiro. Ithaca, N.Y. and London: Cornell University Press, 1976), pp. 42, 36-38.

7.1367 *_____ "Hampstead". Edmund Keeley, tr. Ἑλληνισμός Ἀμερικῆς 10, No. 93 (Mar. 1959), p. 27.

7.1368 *_____ "A Harsh Clarity. From the Early Journals of George Seferis". Athan Anagnostopoulos, tr. *Boston Review* (Aug. 1982), pp. 16-18.

7.1369 _____ "His Last Poem—George Seferis". Ruth Whitman, tr. *Eleutheria* 2, No. 6-7 (Sept.-Oct. 1971), pp. 8-9.
    "On the Thornbushes".

7.1370 _____ "The King of Asine". Edmund Keeley, tr. *Partisan Review* 23, No. 3 (Summer 1956), pp. 334-336.

7.1371 _____ "Language in Our Poetry". Peter Thompson, tr. *Labrys* 8 (Apr. 1983), pp. 35-45 {7.1442}.

7.1372 _____ "The Last Chorus". Edmund Keeley, tr. *The Charioteer* 27 (1985), pp. 12-13 {7.1440}.

7.1373 _____ "The Last Stop". Edmund Keeley, tr. *The Colorado Quarterly* 8, No. 4 (Spring 1960), pp. 318-320 {4.78}.

7.1374 _____ "A Letter on 'Thrush'". James Stone, tr. and intro. *JHD* 7, No. 2 (Summer 1980), pp. 5-26.
    The first translation of the complete text, with notes.

7.1375 _____ "Letter to a Foreign Friend". Nanos Valaoritis, tr. and appended by Edmund Keeley. *Poetry* 105, No. 1 (Oct. 1964), pp. 50-59 {3.27}.
    Subsequently revised. In his *On the Greek Style* (Boston and Toronto: Little, Brown and Company, 1966), pp. 165-181 {7.1342}.

7.1376 _____ "Letter to Rex Warner (resident of Storrs, Connecticut, U.S.A., on his sixtieth birthday)". Edmund Keeley, tr. *Encounter* 34, No. 2 (Feb. 1970), pp. 68-69.
    Also as a separatum. See Γράμμα στόν Rex Warner above {7.1338}.

7.1377 _____ "Letters to Henry Miller". John Stathatos, ed. *Labrys* 8 (Apr. 1983), pp. 51-59 {7.1442}.

7.1378 *_____ "The Mood of a Day". Edmund Keeley, tr. In *Modern Writing* 3 (William Phillips and Philip Rahv, eds. New York: Berkeley Publishing Co., 1956), pp. 69-70.

7.1379 *_____ "Morning". Edmund Keeley and Philip Sherrard. trs. *Poetry Pilot* (Dec. 1970), p. 1.

7.1380 *_____ "Mr. Stratis Thalassinos (3 excerpts)". Edmund Keeley and Philip Sherrard, trs. In *Daniel Martin* (John Fowles. Boston: Little, Brown and Co., 1977), pp. 3, 75, and 615.

7.1381 _____ "from *Mythical Story*". Edmund Keeley, tr. *Perspective* 9, No. 4 (Summer 1957), pp. 184-187.

7.1382 *_____ "from *Mythical Story*, No. 4"; "Stratis the Mariner on the Dead Sea"; "Old Man on the River Bank"; "from *Mythical Story*, No. 8". Edmund Keeley, tr. *Atlantis* (Dec. 1963), pp. 24-29.

7.1383 _____ "from *Mythical Story*, Nos. 9, 12, 22". Edmund Keeley, tr. *The Beloit Poetry Journal* 7, No. 3 (Spring 1957), pp. 11-13.
    In anthology "Four Greek Poets" {4.73}.

7.1384 *_____ "Mythistorema". Vassilis Zambaras, tr. *Madrona* 2, No. 6 (1973).

7.1385 *_____ "Narration". Edmund Keeley and Philip Sherrard, trs. In *Compass II* (David Lee, et al. Glenview, Ill.: Scott, Foresman and Co., 1971), p. 107 {4.47}.

7.1386 *_____ "Nijinski". Edmund Keeley and Philip Sherrard, trs. *Dance Perspectives* 52 (Winter 1972), pp. 19-20.

7.1387 _____ "Nobel Acceptance Speech". John E. Rexine, tr. *The Charioteer* 27 (1985), pp. 25-27 {7.1440}.

7.1388 _____ "On a Ray of Winter Light". Edmund Keeley and Philip Sherrard, trs. *Columbia* 4 (Spring/Summer 1980), pp. 33-35.

7.1389 _____ "On Stage". Edmund Keeley and Philip Sherrard, trs. *The Georgia Review* 34, No. 2 (Summer 1980), pp. 357-359.

7.1390 _____ "On the Aspalathos". Robert Zaller, tr. *Boston University Journal* 23, No. 1 (Winter 1975), p. 56.

7.1391 _____ "Poems". Kimon Friar, tr. with notes. *Greek Heritage* 1, No. 2 (Spring 1964), pp. 105-115 {7.1441}.

7.1392 _____ "Poems". John Stathatos, tr. *Labrys* 8 (Apr. 1983), pp. 2-15 {7.1442}.

7.1393 _____ "from *A Poet's Journal*". Athan Anagnostopoulos, tr. In *The Poet's Work: 29 Masters of 20th Century Poetry on the Origins and Practice of their Art* (Reginald Gibbons, ed. Boston: Houghton Mifflin Company, 1979), pp. 71-81.

7.1394 _____ "Preface to a New Edition of the Poetics of Music". In *Poetics of Music in the Form of Six Lessons* (Igor Stravinsky. Arthur Knodel and Ingolf Dahl, trs. Cambridge, Mass.: Harvard University Press, 1970), pp. v-ix.

7.1395 _____ "Salva Nos Vigilantes". John Chioles, tr. *The Coffeehouse* 9 (Winter 1979), p. 26.

7.1396 _____ "Santorini"; "Salamis in Cyprus"; "Three Mules". Edmund Keeley and Philip Sherrard, trs. *Poetry* 105, No. 1 (Oct. 1964), pp. 44-49 {3.27}.

7.1397 _____ "Seferis to Miller" [a letter, 7 Dec. 1948]. *The Coffeehouse* 9 (Winter 1979), pp. 24-25.

7.1398 _____ "A Selection of Letters to Friends and Family". John Stathatos, ed. and tr. *Labrys* 8 (Apr. 1983), pp. 61-74 {7.1442}.

7.1399 _____ "A Selection of Poems of George Seferis (1924-1955)". Edmund Keeley and Philip Sherrard, trs. *The Charioteer* 9 (1967), pp. 8-43.
   Includes Edmund Keeley and Philip Sherrard, "Foreword to *George Seferis: Collected Poems (1924-1955)*", pp. 8-13.

7.1400 _____ "from *Six Nights on the Acropolis*". Athan Anagnostopoulos, tr. *The Charioteer* 27 (1985), pp. 29-40 {7.1440}.

7.1401 _____ "Stratis the Mariner Among the Agapanthi". Edmund Keeley, tr. *Chicago Review* 12, No. 2 (Summer 1958), pp. 87-88.

7.1402 _____ "Summer Solstice". Edmund Keeley and Philip Sherrard, trs. *Antaeus* 36 (Winter 1980), pp. 44-51. Also in **The Antaeus Anthology* (Daniel Halpern, ed. Toronto: New York: Bantam Books, 1986) {4.39}.

7.1403 _____ "Summer Solstice". M. Byron Raizis, tr. *Prism International* 9, No. 3 (Spring 1970), pp. 102-103.
    Three Sections.

7.1404 _____ "Summer Solstice". M. Byron Raizis, tr. *Prism International* 23, No. 2 (Winter 1984), pp. 63-64.

7.1405 _____ "from *Summer Solstice*". Byron Raizis, tr. *The Southern Review*, N.S. 5, No. 2 (Spring 1969), pp. 522-527. Bilingual version.

7.1406 _____ "T.S.E.—Pages from a Diary". Rowena Fowler, tr. with an introduction by R.M. Beaton. *The Critical Survey* 5, No. 4 (Summer 1972), pp. 305-316.

7.1407 _____ "T.S.E. (Pages from a Diary)". Edmund and Mary Keeley, trs. *Quarterly Review of Literature* 15, Nos. 1/2 (1967), pp. 209-228. Reprinted in Vol. 20, Nos. 3-4 (1977), pp. 302-320.

7.1408 _____ "Three Last Poems". Peter Thompson, tr. *Labrys* 8 (Apr. 1983), pp. 17-20 {7.1442}.

7.1409 _____ "Three Poems". Peter Dreyer, tr. *Omphalos* 1, No. 1 (Mar. 1972), pp. 2-9. Bilingual version.
    "Tuesday"; "Wednesday"; "Postscript to Gymnopaedia, January 1945".

7.1410 _____ "Three Poems". Kimon Friar, Lawrence Durrell, Bernard Spencer, and Nanos Valaorites, trs. *The Atlantic Monthly* 195, No. 6 (June 1955), pp. 158-159 {3.3}.
    "The King of Asine"; "The Smile of the Statues"; "Calligraphy".

7.1411 _____ "Three Poems". Edmund Keeley and Philip Sherrard, trs. *Poetry* 105, No. 1 (Oct. 1964), pp. 44-49 {3.27}.
    "Santorini"; "Salamis in Cyprus"; "Three Mules".

7.1412 _____ "[Three] Poems by George Seferis". Edmund Keeley and Philip Sherrard, trs. *Encounter* 27, No. 3 (Sept. 1966), pp. 40-41.
    "Narration"; "Memory, II"; "Our Sun".

7.1413 _____ "Three Poems for Cyprus". Kimon Friar, tr. In *Cyprus '74: Aphrodite's Other Face* (Emmanuel C. Casdaglis, ed. Athens: National Bank of Greece, 1976), pp. 143-147 {4.87}.
    "Enkomi"; "Memory I"; "Salamis in Cyprus".

7.1414 _____ "Three Poems: George Seferis". Rex Warner, tr. *The Charioteer* 6 (Spring 1964), pp. 14-23.
   "Santorine"; "Mycenae"; "In the Manner of G.S.".

7.1415 _____ "Three Private Poems". Peter Thompson, tr. *Agenda* 7, No. 1 (Winter 1969), pp. 35-49 {3.1}.

7.1416 _____ *"Three Secret Poems"*. Edmund Keeley and Philip Sherrard, trs. *Temenos* 1 (1981), pp. 171-183.
   "On a Ray of Winter Light"; "On Stage"; "Summer Solstice".

7.1417 _____ *"Thrush"*. Edmund Keeley and Philip Sherrard, trs. *Accent* 17, No. 4 (Autumn 1957), pp. 195-201.

7.1418 _____ "The Thrush". Rex Warner, tr. *Orpheus* 1 (1948), pp. 49-55.

7.1419 _____ "Two Poems". Edmund Keeley, tr. *New World Writing* 20 (1962), pp. 42-45.
   "Helen"; "Pedlar from Sidon".

7.1420 _____ "Two Poems". Edmund Keeley, tr. *Quarterly Review of Literature* 16, Nos. 1-2 (1969), pp. 213-215.
   "Tuesday"; "Wednesday".

7.1421 _____ "Two Poems". Edmund Keeley, tr. *Shenandoah* 17, No. 1 (Autumn 1965), pp. 80-81.
   "Days of June '41"; "Rhyme".

7.1422 *_____ "Two Poems". Edmund Keeley and Philip Sherrard, trs. *Greece* (Dec. 1975), pp. 14-18.

7.1423 _____ "Two Poems". *Prairie Schooner* 32, No. 4 (Winter 1958-59), pp. 323-325.
   "Agianapa" [Edmund Keeley, tr.]; "Engomi" [Edmund Keeley and Philip Sherrard, trs.].

7.1424 _____ "Two Poems". M. Byron Raizis, tr. *The Literary Review* 16, No. 3 (Spring 1973), pp. 295-302 {3.15}.
   "On Stage"; "from 'Summer Solstice'".

7.1425 _____ "Two Poems". Nanos Valaoritis and Bernard Spencer, trs. In *New Writing and Daylight* 7 (John Lehmann, ed. London: John Lehmann, 1946), p. 47.
   "Remember the Baths in Which You Plunged"; "And the Name Is Orestes".

7.1426 _____ "Two Poems by George Seferis". Edmund Keeley, tr. *Western Humanities Review* 13, No. 3 (Summer 1959), pp. 246-247.
   "An Old Man on the River Bank"; "from *Mythical Story*".

7.1427 _____ "Two Prose Excerpts". Athan Anagnostopoulos, tr. *Ploughshares* 11, No. 4 (June 1986), pp. 31-37 {3.25}.
   From *A Poet's Journal: Days of 1925-31* and from *Six Nights on the Acropolis*.

7.1428 _____ "Upon a Ray of Winter Sun: Three Secret Poems (1966)". M. Byron Raizis, tr. *Contemporary Literature in Translation* 9 (Winter 1970), p. 5.

c.

7.1429 Burns, Richard. *Black Light: Poems in Memory of George Seferis*. Cambridge: Los Poetry Press, 1983. 28 p.

7.1430 Capri-Karka, C. *Love and the Symbolic Journey in the Poetry of Cavafy, Eliot and Seferis*. An interpretation with detailed poem-by-poem analysis. New York: Pella Publishing Company, 1982. 374 p.
   Especially Part 3 (pp. 155-320) concerns Seferis.

7.1431 Capri-Karka, C. *War in the Poetry of George Seferis: A poem-by-poem analysis*. New York: Pella Publishing Company, 1985. 235 p.

7.1432 Casey, Gerard. *Between the Symplegades: Re-visions from "A Mythological Story" by George Seferis*. London: Enitharmon Press, 1980. 37 p.

7.1433 *George Seferis: A Relationship with Britain. Γιῶργος Σεφέρης: Ἕνας Δεσμός μέ τή Βρεττανία*. A Commemorative Exhibition arranged by the British Council, Athens, November 1972. 33p. Bilingual edition.
   Contains: Ian Scott-Kilvert, "Introduction" (pp. 2-5), Lawrence Durrell, "On George Seferis" (pp. 6-9), and a catalogue of the exhibition.

7.1434 *George Seferis, 1970-1971*. London: The National Book League and The British Council, 1975. 42 p.
   Catalogue of exhibition. Includes: Ian Scott-Kilvert and Clifford Simmons, "Preface" (p. 4); P.A. Zannas, "Introduction" (pp. 5-6); Lawrence Durrell, "On George Seferis" (pp. 7-8); Ian Scott-Kilvert, "Seferis and Britain" (pp. 9-10). The entries of the exhibition follow, arranged in eleven units.

7.1435 Hadas, Rachel. *Form, Cycle, Infinity: Landscape Imagery in the Poetry of Robert Frost and George Seferis*. Lewisburg: Bucknell University Press; London and Toronto: Associated University Presses, 1985. 221 p.

7.1436 *Keeley, Edmund. *Constantine Cavafy and George Seferis and their Relation to English and American Poetry*. Unpublished doctoral dissertation. University of Oxford, 1952.

7.1437 Keeley, Edmund. *Συζήτηση μέ τόν Γιῶργο Σεφέρη. Μετάφραση: Λίνα Κάσδαγλη. Conversation with George Seferis*. Athens: Agra, 1982. 139 p. Bilingual edition. Second edition, with photographs, 1987.
   First published as "The Art of Poetry XIII: George Seferis". *The Paris Review* 50 (Fall 1970), pp. 56-93 {7.1477}.

7.1438 Levi, Peter. *The Hill of Kronos*. *London, St. James Place: Collins, 1980. 222 p. Also New York: E.P. Dutton, 1981. 222
   Esp. pp. 15, 28, 33f., 110, 125f., 132f., 137, 151f., 156f., 174-176, and 177 of the American edition.

7.1439 Tsatsos, Ioanna. *My Brother George Seferis*. Jean Demos, tr.; Eugene Current-Garcia, pref. A Nostos Book. Minneapolis, Minn.: North Central Publishing Company, 1982. 257 p.

Special issues of periodicals

7.1440 *The Charioteer* 27 (1985). Special issue: George Seferis.
   Contains: George Seferis, "Argo" [Edmund Keeley, tr.] (pp. 10-11), "The Last Chorus" [Edmund Keeley, tr.] (pp. 12-13), "All Things are Full of Gods", an essay [Peter Bien, tr.] (pp. 15-23), "Nobel Acceptance Speech" [John E. Rexine, tr.] (pp. 25-27), from *Six Nights on the Acropolis*" [Athan Anagnostopoulos, tr.] (pp. 29-40), from *Days 'B'*" [Athan Anagnostopoulos, tr.] (pp. 41-54); Alexandros Argyriou, "Suggestions about *The Thrush:* A First Approach" (pp. 55-99); Costas G. Papageorgiou, "Notes on the *Three Secret Poems*" (pp. 101-156); Costas G. Papageorgiou, "In Seferis' Poetic Workshop" (pp.157-168); Carmen Capri-Karka, "War in the Poetry of George Seferis" (pp. 169-230); John E. Rexine, "Nobel Prize Winner George Seferis: Two Anniversaries", a TV film documentary report (pp. 233-237). Also contains photographs.
   Address: Pella Publishing Co., Inc., 337 W. 36th St., New York, N.Y. 10018.

7.1441 *Greek Heritage* 1, No. 2 (Spring 1964). *Homage to George Seferis*. Kimon Friar, ed.
   Includes: George Seferis, "By the Name of Orestes" [Kimon Friar, tr.] (p. 11); Menis Koumandareas, "The Bath": A Story [Amy Mims tr.] (pp. 30-35); Nikos Kazantzakis, *"Burn Me to Ashes:* An Excerpt" [Kimon Friar, tr.] (pp. 61-64); Vassilis Vassilikos, *"The Plant:* An Excerpt" [Edmund Keeley and Mary Keeley, trs.] (pp. 74-77); Andreas Karandonis, "George Seferis" [Kay Cicellis and Kimon Friar, trs.] (pp. 96-103); Henry Miller, "George Seferiadhis" (p. 104); George Seferis, "Poems" [Kimon Friar, tr. with notes] (pp. 105-115).
   Address: *Greek Heritage,* 360 North Michigan Avenue, Chicago, Ill. 60601.

7.1442 *Labrys* 8 (Apr. 1983). *George Seferis*. Grahaeme Barrasford Young, ed.; John Stathatos, guest editor, George Seferis Section.
   Contains: John Stathatos, "Introduction" (p. 1); George Seferis, "Poems" [John Stathatos, tr.] (pp. 2-15); George Seferis, "Three Last Poems" [Peter Thompson, tr.] (pp. 17-20); Patrick Leigh Fermor, "Men of the Marmion Class: A Personal Memoir of Seferis" (pp. 21-22); Roderick Beaton, "The Poetic Quest of George Seferis" (pp. 23-34); George Seferis, "Language in Our Poetry" [Peter Thompson, tr.] (pp. 35-45); Steven Runciman, "Some Personal Memories" (pp. 47-49); George Seferis, "Letters to Henry Miller" [John Stathatos, ed.] (pp. 51-59); George Seferis, "A Selection of Letters to Friends and Family" [John Stathatos, ed. and tr.] (pp. 61-74); Takis Sinopoulos, "The Open and Closed Poem in George Seferis" [John Stathatos, tr.] (pp. 75-80); Peter Thompson, "Seferis Against the Colonels" (pp. 81-83); Nassos Vayenas, "George Seferis—T.S. Eliot: Parallels" (pp. 84-94); Bibliographical Note (pp. 95-96). Also includes photographs.
   Address: The Editor, 45 Milk Street, Frome, Somerset, United Kingdom.

d.

7.1443 Argyriou, Alexandros. "Suggestions about *The Thrush:* A First Approach". *The Charioteer* 27 (1985), pp. 55-99 {7.1440}.

7.1444 Arnakis, G. Georgiades. "The Tragedy of Man in the Poetry of George Seferis". *The Texas Quarterly* 7, No. 1 (Spring 1964), pp. 55-67.

7.1445 Bachtin, Nicholas. "English Poetry in Greek: Notes on a Comparative Study of Poetic Idioms". *Poetics Today* 6, No. 3 (1985), pp. 333-356.
   A commentary on Seferis' Greek language translation of T.S. Eliot, *The Waste Land*. First published, as Parts 1 and 2, in *The Link*, No. 1 (June 1938), pp. 77-84 and No. 2 (June 1939), pp. 49-63.

7.1446 Baud-Bovy, S. "A Greek Poet (G. Seferis)". *The Link,* No. 1 (June 1938), pp. 1-6.

7.1447 Beaton, Roderick. "From Mythos to Logos: The Poetics of George Seferis". *JMGS* 5, No. 2 (Oct. 1987), pp. 135-152.

7.1448 Beaton, Roderick. "The Poet's Predicament". *TLS* (14 Nov. 1975), p. 1364.

7.1449 Beaton, Roderick. "The Poetic Quest of George Seferis". *Labrys* 8 (Apr. 1983), pp. 23-34 {7.1442}.

7.1450 *Bournas, Helen. "The Journey Beyond Symbolism: Valery, Rimbaud, Eliot and their Relationship to George Seferis". *Dissertation Abstracts International* 45, No. 2 (Aug. 1984), p. 513A.

7.1451 Capri-Karka, C. "Love and the Symbolic Journey in Seferis' *Mythistorema*". *JHD* 8, No. 3 (Fall 1981), pp. 25-75.

7.1452 Capri-Karka, C. "Seferis' *Turning Point:* A Textual Analysis". *JHD* 9, No. 2 (Summer 1982), pp. 7-35.

7.1453 Capri-Karka, Carmen. "War in the Poetry of George Seferis". *The Charioteer* 27 (1985), pp. 169-230 {7.1440}.

7.1454 Davis, Mark L. "Seferis's 'Thrush'". *Neo-Hellenika* 2 (1975), pp. 280-298.

7.1455 Decavalles, Andonis. "Greekness and Exile". *Spirit* 35 (Sept. 1968), pp. 111-115.

7.1456 Decavalles, Andonis. "The Nobel Prize for Literature: Ghiorgos Seferis". *The Charioteer* 6 (Spring 1964), pp. 7-12.

7.1457 Decavalles, Andonis. "Three Poets: Notes in Passing". *The Charioteer* 22 and 23 (1980/1981), pp. 16-22 {7.631}.
   Re. Kazantzakis, Seferis, and Elytis.

7.1458 Dimiroulis, Dimitris. "The 'Humble Art' and the Exquisite Rhetoric: Tropes in the Manner of George Seferis". In *The Text and its Margins* (Margaret Alexiou and Vassilis Lambropoulos, eds. New York: Pella Publishing Company, 1985), pp. 59-84 {5.8}.

7.1459 Doulis, Thomas. "George Seferis and the Erosion of Memory". *The American Scholar* 37, No. 2 (Spring 1968), pp. 336, 338, 340, 342, 344, 346.

7.1460 Doulis, Thomas. "The Strategy of George Seferis: The Individual Poet and the Greek Tradition". *The Texas Quarterly* 11, No. 4 (Winter 1968), pp. 72-88.

7.1461 Evangelides, Constantinos E. "Some Common Features in the Technique of T.S. Eliot and G. Seferis". Ἐπιστημονική Ἐπετηρίς τῆς Φιλοσοφικῆς Σχολῆς τοῦ Πανεπιστημίου Ἀθηνῶν 24, No. 2 (1973-1974), pp. 1031-1035.

7.1462 Fermor, Patrick Leigh. "Men of the Marmion Class: A Personal Memoir of Seferis". *Labrys* 8 (Apr. 1983), pp. 21-22 {7.1442}.

7.1463 Fowler, Rowena. "Ἡ Ἔρημη Χώρα: Seferis' Translation of *The Waste Land*". *Comparative Literature Studies* 9, No. 4 (Dec. 1972), pp. 443-454.

7.1464 Friar, Kimon. "George Seferis: The Greek Poet Who Won the Nobel Prize". *Saturday Review* 46 (30 Nov. 1963), pp. 16-20.
  Compares Seferis and Kazantzakis. Includes a translation of "The King of Asine".

7.1465 G.N.B. "'Angelic and Black Day': Seferis' Death". [E.W.F., tr.]. *Boston University Journal* 22, No. 1 (Winter 1974), pp. 9-19.
  With a picture of Angelos Sikelianos marked "George Seferis" on p. 9.

7.1466 Gifford, Henry. "George Seferis during the War". *Grand Street* 5, No. 2 (Winter 1986), pp. 175-186.

7.1467 Gifford, Henry. "Seferis and Cavafy". *Grand Street* 6, No. 4 (Summer 1987), pp. 245-256.

7.1468 Gifford, Henry. "Seferis and the Fate of Cyprus: The Voice of the Soothsayer". *TLS* (12 Dec. 1986), pp. 1391-1392.

7.1469 *Hadas, Rachel. "Form, Cycle, Infinity: Landscape Imagery in the Poetry of Robert Frost and George Seferis". *Dissertation Abstracts International* 42, No. 11 (May 1982), p. 4820A. {Cf. 7.1435}.

7.1470 *Hadjistephanou, Costas E. "Seferis on the 'Homeric World' of Cyprus". Στασῖνος 7 (1979-1980), pp. 27-36.

7.1471 Hartigan, Karelisa V. "The Message of Elpenor in Homer, Giraudoux, and Seferis". *CML* 1, No. 1 (Fall 1980), pp. 39-45.

7.1472 Honig, Edwin. "Edmund Keeley". Chapter 8 in *The Poet's Other Voice: Conversations on Literary Translation* (Edwin Honig, ed. Amherst: The University of Massachusetts Press, 1985), pp. 133-149.
  Esp. re. Edmund Keeley's translations of Seferis and Cavafy.

7.1473 Kaiser, Walter. "Translators of Seferis". *TLS* (25 June 1970), pp. 686-687.

7.1474 Kakava, Maria. "Seferis and the Homeland". *JMH* 1 (Apr. 1984), pp. 55-62.

7.1475 Karandonis, Andreas. "George Seferis". Kimon Friar and Kay Cicellis, trs. *Greek Heritage* 1, No. 2 (Spring 1964), pp. 96-103 {7.1441}.

7.1476 Karavidas, Yannis. "'[...] all poetry is difficult [...]': The Limitations of Seferis' Modernist Poetics". *BMGS* 11 (1987), pp. 93-113.

7.1477 Keeley, Edmund. "The Art of Poetry XIII: George Seferis" [interview]. *The Paris Review* 50 (Fall 1970), pp. 56-93. Also appeared as "George Seferis". In *Writers at Work: The Paris Review Interviews. Fourth Series* (George Plimpton, ed.; Wilfrid Sheed, intro. New York: The Viking Press, 1976), pp. 147-178. Also as "Postscript: A Conversation with George Seferis" in his *Modern Greek Poetry: Voice and Myth* (Princeton, N.J.: Princeton University Press, 1983), pp. 180-217 {5.2}.

7.1478 *Keeley, Edmund. "Everyone's Ithaca: On the 'Poverty' of a Nobel Poet". *Book Week* (15 Dec. 1963), pp. 1 and 12.

7.1479 Keeley, Edmund. "George Seferis". *Encounter* 38, No. 3 (Mar. 1972), pp. 37-43.
   Is first publication of one part of "Seferis' 'Political' Voice" found in his *Modern Greek Poetry: Voice and Myth* (Princeton, N.J.: Princeton University Press, 1983), pp. 95-118 {5.2}.

7.1480 Keeley, Edmund. "George Seferis and Stratis the Mariner". *Accent* 16, No. 3 (Summer 1956), pp. 153-157.

7.1481 Keeley, Edmund. "On Translating Cavafy and Seferis". *Shenandoah* 23, No. 2 (Winter 1972), pp. 39-49.

7.1482 *Keeley, Edmund. "The Poet George Seferis". *Fulbright Review* (Athens) (Fall 1964), pp. 11-13.

7.1483 Keeley, Edmund. "Poet Laureate of Greece". *University* 22 (Fall 1964), pp. 30-31.

7.1484 Keeley, Edmund. "Seferis and the 'Mythical Method'". *Comparative Literature Studies* 6, No. 2 (June 1969), pp. 109-125.
   Substantially expanded in his *Modern Greek Poetry: Voice and Myth* (Princeton, N.J.: Princeton University Press, 1983), pp. 68-94 {5.2}.

7.1485 Keeley, Edmund. "Seferis' Elpenor: A Man of No Fortune". *The Kenyon Review* 28, No. 3 (June 1966), pp. 378-390.
   Also in his *Modern Greek Poetry: Voice and Myth* (Princeton, N.J.: Princeton University Press, 1983), pp. 53-67 {5.2}.

7.1486 Keeley, Edmund. "Seferis' 'Political' Voice". In his *Modern Greek Poetry: Voice and Myth* (Princeton, N.J.: Princeton University Press, 1983), pp. 95-118 {5.2}.

Part of the article was first published as "George Seferis" in *Encounter* 38, No. 3 (Mar. 1972), pp. 37-43 {7.1479}.

7.1487 Keeley, Edmund. "T.S. Eliot and the Poetry of George Seferis". *Comparative Literature* 8, No. 3 (Summer 1956), pp. 214-226.

7.1488 Krikos-Davis, Katerina. "Cats, Snakes and Poetry: A Study of Seferis' *The Cats of Saint Nicholas*". *JMGS* 2, No. 2 (Oct. 1984), pp. 225-240.

7.1489 Krikos-Davis, Katerina. "Notes on Seferis' Last Poem". *SSMG* 7-8 (1984), pp. 101-106.
  Re. "Ἐπὶ Ἀσπαλάθων...".

7.1490 Krikos-Davis, Katerina. "On Seferis' 'Helen'". *BMGS* 5 (1979), pp. 57-76.

7.1491 Leontis, Artemis. "'The Lost Center' and the Promised Land of Greek Criticism". *JMGS* 5, No. 2 (Oct. 1987), pp. 175-190.

7.1492 Lester, Eva P. and Dmitri Kyriazis. "George Seferis: His Poetic Insight". *American Imago* 41, No. 2 (Summer 1984), pp. 129-154.

7.1493 Levi, Peter, S.J. "Seferis' Tone of Voice". In *Modern Greek Writers* (Edmund Keeley and Peter Bien, eds. Princeton: Princeton University Press, 1972), pp. 171-189 {5.9}.

7.1494 Lorenzatos, Zissimos. "The Lost Center". In his *The Lost Center and Other Essays in Greek Poetry* (Princeton, N.J.: Princeton University Press, 1980), pp. 85-146 {5.3}.
  Especially re. George Seferis.

7.1495 Matsukis, Corinna. "Seferis and South Africa". *Greek Letters* 4 (1986-1989), pp. 41-61.
  Includes: Appendix A, "My Personal Associations with George Seferis" by Alexander Pilavachi; Appendix B, "My Recollections of George Seferis in Pretoria" by Paul Voutsas; and Appendix C, "Stratis Thalassinos Among the Agapanthi" (bilingual).

7.1496 McCarthy, Eugene J. "Reflections on George Seferis". *MGSY* 1 (1985), pp. 145-151.

7.1497 Miller, Henry. "George Seferiadhis". *Greek Heritage* 1, No. 2 (Spring 1964), p. 104 {7.1441}.

7.1498 *Miranda, Gary. "Going: To George Seferis 1900-1971" [a poem]. In his *The Seed that Dies: Twelve Elegies* (Athens: Kedros, 1973), p. 23.

7.1499 **Nobel Prize Library*. Published under the sponsorship of the Nobel Foundation of the Swedish Academy. Giorgos Seferis, Mikhail Sholokhov, Henryk Sienkiewicz, Carl Spittaler. New York: Alexis Gregory and Del Mar, Calif.: CRM Publishing, 1971.
  Especially pp. 1-33 concern Seferis.

7.1500 Padel, Ruth. "Homer's Reader: A Reading of George Seferis". *Proceedings of the Cambridge Philological Society* 211, N.S. No. 31 (1985), pp. 74-132.

7.1501 *Pahdi, Bibhu. "Carvings of a Humble Art: The Poetry of George Seferis". *Interpretations* 13, No. 1 (Fall 1981), pp. 73-79.

7.1502 Papageorgiou, Costas G. "In Seferis' Poetic Workshop". *The Charioteer* 27 (1985), pp. 157-168 {7.1440}.

7.1503 Papageorgiou, Costas G. "Notes on the *Three Secret Poems*". *The Charioteer* 27 (1985), pp. 101-156 {7.1440}.

7.1504 Philipe, Anne. "An Interview with George Seferis". *Eleutheria* 2, No. 6-7 (Sept.-Oct. 1971), pp. 15-21.
    Tr. from *Le Monde*.

7.1505 Raizis, Marios Byron. "The Poetic Manner of George Seferis". *Folia Neohellenica* 2 (1977), pp. 105-126.

7.1506 Raizis, M. Byron. "The Vindication of George Seferis". *Greek World* (May-June 1976), pp. 32-34.
    Includes a translation of "'Επί 'Ασπαλάθων".

7.1507 Rexine, John E. "The Classical Tradition in the Poetry of George Seferis". *The Indiana Social Studies Quarterly* 32, No. 1 (Spring 1979), pp. 28-42. Also in *Hellenic Perspectives: Essays in the History of Greece* (John T.A. Koumoulides, ed. Lanham, Md.: University Presses of America, 1980), pp. 29-56.

7.1508 Rexine, John E. "The Diaries of George Seferis as a Revelation of His Art". *WLT* 61, No. 2 (Spring 1987), pp. 220-223.

7.1509 Rexine, John E. "From Lincolnshire to Zakynthos; Two Greek Poets in England: Andreas Kalvos and George Seferis". *JHD* 7, No. 2 (Summer 1980), pp. 51-64.

7.1510 Rexine, John E. "Nobel Laureate George Seferis and the Continuity of the Greek Tradition". *JMH* 1 (Apr. 1984), pp. 33-54.

7.1511 Rexine, John E. "Nobel Laureate George Seferis, Holy Scriptures, and the Greek Orthodox Tradition". *The Patristic and Byzantine Review* 4, No. 1 (1985), pp. 51-58.

7.1512 Rexine, John E. "Nobel Prize Winner George Seferis: Two Anniversaries", a TV film documentary report. *The Charioteer* 27 (1985), pp. 233-237 {7.1440}.

7.1513 Rexine, John E. "The Poet George Seferis and his Greek Critics" [review essay]. *JHD* 7, Nos. 3-4 (Fall-Winter 1980), pp. 145-154.

7.1514 Rexine, John E. "The Poetic and Political Conscience of George Seferis" [review article]. *MGSY* 3 (1987), pp. 311-320.

7.1515 Rexine, John E. "Seferis". *Books Abroad* 41, No. 1 (Winter 1967), pp. 37-38.

7.1516 Runciman, Steven. "Some Personal Memories". *Labrys* 8 (Apr. 1983), pp. 47-49 {7.1442}.

7.1517 Savidis, George P. "The Tragic Vision of Seferis". *Grand Street* 5, No. 2 (Winter 1986), pp. 153-174.

7.1518 Savidis, Theodora. "The Role of the Greek Past and of Greek Mythology in Seferis' Μυθιστόρημα". *Το Γιοφύρι* 2 (June 1978), pp. 14-17.

7.1519 Sherrard, Philip. "George Seferis". In his *The Marble Threshing Floor: Studies in Modern Greek Poetry* (Athens: Denise Harvey, 1982), pp. 185-231 {5.6}.

7.1520 Sherrard, Philip. "George Seferis 1900-1971: The Man and his Poetry". In his *The Wound of Greece: Studies in Neo-Hellenism* (London: Rex Collings Ltd. with Athens: Anglo-Hellenic, 1978), pp. 94-117 {5.7}.

7.1521 "A Short Ἀφιέρωμα [Festschrift] to George Seferis". *The Amaranth* 10 (1987), pp. 1-10.

7.1522 Sinopoulos, Takis. "The Open and Closed Poem in George Seferis". John Stathatos, tr. *Labrys* 8 (Apr. 1983), pp. 75-80 {7.1442}.

7.1523 Taktsis, Kostas. "My Short Life with Seferis". Mary Keeley tr. *Grand Street* 5, No. 2 (Winter 1986), pp. 187-200.

7.1524 Thaniel, George. "George Seferis's 'Thrush': A Modern Descent". *Canadian Review of Comparative Literature* 4, No. 1 (Winter 1977), pp. 89-102.

7.1525 Thaniel, George. "George Seferis' 'Thrush' and T.S. Eliot's 'Four Quartets'". *Neohelicon* 4, Nos. 3-4 (1976), pp. 261-282. Also published as a separatum: *Acta Comparationis Litterarum Universarum. Budapest: Akadémiai Kiadó and Amsterdam: John Benjamins B.V., 1976, pp. 261-282.

7.1526 Thaniel, George. "George Seferis' *Thrush* and the Poetry of Ezra Pound". *Comparative Literature Studies* 11, No. 4 (Dec. 1974), pp. 326-336.

7.1527 Thaniel, George. "A Landmark Book on Seferis". *Neo-Hellenika* 4 (1981), pp. 189-199.
   Re. Nassos Vayenas, *Ὁ Ποιητής καί ὁ Χορευτής*. Athens: Kedros, 1979.

7.1528 Thaniel, George. "A Modern Greek View [Seferis'] of Homer". *Πλάτων* 30, Nos. 59/60 (1978), pp. 58-61.

7.1529 Thaniel, George. "Seferis and England: A Greek Poet in an English Landscape". *JMGS* 5, No. 1 (May 1987), pp. 85-109.

7.1530 Thaniel, George. "Sixteen English Letters to George Seferis: Presented with an Introduction". *MGSY* 2 (1986), pp. 121-142.

7.1531 *"This Day in History". *The Boston Globe,* 13 Mar. 1984; and Harvard Professor [G.P. Savidis] criticizes description of George Seferis as a 'Turkish Poet'. Weekly Review, Πρωϊνή (New York), 13 Apr. 1984.

7.1532 Thompson, Peter. "Seferis Against the Colonels". *Labrys* 8 (Apr. 1983), pp. 81-83 {7.1442}.

7.1533 Topping, Eva Catafygiotu. "Seferis' 'Mycenae': A Tragic Lyric". *Neo-Hellenika* 1 (1970), pp. 128-140.

7.1534 Tsirkas, Stratis. "Seferis' Last Days". Minas Savvas, tr. *Quarterly Review of Literature* 18, Nos. 3-4 (1973), pp. 504-510. Republished in Vol. 20, Nos. 3-4 (1977), pp. 339-345.

7.1535 Vayenas, Nassos. "George Seferis-T.S. Eliot: Parallels". *Labrys* 8 (Apr. 1983), pp. 84-94. {7.1442}.

7.1536 Zahareas, Anthony N. "George Seferis: Myth and History". *Books Abroad* 42 (Spring 1968), pp. 190-198.

Sikelianos, Angelos (1884-1951)

a.

7.1537 *_____ *Akritan Songs.* Paul Nord, tr. New York: Spap, 1944. 33 p. Bilingual edition.

7.1538 _____ *The Delphic Word. "The Principle of the Aristoï": The Dedication.* Alma Reed, tr. New York: Harold Vinal Ltd., 1928. 53 p.

7.1539 _____ *The Dithyramb of the Rose.* Frances Sikelianos, tr. Privately printed for Ted Shawn, 1939. Ca. 29 unnumbered p. A limited edition of five hundred copies.

7.1540 _____ *Selected Poems.* Edmund Keeley and Philip Sherrard, trs. and intro. Princeton, N.J.: Princeton University Press, 1979. 150 p. Bilingual edition. *Also London: George Allen & Unwin, 1980. 75 p. English only. London: The Anvil Press, 1983.

7.1541 *Six Poems from the Greek of Sikelianos and Seferis.* Lawrence Durrell, [tr.]. Rhodes, 1946. 18 p.

b.

7.1542 _____ "Caique"; "Sparta". Edmund Keeley and Philip Sherrard, trs. *Pequod*, No. 11 (Winter 1980-81), pp. 38-39.

7.1543 _____ "The Death Feast of the Greeks". Lawrence Durrell, tr. In *New Writing and Daylight* 7 (John Lehmann, ed. London: John Lehmann, 1946), pp. 44-46.

7.1544 _____ "Eleven Poems by Anghelos Sikelianos". Philip Sherrard, Edmund Keeley, and Kimon Friar, trs. *The Charioteer* 1, No. 1 (Summer 1960), pp. 69-88.

7.1545 _____ "Four Poems". Edmund Keeley and Philip Sherrard, trs. *The Malahat Review* 52 (Oct. 1979), pp. 98-103.

7.1546 _____ "The Mother of Dante"; "Pan". Edmund Keeley and Philip Sherrard, trs. *Sequoia* 21, No. 2 (Spring 1977), pp. 24-25.

7.1547 _____ "The Oath to Mother Greece by the Hellenic Communities". Hymn set to music by Eva Sikelianou. *Athene* 4, No. 9 (Dec. 1943), pp. 20-21. Bilingual version.

7.1548 _____ "The Sacred Road". C.A. Trypanis and Thomas Barrie, trs. Ἀγγλο-ελληνικὴ Ἐπιθεώρηση 1, No. 2 (Apr. 1945), pp. 20-21. Bilingual version.

7.1549 *_____ "The Sacred Way". Edmund Keeley and Philip Sherrard, trs. *Footprint Magazine* 4 (Winter 1979/80), pp. 18-20.

7.1550 *_____ "Sibyl". Theofanis G. Stavrou, tr. In *Angelos Sikelianos and the Delphic Idea* (Theofanis G. Stavrou. St. Paul, Minn.: North Central Publishing Company, n.d.) {7.1557}.

7.1551 _____ "Three Poems". Edmund Keeley and Philip Sherrard, trs. *The Ontario Review* 11 (Fall-Winter 1979-80), pp. 82-86.
   "Doric"; "The First Rain"; "Agraphon".

7.1552 _____ "Two Poems". Edmund Keeley and Philip Sherrard, trs. *Translation* 6 (Winter 1978-79), pp. 163-164.
   "Frieze"; "The Suicide of Atzesivano, Disciple of Buddha".

7.1553 _____ "Two Poems by Angelos Sikelianos". Rae Dalven, tr. *Poetry* 120, No. 5 (Aug. 1972), pp. 261-267.
   "Free Dodecanese"; "Supper".

7.1554 _____ "Unrecorded". Kimon Friar, tr. *The Atlantic Monthly* 195, No. 6 (June 1955), p.165 {3.3}.

7.1555 _____ "Unrecorded". Edmund Keeley, tr. *Canto* 1, No. 3 (Fall 1977), pp. 119-120.

c.

7.1556 *Angelos Sikelianos / 1884-1951 / ΑΓΓΕΛΟΣ ΣΙΚΕΛΙΑΝΟΣ*. An Exhibit May 15-July 31, 1981. Modern Greek Collection, Special Collections, 466 Wilson Library, University of Minnesota. 23 p. Pamphlet.
Introduction to the poet and his work by Theofanis G. Stavrou.

7.1557 *Stavrou, Theofanis G. *Angelos Sikelianos and the Delphic Idea*. Including *Life with Angelos Sikelianos* by Anna Sikelianos and *Sibyl* by Angelos Sikelianos. Minneapolis, Minn.: North Central Publishing Company, n.d.

d.

7.1558 Dimaras, C.Th. "The Work of Anghelos Sikelianos". Staff, trs. *The Charioteer* 1, No. 1 (Summer 1960), pp. 65-69.
Preceded by an editorial note: "Anghelos Sikelianos: A Note on His Life" (pp. 63-64).

7.1559 Giannaris, George. "The Oratorio of Theodorakis". *The Greek Report* 14-15 (Mar.-Apr. 1970), pp. 21-23.
The Oratorio 'March of the Spirit' by Mikis Theodorakis is based on the poetic text of Angelos Sikelianos. Translation of Sikelianos' text with commentary on the music.

7.1560 Gregory, Dorothy M.-T. "Kazantzakis and Sikelianos: Complementary Spirits". *JMH* 2 (Oct. 1985), pp. 65-73.

7.1561 Keeley, Edmund. "Ancient Greek Myth in Angelos Sikelianos". *BMGS* 7 (1981), pp. 105-117.
Republished as "Sikelianos and Greek Mythology" in his *Modern Greek Poetry: Voice and Myth* (Princeton, N.J.: Princeton University Press, 1983), pp. 43-52 {5.2}.

7.1562 Keeley, Edmund. "Angelos Sikelianos: The Sublime Voice". *The Ontario Review* 11 (Fall-Winter 1979-80), pp. 73-81.
Republished as "Sikelianos: The Sublime Voice" in his *Modern Greek Poetry: Voice and Myth* (Princeton, N.J.: Princeton University Press, 1983), pp. 31-42 {5.2}.

7.1563 Keeley, Edmund. "Sikelianos and Greek Mythology". In his *Modern Greek Poetry: Voice and Myth* (Princeton, N.J.: Princeton University Press, 1983), pp. 43-52. {Essays.}
First published as "Ancient Greek Myth in Angelos Sikelianos". *BMGS* 7 (1981), pp. 105-117 {7.1561}.

7.1564 Keeley, Edmund. "Sikelianos: The Sublime Voice". In his *Modern Greek Poetry: Voice and Myth* (Princeton, N.J.: Princeton University Press, 1983), pp. 31-42 {5.2}.
First published as "Angelos Sikelianos: The Sublime Voice". *The Ontario Review* 11 (Fall-Winter 1979-80), pp. 73-81 {7.1562}.

7.1565 Liddell, Robert. "The Poetry of Angelos Sikelianos". *The Penguin New Writing* 39 (1950), pp. 72-83.

7.1566 Maskaleris, Thanasis. "The Socially Committed Sikelianos 1941-1951". *JHD* 2, No. 2 (Apr. 1975), pp. 39-43.
   Includes translation of 'March of the Spirit' by Rae Dalven.

7.1567 Pesopoulos, Hero. "A Greek Poet: Angelos Sikelianos". *New Writing and Daylight* 6 (1945), pp. 101-107.

7.1568 Prevelakis, Pandelis. "Kazantzakis-Sikelianos: The Chronicle of a Friendship". Kimon Friar, tr. *JHD* 10, No. 4 (Winter 1983), pp. 5-20.

7.1569 Prevelakis, Pandelis. "'The Light-Shadowed' of Angelos Sikelianos". Ted Sampson, tr. *Greek Letters* 4 (1986-1989), pp. 123-146.

7.1570 Sherrard, Philip. "Anghelos Sikelianos". Chapter 4 of his *The Marble Threshing Floor: Studies in Modern Greek Poetry* (Freeport, N.Y.: Books for Libraries Press, 1956. Reprinted 1970), pp. 125-183 {5.6}.

7.1571 Sherrard, Philip. "Anghelos Sikelianos and His Vision of Greece". In his *The Wound of Greece* (London: Rex Collings Ltd. with Athens: Anglo-Hellenic, 1978), pp. 72-93 {5.7}.
   Previously in *Review of National Literatures* 5, No. 2 (Fall 1974), pp. 90-112 {3.30}.

7.1572 Sikelianos, Anna. "Life with Angelos Sikelianos". In *Angelos Sikelianos and the Delphic Idea* (Theofanis G. Stavrou. Minneapolis, Minn.: North Central Publishing Company, n.d.) {7.1557}.

7.1573 Sikelianou, Eva. "The Poet Anghelos Sikelianos". *Athene* 4, No. 9 (Dec. 1943), pp. 22-35.

7.1574 Sikelianou, Eva. "Upward Panic: The Autobiography of Eva Sikelianou". Excerpts: "Part 1: The Delphic Idea". *The Athenian* (July 1979), pp. 22-28; "Part 2: The First Delphic Festival, 1927". *The Athenian* (Aug. 1979), pp. 24-34; "Part 3: The Second Delphic Festival, 1930". *The Athenian* (Sept. 1979), pp. 28-33.

Sinopoulos, Takis (1917-1981)

a.

7.1575 _____ *Deathfeast*. John Stathatos, tr. London: Oasis Books, 1975. 8 p.

7.1576 _____ *Landscape of Death: The Selected Poems of Takis Sinopoulos*. Kimon Friar, tr. and intro. Columbus, Ohio: Ohio State University Press, 1979. 288 p. Bilingual edition.

7.1577 _____ *Selected Poems*. John Stathatos, tr. and intro. San Francisco: Wire Press; London: Oxus Press, 1981. 94 p.

7.1578 _____ *Stones*. John Stathatos, tr. London: Oasis Books, 1980. 29 p.

b.

7.1579 _____ "The Bell"; "Above the Seasons"; "Defeat"; "If". John Stathatos, tr. *The Coffeehouse* 2 (Spring 1976), pp. 32-35.

7.1580 _____ "Jacob". James Stone, tr. *Grand Street* 2, No. 3 (Spring 1983), pp. 178-179 {7.151}.

7.1581 _____ "Magda"; "Sophia etc."; "Sight and Vision"; "Ioanna's Invitation"; "One of Constantine's Nights"; "The Beheading". Edmund Keeley and George Savidis, trs. *Poetry* 105, No 1 (Oct. 1964), pp. 36-42 {3.27}.

7.1582 _____ "Nights" [from the poem "Chronicle"]. Willis Barnstone, tr. In *Eighteen Texts* (Willis Barnstone, ed. Cambridge, Mass.: Harvard University Press, 1972), pp. 53-62.] {4.1}.

7.1583 _____ "from *The Song of Ioanna and Constantinos*". George Economou, tr. *The Charioteer* 14 (1972), pp. 12-14.

7.1584 _____ "Three Greek Poets: Yannis Ritsos, Takis Sinopoulos, George Pavlopoulos". Translated respectively by Peter Levi and Nikos Stangos; Ian Scott-Kilvert; and Peter Levi. *TLS* (14 Nov. 1975), p. 1365.

7.1585 _____ "Two Poems". Kimon Friar, tr. *The Literary Review* 16, No. 3 (Spring 1973), pp. 338-341 {3.15}.
   "Elpenor"; "Song of Songs".

7.1586 _____ "Waiting Room". Kimon Friar, tr. *Mundus Artium* 4, No. 1 (Winter 1970), pp. 10-11 {4.82}.

d.

7.1587 Beaton, Roderick. "Space Between Armies". *TLS* (10 Oct. 1980), p. 1154.
   Re. K. Friar's translation *Landscape of Death* {7.1576}.

7.1588 Karampetsos, E.D. and Donald D. Maddox. "Greece's Poet-Chronicler Takis Sinopoulos (1917-81): An Interview". *WLT* 57, No. 3 (Summer 1983), pp. 403-408.

7.1589 Savidis, George. "A Note on Takis Sinopoulos". *Poetry* 105, No. 1 (Oct. 1964), p. 43 {3.27}.

Siotis, Dino (b. 1946)

a.

7.1590 *_____ *So What: Poems*. John Chioles, Th. Frangopoulos, Loukas Skipitaris, Th. Maskaleris, and J. Massa, trs.; illustrated by the poet; Nanos Valaoritis, intro. San Francisco: Panjandrum Press, 1972. 60 p.

Skaros, Zissis (b. 1917)

a.

7.1591 *_____ *The Cry of the Greek People*. Montréal: Éditions Nouvelle Frontière, 1971. 37 p.

Skiadaresis, Spyros (1904-1967)

b.

7.1592 _____ "The Kospetonis Barracks: A Cephalonian Story". G. Michael Razi and Alec Reid, trs. and intro. With an intro. by Theofanis G. Stavrou. *MGSY* 2 (1986), pp. 201-220.

Skipis, Sotiris (1881-1952)

a.

7.1593 _____ *Patterns from a Grecian Loom: Selections from the Works of Sotiris Skipis*. J. Harwood Bacon, tr. from the French with an introduction by Sir Edmund Gosse and a biographical sketch by Christine Galitzi. London: Unwin Brothers, 1928. 141 p.

Solomos, Dionysios (1798-1857)

a.

7.1594 _____ *The Greek National Anthem*. The Poem by D. Solomos (1823). The Music by N. Mantzaros. English version by Rudyard Kipling. London: Novello & Co., Ltd., 1918.
   This version includes the music. The translation (six stanzas) was published in Ἡ Ἑσπερία, 25 Ὀκτωβρίου 1918 and had originally been published in the *Daily Telegraph* of the previous Thursday {7.1600}.

7.1595 _____ *The Hymn to Liberty: The Greek National Anthem. Dionysios Solomos 1798-1857*. Warren E. Blake, tr. Ann Arbor, Mich., 1957. 8 p.
   The first four stanzas. Printed as two stanzas on a folded sheet.

7.1596 *_____ *Ode to Liberty*. George D. Canale, tr. into both prose and verse with a biographical sketch of the poet and notes. Zante: Constantine Rossolimo Publisher, 1861. 13 p. Bilingual edition.

b.

7.1597 _____ "The Destruction of Psara". Cedric Whitman, tr. *Eleutheria* 1, No. 1 (Apr. 1970), p. 2.

7.1598 _____ "Dithyrambics to Liberty". In *The Songs of Greece, from the Romaic text* (Charles Brinsley Sheridan, tr. into English verse; M.C. Fauriel, ed. London, 1825), pp. 249-288 {4.56}.
   158 stanzas. By "Mr. Salomos".

7.1599 *_____ "Extract from an Ὠδή (sic) εἰς τήν ἐλευθερίαν, composed by Dionysius Solomon, of Zante. George Lee, tr. *The Literary Gazette and Journal of the Belles Lettres* (11 Sept. 1824), p. 587.
   Translation of stanzas 151-158. The first publication and translation of stanzas 151-158 of Solomos' *Hymn*. See the article *"Η πρώτη δημοσίευση καί μετάφραση τῶν στρ. 151-158 τοῦ σολωμικοῦ Ὕμνου" by Loukia Droulia in *Ὁ Ἐρανιστής* 67 (Feb. 1975), pp. 1-6. For all the known translations into English of the *Hymn to Liberty* see Ντίνος Χριστιανόπουλος, "Οἱ μεταφράσεις τοῦ Ὕμνου εἰς τήν ἐλευθερίαν τοῦ Σολωμοῦ". In *Ἀφιέρωμα στόν καθηγητή Λίνο Πολίτη* (Θεσσαλονίκη, 1979), pp. 99-113.

7.1600 *_____ "The Greek National Anthem". Rudyard Kipling, tr. *Daily Telegraph* (17 Oct. 1918). Reprinted in *Rudyard Kipling's Verses. Inclusive edition 1885-1918.* 3 vols. London: Hodder and Stoughton, 1919, pp. 121-122. Also in *A Choice of Kipling's Verse*, made by T.S. Eliot, with an essay on Rudyard Kipling's poetry. London: Faber and Faber, [1941], pp. 47-48.
   Translation of stanzas 1-5 and 15.

7.1601 _____ "The Greek National Anthem. Poem by D. Solomos, 1823. Music by N. Mantzaros. English version by Rudyard Kipling". On inside back cover of *Navarino Centenary Dinner: 20th October 1927.* Ca. 22 unnumbered pages.
   The same six stanzas as in {7.1600}.

7.1602 _____ "A Hymn to Liberty". Written by Dionysios Solomos, of Zante, in the Month of May 1823. Arnold Green, tr. In his *Greek and what Next? An Address. Solomos' Hymn to Liberty. A Poem* (Read before the Alumni Association of Brown University, 17 June 1884. Providence: Sidney S. Rider, 1884), pp. 35-52.
   The entire poem. Part of {7.1610}.

7.1603 *_____ "Hymn to Liberty". Thanasis Maskaleris, tr. *Hellenic Journal* (11 Mar. 1976).
   Several stanzas.

7.1604 _____ "Hymn to Liberty". Th.P. Stephanides and G.C. Katsimbalis, trs. *Ἀγγλο-ελληνική Ἐπιθεώρηση* 1, No. 1 (Mar. 1945), pp. 6-7. Bilingual version.
   The first 15 stanzas.

7.1605 _____ From "The Ode to Liberty". Florence McPherson, tr. In her *Poetry of Modern Greece* (London, 1884), pp. 61-79 {4.49}.
   Seventy-three stanzas.

7.1606 _____ "The Woman of Zakynthos": Narrative Poem. Marianthe Colakis, tr. *The Charioteer* 24 and 25 (1982/1983), pp. 118-136 {7.392}.

7.1607 _____ "The Woman of Zakythos". Peter Colaclides and Michael Green, trs. and intro. *MGSY* 1 (1985), pp. 153-171.

7.1608 _____ "Xanthoula". David Mason, tr. *Translation* 16 (Spring 1986), pp. 143-144.

c.

7.1609 Coutelle, Louis, Theofanis G. Stavrou and David R. Weinberg. *A Greek Diptych: Dionysios Solomos and Alexandros Papadiamantis* A Nostos Book. Minneapolis, Minn.: North Central Publishing Company, 1986. 113 p.

7.1610 Green, Arnold. *Greek and What Next?* An Address. *Solomos' Hymn to Liberty.* A Poem. Read before the Alumni Association of Brown University, June 17, 1884, by Arnold Green. Providence: Sidney S. Rider, 1884. 52 p.

7.1611 *Jenkins, Romilly. *Dionysius Solomos.* Cambridge: Cambridge University Press, 1940. 225 p. Reprinted, Athens: Denise Harvey & Company, 1981. 226 p.

7.1612 Lorenzatos, Zissimos. *The Lost Center and Other Essays in Greek Poetry.* Kay Cicellis, tr. Princeton, N.J.: Princeton University Press, 1980. 200 p {5.3}.
    Contains: "Solomos" (pp. 3-69); "A Definition of Style by Solomos" (pp. 70-84); "The Lost Center" [esp. re. George Seferis] (pp. 85-146); "Solomos' *Dialogos* and Dante" (pp. 147-180); "'Ultima Verba': Solomos" (pp. 181-194).

7.1613 Raizis, M. Byron. *Dionysios Solomos.* Twayne's World Authors Series, No. 193. New York: Twayne Publishers, 1972. 158 p.

7.1614 Stavrou, Theofanis G. *Dionysios Solomos / 1798-1857 / Διονύσιος Σολωμός.* An Exhibit May 13-June 30, 1983. Modern Greek Collection, Special Collections, University of Minnesota, Minneapolis, Minn. Pamphlet. 25 p.

d.

7.1615 Beaton, Roderick. "Dionysios Solomos: The Tree of Poetry". *BMGS* 2 (1976), pp. 161-182.

7.1616 Belleli, L. *A Misconception about a Poem of Dionisios Solomos. Remarks.* Reprint from the *Hellenic Herald* (Oct. 1906), pp. 3-7.
    Re. "Ὁ θάνατος τῆς ὀρφανῆς".

7.1617 Georgacas, Demetrius J. "The Learned Elements in Dionysios Solomos' Work". In *Studies Presented to David Moore Robinson on His Seventieth Birthday.* Vol. 2 (George E. Mylonas and Doris Raymond, eds. St. Louis, Miss.: Washington University, 1953), pp. 732-742.

7.1618 Jenkins, R.J.H. "A Link between Lord Byron and Dionysius Solomos". *The Journal of Hellenic Studies* 66 (1946), p. 66 and plate VI.

7.1619 Lambropoulos, Vassilis. "Dionysios Solomos and the Fictions of Criticism: Polylas' *Prolegomena* as Künstlerroman". *JMGS* 3, No. 1 (May 1985), pp. 29-43.

7.1620 Lorenzatos, Zissimos. "Solomos' *Dialogos:* A Survey". In *Modern Greek Writers* (Edmund Keeley and Peter Bien, eds. Princeton: Princeton University Press, 1972), pp. 23-65 {5.9}.

7.1621 Mackridge, Peter. "Time out of Mind: The Relationship between Story and Narrative in Solomos' *The Cretan*". *BMGS* 9 (1984/85), pp. 187-208.

7.1622 Polylas, Iakovos. "Prolegomena to Dionysios Solomos". *Greek Letters* 2 (1983), pp. 196-228.

7.1623 Raizis, M. Byron. "Solomos and the Britannic Muses". *Neo-Hellenika* 1 (1970), pp. 94-121.

7.1624 Sherrard, Philip. "Dionysios Solomos". Chapter 1 of his *The Marble Threshing Floor: Studies in Modern Greek Poetry* (Freeport, N.Y.: Books for Libraries Press, 1956), pp. 1-37 {5.6}.

7.1625 Tomadakis, Nikolaos B. "The Proclamation of Ypsilantis Μάχου ὑπέρ Πίστεως καί Πατρίδος and the *Hymn to Liberty* by Solomos". *Neo-Hellenika* 2 (1975), pp. 120-126.

Sotiropoulou, Ersi (b. 1953)
d.
7.1626 _____ "Interview". Kay Cicellis, tr. *Translation* 14 (Spring 1985), pp. 15-22 {3.34}.
    A reporter from the periodical *Art News* interviews the author of *Holiday without a Corpse*.

Souliotis, Mimis (b. 1949)
b.
7.1627 _____ "Mr. Tsimbas"; "Aspirins". Minas Savvas, tr. *The Coffeehouse* 3 (Fall 1976), pp. 41-43.

Souris, Giorgos (1853-1919)
d.
7.1628 Phoutrides, Aristides E. "George Soures". *The Classical Journal* 15, No. 4 (Jan. 1920), pp. 235-238.

7.1629 Phoutrides, Aristides E. "Soures and His World". *The Classical Journal* 15, No. 8 (May 1920), pp. 494-498.

Spanias, Nikos (b. 1925)
b.
7.1630 _____ "Poems". C. Otis, tr. *Aegean Review* 2 (Spring/Summer 1987), pp. 46-48.
    "American Moments"; "The Angel"; "Death Will Come".

Spanou Stratis, Giota

a.

7.1631 *_____ Στήν Ἄλλη Ὄχθη / At the Other Side. Ποιήματα / Poems. Athens and New York: Δρυμός, 1986. 41 p.

Spatharis, Sotiris (1892-1973)

a.

7.1632 _____ *Behind the White Screen: Memoirs.* Mario Rinvolucri, tr. and intro.: "The History and Art of Karagiosis" [Leslie Finer, tr.]. New York: Red Dust, 1976. 150 p. *Also, with subtitle: *An Autobiography.* London: Alan Ross, 1967. 163 p.

Spyropoulos, N.J. (1893-1958)

a.

7.1633 *_____ *Bellerophon* [a play in verse]. Clarence A. Manning, tr. New York: Bookman Associates, 1955. 71 p.

Stavrou, Gerasimos

d.

7.1634 Krili-Kevans, Yota. "Καληνύχτα Μαργαρίτα, by Gerasimos Stavrou: An Introduction". Το Γιοφύρι 6 (Aug. 1979), pp. 43-52.
The play is a dramatization of the short story "Μαργαρίτα Περδικάρη" by Dimitris Chatzis.

Stefanou, Lydia (b. 1927)

d.

7.1635 Dobson, Rosemary. "A Letter to Lydia" (a poem). *Quadrant* 25, Nos. 1-2 (Jan.-Feb. 1981), pp. 22-23.

Stergiopoulos, Kostas (b. 1926)

b.

7.1636 _____ "The Disinterment". Jack Gaist, tr. Πνευματική Κύπρος 183 (Dec. 1975), p. 86.

7.1637 _____ [3 Poems]. Jack Gaist, tr. Πνευματική Κύπρος 184 (Jan. 1976), pp. 125-126
"The Crime"; "Silence"; "Disinterment" (revised translation).

Steriadis, Vasilis (b. 1947)

b.

7.1638 _____ "Aunt Lito"; "Identity Card"; "Mr. Ivo". Kimon Friar, tr. *The Coffeehouse* 5 (Winter 1977), pp. 47-50.

Tachtsis, Kostas (1927-1988)

a.

7.1639 _____ *The Third Wedding*. Leslie Finer, tr. New York: Red Dust, 1971. 303 p.
*Also London: Alan Ross, 1967; Harmondsworth, England: Penguin Books, 1969. 256 p.

7.1640 _____ *The Third Wedding Wreath*. In a new translation with an introduction by John Chioles. Athens: Hermes, 1985. 322 p.

b.

7.1641 _____ "The First Image". D.W. Blewitt, tr. *The London Magazine*, N.S. 11, No. 1 (Apr./May 1971), pp. 129-135.

7.1642 _____ "The First Image". N.C. Germanacos, tr. *Shenandoah* 27, No. 1 (Fall 1975), pp. 89-94 {3.32}.

7.1643 _____ "My Short Life with Seferis". Mary Keeley, tr. *Grand Street* 5, No. 2 (Winter 1986), pp. 187-200.

7.1644 _____ "On Being a Student". John Chioles, tr. *Translation* 14 (Spring 1985), pp. 76-85 {3.34}.

7.1645 _____ "Small Change". A Story. N.C. Germanacos, tr. *Boundary 2*, Vol. 1, No. 2 (Winter 1973), pp. 519-523 {3.5}.

7.1646 _____ "A Visit". Philip Ramp, tr. *Descant XVIII*, Vol. 8, No. 2 (1977), pp. 85-88 {3.8}.

d.

7.1647 Kazazis, Kostas. "Learnedisms in Costas Taktsis's *Third Wedding*". *BMGS* 5 (1979), pp. 17-27.

7.1648 Kazazis, Kostas. "Men vs. Women in *The Third Wedding*". *JMGS* 1, No. 1 (May 1983), pp. 131-140.

7.1649 Tannen, Deborah. "Introducing Constructed Dialogue in Greek and American Conversational and Literary Narrative". In *Direct and Indirect Speech* (Florian Coulmas, ed. Trends in Linguistics: Studies & Monographs, 31. Berlin: Mouton de Gruyter, 1986), pp. 311-332.

Terzakis, Angelos (1907-1978)

a.

7.1650 _____ *Homage to the Tragic Muse*. Athan H. Anagnostopoulos, tr.; Cedric H. Whitman, foreword. Boston, Mass.: Houghton Mifflin Company, 1978. 206 p.

7.1651 *_____ *Theophano*. M. Rethis and George Crocker, trs. Emporia, Kansas, 1961.

7.1652 *_____ *Thomas with Two Souls*. Athan Agnos, tr. Medford, Mass., 1964.

b.

7.1653 _____ "Anghelos Terzakis: Excerpts from Two Novels and a Play". JoAnne Cacoullos, Tedd Athas, John Karkas, Katherine Hortis, and staff, trs. *The Charioteer* 4 (1962), pp. 15-49.
   From *Princess Izabo;* from *Without God;* from *Emperor Michael*.

7.1654 _____ "Calm". Theodore Sampson, tr. In *Modern Greek Short Stories*. Vol. 2 (Kyr. Delopoulos, ed. Athens: Kathimerini Publications, 1981), pp. 387-395 {4.13}.

7.1655 _____ "Matesis' *Vassilikos:* The First Drama of Ideas". In *Modern Greek Writers* (Edmund Keeley and Peter Bien, eds. Princeton, N.J.: Princeton University Press, 1972), pp. 93-107 {5.9}.

7.1656 _____ "Palamidi". From *April*. JoAnne Cacoullos, tr. *The Charioteer* 5 (1963), pp. 115-118.

7.1657 _____ "To an Angry Young Man" (Letter from Athens). Byron Raizis and Catherine Sempepos, trs. *The Charioteer* 5 (1963), pp. 125-127.

d.

7.1658 *Anagnostopoulos, Athan H. "Angelos Terzakis' Existential and Aesthetic Theory of Tragedy". *Dissertation Abstracts International* 38 (1978), p. 5799A.

7.1659 Dimaras, C. and K. Dedopoulos, Y. Hatzinis, A. Karandonis, A. Thryllos, and others. "Anghelos Terzakis: A Critical Mosaic". Tedd Athas, tr. and adapted by the staff. *The Charioteer* 4 (1962), pp. 50-54.

7.1660 *Proussis, Costas M. "The Novels of Angelos Terzakis". In *Fiction in Several Languages* (Henri Peyre, ed. Daedalus Library, 9. Boston: Houghton Mifflin, 1968), pp. 80-104.

Thaniel, George (b. 1938)

a.

7.1661 _____ *Beyond the Moment: Selected Poems 1960-1976*. Edward V.S. Phinney, tr., intro. and notes. New York and Washington: Vantage Press, 1983. 60 p.

7.1662 _____ *Homage to Byzantium: The Life and Work of Nikos Gabriel Pentzikis*. A Nostos Book. Minneapolis, Minn.: North Central Publishing Company, 1983. 156 p.

7.1663 *_____ *The Linchpin*. Ten Poems. Montreal: Anthelion Press, 1969.

7.1664 *_____ *Seawave and Snowfall: Selected Poems 1960-1982*. Edward Phinney, tr. Toronto: Amaranth Editions, 1984. 120 p.
   Contains both translations from the Greek and poems written in English.

b.
7.1665 _____ "The Prefaces of Nikos Kachtitsis". *Études Helléniques* 2, No. 1 (Spring 1984), pp. 63-68.

7.1666 _____ "Secular Song"; "Let the Ideas"; "The Lustrous Landmarks"; "When They Go"; "Literno". Edward Phinney, tr. *The Coffeehouse* 6 (Summer 1978), pp. 27-31.

Themelis, Giorgos (1900-1976)
b.
7.1667 _____ "De Rerum Natura" [a poem]. Kimon Friar, tr. *Boundary 2,* Vol. 1, No. 2 (Winter 1973), pp. 441-453 {3.5}.

Theodorou, Nelly (b. 1938)
a.
7.1668 _____ *Pastorale.* Abbott Rick, tr. New York: Thomas Y. Crowell Company, 1961. 180 p. Also as **Pastorale: A Classic Novel of Man and Nature.* London: Redman, 1962.

b.
7.1669 _____ "from *Pastorale*". Abbott Rick, tr. *The Charioteer* 3 (1961), pp. 48-51.

Theotoka, Koralia (1926-1976)
b.
7.1670 _____ "Two Poems". Theodore Vasils, tr. *The Charioteer* 14 (1972), pp. 29-31.

Theotokas, Giorgos (1906-1966)
a.
7.1671 _____ *Argo.* A Novel. E. Margaret Brooke and Ares Tsatsopoulos, trs. London: Methuen & Company, 1951. 357 p.

7.1672 _____ *Leonis.* A Novel. Donald E. Martin, tr.; Theofanis G. Stavrou, pref. A Nostos Book. Minneapolis, Minn.: North Central Publishing Company, 1985. 145 p.

b.
7.1673 _____ "Alcibiades": A play in three acts and seven scenes". *Thespis* 4-5 (June 1966), pp. 217-245.

7.1674 _____ "Excerpts from Two Novels and a Play". E. Margaret Brooke, Ares Tsatsopoulos, Dina Kyriazi, and Alice-Mary Maffry, trs. *The Charioteer* 5 (1963), pp. 16-59.
   From *Argo:* "Sergeant Pikios and the Fair Vision" and "Meeting under the Pepper-Trees"; from *Alcibiades;* from *Leonis.*

7.1675 _____ "The Fate of John Keats". Ἀγγλο-ελληνική Ἐπιθεώρηση 1, No. 1 (Mar. 1945), pp. 8-11. Bilingual version.

7.1676 _____ *"Free Spirit"*. Soterios G. Stavrou, tr. and intro. *MGSY* 2 (1986), pp. 153-200.

7.1677 _____ "The Man who Wrote a Book". Themi Vasils, tr. *The Coffeehouse* 10 (Summer 1981), pp. 36-39.

7.1678 _____ "The Modern Greeks". Conn Hadjilia, tr. *The Atlantic Monthly* 195, No. 6 (June 1955), pp. 101-105 {3.3}.

7.1679 _____ "On the Folk Element in Modern Greek Literature". Th. Sampson tr. *Greek Letters* 3 (1984-1985), pp. 55-74.

7.1680 _____ "Simone". Theodore Sampson, tr. In *Modern Greek Short Stories*. Vol. 2 (Kyr. Delopoulos, ed. Athens: Kathimerini Publications, 1981), pp. 277-286 {4.13}.

7.1681 _____ "Some Questions of the Psychology of the Modern Greeks". *The Link*, No. 1 (June 1938), pp. 66-70.

7.1682 _____ "Three Monologues" from *Sick Persons and Travellers*. Theodore Sampson, tr. *Greek Letters* 1 (1982), pp. 232-241.

7.1683 _____ "Vardekis' Monologue". Theodore Sampson, tr. *The Athenian* (Mar. 1975), pp. 29-30.
   From "The Survivors", the last chapter of *The Sick and the Lame*.

7.1684 _____ "Westminster" [short story]. Themi Vasils, tr. *The Charioteer* 19 (1977), pp. 88-94.

c.
7.1685 Doulis, Thomas. *George Theotokas*. Twayne's World Authors Series, No. 339. Boston, Mass.: Twayne Publishers, 1975. 185 p.

d.
7.1686 Mackridge, Peter. "Bibliography of George Theotokas and Kosmas Politis". Μαντατοφόρος 3 (1973), pp. 17-21.

7.1687 Mackridge, Peter. "The Two-Fold Nostalgia: Lost Homeland and Lost Time in the Work of G. Theotokas, E. Venezis and K. Politis". *JMGS* 4, No. 2 (Oct. 1986), pp. 75-83.

7.1688 Martin, Donald E. "Theotokas's Constantinople: Nostalgia as a Source of Literary Creativity". *MGSY* 2 (1986), pp. 113-120.

7.1689 Panayotopoulos, I.M., Andreas Karandonis and Apostolos Sahinis. "George Theotokas: A Critical Mosaic". Andonis Decavalles and Lee Hatfield trs. *The Charioteer* 5 (1963), pp. 60-64.

Theotokis, Konstantinos (1872-1923)

b.

7.1690 _____ "Face Down!". Theodore Sampson, tr. In *Modern Greek Short Stories*. Vol. 1 (Kyr. Delopoulos, ed. Athens: Kathimerini Publications, 1980), pp. 267-271 {4.12}.

d.

7.1691 Eklund, Bo-Lennart. "The Socialism of Constantinos Theotokis: An Analysis Based on the Concepts "ΤΙΜΗ" and "ΧΡΗΜΑ" in Two of his Works". *SSMG* 3 (1979), pp. 3-27.

Tsagris, Kleomenis G. (b. 1890)

a.

7.1692 *_____ *A Spring Ramble*. Athens, 1961. 32 p.

Tsaloumas, Dimitris (b. 1921)

a.

7.1693 _____ *The Book of Epigrams*. Philip Grundy, tr. St. Lucia; London; New York: University of Queensland Press, 1985. 207 p. Bilingual edition.

7.1694 _____ *The Observatory*. Philip Grundy, tr. St. Lucia; London; New York: University of Queensland Press, 1983. 170 p. Second edition [with notes], 1984. 175 p. Bilingual edition.

b.

7.1695 _____ "Two Poems". Philip Grundy, tr. *Scripsi* 4, No. 2 (Nov. 1986), pp. 124-130.
   "Heracles at the 'Stymphalos'"; "Three Night Pieces".

d.

7.1696 *Perkins, Elizabeth. "Dimitris Tsaloumas: Interview". *Literature in North Queensland* 15, No. 1 (1987), pp. 96-103.

7.1697 Rodriguez, Judith. "Dimitris Tsaloumas Observed". *Meanjin* 42, No. 1 (Mar. 1983), pp. 104-109.

Tsangarakis, Odysseas

a.

7.1698 *_____ *Open Roads*. Jean H. Woodhead, tr. Great Neck, N.Y.: Todd and Honeywell Inc., 1981.

Tsatsos, Konstantinos D. (1899-1986)

a.

7.1699 _____ *Dialogues in a Monastery*. Jean Demos, tr.; John Brademas, pref. Brookline, Mass.: Hellenic College Press, 1986. 182 p.

d.

7.1700 Morrison, Karl F. "Understanding Conversion: Reflections upon Reading the *Dialogues* of Constantine Tsatsos". *MGSY* 3 (1987), pp. 99-127.

Tsatsou, Ioanna (b. 1904)

a.

7.1701 _____ *Empress Athenais-Eudocia: A Fifth Century Byzantine Humanist*. Jean Demos, tr. Brookline, Mass.: Holy Cross Orthodox Press, 1977. 141 p.

7.1702 _____ *Hours on Sinai*. Jean Demos, tr. Brookline, Mass.: Hellenic College Press, 1984. 78 p.

7.1703 _____ *My Brother George Seferis*. Jean Demos, tr.; Eugene Current-Garcia, pref. A Nostos Book. Minneapolis, Minn.: North Central Publishing Company, 1982. 257 p.

7.1704 _____ *Poems*. Jean Demos, tr.; C.A. Trypanis, intro. A Nostos Book. Minneapolis, Minn.: North Central Publishing Company, 1984. 200 p. Bilingual edition.

7.1705 _____ *The Sword's Fierce Edge: A Journal of the Occupation of Greece, 1941-1944*. Authorized English translation by Jean Demos. Nashville, Tenn.: Vanderbilt University Press, 1969. 130 p.

Tsiamis, Christos (b. 1950)

b.

7.1706 _____ "Greeks"; "Polychromatic"; "Soliloquy"; "I Will Die One Day Means..."; "Incident". Nikos Spanias, tr. *The Coffeehouse* 10 (Summer 1981), pp. 52-56.

Tsirkas, Stratis (1911-1980)

a.

7.1707 _____ *Drifting Cities: A Trilogy*. Kay Cicellis, tr. New York: Alfred A. Knopf, 1974. 710 p.

b.

7.1708 _____ "The Fight with the Moray-Eel" [a story]. Kevin Andrews, tr. *Boundary 2*, Vol. 1, No. 2 (Winter 1973), pp. 315-320 {3.5}.

7.1709 _____ "from *The Journal of the Trilogy*". Kay Cicellis, tr. *Shenandoah* 27, No. 1 (Fall 1975), pp. 99-103 {3.32}.

7.1710 _____ "from *The Lost Spring*". Kay Cicellis, tr. *Descant XVIII,* Vol. 8, No. 2 (1977), pp. 73-80 {3.8}.

7.1711 _____ "Seferis' Last Days". Minas Savvas, tr. *Quarterly Review of Literature* 18, Nos. 3-4 (1973), pp. 504-510. Republished in Vol. 20, Nos. 3-4 (1977), pp. 339-345.

7.1712 _____ "Weather-Change". Kevin Andrews, tr. In *Eighteen Texts* (Willis Barnstone, ed. Cambridge, Mass.: Harvard University Press, 1972), pp. 97-102 {4.1}.

d.
7.1713 Boatwright, James. "Are You Tourists?". *Shenandoah* 26, No. 3 (Spring 1975), pp. 156-171 {3.31}.
  A journal/review dated June 5-Aug. 16, 1974; esp. re. Stratis Tsirkas and Kay Cicellis.

7.1714 Doulis, Thomas. "Stratis Tsirkas, the Voice from the Cellar". *JHD* 3 (July 1975), pp. 27-36.
  Also discusses L. Durrell's *Alexandria Quartet.*

7.1715 Germanacos, N.C. "An Interview with Three Contemporary Greek Prose Writers (May 1972): Stratis Tsirkas, Thanassis Valtinos, George Ioannou". *Boundary 2,* Vol. 1, No. 2 (Winter 1973), pp. 266-313 {3.5}.

7.1716 Karampetsos, E.D. "Stratis Tsirkas and the Arabs". *JMGS* 2, No. 1 (May 1984), pp. 39-51.

Vafopoulos, G.T. (b. 1903)
b.
7.1717 _____ "The Transfusion" (a poem). Marios-Byron Raizis, tr. *Greek Letters* 1 (1982), pp. 12-13.

7.1718 _____ "The Fire of the Century". K. Mitsakis, tr. *Greek Letters* 1 (1982), pp. 14-16.

7.1719 *_____ [7 Poems]. Kimon Friar, tr. *Chapman* 2, No. 4 (1973).

Vagenas, Nasos (b. 1945)
a.
7.1720 *_____ *Biography.* Richard Burns, tr. Cambridge, England: Lobby Press, 1978. Unpaginated. Bilingual edition.

7.1721 _____ *Biography and Other Poems.* John Stathatos, tr. London: Oxus Press, 1979. 32 p.

b.
7.1722 _____ "Apologia"; "A Game of Chess"; "Death in Exarchia". Kimon Friar, tr. *Mews* 1 (Apr. 1975), pp. 20-21.

7.1723 *_____ "Beautiful Summer Morning (unfinished painting)". John Stathatos, tr. *The Literary Review* (Edinburgh) 25 (19 Sept.-20 Oct. 1980), p. 21.

7.1724 *_____ "Biography I, II". Nina Nickles, tr. In *Translations, Works-Words, Old-New, 5. A Folio of Poetry Translations* (Binghamton, N.Y.: National Resource and Interpretation, 1984), p. 17.

7.1725 _____ "from *Biography* II, III, XI, XVII, XIX". Richard Burns, tr. *Perfect Bound* 6 (Autumn 1978), pp. 21-23.

7.1726 _____ "Biography IV, VIII, IX, XVI". Richard Burns, tr. *Modern Poetry in Translation* 34 (Summer 1978), pp. 21-22 {3.21}.

7.1727 *_____ "Biography XVI"; "Ode to my Country"; "Death Will Come". Kimon Friar, tr. *Footprint Magazine* 5 (Autumn 1980), pp. 87-89.

7.1728 *_____ "Biography XVI, XVIII, XIX". Richard Burns, tr. *Small Moon* 7/8 (Spring 1979), p. 4.

7.1729 _____ "*Biography:* The Poetry of Nasos Vayenas". Richard Burns, tr. *JHD* 7, No. 1 (Spring 1980), pp. 53-71. Bilingual version.

7.1730 _____ "Borges and the Labyrinth of Irony". John Solman, tr. *Aegean Review* 2 (Spring/Summer 1987), pp. 33-40.

7.1731 *_____ "Constitution Square". Kimon Friar, tr. *Grove* 5 (Winter 1979), p. 49 {3.12}.

7.1732 _____ "Death in Exarchia"; "Night Watches"; "The Performance"; "The Trees"; "Saturday". John Stathatos, tr. *Contemporary Literature in Translation* 27 (Summer 1977), pp. 19-20 {3.7}.

7.1733 _____ "Death Will Come". Kimon Friar, tr. *Poetry Wales* 11, No. 3 (Winter 1976), pp. 29-30. Bilingual {4.84}.

7.1734 *_____ "Eden"; "Biography IX". John Stathatos, tr. *Poetry Review* 69, No. 2 (Dec. 1979), pp. 10-11.

7.1735 _____ "Episode". Kimon Friar, tr. *The International Portland Review* (1980), p. 166. Bilingual.

7.1736 _____ "Foreword to the Second Edition of *Vertigo*". Kay Cicellis, tr. *Descant* XVIII, Vol. 8, No. 2 (1977), pp. 60-63 {3.8}.

7.1737 *_____ "Inca". John Stathatos, tr. *Central Park* 3 (Spring 1982), p. 17.

7.1738 _____ "Justification"; "Death in Exarchia" [John Stathatos, tr.]; "National Gardens" [Richard Burns, tr.]. *Perfect Bound* 7 (1979), pp. 13-15.

7.1739 _____ "Saturday". John Stathatos, tr. *Zenos* 2 (1978), p. 41 {3.35}.

7.1740 _____ "Sonnet". G. Thaniel, tr. *The Amaranth* 3 (1982), p. 25 {4.65}.

7.1741 _____ "Three Poems". Donald Hall, tr. *The Amaranth* 8 (1984), pp. 41-43 {4.70}.
"Apology"; "Death at Exarhia"; "The Room".

7.1742 *_____ "Two Poems". Christopher Williams, tr. *Iron* 47 (Oct. 1985-Jan. 1986), pp. 58-59.
"Beautiful Summer Morning"; "Rhapsody".

Vakalo, Eleni (b. 1921)

a.
7.1743 _____ Γενεαλογία / *Genealogy*. Paul Merchant, tr. Exeter, England: Rougemont Press, 1971. 87 p. 450 numbered copies. Bilingual edition. New and revised edition: *Egham, England: Interim Press, 1977. 22 p.

b.
7.1744 _____ "The House" [a poem]. Kimon Friar, tr. *Aegean Review* 3 (Fall/Winter 1987), pp. 56-57.

7.1745 _____ "The Mythology of Taste". Kimon Friar, tr. *The Literary Review* 16, No. 3 (Spring 1973), p. 308 {3.15}.

7.1746 _____ "Selected Poems". Kimon Friar, tr. *JHD* 9, No. 4 (Winter 1982), pp. 28-43. Bilingual version.

d.
7.1747 Friar, Kimon. "Eleni Vakalo: Beyond Lyricism". *JHD* 9, No. 4 (Winter 1982), pp. 21-27.

Valaoritis, Aristotelis (1824-1879)

c.
7.1748 *Santas, Constantine. *Aristotelis Valaoritis*. Twayne World Authors Series, No. 406. Boston, Mass.: Twayne Publishers, 1976. 174 p.

d.
7.1749 Menardos, Simos. "A Modern Greek Poet: Aristotle Valaoritis". *The New World* (Aug. 1910). 4 p. Reprint.

7.1750 Rodd, Rennell. "The Poet of the Klephts: Aristoteles Valaoritis". *The Nineteenth Century*, No. 173 (July 1891), pp. 130-144.

Valaoritis, Nanos (b. 1921)

a.

7.1751 _____ *Flash Bloom*. Illustrations by Marie Wilson. San Francisco: Wire Press, 1980. 140 p.

b.

7.1752 _____ "The Gods". Kimon Friar, tr. *The Literary Review* 16, No. 3 (Spring 1973), pp. 350-351 {3.15}.

7.1753 _____ "How I Met Ionesco" [essay]. *Aegean Review* 3 (Fall/Winter 1987), pp. 47-48.

7.1754 _____ "Postscript"; "Orpheus and Eurydice"; "They". *The Coffeehouse* 1 (Fall 1975), pp. 26-29.
   No translator mentioned.

7.1755 _____ "Untitled"; "Postscript Poem". *Eleutheria* 1, No. 8 (Nov. 1970), pp. 18-19.
   No translator mentioned.

7.1756 _____ "World War". Nikos Stangos, tr. *Agenda* 7, No. 1 (Winter 1969), p. 79 {3.1}.

Valtinos, Thanasis (b. 1932)

b.

7.1757 _____ "August '48". N.C. Germanacos, tr. *Shenandoah* 27, No. 1 (Fall 1975), pp. 20-25 {3.32}.

7.1758 _____ "The Descent of the Nine". A Story. N.C. Germanacos, tr. *Boundary 2*, Vol. 1, No. 2 (Winter 1973), pp. 321-347 {3.5}.

7.1759 _____ "Panayotis: A Biographical Note". John Taylor, tr. *Aegean Review* 2 (Spring/Summer 1987), pp. 49-51.

7.1760 _____ "The Plaster Cast". Theodora Vasils, tr. *The Coffeehouse* 4 (Summer 1977), pp. 3-9. Also in *Eighteen Texts* (Willis Barnstone, ed. Cambridge, Mass.: Harvard University Press, 1972), pp. 153-159 {4.1}.

d.

7.1761 Germanacos, N.C. "An Interview with Three Contemporary Greek Prose Writers (May 1972): Stratis Tsirkas, Thanassis Valtinos, George Ioannou". *Boundary 2*, Vol. 1, No. 2 (Winter 1973), pp. 266-313 {3.5}.

Varnalis, Kostas (1884-1974)

a.

7.1762 _____ *The True Apology of Socrates: A Satire.* Stephen Yaloussis, tr. London: Zeno Publishers, 1955. 79 p.

b.

7.1763 _____ "Aphrodite" and "The 4 Mistakes of the 'Unknown Soldier'". Kimon Friar, tr. *The Athenian* (Feb. 1975), p. 33.

Varvitsiotis, Takis (b. 1916)

b.

7.1764 _____ "Clasped Hands". Kimon Friar, tr. *Greek Letters* 4 (1986-1989), pp. 229-260.

7.1765 _____ "Two Poems". Kimon Friar, tr. *The Literary Review* 16, No. 3 (Spring 1973), pp. 293-294 {3.15}.
  "Dreams are Hung by a Thread"; "October Blood".

Vasilikos, Vasilis (b. 1933)

a.

7.1766 _____ *The Harpoon Gun.* Barbara Bray, tr. New York: Harcourt Brace Jovanovich, 1973. 246 p.

7.1767 _____ *The Monarch.* Mary Keeley, tr. Indianapolis and New York: Bobbs-Merrill, 1976. 216 p.

7.1768 _____ *Outside the Walls.* Mike Edwards, tr. New York: Harcourt Brace Jovanovich, 1973. 192 p.

7.1769 _____ *The Photographs.* Mike Edwards, tr. New York: Harcourt Brace Jovanovich, 1971. 181 p. *Also London: Secker and Warburg, 1971. 181 p.; London: Sphere, 1972. 155 p.

7.1770 _____ *The Plant, The Well, The Angel: A Trilogy.* Edmund and Mary Keeley, trs. New York: Alfred A. Knopf, 1964. 272 p.

7.1771 _____ *Z.* Marilyn Calmann, tr. New York: Farrar, Straus, and Giroux, 1968. 406 p. Also New York: Ballantine Books, 1969. 377 p.; *London: Macdonald & Co., 1969. 406 p.; London: Sphere, 1970. 317 p.

b.

7.1772 _____ "Anatomy Lesson". Athan Anagnostopoulos, tr. *JHD* 6, No. 1 (Spring 1979), pp. 5-37. Bilingual version.

7.1773 _____ "The Author in Exile to His Publisher in Prison". James Merrill, tr. *Eleutheria* 1, No. 6-7 (Sept.-Oct.1970), p. 23.
   From *The Greek Report*.

7.1774 _____ "The Departure". M. Byron Raizis, tr. *The Literary Review* 16, No. 3 (Spring 1973), pp. 342-349 {3.15}.

7.1775 _____ "I/He" [essay]. John Chioles, tr. *Translation* 14 (Spring 1985), pp. 106-109 {3.34}.

7.1776 _____ "Letter from Athens". Kriton Hourmousiades, tr. *Poetry* 105, No. 1 (Oct. 1964), pp. 60-64 {3.27}.

7.1777 _____ "*The Plant*: An Excerpt". Edmund and Mary Keeley, trs. *Greek Heritage* 1, No. 2 (Spring 1964), pp. 74-77 {7.1441}.

7.1778 _____ "The Silly Thighs". Soteroulla Syka-Karampetsou, tr. *The Coffeehouse* 9 (Winter 1979), pp. 38-41.

7.1779 _____ "The Three T's". James Merrill, tr. *Shenandoah* 27, No. 1 (Fall 1975), pp. 44-48 {3.32}.

d.

7.1780 Bouyoucas, Pan. "Vassilis Vassilikos: The Writer as Chronicler". *The Athenian* (July 1979), pp. 30-32.

7.1781 Decavalles, Andonis. "A Poet's Novel". *Poetry* 105, No. 1 (Oct. 1964), pp. 65-67 {3.27}.
   Re. *The Plant, The Well, The Angel: A Trilogy*, by Vassilis Vassilikos. Tr. by Edmund and Mary Keeley {7.1770}.

7.1782 Georgakas, Dan. "Two Greek Commentaries". *Chicago Review* 21, No. 2 (Aug. 1969), pp. 109-114 {3.6}.
   Refers respectively to the translations of Vassilis Vassilikos, *Z* and Miltos Sahtouris, *With Face to the Wall* {7.1771, 7.1309}.

7.1783 Georgakas, Dan and Peter Pappas. "To Be a Writer in Greece: A Discussion with Vasilis Vasilikos". *JHD* 7, Nos. 3-4 (Fall-Winter 1980), pp. 7-26.

Venezis, Ilias (1904-1973)

a.

7.1784 *_____ *Aeolia*. Elisabeth D. Scott-Kilvert, tr. Lawrence Durrell, preface. London: Campion Editions, 1949; Denver: University of Denver Press, 1951. 259 p.

7.1785 *_____ *Beyond the Aegean*. E.D. Scott-Kilvert, tr. With a preface by Lawrence Durrell. New York: The Vanguard Press, 1956. 259 p.
   Same novel as in the previous entry.

b.

7.1786 ____ "A Small Anthology of Elias Venezis". Gabriel Drachman and E.D. Scott-Kilvert, trs. *The Charioteer* 1, No. 2 (Autumn 1960), pp. 90-126.
From *Theonikos and Mnisareti;* from *Beyond the Aegean;* from *Number 31328;* from *Serenity;* from *The Ocean.*

7.1787 ____ "The Final Hour"; "Mystra". From *Winds*. Alice-Mary Maffry, tr. *The Charioteer* 5 (1963), pp. 104-114.

7.1788 ____ "On the Mount of Olives" [a short story]. D.V. Elliott, tr. *The Athenian* (Apr. 1979), pp. 28-30.

7.1789 ____ "The Sea Gulls". Robert Liddell and Constantine Trypanis, trs. *The Atlantic Monthly* 195, No. 6 (June 1955), pp. 117-119 {3.3}.

7.1790 ____ "The Sea Gulls". Theodore Sampson, tr. In *Modern Greek Short Stories*. Vol. 2 (Kyr. Delopoulos, ed. Athens: Kathimerini Publications, 1981), pp. 245-256 {4.13}.

c.

7.1791 Karanikas, Alexander and Helen Karanikas. *Elias Venezis*. Twayne World Authors Series, No. 74. New York: Twayne Publishers Inc., 1969. 158 p.

d.

7.1792 Doulis, Thomas. "Ilias Venezis: The Failure of Love". *Neo-Hellenika* 3 (1978), pp. 102-126.

7.1793 Mackridge, Peter. "The Two-Fold Nostalgia: Lost Homeland and Lost Time in the Work of G. Theotokas, E. Venezis and K. Politis". *JMGS* 4, No. 2 (Oct. 1986), pp. 75-83.

7.1794 Sahinis, Apostolos. "The Fiction of Elias Venezis". Gabriel Drachman, tr. *The Charioteer* 1, No. 2 (Autumn 1960), pp. 84-90.

Vikelas, Dimitrios (1835-1909)

a.

7.1795 ____ *Loukis Laras: Reminiscences of a Chiote Merchant during the War of Independence*. J. Gennadius, tr. with preface and notes. London: Macmillan & Co., 1881. 273 p.

7.1796 ____ *Loukis Laras*. J. Gennadios, tr.; D. Trollope revised the translation. London: Doric Publications, 1972. 128 p.

7.1797 *____ *Seven Essays on Christian Greece*. John, marquess of Bute, tr. Paisley and London: Alexander Gardner, 1890. 298 p.

7.1798 ____ *Tales from the Aegean.* Leonard Eckstein Opdycke, tr.; Henry Alonzo Huntington, intro. Chicago: A.C. McClurg and Company, 1894. 258 p.

b.
7.1799 ____ "The Rabid Boy". Theodore Sampson, tr. In *Modern Greek Short Stories.* Vol. 1 (Kyr. Delopoulos, ed. Athens: Kathimerini Publications, 1980), pp. 29-41 {4.12}.

7.1800 ____ "Why I Remained A Lawyer". Alice-Mary Maffry, tr. *The Charioteer* 4 (1962), pp. 82-93 {4.17}.

Vistonitis, Anastasis (b. 1952)
b.
7.1801 ____ "Egnatia 1958" [a poem]. John Chioles, tr. *Translation* 14 (Spring 1985), pp. 103-105 {3.34}.

Vitsaxis, Vasilis (b. 1920)
a.
7.1802 ____ *Like Candle Drops.* The author, tr. New Delhi: Samkaleen Prakashan, 1979. 53 p.

7.1803 ____ *My Trails.* Pauline W. Innis and the author, trs. Bombay and Sydney: Thomson Press, 1975. 41 p.

b.
7.1804 ____ "Help me Sing of Men". M. Byron Raizis, tr. *Greek Letters* 4 (1986-1989), pp. 219-228.

7.1805 *____ "The Secret Path". In *World Poetry. 2. Poetry Europe* (Krishna Srinivas, ed. Madras, India. June 1982), p. 212.
   This poem represented Greece in the volume.

7.1806 ____ "Three Poems". *Greek Letters* 3 (1984-1985), pp. 183-186.
   "O! Listen to the Silence Singing"; "I Feel the Coming of the Night"; "A Question". No translator mentioned.

7.1807 *____ "The Window". Vasilis Vitsaxis, tr. In *Intercontinental Poetry: An Anthology* (R.A. Joshi and O.P. Bhatnagar, eds. Jaipur: Raj Kumari Sharma [Rachna Prakashan], 1979), p. 15.

Vizyinos, Georgios (1849-1896)
b.
7.1808 ____ "My Mother's Sin". Theodore Sampson, tr. In *Modern Greek Short Stories.* Vol. 1 (Kyr. Delopoulos, ed. Athens: Kathimerini Publications, 1980), pp. 55-83 {4.12}.

7.1809 _____ "The Sin of my Mother". In *Modern Greek Stories* (Demetra Vaka and Aristides Phoutrides, trs. New York: Duffield and Company, 1920), pp. 55-89 {4.16}.

d.

7.1810 Wyatt, William F. "Vizyenos and his Characters". *JMGS* 5, No. 1 (May 1987), pp. 47-63.

Vlachodimitris, Thodoris (b. 1925)

a.

7.1811 _____ Κύμβαλα—*Cymbals*. William Beck, tr. from the second edition. Athens: Σήμερα κι Αὔριο, 1978. 67 p. Bilingual edition.

Vlachos, Angelos (b. 1915)

a.

7.1812 _____ *Their Most Serene Majesties*. Kay Cicellis, tr. London: The Bodley Head, 1963. 318 p. *Also New York: Putnam's, 1963; New York: Vanguard Press, 1964. 318 p.

b.

7.1813 _____ "Hours of Life". Peter Bien, tr. *The Charioteer* 14 (1972), pp. 37-87.

d.

7.1814 Bien, Peter. "Ange Vlachos: Biographical Note". *The Charioteer* 14 (1972), pp. 35-36.

Vlachos, Helen (b. 1911)

a.

7.1815 _____ *House Arrest*. London: André Deutsch, 1970. 158 p. *Boston, Mass.: Gambit, 1970. 183 p.

7.1816 _____ *Mosaic (A Greek Notebook)*. Mark Ogilvie-Grant, tr.; Minos Argyrakis, illustr. Athens: "Eklogi", 1959. 176 p.

Vlami, Eva (1914-1974)

a.

7.1817 _____ *Skeletovrahos*. Athens: Efstathiadis Group, 1985. 173 p.

d.

7.1818 Doulis, Thomas. "Eva Vlami and the Imprisonment of the Past". *Balkan Studies* 10, No. 1 (1969), pp. 95-104.

Vlavianos-Arvanitis, Agni

a.

7.1819 _____ *Oscillations: Poems.* Ταλαντώσεις: Ποιήματα. Tr. by the author. [Athens], 1983. 79 p. Bilingual edition.

7.1820 _____ *Reflections: Poems.* Στοχασμοί: Ποιήματα. Tr. by the author. [Athens], 1982. 127 p. Bilingual edition.

7.1821 _____ *Roots: Poems.* Ρίζες: Ποιήματα. Tr. by the author. [Athens], 1983. 159 p. Bilingual edition.

Vraïlas-Armenis, Petros (1813-1884)

c.

7.1822 Moutsopoulos, Evanghelos A. *Petros Brailas-Armenis.* Twayne's World Authors Series, 261. New York: Twayne Publishers, 1974. 154 p.

Vrettakos, Nikiforos (b. 1912)

b.

7.1823 _____ "Dialogue with Poetry: Fourteen Poems by Nikiphoros Vrettakos". Thomas Doulis, tr. *JHD* 6, No. 2 (Summer 1979), pp. 59-73. Bilingual version.

7.1824 _____ "Fever". M. Byron Raizis, tr. *The Literary Review* 16, No. 3 (Spring 1973), p. 273 {3.15}.

7.1825 _____ "Five Poems". Thomas Doulis and Nikos Samaras, trs. *The Texas Quarterly* 10, No. 2 (Summer 1967), pp. 97-108.

7.1826 _____ "Four Poems". Nikos and Zoe Samaras, trs. *The Charioteer* 14 (1972), pp. 26-28.

7.1827 _____ "14 Poems for the Same Mountain". M.B. Raizis, tr. *Greek Letters* 4 (1986-1989), pp. 13-40. Bilingual version.

7.1828 _____ "In Memoriam"; "A Different Citizen"; "The Price" [Thanasis Maskaleris, tr.]; "Attempt at a Surgical Intervention"; "Man and Horse"; "Love" [Thomas Doulis, tr.]. *The Coffeehouse* 5 (Winter 1977), pp. 25-30.

7.1829 _____ "Liturgy under the Acropolis". *Greek Letters* 2 (1983), pp. 9-41.

7.1830 *_____ "Muster". Agnes Sotiracopoulou, tr. *Poetry* (Madras) 9, No. 2 (1968), p. 3 {3.29}.

7.1831 _____ "Return from Delphi". Konstantinos Lardas, tr. *The Charioteer* 1, No. 1 (Summer 1960), pp. 138-139.

7.1832 _____ "Solacing City". Frederick Ragovin, tr. *Eleutheria* 3, No. 2 (Winter 1973), pp. 12-13.

7.1833 _____ "Two Poems by Nikephoros Vrettakos". M. Byron Raizis, tr. *Prism International* 11, No. 1 (Summer 1971), p. 62.
"An Almond Tree"; "Peace".

d.
7.1834 Doulis, Thomas. "Nikiphoros Vrettakos". *The Texas Quarterly* 10, No. 2 (Summer 1967), pp. 95-96.

Xenopoulos, Grigorios (1867-1951)

a.
7.1835 *_____ *Red Rock: From Ecstasy to Tragedy*. William Spanos, tr. New York: Pageant Press Inc., 1955. 202 p.

7.1836 _____ *The Stepmother: A Tale of Modern Athens*. Done into English by Mrs. Edmonds. London & New York: John Lane (The Bodley Head), 1897. 143 p.

b.
7.1837 _____ "C.P. Cavafy: A Greek Poet". Th. Sampson, tr. *Greek Letters* 2 (1983), pp. 317-327.

7.1838 _____ "Mangalos". In *Modern Greek Stories* (Demetra Vaka and Aristides Phoutrides, trs. New York: Duffield and Company, 1920), pp. 103-129 {4.16}.

7.1839 _____ "Warblings". Theodore Sampson, tr. In *Modern Greek Short Stories*. Vol. 1 (Kyr. Delopoulos, ed. Athens: Kathimerini Publications, 1980), pp. 225-235 {4.12}.

c.
7.1840 *Gregorios Xenopoulos / 1867-1951 / ΓΡΗΓΟΡΙΟΣ ΞΕΝΟΠΟΥΛΟΣ*. An exhibit May 31-July 31, 1985. Special Collections Library, O. Meredith Wilson Library, University of Minnesota, Minneapolis. Eighth Annual Celebration of Greek Letters. 35 p.
Pamphlet with introduction to Gregorios Xenopoulos and his work written by Theofanis G. Stavrou.

Xenos, Stefanos Theodoros (1821-1894)

a.
7.1841 _____ *Andronike: The Heroine of the Greek Revolution*. Edwin A. Grosvenor, tr. Boston: Roberts Brothers, 1897. 527 p. Also *London, 1861.

7.1842 _____ *The Devil in Turkey or Scenes in Constantinople*. Tr. from the author's unpublished Greek manuscript by Henry Corpe. 3 vols. London: Effingham Wilson, Royal Exchange, 1851. Vol. 1 = 426 p.; Vol. 2 = 468 p.; Vol. 3 = 532 p.

Zakythinos, Alexis (b. 1934)

b.
7.1843 _____ "Buoys and Stars". George Thaniel, tr. *Greek Letters* 3 (1984-1985), pp. 187-199.

d.

7.1844 Thaniel, George. "The Poetry of Alexis Zakythinos". *The Amaranth* 4 (1982), pp. 23-33.

Zalokostas, Christos (1805-1858)

a.

7.1845 _____ *Rupel.* Woodcuts by Yanni Kephallinos; Alexander Papagos, intro. Athens: Stef. N. Taroussopoulos Printing Press, 1945. 90 p.

Zannas, Pavlos A. (1929-1989)

b.

7.1846 _____ "Bottle in the Sea". Rick M. Newton, tr. *Rackham Literary Studies* 5 (1974), pp. 1-7.

Zarambouka, Sofia (b. 1939)

a.

7.1847 *_____ *Flit Goes on a Trip.* The author, tr. Athens: Kedros, 1972.

7.1848 *_____ *Aristophanes' Irene / Peace.* The author, tr. and illustr. for young children. Washington, D.C.: Tee Loftin Publishers, 1979. [40 p.]

Zatelli, Zirana

b.

7.1849 _____ "Birds" [a short story]. Kay Cicellis, tr. *Translation* 14 (Spring 1985), pp. 28-37 {3.34}.

Zeï, Alki (b. 1925)

a.

7.1850 _____ *Petros' War.* Edward Fenton, tr. New York: E.P. Dutton, 1972. 236 p. Also *London: Gollancz, 1972. 236 p.

7.1851 _____ *The Sound of the Dragon's Feet.* Edward Fenton, tr. New York: E.P. Dutton, 1979. 116 p.

7.1852 _____ *Wildcat Under Glass.* Edward Fenton, tr. New York: Holt, Rinehart and Winston, 1968. 178 p. Also *London: Gollancz, 1969. 180 p.

Zevgoli-Glezou, Dialechti (b. 1907)

c.

7.1853 Papazoglou-Margaris, Theano. *Poetess Dialechti Zevgoli-Glezou and her Poetry. A Lecture.* Fotios K. Litsas, ed. and intro.; Charles Stewart, tr. Chicago, Ill.: Modern Greek Studies Series (University of Illinois at Chicago), 1986. Bilingual edition.

English sections include: "A Lecture on Greek Poetry and Poetess D. Zevgoli-Glezou: A Summary" (pp. 45-48) and "An Anthology" (pp. 49-76).

INDEX

The index contains in a single alphabet: (1) all the Greek authors (page numbers in bold type refer to main headings in Chapter 7; those in regular type, to all other entries); (2) the translators, editors, or authors of essays, introductions or comments (page numbers in italics); (3) titles of anonymous works; (4) Καραγκιόζης and the category "folk song".

To facilitate the use of the index the spelling of the Greek authors' names has been reduced to a standardized form. The variant spellings encountered in the publications are given collectively in parentheses immediately after the standardized form; they are also listed separately with a cross-reference.

The index records only once the appearance of any name on a page.

For further information see the sections "Index", "Transcription", and "Caveat lector" in the introduction.

Abatzopoulou, Frangiski 9, 12
Abbott, George F. *20*
Achilleis 27, 46
Aerts, W.J. *42*
Afentoulis, Theodoros 25 (Aphentoules)
Agnos, Athan: see Anagnostopoulos, Athan H.
Agras, T. 23
Akritas, Loukis 18, 30, 31
Alastos, Doros *85*
Aldridge, A. Owen *127*
Alevizos, Susan *20*
Alevizos, Ted *20*
Alexakis, Orestis 28
Alexander, John C. *37, 53*
Alexander, Thomasina *159*
Alexander Romance 44, 46
Alexandhrou, Aris: see Alexandrou
Alexandrou, Aris 9, 14, 22, 26, 71 (also Alexandhrou)
Alexiou, Christos *40*
Alexiou, Elli **71-72**
Alexiou, Georgia 72
Alexiou, Margaret *36, 37, 42, 53, 57, 85, 91*
Alithersis, Glafkos 30, 31
Allatios, Leon 47
Anaghnostakis, Manolis: see Anagnostakis
Anaghnostopoulos, M.: see Anagnostopoulos
Anagnostaki, Loula **72**
Anagnostaki, Nora 17 (Anagnostakis)

Anagnostakis, Manolis 9, 10, 11, 22, 25, 26, 29, 32, 67, **72-73** (also Anaghnostakis)
Anagnostakis, Nora: see Anagnostaki, Nora
Anagnostopoulos, Athan H. *9, 12, 31, 99, 101, 102, 103, 115, 141, 162, 163, 167, 174, 186, 188, 190, 193,* 211, 212, 221
Anagnostopoulos, M. 18 (Anaghnostopoulos)
Analytis, Panagiotis **73**
Anapliotes, John *125*
Andreou, Andreas 30
Andreou, Peter *146, 148, 157*
Andrews, Kevin *57, 164, 216, 217*
Andriopoulos, Dimitri Z. *127*
Andronikos, Pavlos *7, 146, 147*
Angelaki Rooke, K: see Angelaki-Rooke
Angelaki-Rooke, Katerina 11, 12, *13*, 15, 22, 26, 28, 29, *57*, **73**, *119, 123, 127, 163* (also Angelaki Rooke, Anghelaki Rooke, Anghelaki-Rooke)
Angelakis, Andreas 12, 27, *64* (also Anghelakis)
Angelopoulos, Aris *37*
Anghelaki Rooke, Katerina: see Angelaki-Rooke
Anghelaki-Rooke, Katerina: see Angelaki-Rooke
Anghelakis, And(h)reas: see Angelakis
Anghelidis-Spinedi, Nina *105*
Anthias, Tefkros 21, 30, 31, **73-74**
Anthonakes, Michael A. (sic): see Antonakes
Anthrakites, Methodios: see Anthrakitis
Anthrakitis, Methodios 51 (Anthrakites)
Anton, John P. *51, 66, 85, 127, 157*

Antonakes, Michael A. *127, 184* (also Anthonakes (sic))
Antoniadou, Eleni *68*
Antoniou, D.I. 9, 13, 21, 22, 23, 24, 28, 29, 62, **74**, *186* (also Antoniou, Captain; Demetrios)
Antoniou, Takis 25, 26, **74**
Antoniou, Theodore *10*
Aphentoules, Theodore: see Afentoulis
Apollonius of Tyre 46
Aragon, Louis *166*
Aravandinou, Mando: see Aravantinou
Aravantinou, Manto 10, 11, 22, 28, 29, **75** (also Aravandinou)
Argenti, Philip P. *32*
Arghyriou, Alexandros: see Argyriou, Alexandros
Argoe, Kostis T. *153*
Argyrakis, Minos *57*
Argyriou, A. *15*
Argyriou, Alexandros *57, 194*
Argyropoulos, George *26*
Arnakis, G. Georgiades *194*
Arsenios *48*
Ascreo *158*
Aslanoglou, Nikos-Alexis 9, 22, 25, 32
Assmus, Merella Psarakis *145*
Atchity, Kenneth *80*
Athanas, George 19, 23, 26
Athanasiadis, Nikos *75* (also Athanassiades)
Athanasoulis, Kriton 15, 21, 22, 28
Athanassakis, Apostolos N. *56, 148, 167*
Athanassiades, Nikos: see Athanasiadis
Athas, Theodosis *26, 155, 212*
Auden, W.H. *77, 79, 88*
Aufrère, Gaston-Henri *158*
Avatanghelos, Henriette *57*
Averof-Tositsas, Evangelos *75* (also Averoff-Tossizza)
Averoff-Tossizza: see Averof-Tositsas
Avgeris, Markos 21, 25, **75** (also Avyeris)
Avyeris, Markos: see Avgeris
Axelos, Loukas *57*
Axiote, Melpo: see Axioti
Axioti, Melpo 22, **75** (also Axiote)
Aycock, Wendell M. *58*
Bachtin, Nicholas *57, 195*
Bacon, J. Harwood *206*
Bacopoulou-Halls, Aliki *39, 61, 72* (also Halls)
Baggally, John W. *54*
Bailey, David *31, 120*
Bakker, Wim F. *41, 42, 43, 48, 49*
Balakian, Anna *61*
Bali, Tilla *14*
Bancroft-Marcus, Rosemary E. *49*
Banks, Arthur C. *127*
Baraheni, Reza *83*

Baras, Alexandros 12, 18, 22, 23, **75**
Bardsley, Beverly *173*
Barker, J.W. *46*
Barnstone, Aliki *20*
Barnstone, Halle Tzalopoulou *140*
Barnstone, Willis *17, 20, 21, 57, 81, 85, 95, 140, 205*
Barrie, Thomas *202*
Bassett, Nicholas *144*
Bastias, Kostis **75-76**
Baud-Bovy, Samuel *107, 195*
Beaton, Roderick M. *43, 54, 57, 85, 94, 105, 115, 120, 128, 191, 195, 205, 208*
Becatoros, Stefanos: see Bekatoros
Beck, William *225*
Bédé, Jean-Albert *40*
Bekatoros, Stefanos 12, 26, 27, **76** (also Becatoros)
Bekes, Homer 26
Belisariada 43
Belleli, L. *208*
Belthandros and Chrysantza 45
Benjamin of Lesvos 50, 51
Beratis, Giannis *76*
Berza, M. *44*
Bessa, Maria *128*
Betts, Gavin *184*
Beukas, Anthony S. *128*
Bhatnagar, O.P. *224*
Biancolli, Louis *188*
Bien, Peter A. *10, 35, 36, 40, 57, 58, 83, 86, 88, 94, 98, 121, 122, 123, 124, 125, 128, 130, 131, 133, 146, 164, 168, 173, 174, 180, 187, 225*
Bikelas, Demetrios: see Vikelas
Birnbaum, Henrik *52*
Bislani-Dalipi, Bessie *1*
Bita, Lili 22, 176
Black, Penelope *162*
Blake, Warren *206*
Blewitt, D.W. *211*
Bloch, Adèle *129, 130*
Boatwright, James *14, 97, 217*
Boegehold, Alan L. *79, 80, 82, 103*
Boeschoten, Riki van *54*
Boissin, Henri *158*
Bold, Alan *174*
Bombas, Leonidhas 28
Bonos, V.N. 9
Boumi-Papa, Rita: see Boumi-Pappa
Boumi-Pappa, Rita 12, 14, 21, 22, 23, 25 (also Boumi-Papa, Boumi-Pappas, Boumy Pappas)
Boumi-Pappas/Boumy Pappas, Rita: see Boumi-Pappa
Bourboulis, Photeine P. *54*
Bournas, Helen *195*

Boustronios, George 47
Bouvier, Bertrand *116*
Bouyoucas, Pan. *222*
Bowersock, Glen W. *86*
Bowra, C.M. *86, 88*
Brademas, John *216*
Brailas-Armenis, Petros: see Vraïlas-Armenis
Bratsos, Fontas 27
Bray, Barbara *221*
Breuer, Bessie *147*
Brittain, Maryanne 58, *180, 184*
Brodsky, Joseph *86*
Brooke, E. Margaret *213*
Broumas, Olga *101*
Brown, Marcia *61*
Burkhalter, F. *86*
Burns, Richard 13, *184, 193, 217, 218, 219*
Bury, J.B. *43*
Butler, Francelia *60, 95*
Butterworth, Katharine *21*
Byzantine Iliad 42
Cachtitsis, Nikos: see Kachtitsis
Cacoullos, JoAnne *136, 156, 212*
Caires, Valerie A. *86*
Calas, Nicolas 22, 23
Callimachus and Chrysorrhoe: see *Kallimachos and Chrysorrhoe*
Calmann, Marilyn *221*
Calvos, Andreas: see Kalvos
Cambas, Andreas *162*
Cameris, Christos *97*
Campbell, Finley C. *127*
Campbell, John 40
Canale, George D. *206*
Canellopoulos, Panayiotis: see Kanellopoulos
Capetanakis, Demetrios 9, 41, **76**
Capri-Karka, Carmen **76-77**, *83, 160, 169, 170, 171, 174, 178, 193, 195*
Caradja, Marie G.: see Karatza
Caraveli, Anna *54*
Carion, Daniel *158*
Caro, F.A. de *129*
Carroll, Margaret G. *75, 86, 153, 180*
Carson, Jeffrey *104*
Caryotakis, Constantine: see Karyotakis
Casdaglis, Emmanuel C. *30*
Case-Kessissoglou, Jacques A. *147*
Casey, Gerard *193*
Casseres, Benjamin de *152*
Castan, Con *116*
Catsaouni, Helen *86*
Catselli, Rina: see Katselli
Cavafis, Constantine: see Cavafy, C.P.
Cavafy, C.P. 18, 21, 22, 23, 24, 25, 26, 27, 40, 41, 64, 67, **77-93** (also Cavafis, Kavafis; Constantine P.)
Cavafy, John C. *78, 80, 81*

Cavarnos, Constantine *50*
Chaconas, Stephen George *51*
Chakkas, Marios **93-94** (also Hakkas)
Challoumas, Savvas 31 (Halloumas)
Chambers, Marjorie *171, 172, 174*
Chamboulidis, Dimitris 31 (Hamboulides)
Charalambides, Kyriakos: see Charalambidis
Charalambidis, Kyriakos 22, 30 (also Charalambides, Haralambhidhis)
Charis, Petros 18, **94** (Haris)
Charkianakis, Stylianos 27, 28, **9 4** (Harkianakis)
Chatzidaki, Natasa 15, 22, 26, **94** (also Hadjidaki, Hadjidhaki, Hatzidaki)
Chatzidaki, Rena 17 (Hatzidaki)
Chatzigeorgiou, Kypros 31 (Hadjigeorghiou)
Chatzis, Dimitris **94-95**, 210 (also Hadjis, Hadzis, Hatzis)
Chatzopoulos, Kostas 18, 19, 21, 25, 26, 27 (also Hadjopoulos, Hadzopoulos, Hatzopoulos)
Chatzopoulou-Karavia, Lia *60,* **95** (also Hadzopoulou-Caravia/Karavia)
Chaves, Anna C. *54*
Cheimonas, Georgos: see Chimonas
Cheliakis, Antonis 31 (Heliakis)
Chianis, Sotirios (Sam) *32*
Chiensis 67
Chilson, Richard W. *129*
Chimarridis, Giorgos 31 (Himarrides)
Chimonas, Giorgos **95** (Cheimonas, Heimonas, Himonas)
Chioles, John/Yannis *15, 24, 26, 30, 76, 86,* **95**, *102, 103, 135, 142, 168, 190, 205, 211, 222, 224*
Chionis, Argyris 13, 27, **95** (also Hionis)
Chondrogiannis, Giannis 14 (Hondroyannis)
Chortatses, Georgios: see Chortatsis
Chortatsis, Georgios 25, 27, 41, 48, 49, 50 (also Chortatses, Chortatzis, Hortatzis)
Chortatzis, George: see Chortatsis
Chouliaras, Yiorgos 15, 30, *54*
Choumnos, Georgios 47 (Chumnos)
Christ, Robert L. (sic): see Crist, Robert L.
Christakes, George *37*
Christianopoulos, Dinos 9, 10, 21, 22, 25, 28, 29, 32, **96**, *207*
Christodoulou, Dimitra 26, **96** (also Hristodhoulou)
Christodoulou, Dimitris 9, 12, 23, **96**
Christofidis, Andreas 30, 32 (Christophides)
Christophides, Andreas: see Christofidis
Christopoulos, Athanasios 21 (Chrystopoulos)
Chronas, Giorgos 11, 12, 15, 22, 26, 28, 30, **96** (also Hronas)
Chronicle of the Morea 42, 44, 45, 46
Chrysanthis, Kypros 23, 25, 30, 31, 32, *68,* **97**

Chryssopoulos, Ninos *167, 168*
Chrystopoulos, Athanasius: see Christopoulos
Chumnos, George: see Choumnos
Cicellis, Kay *11, 17,* 18, *29, 35, 93, 94, 95, 97, 108, 174, 197, 208, 209, 216, 217, 218, 225, 228*
Clark, Richard C. *1, 58*
Clay, Diskin *84, 87*
Clement, Eugene *152*
Clifford, Craig Edward *80*
Cline, Leonard Lanson *152*
Clogg, Mary Jo *1*
Clogg, Richard *1, 4, 51, 52, 64, 183*
Cochrane, P.N. *140*
Cokkinos, Dionysios: see Kokkinos, Dionysios
Colaclides, Helen *19*
Colaclides, Peter *88, 129, 207*
Colakis, Marianthe *58, 87, 180, 207*
Cole, Heather Ellen *12*
Collette, Charles Hastings *182*
Condos, Theony *118*
Constantaras, D. *116*
Constantinides, Elizabeth/Liza *54, 58, 112, 116, 129, 156*
Constantinides, Stephanos: see Konstantinidis
Constantinidis, Stratos E. *58, 153*
Constantinidou, Loula D.: see Konstantinidou
Constantis, Yiorghos: see Konstantis
Corn, Alfred *87*
Cornaros, Vincenzo/Vizentzos: see Kornaros
Corpe, Henry *227*
Corres, Manolis: see Korres
Cosmas Aitolos: see Kosmas Aitolos
Costas, Procope S. *3*
Coulmas, Florian *69, 211*
Coutelle, Louis *156, 208*
Coutsoheras, John: see Koutsocheras
Couyialis, Theoklis: see Kougialis
Coxe, Louis O. *129*
Creekmore, Hubert *21*
Crist, Despina *158, 184*
Crist, Robert L. *71, 95, 158, 184* (also Christ (sic))
Crocker, George *211*
Crystallis, Costas: see Krystallis
Current-Garcia, Eugene *194, 216*
Cyril Lucaris: see Kyrillos Loukaris
Dafni, Emilia 26, 27 (also Daphne)
Dahl, Ingolf *190*
Dalakoura, Veroniki 26, 27, **98** (also Dhalakoura)
Dallas, Athena G.: see Gianakas-Dallas
Dallas, Yannis 9, 22, 26 (also Dhallas, Thallas)
Dallas-Damis, Athena: see Gianakas-Dallas
Dalven, Rae *21, 25, 40, 54, 58, 74, 77, 78, 82, 91, 92, 100, 151, 167, 172, 175, 176, 177, 178, 180, 202, 204*

Damaskos, James *9*
Damodos, Vikentios 51
Dancingsun, Kathryn *58*
Danforth, Loring M. *59*
Daniil, Giorgos: see Thaniel, George
Daphne, Emily S.: see Dafni
Daraki, Zefi 12, 22, 27, 28, **98** (also Dharaki)
Dash, Barbara L. *3*
Daskalopoulos, Akos 23
Daskalopoulos, Dimitris 27 (Dhaskalopoulos)
Davies, H.S. *59*
Davis, Mark L. *195*
Dawkins, R.M. *19, 32, 47*
Dawson, C.M. *54*
Dazla, Maza 20
Decavallas, Adonis: see Decavalles
Decavalles, Andonis C. 9, 10, 12, 13, 14, 22, 28, 29, *30, 55, 59, 87,* **98-99**, *102, 104, 105, 106, 129, 161, 162, 165, 178, 180, 185, 195, 214, 222* (also Decavallas)
Dedopoulos, K. *212*
Deligiorgis, Stavros *9, 12, 26, 95, 106, 139, 160*
Delis, George 26
Delopoulos, Kyr. *19*
Demetriades, Demetres: see Dimitriadis
Demetriou, Nadina: see Dimitriou
Demetrius, James K. *129*
Demos, Jean *194, 216*
Demos, Raphael *83*
Denegris, Tasos 11, 22, 25, 28, 29, **99**
Depountis, Iason 26
Dhalakoura, Veroniki: see Dalakoura
Dhallas, Yannis: see Dallas
Dharaki, Zephi: see Daraki
Dhaskalopoulos, Dhimitris: see Daskalopoulos, Dimitris
Dhikteos, Ares/Aris: see Diktaios
Dhimakis, Minas: see Dimakis
Dhimitriou, Nadhina: see Dimitriou
Dhimoula, Kiki: see Dimoula
Dhimoulas, Athos: see Dimoulas
Dhoukaris, Dhimitris: see Doukaris, Dimitris
Diamandouros, Nikiforos P./P. Nikiforos *37, 55*
Diamantis, Antoinette *73*
Dicteos, Aris: see Diktaios
Diehl, Charles *149, 151*
Digenis Akritas 27, 41, 42, 43, 44, 45, 46 (also *Digenis Akrites*)
Diktaios, Aris 10, 12, 14, 15, 21, 22, 25, 28, 29 (also Dhikteos, Dicteos, Dikteos)
Dikteos, A.: see Diktaios
Dillistone, F.W. *129*
Dimadis, C. *2*
Dimakis, Minas 10, 14, 21, 22, 25, 28, 29,*155* (also Dhimakis)
Dimaras, C.Th. *1, 10, 36, 39, 59, 87, 203, 212*

Dimiroulis, Dimitris *87, 195*
Dimitriadis, Dimitris 30 (Demetriades)
Dimitriou, Nadina 12, 25, 30 (also Demetriou, Dhimitriou)
Dimoula, Kiki 12, 22, 28, **99** (also Dhimoula)
Dimoulas, Athos 14, 22 (Dhimoulas)
Dobson, Rosemary *210*
Dodd, Charles *145*
Dokas, Nikos 11
Dombrowski, Daniel A. *129*
Doolaard, A. den *122*
Dorson, Richard M. *19*
Doukaris, Dimitris 9, 12, 14, 22, 25, 26, 27, 29, *74* (also Dhoukaris)
Doukas, Neophytos 51
Doulis, Thomas *10, 24, 59, 72, 76, 114, 115, 120, 129, 195, 196, 214, 217, 223, 225, 226, 227*
Dounavi, Lucretia 15
Doxas, Takis 18, **99**
Doxiadis, Calliope *114*
Drachman, Gabriel *223*
Dracontaidis, Philippos: see Drakontaïdis
Dragoumi, Julia D. **99** (also Dragoumis)
Dragoumis, Julia D.: see Dragoumi
Dragoumis, Markos 21
Drakodaides, Ph.D./Philip: see Drakontaïdis
Drakontaïdis, Filippos 12, 25 (also Dracontaidis, Drakodaides)
Dreyer, Peter R. *115, 141, 160, 191*
Drosines, George: see Drosinis
Drosinis, Georgios 18, 21, 25, 26, 27, **99-100** (also Drosines, Drossinis)
Drossinis, Georgios: see Drosinis
Droulia, Loukia *1, 207*
Droussiotis, Pythagoras 30
Ducrey, Pierre *86*
Dugan, Alan *13*
Durack, Reg *116*
Durrell, Lawrence 22, *84, 87, 91, 92, 104, 106, 182, 186, 187, 191, 193, 201, 202, 217, 222*
Dyck, Andrew R. *43*
E.W.F. *196*
Eade, J.C. *51, 52*
Economou, George *9, 12, 53, 87, 98, 103, 180, 205*
Economou, Georgia *57*
Economou, Zisis: see Ikonomou
Edgerton, William B. *40*
Edmonds, Mrs. Elizabeth M. *21, 51, 99, 100, 118, 136, 139, 227*
Edwards, Epy *10*
Edwards, Grace *181*
Edwards, H.L.R. *10*
Edwards, Mike *221*
Efestios, Pan. *74*

Efstathiadis, Yannis 10
Eftaliotes, Argyres: see Eftaliotis, Argyris
Eftaliotis, Argyris 25, 26, **100** (also Eftaliotes, Ephtaliotis)
Egan, Desmond *167*
Eideneier, Hans *43, 46, 49*
Eklund, Bo-Lennart *151, 215*
Eligia, Giosef 21, **100** (also Eliyia)
Eliot, T.S. *77, 83, 84, 93, 107, 186, 191, 193, 194, 195, 196, 198, 201, 207*
Elitis, Odysseas: see Elytis
Eliyia, Joseph: see Eligia
Elliott, D.V. *223*
Ellis, J.R. *52*
Elsman, Kenneth R. *130*
Elytis, Odysseas/Odysseus 12, 13, 18, 21, 22, 23, 24, 25, 26, 27, 29, 30, 40, 41, 62, 68, **100-108** (also Elitis)
Emberikos, Andreas: see Embirikos
Embiricos, Andreas: see Embirikos
Embirikos, Andreas 10, 12, 13, 18, 21, 22, 23, 24, 25, 29, 41, **108-109**, *151* (also Emberikos, Embiricos)
Emilios, Achilleas 30
Emmanuel, Artemis P. *18*
Emmanuel, Kassaris: see Emmanouil
Emmanuel, Philip D. *18*
Emmanouil, Kaisar 21 (Emmanuel)
Engonopoulos, Nikos 10, 12, 13, 18, 21, 22, 23, 24, 25, 27, 28, **109-110**
Enright, D.J. *80, 87*
Entwistle, William J. *43*
Ephtaliotis, Argyris: see Eftaliotis
Erel-Koumidou, Rea 30
Evangelides, Constantinos E. *196*
Evangelou, Anestis 12, 22, 23, 25, 28, **110** (also Evanghellou)
Evanghellou, Anestis: see Evangelou
Evgeniou, Antonakis 30 (Evyeniou)
Evyeniou, Antonakis: see Evgeniou
Fagles, Robert *80*
Fakinos, Aris **110**
Falconio, Donald *130*
Falieros, Marinos 41, 42, 43 (also Phalieros)
Fanos, Yiorghos 31
Fantazis, Loros 31
Fatouros, A.A. *59, 91*
Fauriel, M.C. *25*
Feeney, Martha J. *1*
Feeney, William R. *1*
Fenton, Edward *94, 228*
Fermor, Patrick Leigh *84, 87, 166, 182, 196*
Fiedler, Theodore *87*
Fielding, Xan *166*
Filippidis, Daniil 51 (Philippides, Daniel)
Finer, Leslie *140, 210, 211*
Flay, Joseph C. *130*

Fleischmann, Wolfgang Bernard *41*
Fletcher, Robin A. *9, 43, 59, 152*
Flogas, Nasos 31
Fludas, John *9*
Fokas, Angelos **110**
Fokas, Nikos 10, 11, 22, 28, 29, **110-111** (also Phocas)
Foley, John Miles *55*
'Folk Song' 9, 10, 12, 18, 20, 21, 22, 23, 25, 27, 30, 32, 33, 44, **53-56**
Fontana, Ernest *87*
Forster, E.M. *79, 84, 87, 88, 92*
Foskolos, Markos-Antonios 49
Fostieris, Antonis 22, 26, 27, 28, **111**
Fotaki, Evanghelia 17
Fotheringham, David Ross *22*
Fotiadis, D. 13
Fotiadis, Thanasis 26
Fouriotis, Angelos *74*
Fourtouni, Eleni *17, 22, 143*
Fouskarinis, Andreas 27
Fowler, Rowena *191, 196*
Fowles, John *189*
Frangopoulos, Th.D. 9, 14, 17, 22, *60, 74, 84, 93, 141, 186, 205*
Fraser, P.M. *88*
Frazee, Charles *47*
Freelander, Ronald *9*
Freese, J.H. *182*
Friar, Kimon *9, 10, 11, 12, 13, 14, 15, 18, 21, 22, 23, 24, 25, 26, 28, 29, 30, 32, 60, 61, 67, 72, 88, 96, 98, 99, 101, 102, 103, 104, 105, 106, 107, 109, 110, 111, 118, 119, 121, 122, 123, 124, 125, 126, 130, 133, 136, 137, 143, 146, 151, 155, 158, 159, 161, 164, 166, 167, 168, 169, 170, 171, 172, 173, 174, 175, 176, 177, 178, 179, 180, 181, 183, 184, 187, 190, 191, 194, 196, 197, 202, 204, 205, 210, 213, 217, 218, 219, 220, 221*
Frye, Ellen *23*
Fylaktou, Takis G. 31, 32 (Phylactou, Phylaktou)
G.N.B. *196*
Gaist, Jack *23, 25, 161, 162, 210*
Galatariotou, Catia *43*
Galatis, Tasos 28 (Ghalatis)
Galatopoulos, Christodoulos 31
Galazi, Pitsa 31
Galitzi, Christine *206*
Gallagher, Timothy *15*
Ganas, Michalis 13, 27, **111** (also Ghanas)
Garbis, Kostas 27 (Gharbis)
Gargilis, Stephen *48*
Garnett, Lucy M.J. *18, 27*
Gaselee, Stephen *48*

Gatsos, Nikos 13, 18, 21, 22, 23, 24, 26, 62, *107*, **111-112**
Gauntlett, Stathis *60*
Gavalas, George *9*
Gavrilovic, Zaga *43*
Gavris, Andreas 31
Gaylin, Willard *81*
Gazes, Anthimos: see Gazis
Gazis, Anthimos 51 (Gazes)
Geanakoplos, Deno John *47*
Gemenaki, S. 18 (Yemenaki)
Gemert, Arnold F. van *41, 42, 43*
Gennadius, John *136, 223* (also Gennadios)
Gensler, Kinereth *31*
Georgacas, Demetrius J. *208*
Georgakas, Dan *10, 23,* **112***, 114, 168, 184, 222*
Georges, Robert A. *55*
Georghiou, Christakis: see Georgiou, Christakis
Georghiou, Tassos: see Georgiou, Tasos
Georgiou, Christakis 30, 31 (Georghiou)
Georgiou, Tasos 31 (Georghiou)
Georgopoulos, N. *130*
Geralis, Georgios 10, 21, 22, 28, 29 (also Yeralis)
Geranis, Stelios 26
Germanacos, N.C. *10, 14, 28,* **112***, 115, 117, 119, 120, 143, 162, 163, 167, 169, 172, 173, 174, 211, 217, 220* (also Germanakos)
Germanakos, N.C.: see Germanacos
Gerolemidou, Xenia 31 (Yerolemidou)
Gerontikos, Arsenis 32
Ghalatis, Tasos: see Galatis
Ghanas, Mihalis: see Ganas
Gharbis, Kostas: see Garbis
Ghika, N.H. *9*
Ghouliamos, Kostas: see Gouliamos
Ghrighoriadhis, Nikos: see Grigoriadis
Giakos, Dimitrios 18 (Yiakos)
Gianakas-Dallas, Athena *121, 122, 123, 124* (also Dallas and Dallas-Damis)
Giannakoulis, Theodore *151*
Giannaris, George *2, 60, 203*
Giannidis, Lefteris 31 (Yiannidis)
Giannopoulos, Alkiviadis **112** (also Yannopoulos)
Gianos, Mary P. *18, 39, 117, 155, 162*
Gibbons, Reginald *190*
Gibson, Gifford Guy *80*
Gifford, Henry *88, 196*
Giokarini, Koula 25 (Yiokarini)
Glassgold, Peter *178*
Gogou, Katerina 26, **112**
Golffing, Francis *84, 88*
Gonatas, E.C. 13, 28, **113**
Gorpas, Thomas 27

Gosse, Sir Edmund *206*
Goudelis, Giannis 12, 14, **113**
Goufas, Vangelis 69
Gouliamos, Kostas 15, 28, 30, *74* (also Ghouliamos)
Goulimi, Alki **113** (also Goulimis)
Goulimis, Alki: see Goulimi
Goumas, Giannis/John A./Yannis 9, *10*, *13*, *15*, 18, *23*, *26*, *75*, *95*, *96*, *109*, *110*, **113**, *137*, *140*, *156*, *163*
Gounelas, C.D. 60
Gounelas, G. 60
Graham, Hugh F. *43*, *44*
Graikos, Costas 31
Grammatopoulos, Kostas *165*
Gransden, K.W. *47*, *64*
Gravalos, P. *24*
Greek Nomarchy 51
Green, Arnold *207*, *208*
Green, Michael *207*
Green, Peter *106*, *130*, *173*
Green, Roger *130*
Gregory, Dorothy M.-T. *130*, *203*
Gregory, Mary *176*
Grégoire, H. *44*
Griffin, Jonathan *122*
Grigoriadis, Nikos 27 (Ghrighoriadhis)
Grigorogiannis, Achilles *74*
Griparis, Yiannis: see Gryparis
Grosvenor, Edwin A. *227*
Grundy, Philip *33*, *215*
Gryparis, John 21, 23, 25, 26, 27
Gudas, Rom 60
Gunderson, Lloyd L. *44*
H., D.: see Haas, Diana
Haas, Diana *87*, *88*, *92* (also D.H.)
Hadas, Rachel *49*, *119*, *141*, *180*, *193*, *196*
Hadgopoulos, Saralyn Poole *131*
Hadjiantoniou, George A. *47*
Hadjidaki, Natassa: see Chatzidaki, Natasa
Hadjidakis, Manolis 10
Hadjidhaki, Natasa: see Chatzidaki, Natasa
Hadjigeorghiou, Kypros: see Chatzigeorgiou
Hadjilia, Conn *10*, *214*
Hadjioannou, Kyriakos 55
Hadjis, Dimitris: see Chatzis
Hadjistephanou, Costas E. *196*
Hadjopoulos, Constantinos/Kostas: see Chatzopoulos
Hadzis, Dimitris: see Chatzis
Hadzopoulos, Konstantinos: see Chatzopoulos
Hadzopoulou-Caravia, Lia: see Chatzopoulou-Karavia
Hadzopoulou-Karavia, Lia: see Chatzopoulou-Karavia
Hakkas, Marios: see Chakkas

Hall, Donald 28, *219*
Halloumas, Savvas: see Challoumas
Halls, Aliki: see Bacopoulou-Halls
Halman, Talât Sait *13*
Halpern, Daniel *23*
Hamboulides, Demetres: see Chamboulidis
Hammel, André *158*
Hanawalt, Emily Albu *3*
Hanson, Kenneth O. *14*
Haralambhidhis, Kyriakos: see Charalambidis
Hardison, O.B. *41*
Haris, Petros: see Charis
Harkianakis, Stylianos: see Charkianakis
Harlow, Michael *18*
Hartigan, Karelisa V. *58*, *61*, *66*, *153*, *196*
Hartocollis, Peter *131*
Hatfield, Lee *214*
Hatton, Thomas *159*
Hatzantonis, Emmanuel *61*, *131*
Hatzidaki, Natassa: see Chatzidaki, Natasa
Hatzidaki, Rena: see Chatzidaki, Rena
Hatzidimitriou, Costas *37*, *61*
Hatzinis, Y. *212*
Hatzis, Dimitris: see Chatzis
Hatzopoulos, Constantine/Kostes: see Chatzopoulos
Haviaras, Stratis 9, *12*, *13*, *17*, **113-114**
Haviland, Virginia *19*
Heimonas, Georgos: see Chimonas
Heldman, Michael *13*
Heliakis, Antonis: see Cheliakis
Henderson, G.P. *51*, *157*
Hermans, Jos. M.M. *42*
Herrey, Maria Sagris *51*
Herzfeld, Michael *36*, *55*, *61*
Hesseling, D.C. *149*
Hill, Victor *15*
Hilty, Hans Rudolf 104, *106*
Himarrides, Yiorghos: see Chimarridis
Himonas, George: see Chimonas
Hionides, Harry T. *47*, *142*
Hionis, Aryiris: see Chionis
Hionis, Peri *20*
Hirschman, Jack *26*, *112*
Hockney, David 77
Hoffman, Frederick J. *131*
Hogan, Maria Papazoglou *136*, *155*
Hogart, Ron *80*
Hokwerda, Hero *119*
Holliday, Vivian L. *131*
Holst, Gail: see Warhaft
Holton, David W. *32*, *42*, *47*, *49*, *55*, *141*
Hondroyannis, Yannis: see Chondrogiannis
Honig, Edwin *61*, *88*, *196*
Horecky, Paul L. *3*, *4*
Hortatzis, G.: see Chortatsis

Hortis, Katherine *30*, *136*, *161*, *162*, *184*, *185*, *212*
Horton, Andrew S. *52*, *61*, *145*, *146*, *184*, *185*
Hourmousiades, Kriton *222*
Hourmouzios, Emil *40*
Howard, Richard *14*, *93*, *123*
Hristodhoulou, Dhimitra: see Christodoulou
Hronas, George/Yorghos: see Chronas
Hull, Denison B. *42*
Huntington, Henry Alonzo *224*
Huxley, George *44*
Iacovides, Mimis: see Iakovidis 31
Iacovou, Andreas: see Iakovou 31
Iatrides, G. El. *52*
Iatridi, Julia **114**
Ierodiaconou, Andriana: see Ierodiakonou
Ierodiakonou, Antriana 26 (Ierodiaconou)
Ifandis/Ifantis, Yannis: see Yfantis
Ikaris, Despoina Spanos *105*, *126*, *131*
Ikonomou, Zisis 23 (Economou)
Imberios and Margarona 44, 45
Indianos, Antonis 31
Innis, Pauline W. *224*
Ioannides, Antis: see Ioannidis, Antis
Ioannides, Costas D.: see Ioannidis, Kostas D.
Ioannides, Kleitos: see Ioannidis, Klitos
Ioannides, Mary *120*
Ioannides, Panos: see Ioannidis, Panos
Ioannidis, Antis 31 (Ioannides, Antis)
Ioannidis, Klitos 31 (Ioannides, Kleitos)
Ioannidis, Kostas D. *32*, *55* (Ioannides, Costas D.)
Ioannidis, Panos 30, 31 (Ioannides, Panos)
Ioannidou, Roula 31
Ioannou, Giorgos 29, 32, **114-115**, *131*
Isaia, Nana: see Isaïa
Isaïa, Nana 11, 12, *13*, 15, 20, 22, 28, 29, **115** (also Isaia, Isaiah, Issaia)
Isaiah, Nana: see Isaïa
Issaia, Nana: see Isaïa
Issaris, Alexandros 13
Ivask, Astrid *103*
Ivask, Ivar *103*, *104*, *105*, *106*
Jackson, Robert F. *4*
Jahiel, Edwin *184*, *185*
Jakobson, Roman *88*
Jeffreys, Elizabeth M. *44*, *45*
Jeffreys, Michael J. *44*, *45*, *52*, *185*
Jenkins, Romilly J.H. *49*, *152*, *208*
John, marquess of Bute *223*
Johnstone, Kenneth R. *53*, *164*
Joshi, R.A. *224*
Joss, Paul Maria Leopold *23*
Jouanny, Robert *61*, *104*, *106*
Junkins, Donald *23*, *101*
Jusdanis, Gregory *62*, *83*, *86*, *89*, *131*
Kachtitsis, Nikos *13*, **115** (also Cachtitsis)

Kafatou, Sarah *9*, *138*, *171*, *183*
Kaftantzis, George 9
Kahane, Henry *45*
Kahane, Renée *45*
Kaiser, Walter *24*, *186*, *187*, *196*
Kakava, Maria *197*
Kakavelakis, Dimitris 28, **115-116**
Kakavoulia, Maria *75*
Kaknavatos, Ektor 9, 22, 28
Kakoulidis, Giannis 26, **116**
Kalamara, Vasso: see Kalamaras
Kalamaras, Vasso **116**, *155*
Kalas, Nikolaos: see Calas, Nicolas
Kallimachos and Chrysorrhoe 27, 45
Kalokyris, Dimitris 15, 30
Kalvos, Andreas 18, 21, 25, 27, 41, **116-117** (also Calvos)
Kambanellis, Iakovos 69, **117**
Kambouroglou, Christos **117**
Kanarakis, George *33*, *62*
Kanellopoulos, Panagiotis 18, *76*, **117** (also Canellopoulos)
Kapetanakis, D.: see Capetanakis
Kapodistrias, Count Ioannis 51
Kapsalis, S.D. *89*
Kapsaskis, Socrates 9
Karachalios, Nikos 9
Karadelis, John N. *159*
Karagatsis, M. 19
Karageorgos, Panos: see Karagiorgos
Karagiorgos, Panagiotis *32*, *33*, *62* (also Karageorgos)
Karagiosis: see Karangiozis
Karakostas, Nikos 27
Karamagianis, Catherine *150*
Karampetsos, E.D. *62*, *205*, *217*
Karandonis, Andreas: see Karantonis
'Karangiozis' 59, 60, 65, 66, 70, 210 (also Karagiosis)
Karanikas, Alexander *62*, *131*, *223*
Karanikas, Helen *223*
Karanikas, Marianthe *37*
Karantonis, Andreas 9, 14, 22, 23, *74*, *107*, *109*, *110*, *147*, *197*, *212*, *214* (also Karandonis)
Karapanou, Margarita 18, **117**
Karasoutsas, John 21, 27 (also Karasutsas)
Karasutsas, John: see Karasoutsas
Karathanassis, A.A. *2*
Karatza, Maria G. **118** (Caradja, Marie G.)
Karatzas, Dionysis 27, 28
Karavasilis, Giorgos 13 (Karavassilis)
Karavassilis, Yorghos: see Karavasilis
Karavidas, Yannis *110*, *197*
Karavitis, Vasilis 27
Karelli, Zoi 12, 18, 21, 22, 23, 25, 32, **118**
Karidhis, Nikos: see Karydis
Kariotakis, Kostas: see Karyotakis

Karka, Ilona *169*
Karkas, John *159*, *212*
Karkavitsas, Andreas 18, 40, **118-119**
Karnezis, George T. *131*
Karoussou, Despo **119**
Karouzos, Nikos D. 9, 10, 12, 14, 21, 22, 28, 29, **119**
Karvounis, Nicholas 21
Karydis, Nikos 22, 28, 29 (Karidhis)
Karyotakis, K.G. 15, 18, 21, 22, 23, 25, 26, 27, 40, **119** (also Caryotakis, Kariotakis; Constantine)
Kasdagli, Lina 20, **119** (also Kasdaglis, Lina)
Kasdagli, Rena 28 (Kasdhaghli)
Kasdaglis, Lina: see Kasdagli, Lina
Kasdaglis, Nikos **120**
Kasdhaghli, Rena: see Kasdagli, Rena
Kassos, Mary 27
Kassos, Vanghellis 27
Kastanakis, Thrasos 19, 20
Kastner, George Ronald *45, 46*
Katartzes, Demetrios: see Katartzis
Katartzis, Dimitrios 51 (Katartzes)
Katevaini, Anna 28
Katope, Christopher G. *89*
Katranides, Aristotle A. *55*
Katsanis, Vangelis **120**
Katsaouni, Niki 31
Katsaros, Michalis 9, 11, 22, 26, **120**
Katselli, Rina 31, **120** (also Catselli)
Katsimbalis, George C. *26*, **121**, *149*, *150*, *151*, *152*, *155*, *207*
Katsouri-Payiasi, Dina 31
Katsoyanis, Katy *188*
Kavadhias/Kavadias, Nikos: see Kavvadias
Kavafis, Constantine: see Cavafy, C.P.
Kavvadias, Nikos 22, 23, 24, 25, 28, **121** (also Kavadhias, Kavadias)
Kazantsakis, Nikos: see Kazantzakis, Nikos
Kazantzaki, Galatea 19, 21
Kazantzaki, Helen: see Kazantzakis, Helen
Kazantzaki, Galatea: see Kazantzaki, Galatea
Kazantzakis, Helen 18, *110*, *122*, *125*, *131*, *143*
Kazantzakis, Nikos 13, 18, 21, 22, 23, 25, 40, 41, 57, 62, 63, *89*, **121-135**, 153
Kazazis, J.N. *89*, *141*
Kazazis, Kostas *211*
Kechaïdis, Dimitris **135** (Kehaides, Kehaidis)
Keeley, Edmund *13*, *15*, *23*, *24*, *25*, *26*, *28*, *29*, *35*, *36*, *40*, *62*, *63*, *64*, *69*, *72*, *77*, *78*, *79*, *80*, *81*, *82*, *83*, *84*, *88*, *89*, *90*, *92*, *98*, *100*, *101*, *102*, *103*, *104*, *106*, *107*, *111*, *112*, *119*, *138*, *167*, *168*, *169*, *170*, *171*, *172*, *173*, *174*, *175*, *176*, *177*, *178*, *179*, *180*, *181*, *182*, *185*, *186*, *187*, *188*, *189*, *190*, *191*, *192*, *193*, *197*, *198*, *201*, *202*, *203*, *205*, *221*, *222*

Keeley, Mary *64*, *72*, *98*, *119*, *148*, *169*, *171*, *177*, *178*, *191*, *200*, *211*, *221*, *222*
Kefala, Antigone *139*
Kefalas, Elias 27
Kefalas, St. Nektarios 50 (Kephalas)
Kehagioglou, George *63*
Kehaides/Kehaidis, Dimitris: see Kechaïdis
Kennedy, Karen *81*
Kentrou-Agathopoulou, Maria 27
Kephalas, St. Nectarios: see Kefalas
Keramianakis, Manolis 15
Kerce, Stephen *13*
Kerényi, Karl *123*, *131*
Keyishan, Marjorie *99*
Khairallah, George *78*
Kindhinis, Kostas: see Kindynis
Kindinis, Kostas: see Kindynis
Kindynis, Kostas 11, 67, **136** (also Kindhinis, Kindinis)
Kingdom (-n?), June *116*, *155*
Kipling, Rudyard *206*, *207*
Kirikopoulos, George *12*
Kirou, Klitos: see Kyrou
Kitroeff, Alec/Alexander *90*, *121*, *145*
Kitromilides, Paschalis M. *37*, *52*, *63*
Klein, Leonard S. *41*
Klein, Theodore M. *58*
Klingopoulos, G.D. *90*
Knapp, John V. *130*
Knodel, Arthur *190*
Koestler, Arthur *185*
Kokkinakes, Constantine 25
Kokkinis, Spyros 26
Kokkinos, Demostenes 32
Kokkinos, Dionysios 19 (Cokkinos)
Kokorovits, Kostes 15, 25
Kolaitis, Memas *84*
Kolokotronis, Theodoros 51, **136**
Kolossiatou, Frossoula 27
Kondos, Yannis: see Kontos
Kondou, Nana: see Kontou
Kondylakis, Ioannis **136**
Konidaris, Dimitris 28 (Konidharis)
Konidharis, Dhimitris: see Konidaris
Konstantas, Gregorios 51
Konstantinidis, Stefanos 30 (Constantinides, Stephanos)
Konstantinidou, Loula D. **136** (also Constantinidou)
Konstantis, Giorgos 30 (Constantis)
Kontoglou, Fotis **136-137**
Kontos, Giannis 10, 11, 12, 13, 15, 22, 26, 27, 28, 29, **137-138** (also Kondos)
Kontos, N. *24*
Kontou, Nana P. **138** (also Kondou)
Kopan, Andrew T. *37*
Koraes/Korais, Adamantios: see Koraïs

Koraïs, Adamantios 41, 51, 52 (also Koraes, Korais)
Korelas, Christos *74*
Korfioti-Panagiotidou, Vera 31 (Korphioti-Panayiotidou)
Korfis, Tasos 12, 27
Kornaros, Vitsentzos 9, 21, 25, 36, 41, 48, 49, 50 (also Cornaros)
Korovesi-Porfiri, Peggy 28
Korovesis, Periklis 18, **138** (also Korovessis)
Korovessis, Pericles: see Korovesis
Korphioti-Panagiotidou, Vera: see Korfioti-Panagiotidou
Korres, Manolis **138** (also Corres)
Korydaleus, Theophilos 51
Kosmas Aitolos 50 (Cosmas Aitolos)
Kotsapa, Koula 31
Kotsiras, Giorgis 10, 21, 22, 25, 28, 29
Kotzamanidou, Maria *13*, *48*, *119*
Kotzias, Alexandros **138-139**
Koufopoulos, Takis 17
Kougialis, Theoklis 30 (Couyialis, Kouyialis)
Koukoulas, Leon 25
Koulis, Vasilis **139**
Koumandareas, Menis: see Koumantareas
Koumantareas, Menis **139** (also Koumandareas)
Koumarianou, C. *1*
Koumas, Konstantinos 51
Koumoulides, John T.A. *59*, *199*
Koundouri, Eleftheria: see Kountouri
Koundouros, Roussos *3*
Kountouri, Eleftheria **139** (also Koundouri)
Kourtidis, Aristotelis **139** (Kourtidos)
Kourtidos, Aristotle: see Kourtidis
Kousoulas, Loukas 9
Koutris, George J. *136*
Koutsocheras, John **139-140** (also Coutsoheras)
Kouyialis, Theoklis: see Kougialis
Kovanis, Kostas 12, 21
Kralis, Manos 25, 30, 31
Kranidiotes, Nikos: see Kranidiotis
Kranidiotis, Nikos 30, 31 (also Kranidiotes)
Kraus, David H. *4*
Krikos, Katerina: see Krikos-Davis
Krikos-Davis, Katerina *49*, *55*, *198* (also Krikos)
Krili-Kevans, Yota *210*
Krinaios, Pavlos: see Krinaios-Michaïlidis
Krinaios-Michaelides, Pavlos: see Krinaios-Michaïlidis
Krinaios-Michaïlidis, Pavlos 30, 31 (also Krinaios, Krinaios-Michaelides)
Kriton, T.D. *182*
Kroetsch, Robert *10*, *173*
Krystallis, Kostas 18, 21, 26, 27, 32 (also Crystallis)
Kyriakides, Stilpon P. *55*
Kyriakidou-Nestoros, Maria-Alke *37*, *55*

Kyriazi, Dina *213*
Kyriazis, Athanasios 26
Kyriazis, Dmitri *198*
Kyriazopoulos, Spyros 32
Kyrillos Loukaris 47 (Cyril Lucaris)
Kyrou, Klitos 10, 22, 26, 29, 32 (also Kirou)
Kyrri-Leontiadou, Eleni 31
Kyrris, Kostas 31, *74*
Ladaki-Filippou, Niki 31, **140** (Ladaki-Philippou, Philippou-Ladaki)
Ladaki-Philippou, Niki: see Ladaki-Filippou
Ladas, Sophia *159*
Laghoureli, Maria: see Lagoureli
Lagoudis Pinchin, Jane: see Pinchin
Lagoureli, Maria 27, 28 (also Laghoureli, Lagourelli)
Lagourelli, Maria: see Lagoureli
Laina, Maria: see Laïna
Laïna, Maria 10, 13, 26, 28, **140** (also Laina)
Lambropoulos, Vassilis 36, *63*, *90*, *208*
Lambros, Spyridon 21
Langnas, Izaak A. *129*
Laos, O. *168*
Laourdas, Basil *44*, *46*, *52*, *63*, *132*
Lapathiotis, Napoleon 25
Lapidus, Jacqueline *110*
Lardas, Konstantinos Nick *53*, *82*, *90*, *112*, *226*
Laskaris, Christos 27
Laughlin, James *109*, *178*
Lavagnini, Renata *90*
Layoun, Mary Nicola *26*, *63*
Layton, Evro *2*, *3*, *4*, *48*
Lazaridis, Markos 18
Lazaris, Nikos 13, 22
Lazarou, Sophoklis 31
Lazou, Maria 28
Lea, James F. *125*, *134*
Leatham, John *10*
Lebesgue, Philéas *152*
Lee, David *24*, *189*
Lee, George *207*
Leedis, Margaret *184*
Lefkis, Giannis 31
Lehmann, John *76*, *79*, *102*, *192*, *202*
Lekatsas, Barbara *63*
Leland, W. *78*
Lendakis, Andreas: see Lentakis
L'Engle, Madeleine *61*
Lentakis, Andreas 14 (Lendakis)
Leondaris, Byron: see Leontaris, Vyron
Leontaris, Vyron 22 (Leondaris)
Leontis, Artemis *63*, *198*
Lester, Eva P. *198*
Leuven, Jon Cloud van *64*
Levesque, Robert *121*
Levi, Peter *9*, *74*, *111*, *146*, *156*, *160*, *177*, *194*, *198*, *205*

INDEX

Levitt, Morton P. *64, 107, 126, 130, 132, 134*
Lewnes, Tula *161*
Légagneux, Claude *97*
Liasides, Pavlos: see Liasidis
Liasidis, Pavlos 30, 31 (also Liasides, Liassides)
Liaskas, Basil 14
Liassides, Pavlos: see Liasidis
Liatsou, Evrydike 31
Liberaki, Margarita: see Lymberaki
Liddell, Robert *9, 40, 84, 90, 92, 146, 162, 203, 223*
Lidderdale, Harold A. *141*
Lidorikis, Alekos 69, **140**
Ligarides, Paisius: see Ligaridis
Ligaridis, Païsios 47 (Ligarides)
Lillios, Anna *148*
Lindsay, Jack *74*
Liontakis, Christoforos 13
Lipertis, Dimitris 25, 30, 31
Litsas, Fotios K. *36, 64, 143, 228*
Littlewood, A.R. *46, 132*
Livadhitis, Tasos: see Livaditis 14, 22
Livaditis, Tasos 14, 15, 25, 26 (also Livadhitis)
Lord, Albert B. *46, 55, 64*
Lorenzatos, Zissimos *15, 35, 64, 198, 208*
Lotris, Konstantinos **140**
Loundemis, Menelaos: see Lountemis
Lountemis, Menelaos 18, 19, 25 (Loundemis)
Loverdos-Streichler, Kali *148*
Lowe, C.G. *49*
Lowe, Robert *96*
Lucas, John *64*
Lurier, H[arold] E. *42*
Lybistros and Rhodamne 27
Lykavyis, Anthos 31
Lymberaki, Margarita **140** (also Liberaki)
Lyssiotis, Xanthos 31
Lyvistros: see *Lybistros and Rhodamne*
MacAlister, Suzanne *46, 56, 90*
Macdougall, Alan Ross *147*
MacEwan, Gwendolyn *11, 166* (also MacEwen, Tsingos)
MacGregor, Alexander 37
Machairas, Leontios 47, 48 (also Makhairas)
MacKinnon, Kenneth 20, 72, *117, 120, 135, 142*
Mackridge, Peter A. *2, 14, 52, 64, 71, 79, 115, 125, 160, 162, 164, 165, 166, 209, 214, 223*
MacLaurin, Lucy *120*
Macrakis, A. Lily 37
MacVeagh, Lincoln 9
Maddox, Donald D. *205*
Maffry, Alice-Mary *136, 162, 166, 213, 223, 224*
Magill, Frank N. *68*
Magowan, Robin *14*

Makaronas, Ch. *44, 46*
Makhairas, Leontios: see Machairas
Makris, Giorgos **140**
Makriyannis, General Yannis: see Makrygiannis
Makrygiannis, Ioannis **141** (also Makriyannis)
Makrynikola, Aikaterini *179*
Maksim the Greek: see Maximos Graikos
Malakasis, Miltiades 21, 26, 27 (also Malakassis)
Malakassis, Miltiades: see Malakasis
Malamas, Lambros 32
Malanos, Timos *89, 91*
Malkoff, Karl *91, 107*
Mandel, Ruth *56*
Mangakis, Georgios-Alexandros **141**
Manglis, Giannis 18, **142**
Mango, Cyril *45*
Maniotis, Giorgos **142**
"Manna" *110*
Manning, Clarence A. *76, 210*
Manousakas, L.T. *171*
Manousakis, Yorgis 26, *132*
Mansfield, Peter *184*
Mantholulis, Rovyros 9
Marangou, Niki 27
Maratheftis, Michalis 31
Maravegias, Dionysis 68 (Maraveyas)
Maraveyas, Dionysis: see Maravegias
Marder, Brenda *64*
Margaris, Vasilis 32
Markides, Costas: see Markidis, Kostas
Markides, Yeorghios: see Markidis, Georgios
Markidis, Georgios 31 (Markides, Yeorghios)
Markidis, Kostas 31 (Markides, Costas)
Markoghlou, Prodhromos: see Markoglou
Markoglou, Prodromos X. 12, 22, 28 (also Markoghlou)
Markopoulos, Giorgos *12*, 13, **142**
Markoras, Gerasimos 21, 26, 27
Marmara, Elli *114*
Maronitis, D.N. *64, 91, 160*
Marshall, Frederick Henry 25, *46, 47, 48*
Martin, Donald E. *213, 214*
Martin, Frederick R. *178*
Martinengo Cesaresco, Countess Evelyn 25
Maskaleris, Thanasis G. *9, 10, 12, 15, 24, 26, 94, 102, 109, 110, 115, 120, 121, 142, 152, 153, 162, 169, 178, 204, 205, 207, 226*
Mason, David *81, 207*
Mason, Hugh J. *147*
Massa, J. *205*
Mastoraki, Jenny/Tzeni 11, 12, 18, 20, 22, 26, 28, **142-143** (also Mastorakis)
Mastorakis, Jenny: see Mastoraki
Mastrodemetres, P.D. *118*
Matesis, Antonios **143**

Matsas, Alexander 13, 18, 21, 22, 23, **143**
Matsas, Nestor **143**
Matsukis, Corinna *198*
Matthews, Carola *144*
Mavilis, Lorentzos 18, 21, 26, 27
Mavrides, Labis/Lambis: see Mavridis
Mavridis, Lambis 27 (Mavrides)
Mavrogordato, John 25, *42*, *48*, *49*, *77*
Mavroidi-Panteleskou, Afroditi **143**
Mavroidi-Papadaki, Sophia 14, 21 (also Mavroidi Papadaky)
Mavroidi Papadaky, Sophia: see Mavroidi-Papadaki
Mavrokordatos, Alexandros 51
Mavrokordatos, Konstantinos 51
Mavrokordatos, Nikolaos 51
Mavromatis, Andreas *140*
Mavroudis, Kostas 13, 15
Maximos Graikos 41, 48 (also Maksim the Greek)
McCarthy, Bryan 25
McCarthy, Eugene J. *198*
McCarthy, Shaun *91*
McDonald, Donna *11*
McDonough, B.T. *126*
McGrew, William *37*
McKeever, Clare *132*
McKinley, Hugh *14*, *15*
McKinsey, Martin *72*, *81*, *104*, *109*, *167*, *170*, *173*, *174*, *175*, *176*, *177*, *178*, *179*
McPherson, Florence 25, *207*
Megalinos, Haris: see Megalynos
Megalynos, Charis 28, **143** (also Megalinos)
Megann, Peter *113*
Megas, Georgios A. *19*, *56*
Meïmaris, Mihalis 28
Melachrinos, Apostolos 21
Melakopides, Constantine *84*, *91*
Melas, Spyros 18, 19
Meleagrou, Hebe 30, 31
Melissanthi 12, 15, 18, 21, 22, 23, **144**
Melissinos, Stavros *84*, **144**
Menardos, Simos *64*, *219*
Meranaios, Kostis *156*
Meranos, Pavlos 31
Merchant, Paul *9*, *12*, *24*, *64*, *167*, *179*, *219*
Merrill, James *80*, *82*, *91*, *222*
Merrill, Reed B. *132*
Merwin, W.S. *14*
Meskos, Markos 9, 22, 23, 28
Michaelides, Costas: see Michaïlidis, Kostas
Michaelides/Michaelidis, Vassilis: see Michaïlidis, Vasilis
Michaïlidis, Kostas 31, *132* (Michaelides, Mihailides)
Michaïlidis, Vasilis 25, 30, 31 (Michaelides, Michaelidis)

Michalaros, Demetrios A. *149*, *150*, *151*, *153*, *154*
Michalopoulos, André *75*
Michalopoulos, Andrew 26
Michalopoulos, Ph. *149*
Michals, Duane *84*
Michanikos, Pantelis 31 (Mihanikos)
Michopoulos, Aristotle *65*
Mihailides, Kostas: see Michaïlidis, Kostas
Mihanikos, Pantelis: see Michanikos
Mikellides, Ninos: see Mikellidis
Mikellidis, Ninos 31 (Mikellides)
Miller, Henry *10*, *110*, *121*, *164*, *165*, *198*
Miller, Joyce *103*
Miller, Julia E. *56*
Mims, Amy 25, *30*, *110*, *122*, *123*, *124*, *125*, *138*, *139*, *155*, *161*, *167*, *170*, *171*
Mira[m]bel, André *65*
Miranda, Gary *198*
Mirza, Baldev 15
Mistakidou, Aekaterina P. *65*
Mitras, Michael **144**
Mitropoulos, Mona: see Mitropoulou, Mona
Mitropoulou, Kostoula **144**
Mitropoulou, Mona **145** (also Mitropoulos)
Mitsakis, Karolos 25, *46*, *65*, *115*, *155*, *166*, *217*
Mitsakis, Michael 19
Mladenovic, Zivomir *56*
Moatti-Fine, J. *132*
Moffatt, Ann *44*
Moisiodax, Iosepos 51
Moles, Ian N. *52*
Moleskis, Yorghos 31
Montgomery, Stuart *24*, *103*
Montis, Kostas 23, 30, 31, 32, **145**
Montis, Marios 31
Moore, Elmer E., Jr. *24*
Moraitis, Makis *142*
Moraïtidis, Alexandros **145**
Moraki, Georgia 15
Morgan, Gareth *49*, *50*, *56*
Morin, Edward *103*
Morrison, Karl F. *216*
Moskof, Kostis **145** (also Moskoff)
Moskoff, Kostis: see Moskof
Moskos, Charles C. *37*
Motsios, Yannis *52*
Moundes, Mattheos: see Mountes
Mountes, Matthaios 9, 28 (also Moundes)
Mourselas, Kostas **145-146**
Moutsopoulos, Evanghelos *226*
Mulhallen, Karen *11*
Murdoch, I.T. *117*
Murray, Penelope *47*, *64*, *175*
Muto, Susan A. *132*
Mylona, Eva 20, 22, 28, **146** (also Mylonas)

Mylonas, Eva: see Mylona
Mylonas, George E. *10, 154, 208*
Myrivilis, Stratis 18, 40, 41, **146-147**
Myrsiades, Kostas J. *11, 15, 65, 117, 119, 137, 158, 159, 163, 167, 168, 169, 170, 171, 172, 173, 174, 175, 176, 177, 178, 179, 180, 181*
Myrsiades, Linda Suny *65, 66*
Myrtiotissa 21, 26, 27, 67, **147**
Nakos, Lilika: see Nakou
Nakou, Lilika **147** (also Nakos)
Nazianzinos, Gregory 14
Negrepontis, Yannis 14, 15
Negris, Alexander *39*
Nehamas, Alexander *91*
Newton, Rick M. *115, 141, 168, 169, 170, 176, 228*
Niarchos, Thanasis 28, **148**
Nicholas, Fotine *118, 136, 161, 162*
Nickels, Mary A. (sic): see Nickles, Mary A.
Nickles, Harry *146*
Nickles, Mary A. *145, 146* (also Nickels (sic))
Nickles, Nina *218*
Nicolaides, Philip L. *74*
Nightingale, Les *138*
Niketas, George *107*
Nikiforou, Tolis 27
Nikolaides, Melis: see Nikolaïdis, Melis
Nikolaides, Nikos: see Nikolaïdis, Nikos
Nikolaidis, Aristotle 14, 22
Nikolaidis, Ioannis 32
Nikolaidis, Kostas N 32
Nikolaïdis, Melis 30, 31 (Nikolaides)
Nikolaïdis, Nikos 30, 31 (Nikolaides)
Niles, Oliver *24*
Nirvanas, Pavlos 19, 26, 27
Nollas, Dimitris **148**
Noonan, J.D. *107*
Nord, Paul *201*
Notopoulos, James A. *46, 56, 132*
Nørgaard, Lars *42*
O' Gorman, Ned *80*
Oates, Joyce Carol *176*
Odysseus, George *66*
Ogilvie-Grant, Mark *68, 225*
Oleson, Claire B. *142*
Olmsted, Hugh M. *48*
Olymbiou, Kika *68*
Opdycke, Leonard Eckstein *224*
Orfanidi, Cali *158*
Orfanidis, Theodoros 21 (Orphanidês)
Orlando, Vito *76*
Orphanidês, Theodore: see Orfanidis
Otis, C. *209*
Ouranis, Kostas 15, 18, 21, 22, 23, 26, **148**
Overmeer, R. *86*
Padel, Ruth *199*

Page, Alan *173*
Pagoulatou, Regina **148**
Pahdi, Bibhu *199*
Paidoussi, Eleni: see Païdoussi
Païdoussi, Eleni 25, *168* (Paidoussi)
Paionidou, Elli 31
Palaeologus of Constantinople, Gregorius: see Palaiologos
Palaiologos, Grigorios 26, *161* (Palaeologus, Paleologos)
Palaiologou-Petronda, Evyenia: see Palaiologou-Petronta
Palaiologou-Petronta, Evgenia 31 (Palaiologou-Petronda)
Palamas, Christian X. *154*
Palamas, Kostis 18, 21, 25, 26, 27, 40, 41, 67, 68, **149-154**, 176
Palamas, Leandros K. *152,* **155**
Paleologos, Gregorios: see Palaiologos
Palli, Angelica 25
Pallis, A.A. *35, 46, 48, 56, 66*
Pallis, Alexandros 21, 26
Palmer, Laura *185*
Pamboudhi, Pavlina: see Pamboudi
Pamboudi, Pavlina 11, 15, 22, 26, 28, **155** (also Pamboudhi, Pampoudhi, Pampoudi)
Pampoudhi/Pampoudi, Pavlina: see Pamboudi
Panagiotopoulos, I.M. 18, 21, 22, 23, *137,* **155**, *214* (also Panayiotopoulos, Panayotopoulos)
Panagiotou, Myrianthi 31 (Panayiotou)
Panagiotounis, Panos N. **155** (also Panayotounis)
Panayiotopoulos, I.M.: see Panagiotopoulos
Panayiotou, Myrianthi: see Panagiotou
Panayotopoulos, I.M./J.M.: see Panagiotopoulos
Panayotounis, Panos N.: see Panagiotounis
Pandelakis, Helene S. *50*
Pandiri, Thalia *181*
Panichas, George A. *128*
Panopoulos-Payne, X.C. *150, 154*
Pantazis, Fotoula *12*
Pantazis, Jim *12*
Paolucci, Anne *14*
Papachrysostomou, Christodoulos 31
Papadhitsas, D.M. (sic): see Papaditsas, D.P.
Papadhitsas, Dimitris P.: see Papaditsas, D.P.
Papadhitsas, P.D. (sic): see Papaditsas, D.P.
Papadhopoulos, Yannis: see Papadopoulos, Giannis K.
Papadiamantis, Alexandros 18, 41, **156**, 208
Papadimas, George *158*
Papadimitrakopoulos, Ilias 10, **156-157**
Papadimitriou, Sakis *66,* **157**
Papaditsas, D.P. 9, 10, 11, 14, 22, 26, 28, 29 (also Papadhitsas; Dimitris, D.M. and P.D. (sic))

Papadopoulos, Giannis K. 12, 14, 22, 25, 28, 30, 31 (also Papadhopoulos)
Papadopoulos, Thanasis 12
Papageorghiou, Spyros: see Papageorgiou, Spyros
Papageorgiou, Kostas G. 13, 28, *199* (also Papayeoryiou)
Papageorgiou, Spyros 30, 31 (Papageorghiou)
Papagos, Alexander *228*
Papaioannou, John G. *132*
Papakonstantinou, Dhimitris 28
Papandoniou, Zacharias: see Papantoniou
Papangelou, Rois 27
Papanikolaou, Mitsos *107*
Papanoutsos, E.P. *66*, *149*, **157**
Papantoniou, Zacharias 21, 25, 26, **157** (also Papandoniou)
Papapetros, Anastos **158**
Paparrhegopoulos, Demetrios: see Paparrigopoulos, Dimitrios
Paparrhigopoulos, [K.]: see Paparrigopoulos, Konstantinos
Paparrigopoulos, Dimitrios 27 (Paparrhegopoulos)
Paparrigopoulos, Konstantinos 61 (Paparrhigopoulos)
Papastamou, Olga **158**
Papathanasopoulos, Thanasis 28
Papatheodorou, Nini *12*
Papatsonis, Takis 13, 18, 22, 23, 25, 30, 41, **158-159** (also Papatzonis)
Papatzonis, Takis: see Papatsonis
Papayeoryiou, Kostas: see Papageorgiou, Kostas G.
Papazoglou-Margaris, Theano *228*
Papoutsakis, G.A. *78*, *79*, *80*, *81*
Pappa, Eleni/Lena 12, 27
Pappageotes, George C. *18*, *40*, *122*
Pappas, Angelos **159**
Pappas, Christina *118*
Pappas, Nikos 14, 15, 21, 22, 23
Pappas, Peter *222*
Pappas, William V. *3*
Paraschos, Achilles 21, 25, 27
Paraschos, Cleon *159*
Parianos, Eleftherios K. *168*, *174*
Parker, Sandra A. *133*
Parkhill, Peter *56*
Parks, George B. *3*
Parnis, Alexis **159**
Paroritis, Costas 19
Parthogh, Lana der *68*
Paschos, Vasilis Th. **159**
Pasicznyk, Uliana *45*
Passiardis, Michalis 31
Pastellas, Andreas 31
Pastras, Philip James *107*, *168*, *172*, *174*, *181*

Patatzis, Sotiris 69
Patilis, Yannis 22, 26, 27, 28
Patrakis, Catherine *138*
Patrikios, Titos 9, 22, **160**
Patriotis, Hector 31
Patsalidis, Savas 27
Pattichi, Maria 31 (Pattihi)
Pattihi, Maria: see Pattichi
Pavleas, Sarandos 22, 29, 32
Pavlides, Lefteris *103*
Pavlides, Leonidas: see Pavlidis
Pavlidis, Leonidas 31 (Pavlides)
Pavlopoulos, George/Giorgis 22, 27, *141*, **160**
Pavlopoulou, Angeliki 22
Pendzikis, Nikos Gavriil: see Pentzikis
Pentzikis, Nikos Gavriil 13, 22, 23, 32, **160** (also Pendzikis)
Perentos, Louis 31
Pergialis, Notis 69
Perkins, Elizabeth *215*
Pernaris, Antis 31
Pernot, H. *67*
Perry, George E. *4*
Pesopoulos, Hero *204*
Petimezas, Nicholas 26
Petrides, Ted *21*
Petropoulos, Ilias *21*, *67*, *107*, **160-161**
Petropoulos, John A. *37*
Petrounias, Evangelos *37*
Petsalis, Thanasis **161** (also Petsalis-Diomedes)
Petsalis-Diomedes, Thanasis: see Petsalis
Peyre, Henri *212*
Phalieros, Marinos: see Falieros
Phelps, Jocelyn M. *132*
Philipe, Anne *199*
Philippides, Daniel: see Filippidis
Philippides, Dia M.L. *50*
Philippides, Marios *132*
Philippou-Ladaki, Niki: see Ladaki-Filippou
Phillip, David *145*
Phillips, William *189*
Phinney, Edward V.S. *27*, *28*, *132*, *165*, *181*, *212*, *213*
Phocas, Nikos: see Fokas, Nikos
Photiades, Marianthi *67*
Photiou, Thanassis *12*
Photos, Basil J. *32*
Phoutrides, Aristides E. *20*, *100*, *118*, *149*, *151*, *152*, *154*, *163*, *209*, *225*, *227*
Phylactou/Phylaktou, Takis G.: see Fylaktou
Piccolos, N.S.: see Pikkolos
Pickford, T.E. *46*
Pierides, George Philippou: see Pieridis, Giorgos Filippou
Pierides, Theodosis: see Pieridis, Theodosis
Pieridis, Giorgos Filippou **161** (also Pierides, George Philippou)

Pieridis, Michalis *78, 80, 81, 82*
Pieridis, Theodosis 31 (Pierides)
Pieris, Michalis *84*
Pikkolos, Nikolaos S. **161** (also Piccolos)
Pilavachi, Alexander *198*
Pilitsis, George *168, 172, 174*
Pillas, Antonis 31
Pilling, John *41*
Pinchin, Jane Lagoudis *84, 88, 91*
Pittas, Triantafyllos 25, **161**
Plante, David *108*
Plaskovitis, Spyros **162**
Plassara, Katerina *181*
Plimpton, George *197*
Plissis, Kyriakos 31
Plomer, William *76*
Ploritis, Marios *24*
Poggioli, Renato *84, 91*
Polemis, John 25, 26, 27
Polentas, Manolis 68
Politis, Kosmas 18, 57, **162**
Politis, Linos *40*
Politis, M.J. *67, 121*
Polydoure, Maria: see Polydouri
Polydouri, Maria 27, 67, **162-163** (also Polydoure)
Polylas, Iakovos **163**, *209*
Pontikas, Marios **163**
Pontis, Timos 15
Porfyras, Lambros 21, 26, 27, **163** (also Porphyras)
Porphyras, Lambros: see Porfyras
Posner, David *73, 118*
Potamitis, Dimitris 11, 22, 28, 31
Poulakidas, Andreas K. *12, 130, 133*
Poulakos, Dimitris *74*
Poulios, Lefteris 11, 12, 15, 22, 26, 28, 30, **163**
Pratsikas, Manolis 27
Preminger, Alex *41*
Presley, Del E. *133*
Prevelakis, P. 41
Prevelakis, Pantelis 18, 22, 23, 25, 63, *126, 130, 133, 134,* **164-166**, *181, 204*
Price, Doug *80*
Pringos, Ioannis 51
Pritsak, Omeljan *45*
Prodromic Poems 41, 42, 43
Prodromos, Theodore 27, 43
Proussis, Costas M. *3, 30, 31, 67, 121, 141, 152, 154, 156, 212*
Provelengios, Aristomenis 18, 21 (also Provilegios)
Provilegios, Aristomenes: see Provelengios
Psalidas, Athanasios 51
Psaropoulos, Tassos 30, 31
Psichari, Jean: see Psycharis, Giannis

Psychares, John: see Psycharis, Giannis
Psycharis, Giannis 18, 40, 41, *67,* **166** (also Psichari, Psychares, Psyharis)
Psychoundakis, George: see Psychountakis
Psychountakis, Giorgos **166** (also Psychoundakis)
Psyharis, Yannis: see Psycharis
Puchner, Walter *50*
Purcell, Sally *111*
Pylioti-Constantinou, Maria: see Pylioti-Konstantinou
Pylioti-Konstantinou, Maria 31 (Pylioti-Constantinou)
Pyliotis, Achilleas 31
Pym, Hilary *9*
Rados, Constantine N. 30
Raffel, Burton *91*
Ragovin, Frederick 25, *33, 144, 226*
Rahv, Philip *189*
Raizis, Catherine *184*
Raizis, Marios Byron 11, 12, 15, 25, 67, 74, 91, *104, 108, 110, 114, 124, 134, 154, 159, 166, 181, 187, 191, 192, 193, 199, 208, 209, 212, 217, 222, 224, 226, 227*
Rallis, P. *51*
Ramp, Philip J. *11, 12, 13, 15, 73, 116, 119, 123, 163, 211*
Rangavis, A.R. 18, 21, 25, 27, **166** (also Rhangabes, Rhizos Rhangabes; Alexander)
Rapsomatis 43
Raubitschek, A.E. *54*
Raymond, Doris *208*
Raysson, A. *74*
Razi, G. Michael *206*
Reed, Alma *201*
Reed, Fred A. *95, 122*
Regas Pheraios: see Rigas Feraios
Regueiro, Helen *188*
Reid, Alec *206*
Reinhold, Meyer *3*
Rethis, M. *211*
Rexine, John E. *41, 67, 116, 134, 190, 199, 200*
Rhangabes, Alexander: see Rangavis
Rhigas Pheraios/Pherrhaios: see Rigas Feraios
Rhodinis, Anthos: see Rodinis
Rhoidis, Emmanouel: see Roïdis
Richards, Lewis A. *125, 134*
Richmond, John 25, *186*
Rick, Abbott *146, 164, 213*
Ricks, D.B. *166*
Rigas Feraios 18, 21, 27, 51 (also Regas/ Rhigas; Pheraios/Pherrhaios)
Rigas Pheraios: see Rigas Feraios
Rigos, Sarah Arnold *75*
Rinvolucri, Mario *210*
Risher, Mary Jo *80*

Ritsonis, Kostas 10
Ritsos, Giannis/Yannis 11, 12, 15, 18, 21, 22, 23, 24, 25, 26, 29, 40, 41, 67, 86, 107, **166-182**
Rizo Neroulos 26
Rizos Rangavis, Alexander: see Rangavis
Robbins, Doren *112*
Robillard, Douglas, Jr. *92*
Robinson, Christopher *67, 68, 104, 108, 147, 154, 163*
Robinson, David M. *154*
Roda, V. 15
Rodas, M. *68*
Rodd, Rennell *219*
Rodinis, Anthos 31 (Rhodinis)
Roditi, Edouard *61, 92*
Rodocanachi, C.P.: see Rodokanaki
Rodokanaki, C.P. 9, **182** (also Rodocanachi)
Rodriguez, Judith *215*
Roides/Roidis, Emmanuel: see Roïdis
Roïdis, Emmanouil 18, 41, **182** (also Rhoidis, Roides, Roidis, Royidis)
Romanos, Christos S. *138, 139*
Rose, H.J. *32*
Ross, Alan *108*
Rossanglogallos 51
Rossides, Zenon: see Rossidis
Rossidis, Zinon 31 (Rossides)
Rotert, Richard *61, 95*
Rotolo, Vincenzo *104, 108*
Roufos, Rodis *17*, 18, **183**
Roumbanis, Theodoros **183**
Roumeliotakis, Christos 28
Rouse, W.H.D. *100*
Roussel, Louis *149, 154*
Roussia, Maria 30, 31
Roussos, Tassos 10, 23
Roussou, Maya-Maria **183** (also Russu)
Rowe, Robert *15, 96*
Royidis, Emmanuel: see Roïdis
Ruehlen, Petroula Kephala *92*
Runciman, Steven *200*
Russell, G.W.E. 22
Russu, Maya-Maria: see Roussou
Sachtouris, Miltos 9, 10, 11, 13, 21, 22, 26, 28, 29, **183-184** (also Sahtouris, Saktouris)
Sacrifice of Abraham 40, 48, 49, 50
Sahas, Daniel *12*
Sahinis, Apostolos *214, 223*
Sahtouris, Miltos: see Sachtouris
Sakalli, Avyi 31
Sakellaropoulos, P. *131*
Saktouris, Miltos: see Sachtouris
Salapassidis, Teos 9
Salomos, Mr. (sic): see Solomos
Samarakis, Antonis **184-185**
Samaras, Nikos *226*
Samaras, Zoe *226*
Sampson, Theodore *19, 71, 74, 75, 93, 94, 95, 100, 109, 110, 112, 114, 115, 118, 124, 136, 137, 145, 146, 147, 150, 155, 156, 157, 161, 162, 163, 164, 165, 166, 182, 204, 212, 214, 215, 223, 224, 227*
Santas, Constantine *68, 219*
Saradis, Giorgis: see Sarantis
Sarandaris, George: see Sarantaris
Sarantaris, George 18, 21, 22, 23 (also Sarandaris)
Saranti, Galatia **185**
Sarantis, Giorgis 14 (Saradis)
Sarejannis, I.A. *84, 92* (also Sareyannis, J.A.)
Savidis, George 15
Savidis, George P. *13, 24, 25, 68, 77, 78, 80, 81, 82, 92, 100, 101, 102, 105, 169, 200, 201, 205* (also Savvides, George)
Savidis, Theodora *200*
Savina, Zoi **185**
Savopoulos, Savas 27
Savvas, Minas 10, *68, 78, 115, 134, 163, 166, 168, 170, 171, 174, 175, 176, 177, 178, 179, 181, 184, 187, 201, 209, 217*
Savvides, G.C.: see Savvidis
Savvides, George: see Savidis, George P.
Savvidis, G.C. 18 (Savvides)
Scarimbas, Yannis: see Skarimbas
Scarpas, Louis: see Skarpas
Schartau, Bjarne *92*
Schmitt, John *42*
Schneider, Sara *21*
Schroeder, Andreas *10*
Schwartz, Benjamin *56*
Scodel, Ruth *93*
Scott-Kilvert, Elisabeth D. *222, 223*
Scott-Kilvert, Ian *79, 83, 124, 160, 177, 193, 205*
Scouffas, George *134*
Scuris, T.K. *9*
Seferiades, Stelios: see Seferiadis
Seferiadis, Stelios 26 (Seferiades)
Seferis, George 12, 13, 15, 18, 21, 22, 23, 24, 25, 26, 27, 30, *35*, 40, 41, *62, 64*, 67, 68, *74, 84, 93, 141*, **185-201**
Sempepos, Catherine *212*
Seremetakis, Nadia C. *56*
Servaki, Maria 22
Sevcenko, Ihor *44, 46*
Sfakianakis, Giannis 21 (Sphakianakis)
Shear, T. Leslie *154*
Sheed, Wilfrid *197*
Sheridan, Charles Brinsley 25, *206*
Sherrard, Philip *13*, 18, *23, 24, 25, 26, 29, 36, 40, 50, 68, 77, 78, 79, 80, 81, 82, 83, 84, 93, 101, 102, 103, 104, 107, 108, 112, 116, 121, 126, 134, 139, 141, 146, 151,*

154, *164*, *169*, *185*, *186*, *187*, *188*, *189*, *190*, *191*, *192*, *200*, *201*, *202*, *204*, *209*
Shirinian, Lorne *12*, *110*
Sholod, Barton *129*
Sibbick, P.M. *50*
Sideris, John/Yannis *40*, *68*
Sikelianos, Angelos 13, 18, 21, 22, 23, 24, 25, 26, 27, 40, 41, 63, *64*, 68, 153, 186, **201-204**
Sikelianos, Anna *204*
Sikelianos, Frances *201*
Sikelianou, Eva *202*, *204*
Silverman, Stuart *9*
Simic, Charles *179*
Simmons, Clifford *193*
Simopoulos, Ilias 27
Simos, Betty *185*
Simpson, Michael *80*
Sinopoulos, Takis 9, 10, 11, 12, 13, 22, 24, 26, 28, 29, *200*, **204-205**
Siomopoulos, Takis 32
Siotis, Dino *6*, 11, 12, 15, 22, *26*, *27*, *27*, 28, 29, 30, *76*, *94*, *98*, *99*, *116*, *140*, *144*, *148*, *156*, *181*, *184*, **205**
Sitas, Amaranth *145*
Sitwell, Edith *76*
Skaltsounis, Ioannis 50
Skarimbas, Yannis 19, 25 (also Scarimbas)
Skaros, Zissis **206**
Skarpas, Louis 26 (Scarpas)
Skiadaresis, Spyros **206**
Skiotis, Dennis *37*
Skipis, Sotiris 21, 32, **206**
Skipitaris, Loukas *205*
Smith, Ole L. *42*, *46*
Smyrniotis, Goula *155*
Sofas, Petros 25, 30, 31 (Sophas)
Sofroniou, Sofronis 31 (Sophroniou)
Sokratous, Costas 31
Solman, John *218*
Solomon, Dionysius (sic): see Solomos
Solomos, Dionysios 18, 21, 25, 27, 40, 41, 68, **206-209** (also Salomos, Solomon (sic))
Sonnenberg, Ben *84*
Sophas, Petros: see Sofas
Sophocleous, Andreas *68*
Sophroniou, Sophronis: see Sofroniou
Sopko, Andrew J. *37*
Sotiracopoulou, A.: see Sotiracopoulou-Skina
Sotiracopoulou-Skina, Agnes *14*, 15, *111*, *113*, *118*, *144*, *171*, *226* (also Sotiracopoulou)
Sotiriou, Popi 28
Sotiropoulou, Ersi 26, **209**
Souliotis, Mimis **209**
Soulis, George Ch. *52*
Soures, George: see Souris
Souris, Giorgos **209** (also Soures)

Sourvinos, Dhimitris 28
Soutsos, Alexander 21, 25, 27
Soutsos, Panagiotes 25
Spanias, Nikos 12, 13, 22, *26*, *27*, *40*, *68*, *74*, *98*, *108*, *139*, **209**, *216*
Spanos, Be(e)be *30*, *155*
Spanos, Nicos S. *31*, *68*
Spanos, William V. *10*, *173*, *174*, *181*, *227*
Spanos Ikaris, Despoina: see Ikaris
Spanou Stratis, Giota **210**
Spatharis, Sotiris **210**
Spencer, Bernard *102*, *186*, *191*, *192*
Spender, Stephen *77*, *84*, *88*, *93*
Sphakianakis, Yiannis: see Sfakianakis
Spilios, Dimitris *144*
Spiropoulos, Tassos: see Spyropoulos, Tasos
Spyropoulos, N.J. **210**
Spyropoulos, Tasos 25 (Spiropoulos)
Srinivas, Krishna *224*
Stanescu, E. *44*
Stanford, Donald E. *92*
Stanford, W.B. *130*, *134*
Stangos, Nikos 9, *24*, *29*, *77*, *108*, *109*, *160*, *167*, *168*, *175*, *177*, *205*, *220*
Stasinopoulos, Michalis 21, 25
Stathatos, John Constantine *10*, *11*, 13, *15*, 26, *101*, *111*, *113*, *120*, *137*, *138*, *142*, *167*, *176*, *183*, *184*, *189*, *190*, *194*, *200*, *204*, *205*, *217*, *218*, *219*
Stavrides, Phoebos: see Stavridis
Stavridis, Foivos 31 (Stavrides)
Stavropoulou, Erasmia-Louiza 2
Stavrou, C.N. *134*
Stavrou, Chrystalleni 31
Stavrou, Gerasimos **210**
Stavrou, Patroclos *135*
Stavrou, Soterios G. *151*, *152*, *214*
Stavrou, Tatiana 19
Stavrou, Theo 30, 31
Stavrou, Theofanis G. *98*, *103*, *105*, *108*, *125*, *151*, *152*, *156*, *157*, *165*, *167*, *202*, *203*, *206*, *208*, *213*, *227*
Stefanou, Lydia 10, 20, 22, 28, 29, **210** (Stephanou)
Steiner, George *26*, *80*
Stephanides, Tassos 31
Stephanides, Theodore Ph. 26, *48*, *53*, *142*, *149*, *150*, *151*, *152*, *155*, *207*
Stephanou, Lydia: see Stefanou
Stergiopoulos, Kostas 22, 23, 28, **210** (Steryiopoulos, Steryopoulos)
Steriadis, Vasilis 11, 22, 26, 28, **210** (also Steryadhis, Steryadis)
Stern, Herbert *138*
Steryadhis/Steryadis, Vasilis: see Steriadis
Steryiopoulos/Steryopoulos, Kostas: see Stergiopoulos

Stevens, David Harrison *154*
Stewart, Charles *36*, *228*
Stogiannidis, Giorgos 23, 25, 27, 29, 32 (also Stoyannides, Stoyannidhis, Stoyiannidhis)
Stone, James *68*, *72*, *137*, *189*, *205*
Stoneman, Richard *18*
Stoyannides, George: see Stogiannidis
Stoyannidhis, George/Yorghos: see Stogiannidis
Stoyiannidhis, G.X.: see Stogiannidis
Strand, Mark *179*
Stravinsky, Igor *190*
Strouse, Jean *108*
Stuart Glennie, John Stuart *18*, *27*
Stylianou, Theodoros 31
Sussex, Roland *51*, *52*
Swanson, Donald C. 2
Syka-Karampetsou, Soteroula *109*, *222*
Szabó, Kálmán *135*
Tachtsis, Kostas 29, *108*, *114*, *200*, **211** (also Tacktsis, Taktsis)
Tacktsis, C.: see Tachtsis
Tagore, Rabindranath *152*
Taktsis, Costas/Kostas: see Tachtsis
Tale of Alexander 42
Tangopoulos, Panos 26
Tannen, Deborah *69*, *71*, *72*, *147*, *211*
Tantalidês, Elias: see Tantalidis, Ilias
Tantalidis, Ilias 21 (Tantalidês)
Tarelli, C.G. *93*
Taylor, John *96*, *139*, *157*, *160*, *161*, *220*
Taylor, Rita *175*, *177*
Taylor, Timothy W. *135*
Temple, Ruth Z. *3*
Tertzetis, G. 136
Terzakis, Angelos *69*, *143*, **211-212**
Thalassinos, Rev. Theodore N. 37
Thallas, Yannis: see Dallas
Thaniel, George 5, 9, 11, *12*, 22, 26, 27, 28, *28*, *67*, *99*, *114*, *115*, *135*, *148*, *160*, *176*, *200*, *201*, **212-213**, *219*, *227*, *228*
Thasites, Panos: see Thasitis
Thasitis, Panos 9, 12, 22, 25, 26, 29, 32 (also Thasites, Thassitis)
Thassitis, Panos K.: see Thasitis
Themelis, Giorgos 12, 18, 21, 22, 23, 25, 32, **213**
Theocharidou, Ianthi 31
Theodorakis, Mikis *25*
Theodorakopoulos, I.N. 50
Theodorakopoulos, Loukas 9, 12
Theodorou, Nelly **213**
Theodorou, Victoria 17, 22
Theofanous, Avra 31 (Theophanous)
Theophanous, Avra: see Theofanous
Theotoka, Koralia **213**
Theotokas, Giorgos 18, 41, 57, 69, **213-214**
Theotokes, Nikephoros: see Theotokis, Nikiforos
Theotokis, Andreas *62*
Theotokis, Konstantinos 18, **215**
Theotokis, Nikiforos 51 (Theotokes)
Therive, André *151*
Theroux, Paul *135*
Theseid 46
Thomas, Jack *130*
Thompson, Peter *11*, *32*, *188*, *191*, *192*, *201*
Thomson, George *149*
Thorlby, Anthony K. *41*
Thrylos, Alkis *154*, *212*
Tobias, Michael *121*
Tofallis, Kypros *40*
Tofallis, Zanettos *159*
Tomadakis, Nikolaos B. *209*
Topping, Eva Catafygiotu *117*, *201*
Topping, Peter *4*
Touliatos-Banker, Diane *37*
Toumazi, Elena 31
Toynbee, Arnold *41*
Traïanos, Alexis 22
Travlantonis, Antonis 19
Trikoupis, Spyridon 23 (Trikupi)
Trikupi, Spiridion: see Trikoupis
Trivizas, Sotiris 28
Trogadis, Pantelis 13, 25
Troilos, Johannes Andreas 49
Trollope, Dorothy *19*, *223*
Trypanis, Constantine A. 25, 27, 37, 40, 41, 47, *152*, *202*, *216*, *223*
Tsagris, Kleomenis G. **215**
Tsaknia, Amalia 28
Tsaloumas, Dimitris **215**
Tsangarakis, Odysseas **215**
Tsatsopoulos, Ares *213*
Tsatsos, Ioanna/Jeanne: see Tsatsou
Tsatsos, Konstantinos D. *10*, *117*, **216**
Tsatsou, Ioanna 23, 28, *194*, **216** (also Tsatsos, Ioanna/Jeanne)
Tsechos, Ilias 27, 28 (Tsehos)
Tsehos, Ilias: see Tsechos
Tselepides, Nikos *100*, *149*
Tsiamis, Christos 68, **216**
Tsiaperas, Solon *118*
Tsingos, Gwendolyn *166* (see also MacEwan)
Tsingos, Nikos *11*, *166*
Tsiovas, Dimitris: see Tziovas
Tsirkas, Stratis 57, *201*, **216-217**
Tsitseli, Kay: see Cicellis
Tsokopoulos, Vasias *145*
Tsoulli-Panagi, Irini 31 (Tsoulli-Panayi)
Tsoulli-Panayi, Eirini: see Tsoulli-Panagi
Tsourdalakis, George 56
Tuffin, Paul *56*
Tumberg, Thomas *183*
Tweed, Gillian *10*, *157*
Typaldos, Julius 21, 27

Tzalias, Kimon 32
Tzilianos, Makis 68
Tziovas, Dimitris *69, 93* (also Tsiovas)
Vacalopoulos, Apostolos: see Vakalopoulos
Vafopoulos, G.T. 18, 21, 22, 23, 32, **217**
Vagenas, Nasos 10, 11, 12, 13, 15, 22, 26, 27, 28, 30, *93, 200, 201*, **217-219** (Vayenas)
Vaka, Demetra *20, 100, 118, 151, 156, 163, 225, 227*
Vakalo, Eleni 9, 10, 11, 12, 14, 20, 21, 22, 26, 28, 29, **219**
Vakalopoulos, Apostolos *52*, 61 (Vacalopoulos)
Valamvanos, George *20, 72, 117, 120, 135, 142*
Valaorites, Aristotle: see Valaoritis, Aristotelis
Valaorites, Nanos: see Valaoritis, Nanos
Valaoritis, Aristotelis 18, 21, 25, 27, 32, 41, **219** (also Valaorites)
Valaoritis, Nanos 9, 10, 12, 13, 21, 22, 24, 25, *26*, 28, 29, 41, *69, 101, 102, 104, 107, 108, 109, 140, 186, 189, 191, 192, 205*, **220** (also Valaorites)
Valassopoulos, George 79
Valavanidhis, Christos: see Valavanidis
Valavanidis, Christos 22, 26, 28 (also Valavanidhis)
Valdasserides, Pavlos: see Valdasseridis
Valdasseridis, Pavlos 31 (Valdasserides)
Valtinos, Thanasis **220**
Valvês, Stamatos: see Valvis
Valvis, Stamatos 21 (Valvês)
Van Dyck, Karen *143*
Van Kaam, Adrian *132*
Varnalis, Kostas 21, 22, 23, 25, 26, 40, **221**
Varveris, Yannis 13, 15, 30
Varvitsiotis, Takis 10, 14, 18, 21, 22, 25, 26, 27, 29, 32, **221**
Vasilikos, Vasilis 12, 18, *168*, **221-222** (also Vassilikos)
Vasiliou, Kostas 31 (Vassiliou)
Vasils, Themi *89, 122, 123, 162, 214*
Vasils, Theodora *89, 121, 122, 123, 161, 220*
Vasils, Theodore *213*
Vassardaki, Lucille *40*
Vassilikos, Vassilis: see Vasilikos
Vassiliou, Costas: see Vasiliou
Vavouris, Stavros 22
Vayenas, Nasos/Nassos: see Vagenas
Veis, Giorgos 15, 30, 68
Velisariada: see *Belisariada*
Velthandros: see *Belthandros and Chrysantza*
Venezis, Ilias 18, 40, 41, **222-223**
Veniamin Lesvios: see Benjamin of Lesvos
Verney, Lady F. *56*
Vickers, John *30, 68*
Vidal-Naquet, Pierre *160*
Vikelas, Dimitrios 21, **223-224** (also Bikelas)
Vilaras, Yiannis 21

Vincent, Alfred L. *50, 181, 182*
Visser, Elizabeth *42*
Vistonitis, Anastasis 68, **224**
Vitsaxis, Vasilis 15, **224**
Vitti, Mario *3, 69*
Viziênós, George: see Vizyinos
Vizinos, Georgios: see Vizyinos
Vizyenos, G.: see Vizyinos
Vizyinos, Georgios 21, 25, 27, **224-225** (also Viziênós, Vizinos, Vizyenos)
Vlachodimitris, Thodoris **225**
Vlachogiannis, Giannis 18, 19 (Vlachoyannis)
Vlachogiannis, Paul *12*
Vlachos, Angelos 21
Vlachos, Angelos (Ange) **225**
Vlachos, Helen *18*, **225**
Vlachoyannis, John/Yannis: see Vlachogiannis
Vlami, Eva **225**
Vlastos, Petros 21, 26
Vlavianos-Arvanitis, Agni **226**
Voelker-Kamarinea, Maria *144*
Voreadis, Agis 31
Voskopoula 48
Votoras, Taki *113*
Voudouris, Dimitrios *1*
Voulgaris, Eugenios 51
Voustronios, Georgios: see Boustronios
Voutsas, Paul *198*
Voutyras, Demosthenes 19
Vozikis, Panos 68
Vrachimis, Nikos 30, 31 (Vrahimis)
Vrahimis, Nikos: see Vrachimis
Vraïlas-Armenis, Petros *50*, **226** (also Braïlas-Armenis)
Vranas, Nikos 9
Vrellis, Pavlos 32
Vretakos, Nikiforos: see Vrettakos
Vrettakos, Nikiforos 13, 18, 21, 22, 23, 24, 25, **226-227** (also Vretakos)
Vryonis, Speros, Jr. *37, 52*
Wagner, Wilhelm *42*
Wallace, Warren *69, 182*
Walton, Francis R. *4*
Walton, Mary Cooper *186*
War of Troy 44
Warhaft, Gail Holst *61, 73, 121* (also Holst)
Warner, Rex *24, 77, 84, 93, 141, 186, 187, 192*
Warnke, Frank J. *41*
Watson, Iain 9
Weick, Karl E. *80*
Weinberg, David Robert *156, 208*
Welsh, Andrew *78*
Wessman, Robert Leo *126*
Wheeler, Sara *84, 92*
Whitman, Cedric H. *17, 70, 206, 211*
Whitman, Ruth *9, 31, 101, 188*
Wildman, Carl *124*

Will, Frederic *3, 12, 135, 149, 150*
Will, Stavroula *159*
Willcox, Jackie *73*
Williams, Christopher *219*
Wilson, Colin *130, 135*
Winnifrith, Tom *47, 64, 175*
Witt, Reginald *72*
Woodhead, Jean H. *98, 165, 215*
Woodhouse, C.M. *141*
Wright, Robert *96*
Wyatt, William F., Jr. *118, 119, 225*
Xanthopoulides, George X. *156*
Xenakis, Manolis *27*
Xenofovos, Orfeas *24* (Xenophobos)
Xenophobos, Orpheus: see Xenofovos
Xenopoulos, Grigorios *18, 93, 227*
Xenos, Stefanos Theodoros *227*
Xydias, Vassilis *70, 141*
Xydis, Stephen G. *9*
Yaloussis, Stephen *221*
Yannopoulos, Alcis: see Giannopoulos
Yemenaki, S.: see Gemenaki
Yeralis, George/Yorghos: see Geralis
Yerolemidou, Xenia: see Gerolemidou
Yfantis, Giannis *13, 22, 26* (also Ifandis, Ifantis)
Yiakos, Demetrios: see Giakos
Yiangoullis, C.G. *68*
Yiannidis, Lefteris: see Giannidis
Yiokarini, Koula: see Giokarini
Young, Kenneth *70*
Yourcenar, Marguerite *79, 93*
Zabatha-Paghoulatou, Phaedra *12*

Zackel, Fred *78*
Zafiris, Spiros *27*
Zahareas, Anthony N. *201*
Zakythinos, Alexis **227-228**
Zakythinos, Dionysios A. *53, 70*
Zalakostas, George (sic): see Zalokostas, George
Zaller, Robert *176, 190*
Zalocosta, Christo: see Zalokostas, Christos
Zalokostas, Christos **228** (also Zalocosta)
Zalokostas, George *21, 25, 27* (also Zalakostas (sic))
Zambaras, Vassilis *189*
Zannas, Pavlos A. *193,* **228**
Zarambouka, Sofia **228**
Zarraftis, Jacob *32*
Zatelli, Zirana **228**
Zeï, Alki **228**
Zenakos, Leonidas *9*
Zenon, Evyenios: see Zinon, Evgenios
Zenon, Victor: see Zinon, Viktor
Zervos, John Cl. *26*
Zervos, John G. *7*
Zervou, Ioanna *26*
Zevgoli-Glezou, Dialechti **228**
Ziatas, Christos *27*
Zinon, Evgenios *31* (Zenon, Evyenios)
Zinon, Viktor *31* (Zenon, Victor)
Ziolkowski, Theodore *135*
Zolder, Anthula *138*
Zotos, Stephanos *75*
Zoumboulakis, Nikos *9*
Zymboulakis, Stephanos *31*